Tort Law

What happens if a driver carelessly crashes into another car? Or a newspaper publishes a story which makes derogatory comments about someone? Or if a resident plays loud music every night so that their neighbour cannot get any sleep? Tort law is a collection of such misbehaviours or misadventures where the law deems it appropriate to intervene with civil remedies.

Tort Law is written to enable students to gain a thorough understanding of tort law in England and Wales, as well as to develop the critical reasoning and problem-solving skills that are needed in an exam situation. The law is explained with clear writing and an accessible approach, relating the subject to everyday examples. There are key learning points to help anchor the reader's basic understanding, and sections of analysis to guide the reader to a more advanced critical engagement. Above all, tort law is interesting, for it covers so much of our daily lives, and is a constant source of evolving litigation.

This second edition has been thoroughly updated throughout to reflect changes in the law, and includes a new chapter on artificial intelligence and emerging technologies.

This book is supported by a range of online multiple choice and essay questions developed to aid your learning, keep you up to date, and help you prepare for assessments.

The **Routledge Spotlights** series brings a modern, contemporary approach to the core curriculum for the LLB and GDL, which will help students:

- move beyond an understanding of the law;
- refine and develop the key skills of problem-solving, evaluation and critical reasoning;
- discover sources and suggestions for taking your study further.

By focusing on recent case law and real-world examples, the Routledge Spotlights series will help you shed light on the law, understand how it operates in practice, and gain a unique appreciation of the contemporary context of the subject.

Timon Hughes-Davies, MA, DPhil (Oxford), FHEA, is a Senior Lecturer at the University of Exeter.

Nathan Tamblyn, MA (Oxford), LLM, PhD (Cambridge), SFHEA, FCIArb, Barrister, is Senior Fellow in Law Reform at the University of Lincoln, and a lawyer at the Law Commission.

Matthew Channon, LLB, LLM, PhD, is Senior Lecturer in Law at the University of Exeter.

SPOTLIGHTS
SHEDDING LIGHT ON THE LAW

Routledge Spotlights Series

A new textbook series designed to help you translate your knowledge of the law to assessment success.

AVAILABLE NOW:

EU Law, Gerard Conway
Equity & Trusts 2nd edition, Scott Atkins
Tort Law, Timon Hughes-Davies and Nathan Tamblyn
English Legal System, Ryan Murphy
Contract Law 2nd edition, Tracey Cooper and Ewan Kirk
Public Law 3rd edition, Michael Doherty and Noel McGuirk
Tort Law 2nd edition, Timon Hughes-Davies, Nathan Tamblyn, and Matthew Channon

SPOTLIGHTS
SHEDDING LIGHT ON THE LAW

Tort Law

SECOND EDITION

TIMON HUGHES-DAVIES,
NATHAN TAMBLYN,
AND MATTHEW CHANNON

Routledge
Taylor & Francis Group
LONDON AND NEW YORK

Designed cover image: borchee/Getty Images

Second edition published 2025
by Routledge
4 Park Square, Milton Park, Abingdon, Oxon, OX14 4RN

and by Routledge
605 Third Avenue, New York, NY 10158

Routledge is an imprint of the Taylor & Francis Group, an informa business

First edition published by Routledge 2020

British Library Cataloguing-in-Publication Data
A catalogue record for this book is available from the British Library

Library of Congress Cataloging-in-Publication Data
Names: Hughes-Davies, Timon, author. | Tamblyn, Nathan, author. | Channon, Matthew, author.
Title: Tort law / Timon Hughes-Davies, Nathan Tamblyn, Matthew Channon.
Description: 2. | New York : Routledge, 2025. | Series: Spotlights | Includes bibliographical references and index.
Identifiers: LCCN 2024060953 (print) | LCCN 2024060954 (ebook) | ISBN 9781032767758 (hardback) | ISBN 9781032767741 (paperback) | ISBN 9781003480051 (ebook)
Subjects: LCSH: Torts—England—Cases. | Torts—Wales—Cases. | LCGFT: Study guides.
Classification: LCC KD1949.6 .H84 2025 (print) | LCC KD1949.6 (ebook) | DDC 346.4203—dc23/eng/20241223
LC record available at https://lccn.loc.gov/2024060953
LC ebook record available at https://lccn.loc.gov/2024060954

ISBN: 978-1-032-76775-8 (hbk)
ISBN: 978-1-032-76774-1 (pbk)
ISBN: 978-1-003-48005-1 (ebk)

DOI: 10.4324/9781003480051

Typeset in Bembo
by Apex CoVantage, LLC

Access the support materials: www.routledge.com/9781032767741

OUTLINE CONTENTS

DETAILED CONTENTS

GUIDE TO THE SPOTLIGHTS SERIES

The Routledge Spotlights series is an exciting new textbook series that has been carefully developed to help give you a head start in your assessments. We've listened to lecturers and examiners to identify what it takes to succeed as a law student and we've used that to develop a brand new series of textbooks that combines detailed coverage of the law together with carefully selected features designed to help you translate that knowledge into assessment success.

AS YOU READ
sections at the start of each chapter introduce you to the key questions and concepts that will be covered within the chapter to help you to focus your reading.

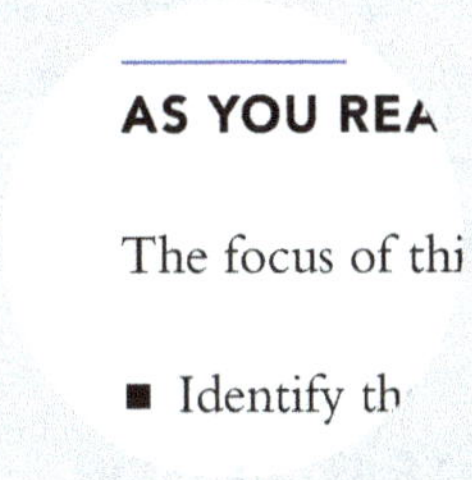

KEY LEARNING POINTS
throughout each chapter highlight important principles and definitions to aid understanding and consolidate your learning.

EXPLAINING THE LAW
brings the subject to life through the use of practical examples to provide valuable context to your learning.

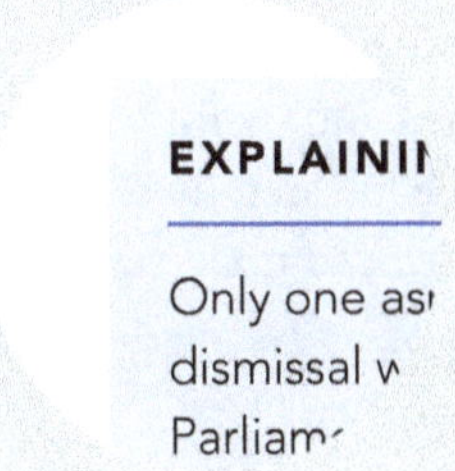

ANALYSING THE LAW
invites you to consider your own response to legal dilemmas and debates. Critical thinking is key to assessment success and with this feature, our authors invite you to critique the law or evaluate conflicting arguments in a debate.

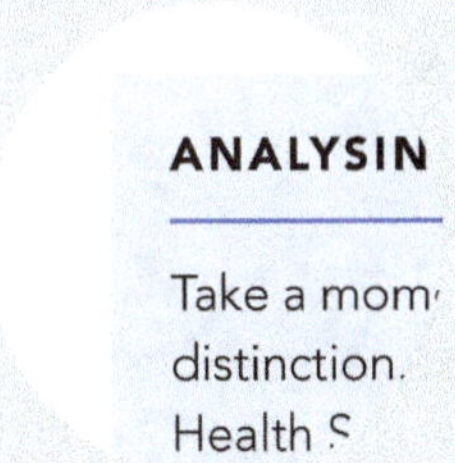

APPLYING THE LAW

Problem questions will form a large part of your assessment and **Applying the law** allows you to develop your problem-solving skills by showing how the law can be applied to a given situation. Learn how to interpret the law and apply it to any problem question.

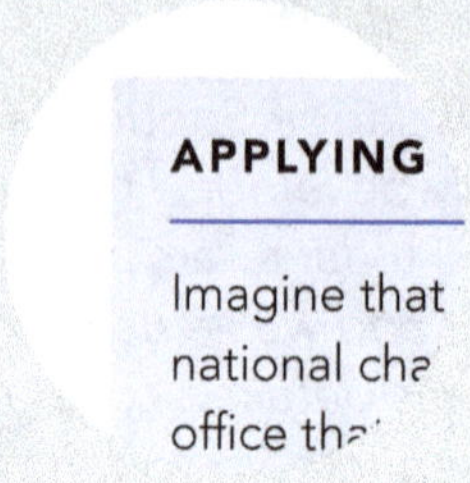

MAKING CONNECTIONS

will help you impress examiners, showing you how a topic fits into the bigger picture, not just of the wider subject but also across the legal curriculum.

POINTS TO REVIEW

bring together all of the principles and themes for the chapter, helping to reinforce your learning.

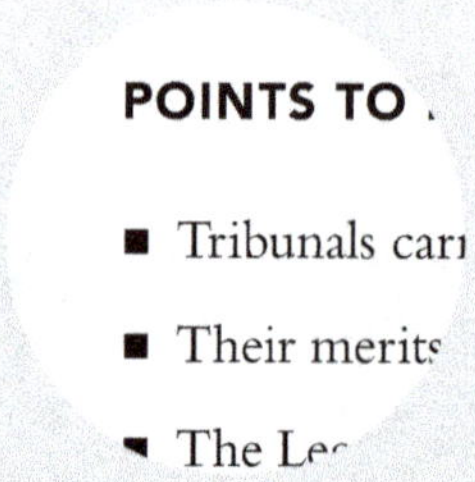

TAKING IT FURTHER

Reading widely impresses examiners! **Taking it further** provides annotated lists of journal articles, book chapters and useful websites for further reading which have been carefully selected to help you to demonstrate an enhanced understanding of the topic.

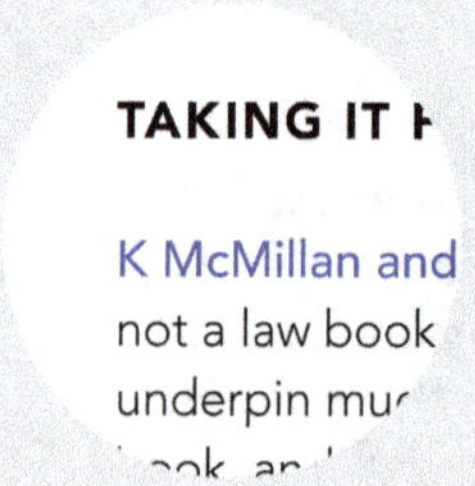

TABLE OF CASES

TABLE OF STATUTES AND OTHER INSTRUMENTS

Table of UK Statutes

Statutory instruments

European Union

United States

1

CHAPTER 1
ABOUT TORT LAW

This chapter considers the following questions: What is tort law? What is the purpose of tort law? How does tort law fit with other areas of law?

The word 'tort' comes from the Old French (via the Norman Conquest), which in turn comes from the Latin (via the Roman Empire), and means a civil wrong. So:

> KEY LEARNING POINT
>
> Tort law is a collection of misbehaviours or misadventures where the law deems it appropriate to intervene with civil remedies.

For example, here is a selection of torts discussed in this book:

If a driver carelessly crashes into another car, they might be liable in the tort of negligence, and have to pay for any damage. If a defendant publishes a story which is derogatory of the claimant, they might be liable in the tort of defamation, and have to issue an apology. If a defendant plays loud music every night so that their neighbour cannot get any sleep, they might be liable in the tort of private nuisance, and be ordered to quieten down.

Each tort is a separate cause of action. In other words, each tort has its own ingredients which a claimant must prove in order to be successful. That said, some ingredients are common to several torts. So too some defences and remedies are common to many torts.

Tort law is not the only form of civil wrong. For example, contract law provides civil remedies where, characteristically, one party does not keep its promises. Or a defendant might incur liability for an equitable wrong, for example for breach of a fiduciary duty (that is, a duty which arises from a special relationship of trust and confidence). Or a defendant might incur liability in unjust enrichment, where they have been enriched at the expense of the claimant in unjust circumstances (for example, where a defendant has taken payment for something, but provided nothing in return). Or a defendant might owe duties under the law of bailment, if they find themselves looking after the claimant's goods.

Why is there such a variety of approaches? The honest answer is, that is just the way it turned out. The common law has been developing for nearly 1,000 years. It has been developed by a range of institutions, sometimes as collaborators, often as rivals. It has been shaped by

DOI: 10.4324/9781003480051-01

political movements and philosophical ideologies. Political movements have come and gone. Philosophical ideologies have waxed and waned. As society has changed, in some areas the law had to innovate; in other areas it became outdated. Just consider the enormity of change: the printing press, democracy, factories, the motor vehicle, the welfare state, the internet. Our knowledge and skills have improved (hopefully). The common law is always a work in progress. Its growth can be both conscientious and haphazard.

Further, life is complicated. We have multiple relationships of different types with different people. We engage in all sorts of activities which interact with other people and their property in diverse ways. The persistent volume of litigation passing before the courts is testament to the ceaseless creativity with which people get into disagreements. It is not possible to resolve all this complexity with a single method. The law has developed multiple approaches, like tort and contract, in its attempt to provide fair or palatable outcomes which respond appropriately to differences in the cases.

What is more, life is not neat, nor is the law. Our behaviours and adventures are rarely compartmentalised in a way that they raise only one issue without broader impact or consequences. For example, on any given set of facts, a claimant might be able to raise arguments in both tort and contract. Or a claimant suing in tort law might be able to raise multiple causes of action. It is important, whether as a student or as a practising lawyer, to identify all the different approaches potentially available to a claimant. Some causes of action might be easier to prove, because their ingredients better suit the narrative of the facts. Other causes of action might provide a more desirable remedy.

All this also means that different areas of law, like contract and tort, are never totally distinct. They are more like the overlapping circles of the Olympic rings. Ideas and principles get shared across the different areas of law.

What if we just started from scratch, and rewrote our law anew? That project would be enormous. But anyway, the following points are worth noting. Yes, some areas of the law need modernising, or just plain improving. Lawyers should always be alert to the benefits of good reform. But some areas of the law work well. Any new law might look different from what we have now, but why give up what works? And any new law will soon enough find itself growing stale, or facing unforeseen challenges, as society continues its wayward journey. No law will suit society perfectly for all time.

If law is this patchwork quilt, how do we divide it up, to make it accessible to study? The tendency is to divide the law according to the problem. The Broken Promise. The Breach of Trust. Tort law is a collection of just such problems: The Careless Accident; The Ruined Reputation; The Inconsiderate Neighbour (and many others besides).

Finally, it is worth remembering that not every wrong is actionable. Life has its natural disappointments. Accidents sometimes happen. There is not always a defendant to blame, or at least to sue. For example, not every promise is enforceable in contract law. And in tort law, a defendant might say something rude about the claimant, and yet incur no liability in the tort of defamation. Or a defendant might play their music loudly enough to annoy their neighbour, but without incurring liability in the tort of private nuisance. Or a driver might crash their car, but without incurring liability in the tort of negligence, because the accident was unavoidable despite the driver taking all reasonable care. Only in some cases of misbehaviour or misadventure will the law intervene. (And we can always ask whether tort law draws that line in the right place.)

The rest of this chapter considers the following issues: what is the function of tort law; how does tort law fit with other areas of law; and how does tort law change over time?

AS YOU READ

- Be aware that tort law is multi-faceted because it has to address a wide variety of circumstances.
- Consider whether all these circumstances should be addressed by tort law. Perhaps they should be addressed in other ways – or not at all.
- Remember that tort law continues to evolve, as it refines itself, or responds to novel situations or changing social attitudes.
- Consider how tort law might be further improved.

1.1 THE FUNCTIONS OF TORT LAW

The ingredients of individual torts might make them more or less straightforward. But tort law as a whole is diverse and complex. The following functions of tort law have been variously identified by authors and judges: to provide compensation for harm suffered; to vindicate people when their rights have been infringed; to ensure activities are carried out in an economically efficient way; to deter undesirable behaviour; to allocate blame. We shall consider each in turn.

1.2 COMPENSATION

Compensation is often seen as the predominant purpose of tort law. For example, in *Fairchild v Glenhaven Funeral Services Ltd*,[1] Lord Bingham said: 'The overall object of tort law is to define cases in which the law may justly hold one party liable to compensate another'. While compensation does often loom large, focusing solely on compensation misses a number of important points.

1 [2002] UKHL 22, [9].

First, some torts are complete without proof of any actual damage. Such torts are said to be 'actionable *per se*'.[2] They include torts like trespass to land, and false imprisonment. We might say these types of behaviour are considered sufficiently wrong that they are proscribed even if they do not cause any harm.

Second, instead of damages, an alternative but important remedy is an injunction. This is a court order which, typically, proscribes certain behaviour, in order to restrain either a threatened tort or the continuation of a current tort. In such a case, the primary purpose is to prevent harm, rather than allow it to happen and provide compensation afterwards. For example, the tort of private nuisance is where the defendant interferes with the claimant's land or its use and enjoyment, like playing loud music late into the night. An injunction is a common remedy, to restrain an interference (here, to stop the loud noise) which might otherwise continue on and on.

Third, if a claimant does seek a money remedy, there are various measures of damages which might not be strictly compensatory. For example, exemplary damages, sometimes called punitive damages, are additional to any loss which the claimant might have suffered. They seek to disgorge the defendant of any ill-gotten gains, to ensure that tort (like crime) does not pay.

LIMITS TO COMPENSATION

If the claimant does seek compensation for harm suffered, still there are practical hurdles. Even for an otherwise successful claimant, these hurdles include the delay of bringing a case to judgment, and the irrecoverable legal costs incurred along the way. The uncertainty of success and the need to fund litigation in the meantime put off further victims from litigating at all. Thereafter, there still remain the difficulties of enforcing a judgment and recovering any money. And all this assumes that the claimant successfully proved every item of loss (right down to every day off work, and every box of plasters bought from the supermarket). As a matter of practice, very few victims will be fully compensated by successful tort litigation.

Further, the law itself does not always guarantee that harm will be compensated: some harms do not attract any compensation; some harms attract compensation more in name than in substance; and with those harms which do attract compensation, still the harm must have been inflicted through proscribed conduct. We shall take each of these points in turn.

First, some harms do not attract any compensation. One example is economic loss suffered by the claimant as a result of damage caused to a third party's property. In *Weller & Co v Foot and Mouth Disease Research Institute*,[3] a virus escaped from the defendant research institute, and infected cattle. Quarantine restrictions meant cattle markets were closed. The claimants were auctioneers, and so lost money. But this type of loss was held by the court not to be recoverable, since it was parasitic on damage to property which was owned not by the auctioneers, but by third parties (the cattle owners).

2 Pronounced 'purr say'.

3 [1966] 1 QB 569 (QBD).

EXPLAINING THE LAW

Every act we do has consequences. It is like dropping a pebble into a pond. The ripples travel outwards. The law says that we are only responsible for those ripples up to a point. Beyond that point, we are not legally liable. So the research institute in *Weller* was liable for harm to the cattle, but not for the further ripple that was harm to those who auctioned the cattle. Perhaps it is not morally fair to hold us to the further ripples. Or perhaps it is simply impractical: it would be too great a financial burden, beyond most of our means, if we attracted such extended liability.

Second, some harms attract compensation more in name than in substance. For example, when a claimant suffers personal injury, they can recover general damages, to compensate them for pain, suffering and loss of amenity. Thus, according to the Judicial College Guidelines,[4] loss of one hand might attract an award of up to £133k. Is that a fair swap?

Personal injury claimants can also recover their itemised out-of-pocket expenses. These are called special damages. These are more likely to provide full compensation for past losses. But the practice of awarding a once-and-for-all lump-sum payment at the end of trial means that any sum awarded represents nothing more than the court's best guess at what future losses might be. Will the claimant ever return to work? How much medical care will they need? As Lord Scarman said in *Lim Poh Choo v Camden and Islington Area Health Authority*:[5] 'There is really one certainty: the future will prove the award to be either too high or too low'.

ANALYSING THE LAW

From a defendant's point of view, how much compensation they must pay depends a lot on luck. For example, if a defendant runs over someone, who then takes time off work, the defendant will likely have to pay compensation for lost earnings. If the victim has a part-time job delivering food orders from restaurant to customer, the lost earnings will be less. If the victim is a high-powered business mogul, the lost earnings will be considerable. Do we feel comfortable that luck has such a significant role to play in determining the financial burden on a tort defendant?

Third, with those harms which do attract compensation, still the harm must have been inflicted through proscribed conduct. Not all harm-causing conduct is proscribed. For example, to sue in the tort of negligence, the claimant must prove that the defendant failed to act with the required standard of care. So if the defendant did act with due care, and still caused harm, then the claimant may have no remedy in tort law.

4 17th edn (2024), para 10.8.

5 [1980] AC 174 (HL), 183.

COMPENSATION OUTSIDE TORT LAW

In 1978, a Royal Commission on Civil Liability and Compensation for Personal Injury, chaired by Lord Pearson, reported as follows.[6] Only around 6.5% of injuries led to tort compensation. About 86% of tort claims were disposed of without the issue of proceedings. Only about 1% reached the courts – but that still accounted for three-quarters of all hearings in the Queen's Bench Division (now King's Bench Division). Further, the operating costs of the tort system (including insurers' costs and legal fees) were about £85 for every £100 paid out in compensation.

So litigation is not the only vehicle we have for compensating a victim. The defendant might be persuaded to make a voluntary payment or enter a settlement agreement. Or the claimant might claim under their insurance. Or the claimant might be eligible for benefits under the welfare state. Any personal injury is likely to be treated under the National Health Service. Or there might be a compensation scheme available to the claimant. For example, there is the Criminal Injuries Compensation Authority, to compensate victims of violent crime. And there is the Motor Insurers Bureau, which deals with claims against uninsured motorists. And there are statutory workers' compensation schemes, paying benefits to those who suffer personal injury at work.

Indeed, the availability of alternative sources of compensation might encourage the courts to withhold liability in tort law in that area. In *Jobling v Associated Dairies Ltd*,[7] the claimant suffered personal injury, and then a naturally occurring illness. In determining how far tort law should provide compensation, the court took into account the fact that the claimant had state benefits, and was covered by their employer's insurance. In *Hill v Chief Constable of West Yorkshire*,[8] the claimants were suing the police for failure to catch a criminal before he harmed another victim. The court said that the police owed no tortious duty to members of the public to catch criminals. And the availability to victims of compensation under the Criminal Injuries Compensation Scheme was said to be a further factor which militated against damages being available against the police in tort.

EXPLAINING THE LAW

We might put it this way. The courts might be encouraged to limit tort law to the nearer ripples of our conduct if the court knows that some of the further ripples are covered anyway by other schemes of compensation.

6 Cmnd 7054 – I: [78], [79], [83].

7 [1982] AC 794 (HL), 803–804. See too: *Lamb v Camden London Borough Council* [1981] QB 625 (CA), 637–638.

8 [1988] QB 60 (CA), 73, upheld at [1989] AC 53 (HL). On the duty of police to prevent crime, see: *Michael v Chief Constable of South Wales Police* [2015] UKSC 2.

1.3 VINDICATION

A tort claim might properly be brought even though the final remedy is merely a declaration vindicating the claimant, rather than, for example, any money remedy. In *Ashley v Chief Constable of Sussex Police*,[9] during a raid, the police shot and killed the suspect. The police admitted negligence, and agreed to pay all damages flowing from the incident. But the court said that the family were still allowed to bring a claim alleging battery, rather than merely negligence, so as to vindicate their contention that the suspect had been intentionally killed. This was despite the fact that the family would likely gain no further damages beyond those which the police had already agreed to pay.

1.4 ECONOMIC EFFICIENCY

Those who subscribe to theories of law and economics tend to make two claims. There is a descriptive claim that tort law often draws lines of liability in a way which secures economic efficiency. There is also the prescriptive claim that tort law *should* use liability to secure economic efficiency.

For example, in *Stovin v Wise*,[10] the claimant was injured in a road accident on a stretch of road owned by a local authority which was known to be dangerous. Should the local authority have spent more money to make the road safer? Lord Hoffmann said this:[11]

> The efficient allocation of resources usually requires an activity should bear its own costs. If it benefits from being able to impose some of its costs on other people (what economists call 'externalities'), the market is distorted because the activity appears cheaper than it really is. So liability to pay compensation for loss caused by negligent conduct acts as a deterrent against increasing the cost of the activity to the community, and reduces externalities.

Overt reasoning in terms of economic analysis is rare, but there is no doubt that judges are well aware that their judgments can have economic consequences. And judges are more likely to dismiss arguments of principle which lead to consequences incompatible with the way the market is currently structured. If tort law is to be respected, and effective in resolving disputes, it must make sense within its social and economic environment.

So, for example, in deciding whether a defendant should have spent money on taking more precautions against injury, the court will balance, on the one hand, the cost of those precautions, and on the other hand, the likelihood and magnitude of harm.[12]

9 [2008] UKHL 25.

10 [1996] AC 923 (HL).

11 Ibid, 944.

12 *Tomlinson v Congleton Borough Council* [2003] UKHL 47, [34].

As for the prescriptive claim that tort law *should* be concerned to secure economic efficiency, we might make the following points:

First, undoubtedly tort law enshrines moral values beyond economic efficiency. For example, it is wrong to falsely imprison someone, even if they suffer little financial loss as a consequence.

Second, if economic efficiency is primarily concerned with allocating resources to those prepared to pay the most for them, it risks tort law becoming a tool for the rich to acquire rights. The courts are alert to this. For example, if a defendant is creating a nuisance, the claimant is ordinarily entitled to an injunction to stop the nuisance. The defendant's ability to pay damages instead should not mean that it can carry on behaving tortiously.[13]

Third, the courts are hardly best placed to decide complex matters of economic policy. That surely requires wide-ranging debate and multiple opinions. It is not suited to the time constraints of two-party litigation.

1.5 DETERRENCE

Liability in tort law is said to deter certain types of undesirable behaviour. Such is the overt rationale, as we have seen, for exemplary damages. But we can point to several factors which are likely to reduce any deterrent effect which the general tort law might have.

First, some torts impose liability in circumstances where the defendant could not have done any better. We might put it this way: there are torts of inadvertence. It is precisely because the defendant did not apply their mind to the matter in hand that the harm was caused. For example, a car accident might follow a momentary lapse of concentration at the wheel. The message of deterrence which liability in tort law seeks to communicate simply cannot be heard when the defendant's mind is elsewhere.

Further, upon death, a claim can be brought by the estate upon any of the causes of action vested in the deceased (except defamation). But also, all actions against the deceased survive against the estate.[14] Deterrence cannot work on a dead person.

Second, often it is not the wrongdoer who has to foot the bill. As Staughton LJ said in *M v Newham London Borough Council*:[15]

> The great expansion of tortious liability over the last hundred and fifty years has had the remarkable feature that the direct financial consequences almost invariably fall on

13 *Shelfer v City of London Electric Lighting Co* [1895] 1 Ch 287 (CA).

14 Law Reform (Miscellaneous Provisions) Act 1934. The dependents of the deceased can also bring claims against the tortious killer for loss of their dependency: Fatal Accidents Act 1976.

15 [1994] 4 All ER 602 (CA), 631, on appeal [1995] 2 AC 633 (HL).

someone whose purse is assumed to be bottomless, such as an insurance company or a large commercial concern or an organ of central or local government.

So let us briefly consider in turn the questions of insurance and vicarious liability.

As for insurance, a repeat tortfeasor might face a higher renewal premium, but any premium will be less than the potential liability insured against. The tortfeasor might face a higher deductible on renewal, but it will be rare for a tortfeasor to be unable to obtain any insurance. The great benefit of insurance is precisely the reason why it diminishes the deterrent effect of liability: the risk of having to pay out is taken from the insured alone and spread across all those who pay premiums. With some activities, insurance is compulsory: for example, when driving, or in the workplace. These are precisely the areas where accident rates are highest.[16]

As for the rules of vicarious liability, this is typically the legal principle whereby, although it is a worker who commits the tort, it is the employer who pays for it. These rules are victim-oriented in as much as they help ensure that the victim has a choice of defendants, usually by going up the chain of command to someone else with deeper pockets, so increasing the victim's chances of finding a solvent defendant. The rules apply even where the employer itself has done nothing wrong. The message seems to be: if you want something done properly, do it yourself; if you get someone else to do it for you, then you take the risk of their mistakes. Of course, a worker who commits a tort might find their career prospects shortened. But if the employer is in court, and the employer is blameless, there is no misconduct on its part to deter.

1.6 BLAME AND FAULT

The sort of behaviour which tort law might seek to deter is often behaviour where we can blame the defendant for being morally at fault. To borrow language from criminal law, there are various types of *mens rea* or 'guilty mind' which tort law acts upon. For example, dishonesty might sound in the tort of deceit (that is, fraud). Intentionally or recklessly interfering with another's person might give rise to liability in the tort of battery. And negligence liability tends to arise when a defendant has behaved unreasonably.

Nevertheless, there are various ways in which tort law is *not* about doing wrong after all.

First, there are torts of strict liability. For example, a defendant can incur liability in defamation for happening to say something derogatory about the claimant, even if the defendant did not mean to say anything derogatory. And the rule in *Rylands v Fletcher* stands for the proposition that if a defendant brings something dangerous onto their land, then they

16 The Department for Transport reports that, in the year ending June 2023 in Great Britain on the road, there were around 133,000 minor injuries, 29,000 serious injuries and 1,600 fatalities. The Health and Safety Executive reports that, in the 2022–2023 period in Great Britain in the workplace, there were 1.8 million people suffering work-related illness, around 561,000 injuries, and 135 fatalities.

are strictly liable for any harm caused by its escape, no matter how much care they took to prevent that escape.[17]

ANALYSING THE LAW

The rule in *Rylands v Fletcher* might sound reasonable at first blush. After all, who *has* to bring something dangerous onto their land? But the court has said that this tort applies to factories using chemicals, even if those chemicals are standard for the industry.[18] How many processes do we rely upon in ordinary life which involve ingredients likely to be dangerous if they escape? Is it fair to make a defendant strictly liable for the escape of something dangerous if all of us benefit from that dangerous process?

Second, some torts do contain a fault element in their definition, but without any sensible prospect of stigma being attached to the defendant. So, for example, a learner driver will be liable in negligence when they fail to drive to the same standard as a reasonable driver.[19] They are not held to the standard of a reasonable learner, and despite their car being decked out with warning symbols. (But any damages will presumably be paid by the insurance cover.) And with any driver however experienced, a momentary lapse of concentration can result in liability in negligence, even though such lapses inevitably happen to everyone sometime. (Most of us are lucky enough that our lapses do not result in harm.)

ANALYSING THE LAW

If tortious liability can be incurred without the defendant being at fault, then liability seems to be a policy decision that victims of certain activities should be compensated for injury. But why should it be the defendant who pays the compensation? Instead, should the cost of such activities be shouldered by society as a whole? In New Zealand, for example, there is a statutory scheme of no-fault compensation for anyone who suffers injury from an 'accident'. Is that a fairer approach?

1.7 HOW TORT FITS WITH OTHER AREAS OF LAW

We have already noted how tort law is not the only form of civil wrong, and how the various areas of law are rarely distinct, but more like the overlapping circles of the Olympic rings. In

17 (1868) LR 3 HL 330.

18 *Cambridge Water Co Ltd v Eastern Counties Leather plc* [1994] 2 AC 264 (HL).

19 *Nettleship v Weston* [1971] 2 QB 691 (CA).

this section we explore some of the overlaps which tort shares with other areas of law. This part is all about 'Making Connections'.

PRIVATE AND PUBLIC LAW

Tort is certainly part of private law. Most litigation is between private citizens or companies, like one neighbour complaining about another's noise, or an employee alleging that their employer failed to provide a safe place of work. But tort can also play a public law role, when citizens sue a public body. For example, a citizen might make an allegation of false imprisonment against the police. Or a patient might sue the NHS for medical negligence. Or a school child might complain that a local authority failed to take reasonable steps to meet their special educational needs.

OBLIGATIONS AND PROPERTY LAW

Tort is part of the law of obligations. It imposes personal duties on people, for example to take reasonable care when driving. The primary remedy for breach of duty is often payment of a sum of money. But tort is also part of the law of property. For example, careless damage to property can be remedied through the tort of negligence. Or interference with land might be restrained through the torts of trespass to land, or nuisance.

TORT AND CONTRACT

Tort overlaps with contract. For example, occupiers' liability in tort includes the duty of occupiers of premises to take reasonable care for their visitors, some of whom might have a contractual licence governing their visit, like a customer who buys a cinema ticket. Further, liability in negligence might arise following an 'assumption of responsibility', and most contracts involve an assumption of responsibility. For example, a customer who buys a ferry ticket, and then suffers injury on board, might be able to sue in either contract or tort.

KEY CASES

In *Henderson v Merrett Syndicates Ltd*,[20] the claimants were underwriting members at Lloyd's (the insurance market), and the defendants were their managing agents. After a period of heavy losses, the claimants sued the defendants, saying that the managers had not taken reasonable care, for example in choosing which risks to underwrite. There were contracts in place between the parties, which contained an implied term to take reasonable care. But the court said that a duty to take care also arose in tort, and the claimants were free to choose whichever cause of action they preferred.

The choice matters particularly where different remedies are available. If the claimant seeks damages, for example: in contract they are usually forward-looking, aiming to put the claimant

20 [1995] 2 AC 145 (HL).

into the position they expected to be in; whereas in tort they are usually backward-looking, aiming to put the claimant back into the position they were in previously. Ordinarily, a claimant will choose the cause of action which is easiest to prove, and which provides the best remedy (like the most money).

ANALYSING THE LAW

If a defendant is liable in both contract and tort, is it fair that the claimant can simply pick the cause of action which is most rewarding for the claimant (and most burdensome for the defendant)? Or is it the defendant's fault for acting in a way which incurred multiple forms of liability?

BAILMENT

Bailment sits at the conjunction of tort and contract and property law. It is a cause of action based upon another's possession of one's property. So if A takes their clothes to dry cleaner B, then B will likely owe A a duty, to take reasonable care of the clothes, in contract and in tort and in bailment. If B sub-bails the clothes to another cleaner C, then A might be able to sue C directly in tort – but the law of bailment means that C might be able to rely in defence upon any terms in the contract between B and C.[21]

TORT AND CRIMINAL LAW

Some crimes are also torts, like battery, and some criminal defences are also defences in tort, like necessity. This is not to say that the tests are identical in both crime and tort. Because criminal liability is more serious, criminal law tends to be stricter in what it labels a crime, and more generous in what it permits as a defence. But there is often coherence between crime and tort, to avoid the mixed message of conduct being permissible in civil law, but proscribed in criminal law. This means that tort law can sometimes look to the criminal case law (and vice versa) when seeking to develop an area it shares in common.

TORT AND EQUITY

At one point, tort and equity were somewhat at odds. England had a number of courts competing for power and influence, with the common law of tort applied by one, and the rules of equity applied by another. Some of those earlier distinctions have broken down. For example, a person holding a fiduciary position (that is, a special role of trust and confidence recognised in equity) may owe a duty to perform their tasks with reasonable care – which is precisely the same duty which would arise in tort, given the relationship between the parties.[22] Also, the equitable remedy of an injunction is now available in tort law. And there

21 *The Pioneer Container* [1994] 2 AC 324 (PC).

22 *Henderson v Merrett Syndicates Ltd* [1995] 2 AC 145, 205.

has even been some cross-over from equity to tort. For example, what started out as a duty of confidentiality in equity has now branched off into a nascent tort of invasion of privacy.[23]

1.8 TORT LAW OVER TIME

Tort law has roots which go back nearly 1,000 years, but it continues to face new problems as society develops. For example, the pervasive use of the internet means that old torts, like defamation, might now arise in new ways. New technologies pose new conceptual challenges. For example, if a self-driving car is involved in an accident, is the driver to blame, or the company which wrote the software? Nor is it always fitting to squeeze new harms into old formulae. For example, an early attempt to provide protection from harassment looked primarily to the tort of private nuisance.[24] That was unpromising: nuisance is about protecting enjoyment of land, whereas modern forms of harassment can be personal, mobile, and virtual. We now have the Protection from Harassment Act 1997.

So it is that we might turn to the legislature for help with modern problems, and sometimes we must. For example, the continuing phenomenon of pollution probably cannot be contained through private actions in nuisance brought by disgruntled home owners. Effective protection of the environment, for its own sake and for the sake of its inhabitants, needs government regulation. But it has always been one of the great virtues of the common law that it can develop in near real time, responding case by case to solve the disputes before it in a way which balances the need to be both coherent and progressive.

Indeed, there is a steady stream of tort law cases heard by the Supreme Court. Between the first and second editions of this book, the Supreme Court has heard cases including the following: the nuisance of Japanese knotweed,[25] a claimant suffering psychiatric harm when witnessing the death of a loved one due to medical negligence,[26] the vicarious liability of an employer when an employee with a grudge leaked private details of colleagues,[27] false imprisonment by curfew of an immigrant pending deportation,[28] and the defence of illegality when a psychiatric patient sued a hospital for failing to prevent the patient from committing a crime.[29]

23 *Campbell v MGN Ltd* [2004] UKHL 22; *PJS v News Group Newspapers Ltd* [2016] UKSC 26.

24 *Khorasandjian v Bush* [1993] QB 727 (CA).

25 *Davies v Bridgend County Borough Council* [2024] UKSC 15. On nuisance, see too: *Fearn v Board of Trustees of the Tate Gallery* [2023] UKSC 4 (nuisance of museum visitors on a viewing gallery looking through into neighbouring flats).

26 *Paul v Royal Wolverhampton NHS Trust* [2024] UKSC 1.

27 *Various Claimants v WM Morrison Supermarkets plc* [2020] UKSC 12. On vicarious liability, see too: *Trustees of the Barry Congregation of Jehovah's Witnesses v BXB* [2023] UKSC 15 (whether a religious order is vicariously liable for crimes committed by an elder); *Various Claimants v Barclays Bank plc* [2020] UKSC 13 (whether bank is vicariously liable for crimes committed by a doctor to whom its employees were sent).

28 *Jalloh v Secretary of State for the Home Department* [2020] UKSC 4.

29 *Henderson v Dorset Healthcare University NHS Foundation Trust* [2020] UKSC 43.

Developments in the common law need not be restricted solely to causes of action. Substantive causes of action matter, but when judgment comes, it is often the remedy which matters most to the litigant. Also, developments in procedure and ancillary relief can be of great practical importance to the litigant. To mention three examples: injunctions to freeze the defendant's assets, so that they cannot be spirited away, out of the jurisdiction, leaving the claimant with an insolvent defendant;[30] injunctions to search the defendant's premises and seize material, so that the defendant cannot destroy evidence;[31] and an order against an innocent third party to disclose the identity of the tortfeasor with which it has unwittingly become involved.[32]

New problems call for new solutions, and there is no reason why resourceful and creative lawyers cannot draw upon its great diversity to find fresh approaches which keep tort law relevant and useful.

APPLYING THE LAW

Alicia buys a car from Brendan. Driving along the road, Cerys carelessly pulls out in front of Alicia. Alicia cannot stop in time, partly because she is driving too fast, partly because the brakes do not work properly. The brakes are made by Denver Ltd, and are faulty because of an error in the manufacturing process. Alicia crashes into Cerys, who suffers a whiplash injury. Alicia is a travelling sales representative for Eagle plc, and she was driving to visit a client when the crash happened. Cerys takes time off work to recover, and is cared for by Fernando. Advise the parties.

We have not yet considered the detail of individual torts. So let us consider this scenario in overview. Alicia might be able to sue Brendan for breach of contract, because he sold her a car with faulty brakes. Alicia might be able to sue Denver in tort for failing to take reasonable care in their manufacturing of the brakes, as a result of which Alicia has suffered a car crash. Cerys could sue Alicia in tort for crashing into her, because Alicia was driving too fast. Indeed, Alicia might risk incurring criminal liability for speeding. But Cerys might have to accept some responsibility for the crash, for pulling out in front of Alicia carelessly. And to that extent, Alicia might have a counterclaim for any damage she suffered. Cerys might also be able to sue Denver in tort for manufacturing faulty brakes, since Cerys was a victim of their mistake. As well as suing Alicia, Cerys might also sue Eagle, who are vicariously liable for Alicia's tort, since they are Alicia's employer, and Alicia was driving for work purposes. The cost of care provided by Fernando could be part of Cerys' claim.

In all likelihood, the car insurers of Alicia and Cerys would discuss together how much should be paid, on balance, to whom, thus avoiding the need for Alicia and Cerys to go to

30 *Mareva Cia Naviera SA v International Bulk Carriers SA, The Mareva* [1980] 1 All ER 213 (CA).

31 *Anton Piller KG v Manufacturing Processes Ltd* [1976] Ch 55 (CA).

32 *Norwich Pharmacal Co v Customs and Excise Commissioners* [1974] AC 133 (HL).

court. They might also seek to involve Eagle's public liability insurers in that discussion. Then the insurers might sue Brendan or Denver to recover their losses. (At which point, Brendan and Denver would notify their own insurers . . .)

ANALYSING THE LAW

Insurance plays such a major part in modern life in terms of compensating people for harm suffered. But are we happy that it is insurers deciding liability, predominantly according to the terms of private insurance contracts, rather than the courts deciding liability according to tort law? And what about people who cannot afford to obtain insurance?

POINTS TO REVIEW

- Tort law is a collection of misbehaviours or misadventures where the law deems it appropriate to intervene with civil remedies.
- Each tort is a separate cause of action with its own ingredients.
- Some ingredients are common to several torts. Some defences and remedies are common to many torts.
- Tort law is multi-faceted and overlapping because it has to address a wide variety of circumstances.
- Tort law continues to evolve, as it refines itself, or responds to novel situations or changing social attitudes.

TAKING IT FURTHER

Lewis, R. and Morris, A. 'Challenging Views of Tort' [2013] J Personal Injury Law 69 & 137
Free access: www.researchgate.net/publication/260203467_Challenging_Views_of_Tort
The authors discuss a range of commonly held views about personal injury litigation, and show how those views do not match the reality of such litigation in practice. In particular, they deny that there is a 'compensation culture' whereby claimants rush to court for every accident, making up fraudulent complaints along the way. The one exception, they suggest, where there is a strong culture of claiming, is road traffic accidents (where whiplash injuries constitute about 70% of claims). We might ask, are injured drivers merely claiming their due? If not, what reforms could we put in place to ensure only meritorious claims are brought forward?

Goudkamp, J. and Murphy, J. 'The Failure of Universal Theories of Tort Law' (2015) 21 Legal Theory 47
Free access: https://papers.ssrn.com/sol3/papers.cfm?abstract_id=2765717
The authors take aim at corrective justice theory, rights theory, and economic theory, saying that none of these theories, presented by their champions as providing a single

and universal account of tort law, adequately fit with the tort case law. Indeed, say the authors, in places there is a gulf between the theory and the case law. We might ask, does this mean that no single theory can account for tort law, or have we just not identified it yet? Why is it important to find moral or philosophical justifications for tortious doctrines?

Howarth, D. 'Three Forms of Responsibility: On the Relationship Between Tort Law and the Welfare State' [2001] Cambridge LJ 553
Free access: www.researchgate.net/publication/231935499_Three_forms_of_responsibility_On_the_relationship_between_tort_law_and_the_welfare_state
The author says that the existence of tort law acknowledges that there are at least some cases in which we must take personal responsibility for the consequences of our actions. It is because we recognise individual responsibility that we can also appreciate when it might be appropriate instead to have collective responsibility for people's misfortunes. The author says that collective responsibility should be seen not as help for victims, but as help for injurers, sharing a burden for which they would otherwise have to take individual responsibility. Where we draw the line between individual and collective responsibility might vary from case to case or evolve over time. We might ask, are there currently any areas of social activity where it would be fairer to share the cost of harm collectively?

Tilley, C. 'Tort Law Inside Out' (2017) 126 Yale LJ 1320
Free access: www.yalelawjournal.org/pdf/TilleyFinalPDF_77fpm6vw.pdf
The author argues that philosophers have sought to explain tort law by imprinting external theories of economic efficiency or moral justice on top of the case law. However, the tort case law reveals its own internal motivation: community. The author says that tort law is the vehicle through which communities perpetually re-examine and develop their values, encouraging individuals to coordinate their activities among themselves, rather than relying on state regulation. However, we might ask, to the extent that tortious disputes require adjudication by judges, does that not involve some form of state supervision after all?

Abraham, H. 'Queering the Reasonable Person' in K. Horsey (ed), *Diverse Voices in Tort Law* (Bristol University Press, 2023)
Free access: https://papers.ssrn.com/sol3/papers.cfm?abstract_id=4206445
The authors argue that the reasonable person standard common throughout tort law tends to equate to white, middle-class, cisgender, heterosexual men – and therefore applies that standard unfairly to everyone else. We might ask, is it possible to have a single standard that is fair to everyone?

2

CHAPTER 2
NEGLIGENCE: DUTY OF CARE

This chapter introduces the tort of negligence and the key concept of the duty of care.

2.1 INTRODUCTION

Negligence has been defined many times by judges and commentators. One definition was given in the case of *Bolam v Friern Hospital Management Committee*:

> [N]egligence in law means a failure to do some act which a reasonable man in the circumstances would do, or the doing of some act which a reasonable man in the circumstances would not do; and if that failure or the doing of that act results in injury, then there is a cause of action.[1]

Negligence claims start with some form of damage, in the form of physical injury,[2] psychiatric injury, property damage, or financial loss. Where a person has suffered damage, and the damage is caused by another person's conduct, there is a potential claim in negligence.

Where, for example, a person is injured by bags of sugar falling onto him from the upper floor of a warehouse, the law requires that the person responsible for the injury should compensate the victim.[3] The compensation will take the form of a financial payment, or damages, for the pain and suffering caused and for any financial loss caused by the injury, such as loss of earnings while he or she recovers. If the injury causes long-term disability, then the compensation for the 'loss of amenity' and the financial costs of dealing with the disability can also be claimed.

The tort of negligence started as a claim for personal injury and damage to property which was caused directly by the defendant. However, during the twentieth century, it developed to cover all sorts of carelessness on the part of another person: there were successful claims against a surgeon for failing to warn a patient of the risks of an operation,[4] against a surveyor who failed to notice that a building was structurally unsound,[5] against a former employer for

1 *Bolam v Friern Hospital Management Committee* [1957] 1 WLR 582 (QB) 586 (McNair J).

2 Personal injury includes psychiatric injury, where there is a diagnosed mental illness.

3 *Scott v The London and St Katherine Docks Co* (1865) 159 ER 665.

4 *Chester v Afshar* [2004] UKHL 41, [2005] 1 AC 134.

5 *Smith v Eric S Bush* [1990] 1 AC 831 (HL).

DOI: 10.4324/9781003480051-02

an inaccurate reference,[6] and against a solicitor who failed to update a father's will before he died, depriving his daughters of their inheritance.[7]

AS YOU READ

- Understand what is meant by negligence in law.
- Identify the elements of the tort that the claimant has to establish.
- Understand the meaning of duty of care.
- Understand the approach taken by the courts in deciding whether a defendant owes a claimant a duty of care.

2.2 HISTORY AND DEVELOPMENT

English law has recognised, since at least the thirteenth century, that if a person is injured by the carelessness of another, he or she is entitled to be compensated for the injury caused. If the injury was caused directly, the claimant could bring a claim in trespass.[8] If the injury was a consequence of the other's actions, then English law recognised a claim known as an 'action on the case'.[9] The difference between the two claims was summarised in the case of *Reynolds v Clarke*:

> If a man throws a log into the highway and in that act it hits me, I may maintain trespass because it is an immediate wrong; but if, as it lies there, I tumble over it and receive an injury, I must bring an action upon the case because it is only prejudicial in consequence.[10]

The old claim of an action on the case is the basis of the modern claim of negligence. The modern law does not distinguish between direct and consequential damage, but between intentional and unintentional harm. If the defendant intends to injure, or even to touch the claimant, there may be a claim in trespass to the person. If the defendant does not intend to injure, but injures the claimant through a failure to take reasonable care, then the claim will be in negligence.[11]

Another difference is that, while action on the case was concerned with direct physical injury and property damage, negligence covers a wider range of damage. The modern tort includes

6 *Spring v Guardian Assurance plc* [1995] 2 AC 296 (HL).

7 *White v Jones* [1995] 2 AC 207 (HL).

8 See Chapter 13.

9 An action on the case was a broad claim, which included other torts, including what is now referred to as nuisance.

10 *Reynolds v Clarke* (1725) 1 Stra 634, 636 (Fortescue J).

11 *Letang v Cooper* [1965] 1 QB 232 (CA) 239 (Lord Denning MR).

psychiatric injury[12] and economic loss.[13] It can also include damage caused by failure to rescue or protect the claimant from damage caused by external causes.[14]

KEY LEARNING POINT

A claim in negligence requires the claimant to show that he or she suffered harm, such as personal injury, damage to property, or financial loss.

2.3 THE ELEMENTS OF NEGLIGENCE

Where a person suffers harm which is caused by the failure of another person to take reasonable care not to cause him or her that harm, the person may have a claim in negligence. A successful claim requires the claimant to establish all of the elements of negligence. Before 2021, these elements were usually summarised as:

- The claimant had suffered a form of harm recoverable in negligence.
- The defendant owed a duty to take reasonable care not to cause harm of the type that the claimant suffered (duty of care).
- The defendant was in breach of their duty (breach of duty).
- The claimant suffered harm which he or she would not have suffered if the defendant had not breached the duty (causation in fact).
- The damage was not too remote and there was no intervening incident which should be regarded as the cause of the harm (legal causation).

In two cases heard in 2021, however, the Supreme Court held that a claim in negligence requires the court to consider six issues, introducing the new issue referred to as the 'duty nexus' which takes into account the link between the harm caused and the extent of the defendant's duty of care:

1 Is the claim actionable in negligence?
2 Did the defendant owe a duty to the claimant to take reasonable care not to cause the type of harm caused (duty of care)?
3 Did the defendant breach his or her duty by act or omission (breach)?
4 Is the harm suffered by the claimant caused by the defendant's act or omission (causation in fact)?
5 Is there a sufficient nexus, or link, between the harm and the defendant's duty to take care (duty nexus)?

12 *Dulieu v White & Sons* [1901] 2 KB 669 (KB).
13 *Hedley Byrne v Heller and Partners* [1964] AC 465 (HL).
14 *Smith v Littlewoods Organisation* [1987] AC 241 (HL).

6 Is the harm unforeseeable or is there another effective cause of the harm, including the claimant's own failure to take effective steps to mitigate or prevent the harm (legal causation)?[15]

This formulation was approved by five of the seven members of the Supreme Court that heard the cases of *Manchester Building Society v Grant Thornton* and *Meadows v Khan* in 2021, but there were reservations expressed by other members of that court. Lord Burrows preferred that the 'duty nexus' question be expressed in terms of the scope of the duty and questioned the inclusion of contributory negligence with legal causation, while Lord Leggatt questioned the need for the novel issue of 'duty nexus', which he regarded as an aspect of causation.

ACTIONABILITY

A claim in negligence is actionable if the claimant has suffered damage of a type that the law recognises. The types of damage that are recognised are physical and psychiatric injury, damage to land or personal property, and financial loss. In addition, courts have recognised that interference with a person's rights can be a form of damage,[16] although this is only applied in specific circumstances. More commonly, claims for interference with a person's human rights are brought under section 7 of the Human Rights Act.

The law does not recognise distress or emotional upset as a form of damage: to be regarded as damage, the claimant must suffer from a recognised psychiatric injury.[17] Nor will the law compensate claimants for injuries that might happen,[18] or for near misses. Endangering a person is not a tort and, although 'reckless endangerment' is recognised in some jurisdictions as a crime, it is not a crime or a tort in England and Wales.

THE DUTY OF CARE

The question of whether the defendant owed the claimant a legal obligation to take reasonable care not to cause the sort of harm that the claimant suffered is usually abbreviated to whether the defendant owed the claimant a duty of care. However, it is important to remember that a particular duty of care will only apply to a specific type of harm: physical or psychiatric injury, property damage, or economic loss. A duty not to cause one type of damage will not automatically imply a duty not to cause another type. It is common to say,

15 *Manchester Building Society v Grant Thornton* [2021] UKSC 21, [2022] AC 852, [8] (Lord Hodge and Lord Sales) and *Meadows v Khan* [2021] UKSC 21, [2022] AC 852, [28] (Lord Hodge and Lord Sales). These cases are intended to be read in combination with each other (see [2021] UKSC 20, [2022] AC 783, [1]).

16 See *Rees v Darlington Memorial Hospital NHS Trust* [2003] UKHL 52, [2004] 1 AC 309, [8] (Lord Bingham); *Chester v Afshar* [2004] UKHL 41, [2005] 1 AC 134, [24].

17 *Hicks v Chief Constable of the South Yorkshire Police* [1992] 1 All ER 690 (HL).

18 Where a claimant has recovered damages in a personal injury claim, the court may award damages for future illnesses that may be caused by the injury: Senior Courts Act 1981, s.32A. But a claimant who has, for example, been negligently exposed to asbestos cannot recover damages for the future possibility of developing mesothelioma or the psychiatric injury caused by worry that they might develop it: see *Rothwell v Chemical & Insulating Co Ltd* [2007] UKHL 39, [2008] 1 AC 281.

without qualification, that all road users owe a duty of care to other road users. However, the duty is not to take reasonable care not to cause all foreseeable types of harm. A car driver does have a legal obligation to use reasonable care not to cause other road users from suffering from personal injury or property damage.[19] But the driver does not owe any duty to prevent other road users from suffering from financial loss. If a driver causes an accident through a failure to take reasonable care, that driver is liable to any road users who are injured in the accident, and for the damage caused to their vehicles. But the driver at fault is not liable for any financial losses suffered, such as loss of business, by other road users who are held up by the traffic jam caused by the accident.

It is not sufficient to say that the defendant owed the claimant a duty of care: the extent, or scope, of the duty must also be considered. A defendant is not liable for any damage, however caused, which is outside the scope of the duty owed to the claimant. An employer owes a duty to take reasonable care not to cause foreseeable physical or psychiatric injury to its employees,[20] but does not owe a duty to protect an employee from having his or her possessions stolen from the workplace,[21] or to prevent an employee from suffering from financial loss by failing to point out the financial consequences of early retirement.[22]

Recent Supreme Court cases have emphasised the importance of the scope of the defendant's duty of care and included this issue as one of the six specific questions to be considered in negligence claims. In the case of *Meadows v Khan*,[23] the Supreme Court considered whether the defendant was liable for falsely reassuring a pregnant mother that her foetus did not have haemophilia. When the claimant's son was born, he was diagnosed with haemophilia and, later, with autism spectrum disorder. The claimant sought to recover damages for the additional costs of bringing up her child with autism spectrum disorder,[24] as well as the haemophilia. However, the Supreme Court held that, while the misdiagnosis of haemophilia was within the scope of the doctor's duty of care, that did not mean that the doctor was liable for unrelated risks which were inherent in all pregnancies. The autism spectrum disorder was outside the scope of the doctor's duty, so he was not liable for the additional costs associated with that condition. Similarly, in the more recent case of *Manchester Building Society v Grant Thornton*,[25] the Supreme Court held that the key issue was not whether the defendant owed a duty of care or was in breach of that duty, but whether the loss caused was within the scope of the defendant's duty.

19 See, for example, *Swadling v Cooper* [1931] AC 1 (HL).

20 *Wilsons and Clyde Coal Co Ltd v English* [1938] AC 57 (HL).

21 *Deyong v Shenburn* [1946] KB 227 (CA).

22 *Crossley v Faithful & Gould Holdings Ltd* [2004] EWCA Civ 293, [2004] 4 All ER 447.

23 [2021] UKSC 21, [2022] AC 852.

24 The costs of bringing up a child with autism spectrum disorder and haemophilia were agreed to be more than six times the costs of bringing up a child with haemophilia alone: see [10] of the judgment.

25 [2021] UKSC 20, [2022] AC 783.

> KEY LEARNING POINT
>
> A duty of care is a legal duty to take reasonable care not to cause the sort of harm that the claimant suffered. The defendant is not liable for harm which is outside the scope of the duty of care.

BREACH

If there is a legal obligation to take reasonable care not to cause a particular type of harm, the next question to consider is whether the defendant breached that obligation. The law of negligence does not impose an absolute duty to prevent the harm: if the defendant can show that he or she took reasonable care, taking all the circumstances into account, then he or she is not negligent, even if he or she caused, or failed to prevent, the harm.[26] This issue is considered in Chapter 3.

CAUSATION IN FACT AND LEGAL CAUSATION

The harm must have been caused by the breach: this involves two elements which are referred to as causation in fact and legal causation. If the claimant can show that the harm would not have happened without the defendant's breach of duty, then causation in fact is established.

To establish legal causation, the claimant has to show that the harm was a foreseeable consequence of the defendant's breach of duty and that there was no intervening incident, between the breach and the harm being suffered, that supersedes the defendant's breach of duty as the primary cause of the harm.

Breach and causation are considered in Chapters 3 and 4.

THE DUTY NEXUS

Manchester Building Society v Grant Thornton[27] and *Meadows v Khan*[28] introduced the issue of the duty nexus as one of the six elements of a claim in negligence. This is related to the issue identified in the second question, which is the nature of the harm which the defendant is under a duty not to cause, or scope of the duty. Once the scope of the duty is identified at the duty of care stage, the duty nexus question asks whether there is a sufficient connection, or nexus, between the scope of the duty of care, the defendant's failure to take reasonable care, and the harm caused to the claimant.

26 *Latimer v AEC Ltd* [1953] AC 643 (HL).

27 [2021] UKSC 20, [2022] AC 783.

28 [2021] UKSC 21, [2022] AC 852.

2.4 THE TEST FOR A DUTY OF CARE

Whether a defendant owes a claimant a duty of care is one of the most intensely litigated issues in English law: the question has been considered by the House of Lords, Supreme Court and Privy Council on more than 50 occasions since the seminal case of *Donoghue v Stevenson*.[29]

The doctrine of precedent means that, once a duty of care has been established in a specific situation, such as between doctor and patient, there is generally no need to reconsider whether there is a duty of care on the next occasion that a claimant sues the defendant for the same type of damage.

However, when novel situations arise, such as when the family of a victim of a serial killer sues the police for failing to arrest the killer,[30] the courts must consider whether the defendant owes the claimant a duty of care. Courts – particularly the House of Lords and Supreme Court – have attempted to set out a test, based on legal principles, which can be applied to new types of claim, to ensure consistency with established duties of care and with the principles of justice.

> KEY LEARNING POINT
>
> The most common way in which the claimant establishes a duty of care is by showing that his or her claim is based on an established duty of care for which there is an existing precedent. An existing precedent means that the court will accept that there is a duty without further consideration.

In *Van Colle v Chief Constable of Hertfordshire Police*,[31] Lord Bingham set out three ways by which the claimant might establish that the defendant owed him or her a duty of care. These were:

- the Caparo or 'tripartite' test;
- assumption of responsibility; or
- special relationship.[32]

Until 2018, the Caparo test was the most commonly applied when courts considered new situations. It is based on principle and policy, rather than on precedent and, if the claimant could establish that the situation met the three elements of the test, he or she would succeed in establishing that there was a duty of care.

29 [1932] AC 562 (HL).

30 *Hill v Chief Constable of West Yorkshire Police* [1989] AC 53 (HL).

31 [2008] UKHL 50, [2009] AC 225.

32 Ibid, [42] (Lord Bingham).

The Caparo test was set out in the case of *Caparo Industries plc v Dickman*,[33] and stated that the defendant would owe the claimant a duty of care if the claimant could establish that:

- there was 'proximity' between the parties;
- it was foreseeable that the defendant would cause injury to the claimant if he or she did not take reasonable care; and
- it was fair, just, and reasonable for the defendant to owe a duty of care to the claimant.

In 2018, the Supreme Court, in the case of *Robinson v Chief Constable of West Yorkshire Police*,[34] re-examined the case of *Caparo*, and concluded that the Caparo or tripartite test, as it had been applied during the previous 28 years, was based on a misunderstanding of the judgment in that case.[35] The correct meaning of the case was that new duties of care should be imposed only by gradual development of existing duties of care, taking into account whether it was fair, just, and reasonable to find a duty.

2.5 PRINCIPLE OR ANALOGY

Negligence is a common law tort: there is no statute that sets out the elements of the tort or imposes a duty of care on the defendant.[36] This means that the claimant, in any case, needs to find an existing precedent, persuade the court to depart from an existing precedent that holds that the defendant did not owe the claimant a duty of care,[37] or persuade the court to find a new duty of care.

Most negligence claims relate to well-established situations, such as road traffic accidents or medical procedures that have gone wrong. In these types of claim, that a duty of care exists will be accepted by the court: a defendant in a road traffic claim would be wasting his or her time and money if he or she tried to persuade the court that car drivers do not owe a duty to take reasonable care when driving not to cause physical injury or property damage to other road users who are physically close to the driver. The defence is much more likely to argue that the defendant did take reasonable care in the circumstances or did not cause the claimant's injuries.

The courts have repeatedly confirmed that 'the categories of negligence are never closed'.[38] If a new set of circumstances arises, it is open to the claimant to bring a claim in negligence,

33 [1990] 2 AC 605 (HL).

34 [2018] UKSC 4, [2018] AC 736.

35 Ibid, [24]–[25] (Lord Reed).

36 There are statutes which amend the common law: for example, the common law defence of contributory negligence was amended by the Law Reform (Contributory Negligence) Act.

37 As, for example, in *Hedley Byrne v Heller & Partners Ltd* [1964] AC 465 (HL), where the House of Lords departed from a Court of Appeal precedent.

38 *Donoghue v Stevenson* [1932] AC 562 (HL) 619 (Lord MacMillan). See also *Michael v Chief Constable of South Wales Police* [2015] UKSC 2, [2015] AC 1732 [102] (Lord Toulson).

even if there is no precedent for the claim. There has been a steady stream of cases heard by the higher courts in which the claimant was attempting to persuade the court to find a new duty of care or to depart from previous precedent. Following *Donoghue v Stevenson*,[39] in which the claimant did persuade the House of Lords that the manufacturer of a soft drink did owe her, as a consumer, a duty of care, claimants have brought many different and novel claims before the courts. These have included claims against highway authorities for failing to put up warning signs,[40] against the police for failing to catch a serial murderer,[41] against a bank for not freezing a person's assets when ordered to do so by the courts,[42] and against a bank for reassuring a creditor that a company was creditworthy.[43] Most of the claims – particularly those heard since 1990 – have failed to establish new duties of care.

There are two main approaches that the courts have historically used to deal with such claims. The first is the principled approach. In this approach, if there is no applicable precedent, the court considers each new set of circumstances on its own facts and merits. The claim is tested against specific legal principles, such as that for a duty of care to arise, the damage caused must be foreseeable. If the court finds that these legal principles are satisfied, then there will be a duty of care, even if there has been no previous similar or analogous case in which a duty has existed.

The second approach is the incremental approach. In this approach, the court considers whether finding that a duty of care exists would be a justifiable extension of an existing duty of care where there is a precedent. If there is no such existing duty, or if finding a new duty of care would involve a 'giant step'[44] from the existing duty, then the court will find that no duty exists.

Since at least 1990, the courts have also considered public policy issues and, if finding a duty of care would conflict with public policy, have not found a duty of care even in circumstances where the legal principles have been satisfied.

KEY LEARNING POINT

The two approaches to the question of whether, in a case in which there is no existing precedent, a duty of care should exist are the **principled approach** and the **incremental approach**. Courts also consider the public policy implications of finding that a duty of care exists.

Until 2018, the primary test for whether there would be a duty of care in new circumstances was the Caparo or tripartite test, which combined a principled approach with consideration

39 [1932] AC 562 (HL).

40 *Gorringe v Calderdale Metropolitan Borough Council* [2004] UKHL 15, [2004] 1 WLR 105.

41 *Hill v Chief Constable of West Yorkshire* [1989] AC 53 (HL).

42 *Customs and Excise Commissioners v Barclays Bank plc* [2006] UKHL 28, [2007] 1 AC 181.

43 *Hedley Byrne v Heller & Partners Ltd* [1964] AC 465 (HL).

44 *Michael v Chief Constable of South Wales Police* [2015] UKSC 2, [2015] AC 1732, [102] (Lord Toulson).

of public policy issues. In *Michael v Chief Constable of South Wales Police*,[45] the Supreme Court signalled a move away from Caparo and, in *Robinson v Chief Constable of West Yorkshire Police*,[46] unequivocally adopted a test which combined an incremental approach with consideration of public policy issues.

The test based on principle was the main approach of English courts until *Robinson*, however, and it is important to understand how this approach was established in *Donoghue v Stevenson*[47] and applied until *Robinson*. The principled approach has been central to the development of the law of negligence, and understanding principles such as 'foreseeability' and 'proximity' is essential to understand the existing case law.

2.6 A PRINCIPLE-BASED TEST

One of the first attempts to create an overarching principle-based test that would encompass all claims in negligence was in the case of *Heaven v Pender*,[48] in which Brett MR said:

> whenever one person is by circumstances placed in such a position with regard to another that every one of ordinary sense who did think would at once recognise that if he did not use ordinary care and skill in his own conduct with regard to those circumstances he would cause danger of injury to the person or property of the other, a duty arises to use ordinary care and skill to avoid such danger.[49]

However, this statement of principle was expressly rejected by the other two judges in the court.[50]

The first successful creation of a general test was in the case of *Donoghue v Stevenson*.[51]

KEY CASE

Donoghue v Stevenson [1932] AC 562 (HL) is one of the best-known cases in English tort law: it concerned a woman who was having a drink at a café with a friend. She drank ginger beer from a bottle which was later found to contain the decomposing body of a snail. The woman suffered from a stomach upset as a result. She sued the

45 [2015] UKSC 2, [2015] AC 1732.
46 [2018] UKSC 4, [2018] AC 736.
47 [1932] AC 562 (HL).
48 (1883) 11 QBD 503 (CA).
49 Ibid, 509 (Brett MR).
50 Cotton LJ, with whom Bowen LJ concurred, stated that he was 'unwilling to concur with the Master of the Rolls in laying down unnecessarily the larger principle': see (1883) 11 QBD 503 (CA) 516.
51 [1932] AC 562 (HL).

manufacturer of the drink in negligence, claiming that the manufacturer owed her, as a consumer of the product, a duty of care.

The House of Lords held, 3–2, that a manufacturer did owe a consumer a duty to take reasonable care to ensure that their products should not cause injury or sickness. There was conflicting authority on the point, as some cases, including *George v Skivington*, held that there was such a duty, but others, such as *Longmeid v Holliday*, held that a manufacturer owed a duty in contract to the buyer, but not to any third party that might use the product. In *Longmeid*, a person who was injured when an oil lamp exploded was unable to recover damages because the oil lamp had been bought by her husband, rather than herself. In *Donoghue*, the claimant's friend had bought the ginger beer from the café, which had, in turn, bought the ginger beer from the manufacturer, Stevenson.

The House of Lords held that the manufacturer's contractual obligation to the purchaser did not prevent them from also having a duty of care to anyone who drank the ginger beer, although Lord Buckmaster, in his dissenting judgment, thought it would be 'little short of outrageous' to hold manufacturers liable to anyone that used their products.

On the specific point of law considered, *Donoghue v Stevenson* held that a manufacturer owed a duty to its consumers to take reasonable care to ensure that its products did not cause physical injury. The case is important, however, for Lord Atkin's statement of the 'neighbour principle':

> You must take reasonable care to avoid acts or omissions which you can reasonably foresee would be likely to injure your neighbour. Who, then, in law is my neighbour? The answer seems to be – persons who are so *closely and directly affected* by my act that I ought *reasonably to have them in contemplation* as being so affected when I am directing my mind to the acts or omissions which are called in question.[52]

The neighbour principle, for the first time, set out a test which could be applied by courts to determine whether the defendant owed the claimant a duty of care in cases where there was no previous case that could be applied.

The neighbour principle includes two key concepts in determining whether a duty of care exists: the claimant should be 'closely and directly' affected by the acts or omissions of the defendant, and the defendant should reasonably have the claimant 'in contemplation as being so affected'. These two concepts are usually referred to as 'proximity' and 'foreseeability', and they have been the foundations of the tests for whether a duty of care should exist.

52 Ibid, 580 (Lord Atkin) (emphasis added).

KEY LEARNING POINT

Donoghue v Stevenson established that, if the relationship between the parties is close, or has the necessary 'proximity', and a reasonable person would foresee that the claimant might suffer a particular type of damage, a duty to take reasonable care to prevent the claimant from suffering that type of damage will be imposed upon the defendant.

While it was well established by the time of *Donoghue v Stevenson* that there was a general obligation to take reasonable care not to cause directly personal injury to others, as well as specific duties, such as the duty occupiers of land owed to visitors, Lord Atkin created a test which could be applied to new types of claim.

In *Dorset Yacht v Home Office*,[53] Lord Reid held that:

> *Donoghue v Stevenson* may be regarded as a milestone, and the well-known passage in Lord Atkin's speech should I think be regarded as a statement of principle. It is not to be treated as if it were a statutory definition. It will require qualification in new circumstances. But I think that the time has come when we can and should say that it ought to apply unless there is some justification or valid explanation for its exclusion.[54]

A similar formulation was set out by Lord Wilberforce[55] in the case of *Anns v Merton London Borough Council*.[56] If the elements of proximity and foreseeability had been established, then the defendant would owe the claimant a duty of care, unless there were some 'considerations which ought to negative, or to reduce or limit the scope of the duty or the class of person to whom it is owed or the damages to which a breach of it may give rise'.[57]

Lord Wilberforce's two-part test, or the Anns test, is now seen as the high point of a period when it was relatively easy for claimants to establish a duty of care in new circumstances. This period came to an end in 1990, with the cases of *Caparo Industries plc v Dickman*[58] and *Murphy v Brentwood District Council*.[59]

THE 'RETREAT FROM ANNS'

Between the 1960s and early 1980s, as Lord Reid's and Lord Wilberforce's statements show, the presumption was that, if the claimant could show proximity and foreseeability, then a duty of care would arise unless the defendant could point to some reason that the duty should not arise.

53 [1970] AC 1004 (HL).
54 Ibid, 1027 (Lord Reid). Viscount Dilhorne, dissenting, disagreed with this approach: see p.1044 of the judgment.
55 Lord Wilberforce's judgment was approved by a majority of the House of Lords.
56 [1978] AC 728 (HL).
57 Ibid, 752.
58 [1990] 2 AC 605 (HL).
59 [1991] 1 AC 398 (HL).

In a series of decisions during this period, the House of Lords expanded the scope of negligence into new areas. New claims were allowed for pure economic loss, where a person gave negligent advice;[60] against the Home Office for allowing young detainees to escape and damage property;[61] against a local council for failure to ensure that the foundations of a building were properly laid;[62] and for psychiatric injury caused by witnessing the immediate aftermath of an accident in which the claimant's daughter was killed.[63]

By the mid-1980s, however, there was increasing concern that the law was leaning too far in favour of the claimant, and that the courts were being overwhelmed by new claims in negligence. In 1988, Lord Templeman, in a judgment that was agreed by the other members of the House of Lords, sharply criticised the effect of *Anns v Merton Borough Council* in increasing the number of negligence claims with the words:

> Since *Anns v Merton London Borough Council* put the floodgates on the jar,[64] a fashionable plaintiff alleges negligence. The pleading assumes that we are all neighbours now . . . that foreseeability is a reflection of hindsight and that for every mischance in an accident-prone world someone solvent must be liable in damages.[65]

In restricting the expansion of new claims in negligence, the House of Lords began to use the duty of care as a 'control mechanism'.[66] If there was no duty owed to the claimant, the case could be struck out before trial, unless the claimant could show that he or she had a realistic prospect of persuading a court that a duty of care should exist.[67] This meant that claims could be dealt with more speedily and more economically. Public policy started to play a prominent role in restricting new duties of care and liability in negligence.

Traditionally, English courts did not pay much attention to public policy considerations. In *Dorset Yacht v Home Office*,[68] Lord Reid had brushed aside the policy argument that finding a duty of care would dissuade public servants from doing their duty with the words: 'Her Majesty's servants are made of sterner stuff'.[69] In a 1982 House of Lords case, Lord Scarman had held that courts could not even consider policy issues. In his dissenting judgment, he stated that if legal principles led to the conclusion that the defendant owed the claimant a

60 *Hedley Byrne v Heller & Partners* [1964] AC 465 (HL).

61 *Dorset Yacht v Home Office* [1970] AC 1004 (HL).

62 *Anns v Merton London Borough Council* [1978] AC 728 (HL).

63 *McLoughlin v O'Brian* [1983] 1 AC 410 (HL).

64 Putting a door 'on the jar' means to leave it slightly open, or ajar: Lord Templeman means that *Anns v Merton Borough Council* left the floodgates open.

65 *CBS Songs Ltd v Amstrad Consumer Electronics plc* [1988] AC 1013 (HL).

66 See *Candlewood Navigation Corp Ltd v Mitsui OSK Lines Ltd* [1986] AC 1 (PC) 25 (Lord Fraser) for an early example of the Privy Council declaring that a control mechanism is needed to limit liability in negligence for economic loss.

67 Many of the leading cases on duty of care, including *Donoghue v Stevenson* [1932] AC 562 (HL), *Caparo v Dickman* [1990] 2 AC 605 (HL) and *Michael v Chief Constable of South Wales Police* [2015] UKSC 2, [2015] AC 1732, were either applications to strike out the claim as having no realistic prospect of success or preliminary hearings to determine whether the defendant owed the claimant a duty of care.

68 *Dorset Yacht v Home Office* [1970] AC 1004 (HL)

69 Ibid, 1033 (Lord Reid).

duty of care, it was not open to the court to deny the duty on the grounds of public policy: that was a matter for Parliament.[70] However, during the 1980s, the House of Lords started to pay more attention to public policy issues, and to use those issues as a basis for denying duties of care.

In *Governors of the Peabody Donation Fund v Sir Lindsay Parkinson*,[71] Lord Keith[72] said that a duty of care should only be found when it was 'just and reasonable' to do so. This was later confirmed in the case of *Caparo Industries plc v Dickman*.[73] This was a sign of the increasing importance of policy issues in determining whether a duty of care would exist.

THE CAPARO TEST

KEY CASE

In *Caparo Industries plc v Dickman* [1990] 2 AC 605 (HL), the claimant was a public company which had bought shares in another public company, Fidelity plc. When the annual report for 1984 was published, the claimant launched a successful takeover bid. The claimant then discovered that the annual accounts were inaccurate, as they had stated that Fidelity had made a profit of £1.3 million rather than the true position, which was that there had been a loss of £400,000. The claimant sued the auditors of Fidelity, arguing that the auditors owed investors and potential investors a duty to take reasonable care to ensure that the accounts were a 'true and fair' view of the company's financial position.

The House of Lords held that the auditors did not owe a duty of care to investors. In *Hedley Byrne v Heller and Partners* [1964] AC 465 (HL), the House of Lords had held that a liability for negligent statements would arise if the defendant assumed responsibility for the claimant's economic well-being, but that required the defendant to make the statement to a known recipient for a specific purpose, and to be aware that the claimant would rely upon the statement. In this case, the 'statement', in the form of the annual accounts, had been put into public circulation and could be used by any investor or potential investor for any purpose.

Lord Bridge also stated that a duty of care would arise if the damage was foreseeable, the relationship between the parties was 'characterised by the law as one of proximity', and that it was 'fair, just and reasonable' to impose the duty on the defendant.

70 *McLoughlin v O'Brian* [1983] 1 AC 410 (HL) 429ff (Lord Scarman).

71 [1985] AC 210 (HL).

72 Lord Keith gave the only judgment.

73 [1990] 2 AC 605 (HL).

Lord Bridge's judgment created what became known as the Caparo, or tripartite, test – the three elements of the test being:

- foreseeability of damage;
- proximity between defendant and claimant; and
- that it is 'fair, just and reasonable' to impose the duty.

In fact, as the recent Supreme Court judgment in *Robinson v Chief Constable of West Yorkshire* has explained, it was never Lord Bridge's intention to create such a test: a careful reading of his judgment reveals that he was summarising the law as it stood at the time, not proposing a new test.[74] The tripartite test was his summary of the Anns test, as it had been developed by the House of Lords in cases such as *Governors of the Peabody Donation Fund*.[75] Immediately after setting out the current law, Lord Bridge went on to say that the law should develop new duties of care incrementally, by analogy with existing cases, rather than by the application of a principle or test.[76]

However, while it might not have been Lord Bridge's intention to create the tripartite test, that is how his judgment was interpreted and applied in the period between 1990 and 2015 by all courts, including the House of Lords and the Supreme Court.[77] While the familiar elements of proximity and foreseeability remained, the qualifying third step required the court to consider policy issues before deciding whether a duty of care existed.

KEY LEARNING POINT

The Caparo test, or tripartite test, required that:

- the damage be of a foreseeable type;
- the relationship between the claimant and defendant had the necessary proximity or closeness; and
- it is 'fair, just and reasonable' to impose a duty on the defendant.

THE THREE ELEMENTS

FORESEEABILITY

Foreseeability is the most straightforward of the three parts of the Caparo test: the test is objective, so it is not necessary to show that the defendant foresaw that the damage might occur. Rather the question is whether a reasonable person in the position of the defendant would foresee the damage. As was stated in *Bourhill v Young*, a duty of care is 'owed to those to

74 [2018] UKSC 4, [2018] AC 736 [24]–[25] (Lord Reed, with whom Baroness Hale and Lord Hodge agreed).

75 [1985] AC 210 (HL). It is worth noting that, in the High Court case of *Caparo v Dickman*, the judge set out the three elements of Lord Bridge's test, and considered foreseeability, proximity and whether it would be 'fair, reasonable and just' to impose liability: *Caparo v Dickman* [1988] BCLC 387 (QB) 392 (Sir Neil Lawson).

76 *Caparo Industries plc v Dickman* [1990] 2 AC 605 (HL) 618 (Lord Bridge). See also *Robinson v Chief Constable of West Yorkshire Police* [2018] UKSC 4, [2018] AC 736 [25] (Lord Reed).

77 See, for example, *Marc Rich v Bishop Rock Marine* [1996] AC 211 (HL).

whom injury may reasonably and probably be anticipated if the duty is not observed'.[78] It is foreseeable that a careless car driver might cause physical injury or property damage to other road users;[79] or that a doctor who examines a patient too hastily may miss something vital.[80] However, it is not foreseeable that an oil-rig worker might suffer from a mental illness if he saw his fellow workers killed when the rig exploded.[81]

KEY LEARNING POINT

For a duty of care to arise, the damage must be of a foreseeable type.

Quite what the reasonable person would foresee is a question to be determined by the court, which will usually be a single judge. This does introduce an element of subjectivity, as was noted by Lord Macmillan in *Glasgow Corporation v Muir*:

> It is still left to the judge to decide what, in the circumstances of the particular case, the reasonable man would have had in contemplation, and what, accordingly, the party sought to be made liable ought to have foreseen. Here there is room for diversity of view, as, indeed, is well illustrated in the present case. What to one judge may seem far-fetched may seem to another both natural and probable.[82]

PROXIMITY

In *Caparo*, Lord Bridge stated that proximity was not capable of being defined precisely, but was a little more than a 'convenient label' to attach to the specific circumstances that gave rise to a duty of care.[83] Other courts have tried to be more precise. In an Australian judgment[84] which has been widely quoted,[85] it was held that the proximity requirement could be met in three ways:

- physical proximity;
- 'circumstantial' or 'relational' proximity; and
- causal proximity.[86]

Physical proximity, or proximity in space, is one way in which this element of the Caparo test can be established: as a rule, everyone owes a duty to those who are physically close to them to take reasonable care not to physically injure them by their acts or omissions. Road users owe a duty to other road users, such as motorists, cyclists and pedestrians, who are in the

78 *Bourhill v Young* [1943] AC 92 (HL) 104 (Lord Macmillan).
79 *Nettleship v Weston* [1971] 2 QB 691 (CA).
80 *Barnett v Chelsea and Kensington Hospital Management Committee* [1969] 1 QB 428 (QB).
81 *McFarlane v EE Caledonia Ltd* [1994] 2 All ER 1 (CA) 14 (Stuart-Smith LJ).
82 *Glasgow Corp v Muir* [1943] AC 448 (HL) 457 (Lord Macmillan).
83 [1990] 2 AC 605 (HL) 618 (Lord Bridge).
84 *Sutherland Shire County v Heyman* (1985) 60 ALR 1.
85 See, for example, *Michael v Chief Constable of South Wales Police* [2015] UKSC 2, [2015] AC 1732, [146] (Lord Kerr).
86 *Sutherland Shire County v Heyman* (1985) 60 ALR 1, 55 (Deane J). See also *Jaensch v Coffey* (1984) 54 ALR 417, 444 (Deane J).

immediate vicinity or 'area of potential danger',[87] but not to other road users outside that area. Likewise, landowners owe a duty to owners of neighbouring land, but not to more remote landowners.[88]

> KEY LEARNING POINT
>
> The proximity element of the Caparo test will be met if the claimant and defendant are physically close to each other.

In the case of physical injury caused directly by the acts of the defendant, physical proximity will suffice: a builder throwing rubble from an upper floor into a skip owes a duty to anyone close by. If a carelessly thrown brick bounces off the edge of the skip and injures a person walking past, the builder would be liable for the injuries. As a passer-by enters the 'danger zone' – the area in which it is foreseeable that a carelessly thrown brick could cause injury – the duty of care to him or her arises and when he or she leaves the danger zone, the duty lapses.

In the case of psychiatric injury caused by witnessing the death of another person or the immediate aftermath of the death, courts have included a requirement of proximity in time as well as proximity in space. Proximity requires that the claimant either witnessed the incident with his or her own eyes, or saw the aftermath of the incident within a period of two hours.[89]

The second way in which proximity can be established is what the High Court of Australia referred to as 'circumstantial proximity': this refers to the circumstances of the case but might be better referred to as 'relational proximity'. This form of proximity arises from a relationship between the parties such as, in the examples cited in the Australian judgment, between employer and employee or between a professional person and his or her client.

Relational proximity is the principal way in which the proximity requirement of the Caparo test may be met. It requires a relationship between the parties, such as between employer and employee, which existed before the event that caused the damage to the claimant. If there is no prior relationship, then unless there is physical or causal proximity, there will be no duty of care, other than in specific circumstances, unless such a duty arises from assumption of responsibility.

Many relationships are well established as imposing a duty of care on one or both parties: a partial list would include employers and employees,[90] occupiers of land to visitors,[91] police to

87 *Bourhill v Young* [1943] AC 92 (HL) 98 (Lord Thankerton).
88 *Goldman v Hargrave* [1967] 1 AC 645 (PC).
89 *Alcock v Chief Constable of South Yorkshire Police* [1992] 1 AC 310 (HL). See Chapter 6.
90 *Smith v Baker & Sons* [1891] AC 325 (HL).
91 *Glasgow Corp v Taylor* [1922] 1 AC 44 (HL).

prisoners,[92] doctors and other healthcare practitioners[93] to patients,[94] solicitors and accountants to clients,[95] manufacturers to consumers,[96] vets to animal owners,[97] schools to pupils,[98] and sports participants to other participants[99] and spectators.[100]

In some of these cases, there will be physical proximity as well as relational proximity: however, the duty will arise even if there is no physical proximity. A doctor owes a duty of care to a patient when he or she is examining him or her in person, in which case there is physical proximity, but the duty continues while the patient is physically absent. For example, if the doctor receives the test results for a patient, he or she is required to use reasonable care when determining what to do about them, even though the patient, at the time, is nowhere near the doctor. Schools owe a duty of care to their pupils which continues even when the pupils are away from the school and being supervised by independent providers.[101] Employers owe a duty of care to their employees while they are at work and while they are working at other places. In the case of the duty of occupiers of land to visitors, the duty arises from the relationship, rather than from physical proximity. The occupier owes a duty to ensure that the land or premises are reasonably safe, but this duty is only owed to visitors whom the occupier has invited or permitted to be on the land, or people who have a legal right to be on the ground. In the case of trespassers, who are in equal physical proximity, a lesser duty is owed.[102]

However, if there is no prior relationship, then there will not be relational proximity: doctors do not owe a duty to the general public and, until the doctor–patient relationship is established, there is no duty of care.[103] In English law, a doctor owes no obligation to a person who is physically close to the doctor and who needs medical attention, but is not the doctor's patient, even if the doctor might easily provide life-saving treatment.[104] Likewise, the police owe a duty to take reasonable care to prevent prisoners from suffering physical injury, but do not owe a duty to members of the public to prevent them from being killed by a serial murderer.[105]

92 *Reeves v Metropolitan Police Commissioner* [2000] 1 AC 360 (HL).
93 Including alternative therapists: *Shakoor v Situ* [2001] 1 WLR 410 (QB).
94 *Bolam v Friern Hospital Management Committee* [1957] 1 WLR 582 (QB).
95 *Wong (Edward) Finance Co Ltd v Johnson Stokes & Master* [1984] AC 296 (PC).
96 *Donoghue v Stevenson* [1932] AC 562 (HL).
97 *Calver v Westwood Veterinary Group* (2000) 58 BMLR 194 (CA).
98 *Woodland v Essex County Council* [2013] UKSC 66, [2014] AC 537.
99 *Condon v Basi* [1985] 1 WLR 866 (CA).
100 *Wooldridge v Sumner* [1963] 2 QB 43 (CA).
101 *Woodland v Essex County Council* [2013] UKSC 66, [2014] AC 537.
102 *British Railway Board v Herrington* [1972] AC 877 (HL). See also Occupiers Liability Act 1984.
103 There is a very limited exception to this rule, established in *ABC v St George's NHS Trust* [2020] EWHC 455 (QB).
104 *Cassidy v Ministry of Health* [1951] 2 KB 343 (CA) 360 (Denning LJ). In other common law jurisdictions, courts have found a duty to intervene on the parts of doctors: *Woods v Lowns* (New South Wales Court of Appeal, 5 February 1996).
105 *Hill v Chief Constable of West Yorkshire Police* [1989] AC 53 (HL).

KEY LEARNING POINT

The proximity element of the Caparo test will be met if there is a relationship between the parties which existed before the event that caused damage to the claimant.

The third type of proximity is causal proximity: this is where the claimant and defendant are not in physical proximity and there is no prior relationship, but there is a direct causal link between the defendant's acts or omissions and the claimant's damage. It does not appear that causal proximity has been expressly applied in English courts. However, courts have referred to 'special relationships' between defendant and claimant, which have been sufficient to create a duty of care where there is neither physical proximity nor a prior relationship.[106]

In *White v Jones*,[107] a father argued with his daughters, and made a will in which they received nothing. Later, the father and his daughters were reconciled, and he decided to make a new will. He instructed solicitors, but because of the solicitors' negligence, the new will had not been signed by the father before he died. The daughters sued the solicitors in negligence, so needed to establish that there was a duty of care. Under ordinary circumstances, a solicitor owes a duty to his or her clients, but not to any third party. However, the House of Lords held that, in the circumstances, the defendant did owe a duty of care. The main discussion in the judgments was whether the defendant had assumed responsibility for the claimant, rather than applying the Caparo test. However, the judgments of the majority all referred to the close causal relationship between the solicitors' negligence and the claimants' loss.[108]

KEY LEARNING POINT

The proximity element of the Caparo test may be met if there is a particularly close causal relationship between the defendant's acts and the damage suffered by the claimant.

FAIR, JUST, AND REASONABLE

The final part of the Caparo test is that it should be fair, just, and reasonable to impose a duty of care. This part has allowed courts to take external matters into account, and to look at the consequences of imposing a duty of care on a particular defendant.

It is natural for the court to feel sympathy for a claimant, and there is an instinct to provide a remedy in a case where the claimant has clearly suffered harm as a result of the defendant's

106 In the Australian case of *Bryan v Maloney* [1995] 1 LRC 562, causal proximity was used to justify the finding of a duty owed by a house builder to a later purchaser of the property.

107 [1995] 2 AC 207 (HL).

108 See [1995] 2 AC 207 (HL) 269 (Lord Goff), 276 (Lord Browne-Wilkinson), and 294 (Lord Nolan). See also the Australian case of *Hills v Van Erp* (1997) 142 ALR 687, which also considered the duty of a solicitor to a beneficiary of a will.

carelessness.[109] During the expansive period of the 1960s and 1970s, when new claims in negligence were being allowed, the courts allowed this sympathy to override any concern that the law was becoming too generous to claimants. By the mid-1980s, however, the courts began to consider the wider implications of a proposed new duty of care, and whether it would be fair, just, and reasonable to the defendant and to the public, as well as to the claimant, to award a remedy.

An early case in which wider issues were considered was a claim brought by the mother of Jacqueline Hill, who was the last victim of a serial murderer who had killed 13 women in West Yorkshire during the 1970s and early 1980s.[110] The investigation carried out by the West Yorkshire Police was widely criticised: in particular, over-reliance on a single piece of evidence,[111] which later turned out to be a hoax, meant that the police overlooked strong evidence pointing to Peter Sutcliffe, who was arrested and convicted of 13 counts of murder in 1981.

The House of Lords held that the police force did not owe a duty of care to the claimant's daughter. Applying the Anns test, they accepted that it was foreseeable that, if the police force did not take reasonable care when investigating crimes, then some criminals would remain free to commit further crimes and cause injury to future victims. However, there was no proximity: there was no prior relationship between the victim and the police force, and there was nothing to distinguish Jacqueline Hill from any other potential victim.[112] That was, as Lord Keith noted, sufficient to decide the claim,[113] but his judgment continued to discuss the policy issues that were relevant. Lord Keith identified a number of policy and public interest issues which were in favour of there not being a duty of care: these included that imposing such a duty would not reinforce the police's sense of public duty or improve the standard of policing; that it would lead the police to act 'defensively'; that it would influence the police's priorities unduly; and that defending such claims would divert police resources from the suppression of crime.[114]

109 See Denning LJ's comments in *Roe v Ministry of Health* [1954] 2 QB 66 (CA) 86, on the 'natural feeling' that the claimants in that case should be compensated for the 'terrible consequences' of a minor operation.

110 *Hill v Chief Constable of West Yorkshire Police* [1989] AC 53 (HL).

111 A hoax audio tape, claiming to be from the murderer, was sent to George Oldfield, the police officer leading the investigation. Oldfield believed the tape to be genuine, even though he was warned by linguistic experts that it was probably a hoax, and instructed his officers to eliminate any suspect who did not have the same distinctive regional accent as was heard on the tape. Sutcliffe, who did not have the accent heard on the tape, was questioned nine times before his eventual arrest. The person responsible for the hoax tape was later convicted of perverting the course of justice. See French, P., Harrison, P., and Windsor Lewis, J., '*R v John Samuel Humble*: the Yorkshire Ripper hoaxer trial' (2006) 13(2) International Journal of Speech, Language and the Law 255–273.

112 [1989] AC 53 (HL) 62 (Lord Keith, with whom Lord Brandon, Lord Oliver, and Lord Goff agreed).

113 Ibid.

114 Ibid.

2.7 POLICY ISSUES

KEY LEARNING POINT

There will not be a duty of care if it would be against public policy to impose one on the defendant.

A 'policy issue' is an issue that is not immediately related to the claim. 'Policy issues' is a term used to describe wider issues, such as the extent of the liability that other potential defendants might face, the cost to the public, or the consequences to society. While determining foreseeability and proximity requires the court to look back at the facts of the case and the relationship between the parties at the time of the damage, the consideration of policy issues requires the court to look to the future and to determine the wider effects of a judgment in favour of the claimant.

In the case of *Hill*, Lord Keith considered whether there was sufficient proximity between claimant and defendant, and whether the claimant's death was foreseeable in the first part of his judgment. On this basis, there was no duty. What might happen in the future as a consequence of finding that the police owed a duty to potential victims of crime was considered in the second part of his judgment. The factors identified reinforced the conclusion that he had already reached: that the detrimental wider effects of finding a duty of care meant that it would not be in the public interest to hold the police liable for the death of Jacqueline Hill.

The third limb of the Caparo test established that consideration of policy issues was necessary in determining whether there was a duty of care in any novel situation. There are many policy issues that the courts have considered, of which the most commonly cited are:

- proliferation of new claims (the 'floodgates');
- disproportionate liability;
- costs to the taxpayer;
- defensive practices; and
- conflict with other duties.

Although the Supreme Court has recently re-examined Caparo and held that the tripartite test should no longer be applied, the new Robinson test still requires a consideration of whether it would be 'fair, just and reasonable' to find a new duty of care.[115] Policy issues will remain central to the issue of duty of care in future cases, and the court will continue to take the above factors into account.

115 [2018] UKSC 4, [2018] AC 736, [27] (Lord Reed).

THE FLOODGATES

The creation of a new duty of care will lead, inevitably, to an increase in the number of claims: if it is possible for a victim of crime to sue the police force for failing to catch a criminal, as was argued in Hill, then there would clearly be a very large number of victims of crime who would be able to claim against the police. This is, strictly speaking, what is meant by the 'floodgates' argument. Such an increase in the number of potential claimants would place an increased workload on the courts, with a resulting increase in public expenditure. Proliferation of claims should be distinguished from indeterminate or disproportionate liability, although 'floodgates' has been used to describe both issues.[116]

An early expression of the floodgates argument was made by the Privy Council in *Victorian Railway Commissioners v Coultas*, a nineteenth-century case:

> Not only in such a case as the present, but in every case where an accident caused by negligence had given a person a serious nervous shock, there might be a claim for damages on account of mental injury. The difficulty which now often exists in case of alleged physical injuries of determining whether they were caused by the negligent act would be greatly increased, and a wide field opened for imaginary claims.[117]

Since then, courts have regularly cited this policy issue as a reason for denying a duty of care. The reliance on floodgates has been criticised on the grounds that the issue is based on the perception of the judges involved, rather than on any actual evidence.[118]

DISPROPORTIONATE LIABILITY

Disproportionate liability is applied when the extent of the liability is disproportionate to the lack of care or fault of the defendant. An early example was seen in the American case, *Ultramares Corporation v Touche*.[119] This was a claim against an accountant for the negligent preparation of a company's accounts, on the basis of which the claimant advanced credit to the company. Cardozo CJ held that, if an accountant owed a duty of care to any person who relied upon the accounts, then a 'thoughtless slip or blunder' or a failure to detect theft or forgery would lead to the accountant facing liability of 'an indeterminate amount for an indeterminate time to an indeterminate class'. This would be disproportionate to the negligence of the defendant.[120] He was not expressing a concern that the court would be

116 'Floodgates' is used to mean an increase in the number of claims in *Gregg v Scott* [2005] UKHL 2, [2005] 2 AC 176 [47]–[48] (Lord Nicholls); *Johnson v Unisys Ltd* [2001] UKHL 13, [2003] 1 AC 518, [27] (Lord Steyn); *Alfred McAlpine Construction Ltd v Panatown* [2001] 1 AC 518 (HL) 590 (Lord Millett); and *White v Chief Constable of South Yorkshire Police* [1999] 2 AC 455 (HL), 465 (Lord Griffiths), and 510 (Lord Hoffmann). By contrast, 'floodgates' is used to refer to disproportionate liability in *Junior Books Ltd v Veitchi Co Ltd* [1983] 1 AC 520 (HL) 532 (Lord Fraser) and *Customs and Excise Commissioners v Barclays Bank plc* [2006] UKHL 28, [2007] 1 AC 181, [100] (Lord Mance).

117 (1887) 13 App Cas 222 (PC) 225–226 (Sir Richard Couch).

118 See, for example, Witting, C. 'Duty of Care: An Analytical Approach' (2005) 25(1) OJLS 33–63.

119 (1931) 255 NY 170.

120 Ibid, 179–180 (Cardozo CJ).

flooded with new claims, but that anyone carrying on the business of accountancy might face such a disproportionate burden as to make their business impossible.

The disproportionate burden argument was cited by Lord Bridge in *Caparo v Dickman* as a reason for holding that there was no duty of care owed by the accountants to anyone who might make use of the published accounts.[121] This applies when a single negligent act can cause damage to an unlimited or unquantifiable number of people. In the case of *Caparo v Dickman*, if the duty of care was owed to anyone who relied upon the company's accounts when making an investment decision, then the potential claimants would include the actual claimants, who were considering a takeover bid. But it would also include the claims of any other shareholders who had bought shares relying on the accounts, or even shareholders who did not sell their shares, but who might reasonably claim that they would have done if they had known the true state of the company. The accountants would have been liable for all the losses suffered by investors, which would be disproportionate to their actual fault. Disproportionate liability would also have consequential effects: it would increase the cost of professional insurance and raise costs for all clients.

Disproportionate liability has also been used as a policy reason to limit the liability of defendants for causing psychiatric injury: where the psychiatric injury is caused by the shock of seeing a person killed or seriously injured, the courts have placed strict limits on the extent of the duty of care. In *McLoughlin v O'Brian*, Lord Wilberforce stated expressly that the duty of care should be restricted to prevent a disproportionate burden on the defendant.[122] In *White v Chief Constable of South Yorkshire Police*, Lord Steyn held:

> Fourthly, the imposition of liability for pure psychiatric harm in a wide range of situations may result in a burden of liability on defendants which may be disproportionate to tortious conduct involving, perhaps, momentary lapses of concentration, eg in a motor car accident.[123]

In these types of claim – for economic loss and for psychiatric injury caused by the shock of seeing a person killed – there is a potential for the defendant's negligence to cause damage to a large number of people: thousands or tens of thousands of people may be shareholders in a public company. In the case of *Alcock v Chief Constable of South Yorkshire Police*,[124] the shocking event which caused the claimants to suffer from psychiatric injury was broadcast live on national television: millions of people were watching as the event occurred.

For other types of damage, such as personal injury or property damage, the potential to cause damage to large numbers of potential claimants is less likely, and disproportionate liability is less likely to be cited as a policy issue.

121 [1990] 2 AC 605 (HL) 621 (Lord Bridge).

122 [1983] 1 AC 410 (HL) 421–422.

123 [1999] 2 AC 455 (HL) 494.

124 [1992] 1 AC 310 (HL).

COSTS TO THE TAXPAYER

In the case of claims against public authorities, who are funded by the taxpayer, the increased costs of dealing with claims in negligence, both in defending the claims and in paying any compensation awarded by the courts, has been held to be a reason that public authorities should not owe a duty of care in the circumstances under consideration.[125] Again, this is a relatively recent development: in *Dorset Yacht v Home Office*, Viscount Dilhorne held that the cost of compensating for damage would fall upon 'the general body of taxpayers',[126] who would be able to afford such compensation, rather than on the individual, who might not be able to bear the cost, was a reason in favour of finding a duty of care, rather than denying that a duty existed.

As policy issues have been increasingly used to limit the expansion of tort, the potential costs to taxpayers has become one of the policy issues relied upon by the courts. In *Hill v Chief Constable of West Yorkshire Police*, Lord Keith referred to the 'police time, trouble and expense' that would be spent defending claims, if the police did owe a duty to victims of crime.[127] The same policy consideration has also been significant in later cases against the police.[128]

DEFENSIVE PRACTICES

In *Hill*, Lord Keith referred to the police carrying out their functions in a 'detrimentally defensive state of mind':[129] he believed that finding a duty of care would cause the police to change their practices and procedures to avoid liability in negligence, rather than doing their job as well as possible. Avoiding liability would become their priority, at the expense of their main function of the suppression and investigation of crime. This would be against the public interest and is a strong policy reason for holding that the police do not owe a duty of care to potential victims of crime, such as Jacqueline Hill. A similar argument had been made in *Dorset Yacht*, which Lord Reid dismissed out of hand, but 'defensive practices' is now accepted as a legitimate reason for denying that a defendant owes the claimant a duty of care.

The defensive practices argument is applicable to the police and other public authorities. It has also been applied in cases of clinical negligence. Defensive medicine has been described as 'the practice of doctors advising and undertaking the treatment which they think is legally safe even though they may believe that it is not the best for their patient'.[130] The example of more litigious jurisdictions, such as the United States, means that English judges are ready to accept 'defensive practices' as a reason to deny a duty of care.

---

125 This policy consideration is sometimes referred to as 'the burden on the public purse'.

126 [1970] AC 1004 (HL) 1045.

127 [1989] AC 53 (HL) 63.

128 See *Brooks v Commissioner of Police of the Metropolis* [2005] UKHL 24, [2005] 1 WLR 1495, [30] (Lord Steyn); *Smith v Chief Constable of Sussex Police* [2008] UKHL 50, [2009] AC 225, [89] (Lord Phillips), and [133] (Lord Brown); and *Michael v Chief Constable of South Wales Police* [2015] UKSC 2, [2015] AC 1732, [122] (Lord Toulson).

129 *Hill v Chief Constable of West Yorkshire Police* [1989] AC 53 (HL) 63 (Lord Keith).

130 *Sidaway v Governors of the Bethlem Royal Hospital and Maudsley Hospital* [1985] AC 871 (HL) 887 (Lord Scarman).

Defensive practices was also cited in the case of *X (minors) v Bedfordshire County Council*.[131] This was a claim against a social services authority by children who had been abused and neglected by their parents for failing to protect them from harm. Lord Browne-Wilkinson said that to impose liability on the authority would cause them to 'adopt a more cautious and defensive approach to their duties'.[132]

CONFLICTING DUTIES

In some cases, a duty to the claimant would conflict with the defendant's wider duties. This conflict has been used as a policy reason for denying a duty of care.

The conflicting duty argument was used in the case of *X (minors) v Bedfordshire County Council*.[133] This was a series of claims against local authorities by children who had received inadequate support from social services and from their schools, which had led to continuing abuse and neglect and educational under-achievement. In respect of the abuse and neglect claims, the House of Lords took into account that local authorities had a statutory duty to protect children from abuse and neglect. If the courts allowed a person, such as a parent whose children had been taken into care, to sue the local authority, that would conflict with the local authority's duty to protect children. A social worker, concerned that a mistake might lead to a claim by a parent, might hesitate before taking action and fail to prevent further harm to a child.

The same reasoning was applied by the House of Lords in *Jain v Trent Strategic Health Authority*,[134] where a public authority had closed a nursing home. Although it was acknowledged that there was no justification for the authority's actions, it was not liable to the owners of the home, whose had lost their business. The aim of the statute under which the authority acted was to protect vulnerable people in residential care homes, and taking into account the economic interests of the owners of those homes would conflict with that duty.

ALTERNATIVE REMEDIES

The availability of alternative remedies, such as an independent body which considers complaints against public authorities, has also been used as a policy reason not to impose a duty of care. In the case of social services authorities, the House of Lords held, in *X (minors) v Bedfordshire County Council*,[135] that the availability of a statutory complaints scheme was one of the reasons that it would not be fair, just, and reasonable to impose a duty of care.[136] Two later House of Lords judgments, however, cast doubt on this.[137]

131 [1995] 2 AC 633 (HL).

132 Ibid, 662.

133 [1995] 2 AC 633 (HL).

134 [2009] UKHL 4, [2009] AC 853.

135 [1995] 2 AC 633 (HL).

136 Ibid, 751 (Lord Browne-Wilkinson). In *Rowling v Takaro Properties Ltd* [1988] AC 473 (PC), the Privy Council cited the availability of judicial review as an alternative remedy as a reason not to impose a duty on a public authority: see p.502.

137 *Phelps v Hillingdon London Borough Council* [2001] 2 AC 619 (HL) 672 (Lord Slynn); *Barrett v Enfield London Borough Council* [2001] 2 AC 550 (HL) 589 (Lord Hutton).

A related argument was accepted in *Marc Rich v Bishop Rock Marine*.[138] In this case, a ship was lost at sea when a marine surveyor allowed it to sail despite the ship not being seaworthy. The cargo owner could not recover for the loss of its cargo: one of the policy reasons given was that there was already a well-established system of risk allocation for carriage of goods by sea, which had been established by international treaty. To hold that cargo owners could recover from marine surveyors would 'disturb the balance' created by this system.[139]

ANALYSING THE LAW

Should policy play such an important role in deciding whether the claimant can succeed?

Sir Thomas Bingham MR said, 'the rule of public policy which has first claim on the loyalty of the law [is] that wrongs should be remedied' (*X (minors) v Bedfordshire County Council* [1995] 2 AC 633, 663). Lord Scarman said that, if legal principle led to a particular result, the court should not deny the claim on policy grounds: that was a matter for Parliament (*McLoughlin v O'Brian* [1983] 1 AC 410, 429ff).

Do you agree? Should it be up to the courts to determine the limits of liability in negligence and how public policy should be applied, or is it a matter for Parliament? Do courts have the capacity to make decisions on policy and public interest?

2.8 *ROBINSON* AND THE END OF THE CAPARO TEST

Between 1990 and 2018, all English courts accepted that the tripartite test was a correct statement of the law, and applied the three elements of foreseeability, proximity and 'fair, just and reasonable' to claims where there was no applicable precedent. In two cases, heard in 2015 and in 2018,[140] the Supreme Court re-examined *Caparo*, and came to a striking conclusion: Lord Bridge had not intended to set out a three-part test. His judgment had intended to move away from a principled test to an incremental approach: he held that the law of negligence should develop new duties of care by analogy with existing duties of care.

138 [1996] AC 211 (HL).

139 Ibid, 240 (Lord Steyn).

140 *Michael v Chief Constable of South Wales Police* [2015] UKSC 2, [2015] AC 1732; and *Robinson v Chief Constable of West Yorkshire Police* [2018] UKSC 4, [2018] AC 736.

Robinson v Chief Constable of West Yorkshire Police[141] sets out the new approach. As before, if there is an applicable precedent, then the court will not need to consider the matter, unless the claimant or defendant is seeking to overturn the precedent. If there is no applicable precedent, then the court will consider existing, analogous precedents. If extending the analogous precedents to the claim would be a modest extension of the existing law, would promote coherence in the law and avoid inappropriate distinctions, and it would be fair, just, and reasonable to extend the analogy to the claim, then the court will find that a duty exists. If there is no analogous precedent, then the claim will fail at the first hurdle. If there is such an analogous precedent, the claimant will still have to persuade the court to extend it to his or her circumstances.

KEY CASE

Robinson v Chief Constable of West Yorkshire Police [2018] UKSC 4, [2018] 2 WLR 595 was a claim made by a woman who was injured during the arrest of a suspected drug dealer: the suspect resisted arrest and there was a struggle between him and two police officers. During the struggle, which took place on a busy shopping street, the three men collided with the claimant, pushing her to the ground and falling on top of her.

The High Court and the Court of Appeal both applied *Hill v Chief Constable of West Yorkshire Police* and subsequent judgments and held that the police owed no duty of care to members of the public, such as the claimant, when carrying out their duties.

The Supreme Court allowed the claimant's appeal. The principle established in *Hill* meant that police were not liable to members of the public for omissions: for failing to rescue or protect a member of public from injury caused by the acts of a third party. However, in this case, the injury was caused directly by the acts of the arresting police officers and the Hill principle did not apply.

The Supreme Court also considered Lord Bridge's judgment in *Caparo v Dickman*, and concluded that Lord Bridge had not intended to create the tripartite test: he had, in fact, expressly endorsed an incremental approach to the question of whether new duties of care should be established.

The tripartite test allowed the court to start with a blank sheet: in the absence of a duty of care established by an applicable precedent, the court examined whether the damage suffered by the claimant was of a foreseeable type and whether the circumstances gave rise to the necessary proximity, whether physical, relational, or causal. If the claimant was able to establish those two elements, the court would then consider the policy issues, and whether it would be fair, just, and reasonable to find a duty of care. This process did not rely upon precedent,

141 [2018] UKSC 4, [2018] AC 736.

although the meaning of the three elements – foreseeability; proximity; and fair, just, and reasonable – was determined by the way in which courts had previously interpreted those terms. In a case such as *Marc Rich v Bishop Rock Marine*,[142] the claimant was not required to find a precedent that showed that a surveyor who had certified a ship as seaworthy owed a duty to the person who owned the cargo being carried by the ship, or even a case that was analogous. If the claimant had been able to establish the three elements of the Caparo test, that would have been enough.

This approach was rejected in *Robinson.*[143] The Supreme Court held that new duties of care would only be found by incremental expansion of existing duties. This means that courts no longer consider each novel claim in isolation: the claimant must find an analogous case in which there is an existing duty of care, and persuade the court that it would be fair, just, and reasonable to extend the existing, analogous duty to the new circumstances. The third element of the tripartite test remains central to the process, but *Robinson* moves the courts' approach from principle to precedent.

KEY LEARNING POINT

Courts will find that a duty of care exists in circumstances where there is no applicable precedent if:

- there is an existing duty of care which is analogous to the circumstances under consideration;
- extending the analogous duty to the new circumstances would be a small change to the existing law;
- applying the analogous duty to the new circumstances would maintain the coherence of the law and avoid inappropriate distinctions; and
- it would be fair, just, and reasonable to extend the existing duty of care.

The case of *James-Bowen v Commissioner of Police of the Metropolis*[144] shows the Supreme Court's new approach. In this case, the claimant police officers had arrested a man, BA, on suspicion of terrorism offences. BA later sued the arresting officers and the commissioner, as their employer,[145] for the use of excessive force during the arrest. The arresting officers argued that the commissioner owed them a duty to take reasonable care to protect their economic well-being and their reputations while defending the claim and that, by settling the claim with an admission of liability and apologising for the use of 'gratuitous violence' during the arrest, the commissioner had breached that duty.

142 [1996] AC 211 (HL). A ship had undertaken temporary repairs on a crack in its hull and had been passed as fit to sail by the marine surveyor. The temporary repair failed, and the ship and its cargo were lost. The claimant, one of the cargo owners, argued that the surveyor had been negligent and should be liable for the loss.

143 [2018] UKSC 4, [2018] AC 736.

144 [2018] UKSC 40, [2018] 1 WLR 4021.

145 Police officers are not employees, but office holders. However, the commissioner of the police force may be sued as if he or she were the police officer's employer under the Police Act 1996 s.88.

The Supreme Court, in considering whether the defendant owed the claimants a duty of care in negligence, followed the process set out in *Robinson*. There was no precedent that was directly applicable, so they moved on to consider whether there were any analogous cases. They identified two such cases: *Calveley v Chief Constable of the Merseyside Police*[146] and *Spring v Guardian Assurance plc.*[147] *Calveley*, which was closest to the facts of *James-Bowen*, had held that a chief constable did not owe a duty to take reasonable care to protect a police officer's economic well-being and reputation when investigating an internal complaint. The later House of Lords case of *Spring*, on the other hand, established that an employer was under a duty to take reasonable care to protect a former employee's economic well-being when providing a reference.

Having identified the analogous precedents, the Supreme Court considered whether allowing the proposed duty would be consistent with maintaining the coherence of the law and avoiding unjustified distinctions, and whether it would be fair, just, and reasonable. Taking these issues into consideration, the Supreme Court found that the defendant did not owe the claimants a duty to protect their economic well-being and reputation in the circumstances.

The same process was followed in *Darnley v Croydon Health Services NHS Trust*:[148] in this case the claimant attended an A&E department with a head injury, where the receptionist told him that he would have to wait four to five hours to be seen by a doctor. The receptionist did not tell him that he would be seen within 30 minutes by a triage nurse. The claimant felt too unwell to wait and he returned home. Some hours later he suffered a brain haemorrhage, which caused severe, permanent disability. The claimant sued the hospital, arguing that the receptionist had a duty to tell him that he would have been seen within 30 minutes: if he had known that he would be seen within that time, he would have remained in the hospital and would have received prompt treatment for the brain haemorrhage,[149] which would have prevented the permanent disability. The High Court and the Court of Appeal both found for the defendant, holding that it would not be 'fair, just and reasonable' to impose the proposed duty on the receptionists.

The Supreme Court applied *Robinson*. The first step in *Robinson* requires the court to identify any precedent applicable to the case before it.[150] In this case, there were two relevant cases: *Barnett v Chelsea and Kensington Hospital Management Committee*[151] and *Kent v Griffiths*.[152] In *Barnett*, a hospital had sent a person away with instructions to see his doctor in the morning. In *Kent*, an ambulance did not attend within the promised time. Both cases established the

146 [1989] AC 1228 (HL).

147 [1995] 2 AC 296 (HL).

148 [2018] UKSC 50.

149 Doctors and surgeons refer to the 'golden hour' following a head injury within which effective treatment of brain haemorrhage can be given. If treatment is delayed beyond that period, death or permanent disability is much more likely. See Brooke Lerner, E. and Moscati, R. M. 'The Golden Hour: Scientific Fact or Medical "Urban Legend"?' (2001) 8(7) Academic Emergency Medicine 758.

150 [2018] UKSC 50, [15] (Lord Lloyd-Jones, giving the only judgment).

151 [1969] 1 QB 428 (QB).

152 [2001] QB 36 (CA).

principle that, in the context of the provision of health services, a duty of care arose at the time that the claimant was accepted as a patient. A hospital, doctor, or ambulance service might not accept a person as a patient, but if they did do so, a healthcare provider–patient relationship was established, with the duty to use reasonable care to prevent the patient from suffering physical injury.[153] The duty was owed by the hospital, and included a duty not to provide misleading information to patients. It was immaterial that the person responsible for giving the misleading information was not medically qualified: in *Kent v Griffiths*, the Court of Appeal had held that ambulance staff should be in the same position as doctors and nurses.[154] That the same level of expertise would not be expected of non-clinical staff was an issue to be considered when determining whether the defendant had taken reasonable care, not when considering whether the hospital owed the claimant a duty of care.[155] The Supreme Court allowed the appeal. The precedents were directly applicable, and the defendant hospital did owe the claimant a duty of care.

2.9 DEVELOPMENTS SINCE *ROBINSON*

Immediately following *Robinson v Chief Constable of West Yorkshire Police*,[156] there was some uncertainty as to the true meaning of the judgment, with some commentators interpreting the judgment to mean that the tripartite test from *Caparo plc v Dickman*[157] retained a role in 'novel situations' and lower courts continuing to apply the tripartite test rather than the incremental approach set out in *Robinson*. In *John Innes Foundation v Vertiv Infrastructure Ltd*[158] and in *BXB v Watch Tower Bible and Tract Society of Pennsylvania*,[159] for example, the High Court expressly stated that the correct approach was the tripartite test of foreseeability, proximity, and whether it would be fair, just, and reasonable to impose the claimed duty on the defendant. More recently, in *Shamsan v 44–49 Lowndes Square Management*,[160] the Court of Appeal noted that the lower court had applied the tripartite test to determine whether there was a duty of care and described the application as 'surprising'.[161]

However, following this period of uncertainty, the incremental approach approved in *Robinson* is now accepted as correct: there are no circumstances in which the court should apply the tripartite test. That is not to say that the elements of the tripartite test are no longer significant, however. The third part of the tripartite test – whether it is fair, just, and reasonable to impose the duty – is expressly retained as part of the incremental approach. And

153 [2018] UKSC 50, [16] (Lord Lloyd-Jones).
154 Ibid, [18] (Lord Lloyd-Jones).
155 [2018] UKSC 50, [17] (Lord Lloyd-Jones).
156 [2021] UKSC 21, [2022] AC 852.
157 [1990] 2 AC 605 (HL).
158 [2020] EWHC 19 (TCC), [53]–[55] (Roger Ter Haar QC).
159 [2020] EWHC 156 (QB), [2020] 4 WLR 42, [177] (Chamberlain J).
160 [2024] EWCA Civ 436.
161 Ibid, [79] (Edis LJ).

issues of foreseeability and proximity remain relevant when deciding whether to extend an existing duty of care to the novel circumstances being considered.

2.10 ASSUMPTION OF RESPONSIBILITY AND SPECIAL RELATIONSHIPS

Lord Bingham identified three ways in which a claimant could establish that a defendant owed him or her a duty to take reasonable care to avoid the type of damage that the claimant suffered.[162] So far, this chapter has focused on the first of these, the Caparo or tripartite test. However, where a defendant assumes responsibility for the claimant's well-being or where there is a special relationship between the defendant and the person who caused the damage to the claimant, there will also be a duty of care.

Assumption of responsibility was established as a way of finding a duty owed by the defendant in the case of *Hedley Byrne & Co Ltd v Heller & Partners Ltd*.[163] It was originally only applicable in cases where the claimant suffered economic loss as a result of relying on a statement – such as financial advice – made by the defendant. It also now applies where the economic loss is caused by negligent acts by the defendant,[164] and has been applied in cases of personal injury and property damage where the defendant has failed to rescue or protect[165] the claimant from harm caused by another person or other factor.[166] The application of this doctrine to economic loss is considered in Chapter 5.

A duty to rescue or protect a person from the acts of a third party may arise where there is a special relationship between the defendant and the third party, although this is no longer the terminology preferred by the court. This is considered in Chapter 7.

POINTS TO REVIEW

- Negligence is a common law tort, which requires a claimant to show that the defendant breached a duty of care owed to him or her and that the breach caused damage.
- The claimant must show that the defendant owed him or her a duty to take reasonable care not to cause or allow the type of damage that the claimant suffered.
- If there is no duty of care, the claim will fail.
- The most common way of establishing a duty of care is by precedent.

162 *Van Colle v Chief Constable of Hertfordshire Police* [2008] UKHL 50, [2009] AC 225, [42].

163 [1964] AC 465 (HL).

164 *Henderson v Merrett Syndicates* [1995] 2 AC 145 (HL).

165 A failure to rescue, warn, or protect a person from harm caused by a third party or external cause is regarded as a 'pure omission' in the law of negligence. Pure omissions are discussed in Chapter 7.

166 See *Barrett v Ministry of Defence* [1995] 1 WLR 1217 (CA).

- In the absence of an applicable precedent, the court will consider similar claims and decide whether the claimed duty of care is a small extension of an existing duty.
- The court will consider the need to maintain the coherence of the law and to avoid inappropriate distinctions when considering whether an existing duty should be extended.
- The court will also consider whether it is fair, just, and reasonable to extend an existing duty, taking into account the claimant's interests, the interests of the defendant and potential future defendants, and the wider effects of extending the duty.
- A duty of care will also arise if the defendant assumes responsibility for the claimant's well-being or where there is a special relationship between the defendant and the principal cause of damage.

TAKING IT FURTHER

Robinson v Chief Constable of West Yorkshire Police significantly changed the approach of courts to the duty of care. Any articles published before *Robinson* must, therefore, be treated with some caution.

Tan, D. 'The End of the Search for a Universal Touchstone for Duty of Care' (2019) 135 LQR 200
Analyses the application of the incremental approach in *Darnley*.

Goudkamp, J. and Nolan, D. '*Robinson v Chief Constable of West Yorkshire Police*: Taking Duty Back to Basics' (2023) 16(1) Journal of Tort Law 125
Analyses the judgment in Robinson and the new approach to duty of care established in that case.

Witting, C. 'Duty of Care: An Analytical Approach' (2005) 25(1) OJLS 33–63

McBride, N. J. 'Duties of Care – Do They Really Exist?' (2004) 24(3) OJLS 417–441

3

CHAPTER 3
NEGLIGENCE: BREACH

3.1 INTRODUCTION

Breach is the second element of the tort of negligence. The claimant has to show that the defendant not only owed him or her a duty of care, but also that the defendant breached the duty.

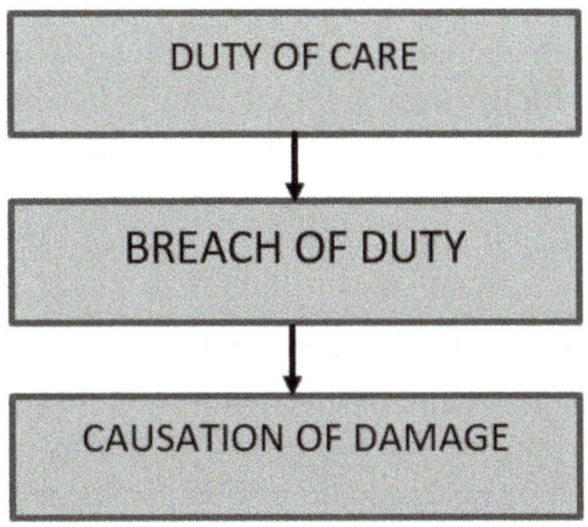

Figure 3.1 The elements of negligence: breach

The law adopts an objective standard: if the defendant did something that a reasonable person would not have done, or did not do something which a reasonable person would have done in the circumstances, then there will usually be a breach of the duty. Why the defendant breached the duty is less important. It does not matter that the defendant was tired, or distracted, or inexperienced.[1] The well-meaning, but incompetent, defendant is just as liable as the lazy or reckless defendant.

The law does, however, take the circumstances into account. Obviously, it would be unreasonable for a driver to go through a red light in ordinary circumstances. But if the person is driving an ambulance, then the same act may be reasonable.

AS YOU READ

- Understand the standard of care and what is meant by breach.
- Identify the duty of care as applied to children.

1 *Nettleship v Weston* [1971] 2 QB 691 (CA).

DOI: 10.4324/9781003480051-03

- Understand the care to be taken when vulnerable people and children may be involved.
- Understand the test applied in professional negligence.

3.2 REASONABLE CARE

The duty of care is a duty to take reasonable care not to cause damage to the claimant. As a nineteenth-century judge put it, 'negligence is the omission to do something which a reasonable man, guided upon those considerations which ordinarily regulate the conduct of human affairs, would do, or doing something which a prudent and reasonable man would not do'.[2] So a duty of care is not an absolute duty not to cause damage: it is possible for the defendant to cause damage without being liable, if his or her acts were reasonable in the circumstances.

So it is not enough to show that the defendant owed the claimant a duty of care, and that the defendant's acts caused the damage. The claimant must show that the defendant acted unreasonably. For example, a surgeon operating on a patient owes a duty of care. If the operation is not successful, however, the question is whether the surgeon used reasonable care. If the claimant cannot show that the surgeon did not do so, then the claim will not succeed.

KEY CASE

In *Glasgow Corp v Muir* [1943] AC 448 (HL), two picnickers were carrying a large urn of hot water through a narrow passage in a café, where a number of children were gathered. One of the picnickers dropped his handle, allowing the hot water to spill out and scald six children. One was particularly seriously injured. The claim was against the manageress of the café: it was argued that, by allowing the picnickers to carry the urn through the café without removing the children, she had not used reasonable care.

The claim failed: the House of Lords held that the claimants had to prove more than that the manageress might have prevented them from suffering injury. They had to show that the defendant had failed to take reasonable steps to prevent foreseeable harm. The manageress was 'not bound to take precautions against dangers which were not apparent to persons of ordinary intelligence and prudence'.

In *Bolton v Stone*,[3] a woman who was standing outside her home was injured when struck by a cricket ball, which had been hit out of a neighbouring cricket ground. The House of Lords accepted that there was a duty of care on the cricketers to avoid injuring members of

2 *Blyth v Birmingham Waterworks Co* (1856) 11 Ex 780, 784, 156 ER 1047, 1049 (Alderson B).
3 [1951] AC 850 (HL).

the public. They also noted that no such incident had happened before, and that it was rare for balls to be hit out of the ground. The House of Lords held that there had been no breach: the chances of a person being hit by a ball hit out of the ground were remote, and it would not be reasonable to expect the cricket club to take any steps to prevent it from happening. A similar conclusion was reached in another case of a member of the public being hit by a cricket ball in *Lewis v Wandsworth Borough Council*:[4] the court held that allowing people to walk close to the cricket pitch was reasonably safe, given the remote possibility of a person being hit, and that the danger was so evident that the Council had not breached its duty by failing to warn of the danger of cricket balls.

> KEY LEARNING POINT
>
> The general duty of care is a duty to take reasonable care to avoid foreseeable harm, not to take any steps necessary to avoid any possible harm.

In another House of Lords case, *Latimer v AEC*,[5] a worker was injured when he slipped on a factory floor. The factory had been flooded, which had caused the floor to become slippery. However, the employer had used sawdust to cover the affected areas. The House of Lords held that the steps taken by the employer had been reasonable in the circumstances, and they were not liable for the injury.

3.3 OBJECTIVE STANDARD

The standard of reasonable care is an objective standard. That means that the court considers the defendant's acts or omissions by reference to a hypothetical person, in the position of the defendant, rather than taking into account the defendant's particular characteristics. In general, where a person is carrying out a particular job or profession, or claims a particular skill, they are judged as a reasonable person in that job or profession, or with that particular skill.[6] If they are carrying out a specific activity, such as driving,[7] playing sports,[8] or carrying out a domestic repair,[9] they are judged as a reasonably competent person carrying out that activity.

So a person driving a car is judged by the standard of a reasonable driver, whether he or she is a learner or an experienced driver. This was established in *Nettleship v Weston*,[10] when a learner driver panicked and drove into a lamppost, injuring the person instructing her. The

4 [2020] EWHC 3205 (QB).
5 [1953] AC 643 (HL).
6 *Bolam v Friern Hospital Management Committee* [1957] 1 WLR 582 (QB).
7 *Nettleship v Weston* [1971] 2 QB 691 (CA).
8 *Condon v Basi* [1985] 1 WLR 866 (CA).
9 *Wells v Cooper* [1958] 2 QB 265 (CA).
10 [1971] 2 QB 691 (CA).

Court of Appeal held that the defendant should be held to the same standard as an ordinary driver, rather than taking her inexperience into account.

Although *Nettleship* was controversial (it was described by the High Court of Australia as 'contrary to common sense'[11]), a similar approach was taken by the Court of Appeal in *Wilsher v Essex Area Health Authority*.[12] A doctor was expected to attain the standard of a reasonable doctor holding the same position, regardless of his or her experience in that position.[13] So a newly appointed GP, starting his or her first job, would be expected to perform to the same standard as a reasonable GP, with years of experience. The same standard has been applied to alternative health practitioners: a traditional Chinese medicine practitioner was judged by reference to a GP.[14]

3.4 CHILDREN

The one characteristic of the defendant that is taken into account is where the defendant is a child. Children are not expected to demonstrate the same foresight and care as adults. In *Orchard v Lee*,[15] a 13-year-old boy was playing tag with another boy. He was running backwards, taunting his friend, when he ran into the claimant, causing her serious injuries. The Court of Appeal held that the defendant did owe a duty of care to the claimant, but his conduct should be considered by reference to other 13-year-olds playing tag. By that standard, the defendant had not breached the duty owed.[16] Likewise, in the case of *Mullin v Richards*,[17] a 15-year-old schoolgirl who had injured her friend when playing was judged by the standard of an 'ordinarily prudent and reasonable 15-year-old schoolgirl'.[18] In the Australian case of *McHale v Watson*,[19] the High Court of Australia noted that 'childhood is not an idiosyncrasy':[20] it is a stage that all people go through, rather than a characteristic of a particular defendant.

3.5 ILLNESS AND MENTAL IMPAIRMENT

In some cases, the breach is involuntary or caused by illness or mental disorder. For example, in *Roberts v Ramsbottom*,[21] a driver suffered from a cerebral haemorrhage, which caused him to

11 *Cook v Cook* (1986) 68 ALR 353, 358.

12 [1987] QB 730 (CA). This judgment was successfully appealed ([1988] AC 1074), but not on this issue.

13 See *FB v Princess Alexandra Hospital* [2017] EWCA 334.

14 *Shakoor v Situ* [2001] 1 WLR 410 (QB).

15 *O v L (sub nom Orchard v Lee)* [2009] EWCA Civ 295.

16 Ibid, [11]–[13] (Waller LJ). See also *Mullin v Richards* [1998] 1 WLR 1304, where 15-year-old schoolgirls were judged by the standard of an ordinarily prudent and reasonable 15-year-old schoolgirl.

17 [1998] 1 WLR 1304 (CA).

18 Ibid, 1308 (Hutchinson LJ).

19 [1966] HCA 13.

20 Ibid, [4] (McTiernan ACJ).

21 [1980] 1 WLR 823 (QB).

lose full control. He continued to drive, and crashed into a parked car, injuring the driver and a passenger. It was held that the claimant could not rely on his incapacity as a defence, unless he could show that he was acting entirely involuntarily, in a state of automatism. Furthermore, as the defendant had continued to drive after the symptoms of the haemorrhage appeared, he was liable.

By contrast, in the case of *Mansfield v Weetabix Ltd*,[22] the defendant, a lorry driver, was suffering from low blood sugar, caused by an undiagnosed cancer. This caused him to lose control and he crashed into a shop. It was held that he was not liable. The Court of Appeal disapproved the rule set out in *Roberts*, that a defendant would be liable unless his acts were entirely involuntary, although it did approve the outcome on the grounds that the defendant had continued to drive after the symptoms had started to appear. However, in *Mansfield*, the driver did not know and could not have realised that he was suffering from the cancer, and was not liable.

ANALYSING THE LAW

Where the defendant is not in full control of him- or herself, should they be liable? For example, if a motorist has a seizure while driving and causes an accident, should he or she be liable? Should it make a difference if the driver had never had a seizure before, or if he or she had been warned by a doctor that it might happen?

In the case of motorists, insurance will be relevant: all motorists are obliged to have insurance, and there is a statutory scheme which covers uninsured drivers. Should courts take into account whether the motorist or the insurance company will actually be liable to pay any damages awarded?

The legal philosopher, Lon Fuller (*The Morality of Law*, Yale University Press, 1964, p.73) makes the point that the aim of civil law is to compensate the claimant, not to punish the defendant. If a defendant takes another person's wallet, but is unable to understand that he or she is doing something wrong, that may be a very good reason not to punish the defendant. However, it is not a good reason not to allow the original owner to have the wallet back. In other words, insanity may be a good defence to a criminal charge of theft, but should not be a defence to a civil claim in the tort of wrongful interference with goods.

Both of these cases were considered by the Court of Appeal in *Dunnage v Randall*.[23] A man suffering from a serious mental illness had soaked himself in petrol. His nephew tried, unsuccessfully, to prevent him from setting fire to himself and was badly burned. It was held that, to be liable in negligence, the defendant had to be acting consciously.

22 [1998] 1 WLR 1263 (CA).
23 [2015] EWCA Civ 673, [2016] QB 639.

The question was whether the defendant should be held to the standard of a reasonable person despite his serious mental illness, which meant that he was not acting rationally and was not in full control of his actions. It was held that the defendant was responsible for his actions, as despite his serious mental illness, he was acting voluntarily. The Court of Appeal held that a person's physical or mental illness should not be taken into account when determining liability in negligence: the only subjective factor that should be taken into account was the defendant's age. The fact that the defendant's conduct was influenced by physical or mental illness was only a defence if the conduct had been entirely involuntary. This would be the case where the person was suffering from somnambulism or automatism, which are states in which the person is unconscious but still physically active. In other states, where any degree of consciousness remained, the defendant would be judged by the objective standard.

KEY LEARNING POINT

Where the defendant's actions or decisions are affected by physical or mental illness, the objective standard is still applied, unless the defendant's actions are entirely involuntary.

3.6 PROFESSIONAL NEGLIGENCE

KEY CASE

The claimant in *Bolam v Friern Hospital Management Committee* [1957] 1 WLR 582 (QB) was being treated for depression with electro-convulsive therapy (ECT). During the procedure, he suffered from a fractured pelvis, caused by the severity of the convulsion induced. He sued in negligence, arguing that he should have been given a muscle relaxant before being treated. The expert witnesses testified that muscle relaxants were commonly used, but some doctors considered that muscle relaxants increased the risk of death, while the risk of fractures was minimal.

McNair J directed the jury that a doctor is not liable in negligence 'if he has acted in accordance with a practice accepted as proper by a responsible body of medical men skilled in that particular art'.

In *Whitehouse v Jordan*,[24] the House of Lords accepted *Bolam* as correctly stating the law in a case involving treatment, and a similar approach was adopted by Lord Scarman (giving the

24 [1981] 1 WLR 246 (HL).

only judgment) in *Maynard v West Midlands Regional Health Authority*.[25] Lord Scarman did not expressly approve *Bolam*, but did state that a doctor's decision would not be a breach of duty if 'a responsible body of medical opinion would have accepted it as proper'. The test approved by the House of Lords in *Maynard* was that a doctor is negligent if he or she is 'guilty of such failure as no doctor of ordinary skill would be guilty of if acting with ordinary care'.

Bolam provides a defence where the defendant has acted in accordance with accepted professional practice. It is recognised that, in any profession, there may be different approaches or schools of thought. It is not sufficient for the claimant to show that another professional might have done things differently and might not have caused the injury. If the defendant can show that there is a body of professional opinion that would have acted in the same way, he or she has not breached the duty of care. To put this another way, to establish a breach of duty by a doctor, the claimant must show that no reasonable doctor would have acted as the defendant did.

KEY LEARNING POINT

The 'Bolam test' is used in cases of professional negligence. It states that a professional is not negligent if he or she has acted in accordance with a practice accepted as proper by a responsible body of professional opinion. Alternatively, the test can be expressed as the claimant has to show that no responsible or reasonable professional would have acted as the defendant did.

Bolam is a controversial case, as it allowed the medical profession to be 'judges in their own cause'. The defendant does not have to provide any justification for his or her acts, other than to show that he or she was acting in accordance with professional practice. In some cases, the body of medical opinion which supported the defendant's approach could be no more than a handful of doctors. In *De Freitas v O'Brien*,[26] the claimant suffered from chronic pain following an operation on her spine. The first defendant was a 'spinal surgeon', one of only 11 in the country. The defence expert witnesses accepted that 'normal medical opinion' would not have supported the defendant's decision to operate, and it was argued that such a small group of doctors could not be a 'body of medical opinion'. The Court of Appeal disagreed: although spinal surgery was not a large specialism, it was well established and a 'small number of tertiary specialists could constitute a responsible body of medical opinion'.

The Bolam test is closely associated with clinical negligence, but the same approach is applied in other areas of professional negligence. If a professional person, such as a lawyer or surveyor, has acted in accordance with a practice which is accepted as proper by a responsible body of professional opinion, then he or she will not have fallen below the standard of the profession and will not have breached his or her duty of care.

25 [1984] 1 WLR 634 (HL).
26 (1995) 25 BMLR 51 (CA).

The Bolam test has been used in a wide variety of professional settings, including claims against auctioneers,[27] veterinary surgeons,[28] education providers,[29] property valuers,[30] accountants,[31] financial advisers,[32] lawyers,[33] expert witnesses,[34] property designers,[35] and engineers[36] in negligence.

3.7 *BOLITHO* AND *MONTGOMERY*: REFINING *BOLAM*

Since it was established, the Bolam test has been refined, in particular by the House of Lords in the case of *Bolitho v City and Hackney Health Authority*.[37] More recently, its scope has been limited by the Supreme Court in the case of *Montgomery v Lanarkshire Health Board*.

The Privy Council case of *Edward Wong Finance v Johnson Stokes & Master*[38] did not accept established professional practice as a defence to a claim in negligence. The case concerned a loan of money for the purchase of part of a factory building in Hong Kong. The lender's solicitors sent the purchase money to the seller's solicitors, subject to an undertaking that he would transfer title to the building within 10 days. Instead, the seller's solicitor took the money and disappeared. The lender sued their solicitors, claiming that it was negligent to send all the money to the seller's solicitor with no more security that the solicitor's undertaking. It was accepted that the buyer's solicitors had been acting in accordance with standard practice within the profession in Hong Kong.

However, the claimant succeeded before the Privy Council. Perhaps surprisingly, the Privy Council did not refer to *Bolam* or, indeed, to any other authority or statute[39] when reaching the conclusion that it was self-evident that the practice was vulnerable to embezzlement and that the defendants had been negligent in trusting the seller's solicitor.

27 *Alchemy (International) Ltd v Tattersalls Ltd* [1985] 2 EGLR 17 (QB).

28 *De Maynard v Streatham Hill Veterinary Surgery* [2001] EWCA Civ 1728; *Calver v Westwood Veterinary Group* (2001) 58 BMLR 194 (CA).

29 *Abramova v Oxford Institute of Legal Practice* [2011] EWHC 613 (QB); *Siddiqui v University of Oxford* [2016] EWHC 3150 (QB).

30 *Singer & Friedlander Ltd v John D Wood* [1977] 2 EGLR 84 (QB); *Zubaida v Hargreaves* [1995] 1 EGLR 127 (CA); *Capita Alternative Fund Services (Guernsey) Ltd v Drivers Jonas* [2011] EWHC 2336 (Comm).

31 *Smith v Revenue and Customs Commissioners* [2011] UKUT 270 (TCC), [2011] STC 1724.

32 *O'Hare v Coutts & Co* [2016] EWHC 2224 (QB).

33 *Arthur JS Hall v Simons* [2002] 1 AC 615 (HL) 737 (Lord Hobhouse).

34 *Jones v Kaney* [2011] UKSC 13, [2011] 2 All ER 671, [180] (Lady Hale).

35 *Adams v Rhymney Valley District Council* [2000] 3 EGLR 25 (CA).

36 *Greaves & Co (Contractors) Ltd v Baynham, Meikle & Partners* [1975] 1 WLR 1095 (CA).

37 [1998] AC 232 (HL).

38 [1984] AC 296 (PC).

39 It is unusual for a judgment of an appellate court to make no reference to any law, in the form of statute or precedent.

A further challenge to *Bolam* appeared in the Court of Appeal in the case of *Sidaway v Board of Governors of Bethlem Royal Hospital*,[40] where it was held, obiter, that 'a judge would be entitled to reject a unanimous medical opinion if he were satisfied that it was manifestly wrong'.[41] This was not upheld on appeal and the House of Lords confirmed that once the defendant had established that he was acting in accordance with professional practice, he had a 'complete defence'.[42]

In *Bolitho v City and Hackney Health Authority*,[43] the House of Lords considered *Edward Wong Finance* when reaching the conclusion that acting in accordance with a body of professional opinion was not a complete defence. Acting in accordance with a body of medical opinion would mean, in most cases, that the defendant had acted reasonably. However, in some cases, it was possible that the professional opinion could not 'withstand logical analysis'[44] and the court was entitled to hold that the body of opinion was not reasonable. In that case, the defendant might be liable, despite having acted in accordance with professional practice. It was emphasised that this would only be in rare cases, and that the judge would have to be satisfied that the professional opinion could not be logically supported before finding that a practice supported by professional opinion was negligent.

Bolitho does not overrule *Bolam*: it is still a defence for the defendant to show that he or she was acting in accordance with a practice accepted as proper by a reasonable and responsible body of professional opinion. What *Bolitho* does is make it clear that the courts can decide whether the body of professional opinion, as expressed by the expert witnesses, is reasonable and responsible. If the professional practice is not reasonable and responsible, as in the case of *Edward Wong Finance*, the court can find the defendant negligent. The mere fact that a practice has been adopted by a profession does not automatically make it responsible and reasonable.

KEY LEARNING POINT

Bolitho allows the court to find that a defendant has been negligent, even if he or she has been acting in accordance with accepted practice within a profession, if the accepted practice does not withstand logical analysis.

As Lord Browne-Wilkinson's judgment in *Bolitho* makes clear, it is rare for professional practice not to be able to withstand logical analysis, and the refinement of the Bolam test has made little difference in practice to the courts' approach to clinical and professional negligence claims. One case in which it was found that the defendant's actions, though supported by expert testimony, did not withstand logical analysis was *Taaffe v West of England Ambulance Service NHS Trust*.[45] In this case, paramedics attending a patient with chest pains did

40 [1984] QB 493 (CA).
41 Ibid, 513–14 (Sir John Donaldson MR).
42 [1985] AC 871 (HL) 901 (Lord Bridge).
43 [1998] AC 232 (HL).
44 Ibid, 243 (Lord Browne-Wilkinson).
45 [2012] EWHC 1335 (QB), (2012) 128 BMLR 71.

not advise her to go to hospital immediately. Although the defendant's expert witness testified that this was a reasonable cause of action, the court held that the expert testimony was not reasonable or logical, and allowed the claim.

A further limitation of the Bolam test was seen in *Montgomery v Lanarkshire Health Board*,[46] in which it was held that *Bolam* did not apply if the issue in question did not require specific technical or professional expertise.

The question in *Montgomery* related to informed consent to a medical procedure, and how much information the doctor should disclose to the patient. On a previous occasion when this had been considered by the House of Lords, in *Sidaway v Board of Governors of Bethlem Royal Hospital*,[47] it had been held that the Bolam test applied to all aspects of a doctor's duty of care, including the duty to obtain consent for an operation or other procedure.[48]

In *Montgomery*, the claimant was a woman seeking damages for her son, who was severely disabled by complications during his birth. The obstetrician was aware that there were factors, including the relative sizes of the mother and foetus, which increased the risk of shoulder dystocia, a 'major obstetric emergency'[49] capable of causing disability to both the mother and foetus. However, the obstetrician did not inform the claimant of the increased risk or offer the option of a caesarean section. During the delivery, shoulder dystocia did occur, and the claimant's son was severely disabled. The claimant argued that the obstetrician was negligent in not informing her of the risk and allowing her to make the decision whether to have a caesarean section. The Scottish Court of Session Inner House applied *Sidaway v Board of Governors of Bethlem Royal Hospital*[50] and held that the question of how much the patient should be told was 'very much a question for the experienced practitioner to decide, in accordance with normal and proper practice'.[51]

The Supreme Court did not follow *Sidaway* and allowed the claimant's appeal. They held that a doctor was obliged to disclose all material facts to the patient, and that a fact was material if a reasonable patient would attach significance to it, or the actual patient being treated would attach significance to it.[52]

The Supreme Court also held that, for questions where medical or professional expertise was not needed, the Bolam test did not apply. Unlike *Sidaway*, where the House of Lords held that the amount of information to be disclosed to the patient was a matter for the doctor, acting in accordance with a body of medical opinion, Lord Reed and Lord Kerr held that no particular

46 [2015] UKSC 11, [2015] AC 1430.

47 [1985] AC 871 (HL).

48 Ibid, 893–894 (Lord Diplock) and 899–900 (Lord Bridge).

49 [2015] UKSC 11, [2015] AC 1430, [8] (Lord Kerr and Lord Reed, quoting Dr Philip Owen, a defence expert witness).

50 [1985] AC 871 (HL).

51 *NM v Lanarkshire Health Board* [2013] CSIH 3, [41].

52 [2015] UKSC 11, [2015] AC 1430, [87] (Lord Kerr and Lord Reed).

medical expertise was needed to determine whether the risks of a medical procedure outweighed the benefits,[53] and the Bolam test should not be applied.

> KEY LEARNING POINT
>
> The Bolam test applies when the professional is exercising professional skill and judgment. It does not apply to issues where professional expertise is not required, such as weighing the risks and benefits of treatment.

3.8 SPECIFIC SITUATIONS

The standard of care depends upon context, and all the circumstances are taken into account. This will include where the defendant is responding to an emergency or in other circumstances which mean that it would not be reasonable for the defendant to exercise the same degree of care in other circumstances.

EMERGENCIES

The police, ambulance, and fire services are all subject to the general law, both criminal and civil, in the same way as any other member of the public, except where there are specific statutory exceptions. If an emergency vehicle is involved in an incident which causes injury, they are, in principle, liable to the injured person in negligence in the same way as any other road user.[54]

The driver of an emergency vehicle owes a duty of care to other road users, and will be liable if he or she breaches that duty and the breach causes injury. However, the standard of care is lowered in the event of an emergency: this is one of the circumstances that the court takes into account when determining whether the claimant acted reasonably.

In *Watt v Hertfordshire County Council*,[55] a fireman was injured by an unsecured trolley-jack in the back of a vehicle while the fire brigade was responding to an emergency. The Court of Appeal held that there was no negligence: in the circumstances, the fire brigade was right to balance the risk of injury to the firemen against the risk to life in the incident to which they were responding.

In other circumstances, however, the emergency services may be held liable: if, even taking the circumstances into account, the defendant did not use reasonable care, he or she will be liable in negligence.[56]

53 Ibid, [82]–[86] (Lord Kerr and Lord Reed).

54 *Gaynor v Allen* [1959] 2 QB 403 (QB); *Marshall v Osmond* [1983] QB 1034 (CA).

55 [1954] 1 WLR 835 (CA).

56 See, for example, *Smith v Chief Constable of Nottinghamshire Police* [2012] EWCA Civ 161.

The same principle applies where the defendant is not a member of the emergency services. In *The Oropesa*,[57] the captain of a ship ordered his crew to take to the lifeboat, and a number of crew members were drowned. Although the ship was not in immediate danger, it was held that, in the circumstances, the captain had acted reasonably.

GOOD SAMARITANS AND SARAH

Good Samaritans, or rescuers, are volunteers who give medical attention, first aid, or other assistance to a person who has been injured or who is in danger. They are so called after the biblical parable, in which a person from Samaria (the 'good Samaritan') gave help to a person who had been set upon by thieves.[58]

Good Samaritans may be members of the public, or 'off-duty' qualified first aiders or health professionals. A first aider or health professional, acting in the course of his or her job, will owe a duty of care and be held to the appropriate professional standard.

In English law, there is no general duty to rescue a person in trouble. However, if a person does voluntarily intervene, the rescuer may come under a duty of care, if he or she assumes responsibility for the injured person. In this case, the rescuer might become liable, if they fail to use reasonable care.[59] This is regarded as particularly problematic for off-duty doctors and other healthcare professionals. For this reason, a number of common law jurisdictions, including all 50 of the states of the United States, have 'Good Samaritan' statutes, which provide some protection to volunteer rescuers from liability in tort.

There do not appear to have been any successful claims in England and Wales against volunteer rescuers. However, there was a perceived problem that fear of litigation was preventing people from volunteering and from trying to give assistance to people in trouble. In response, the Social Action, Responsibility and Heroism Act 2014[60] was enacted. The Act gives the court the power to take into account whether the defendant was 'acting for the benefit of society', whether he or she had 'demonstrated a predominantly responsible approach', and whether he or she was acting 'heroically', by intervening to save another in an emergency.[61]

57 [1943] P 32 (CA).

58 *The Bible*, Luke 10:30–10:35.

59 In the American case of *Torti v van Horn* (2008) 45 Cal 4th 322, the defendant pulled the claimant from her crashed vehicle. Unfortunately, in doing so, she exacerbated the claimant's spinal injury, causing permanent paralysis. The claimant sued.

60 This Act is sometimes referred to as SARAH. Although it is not unknown for UK Acts to be referred to as acronyms, such as UCTA (Unfair Contract Terms Act 1977), this appears to be the first Act to have been specifically named so that its initials formed a word. Parliament appeared to have adopted the US practice in this regard (see, for example, the SPEECH Act 2010, whose full name is the Securing the Protection of our Enduring and Established Constitutional Heritage Act).

61 Ss.2, 3, and 4 of the Act.

The Act was heavily criticised by the legal profession. In the House of Lords, Lord Pannick QC said: 'I cannot remember a more pointless, indeed fatuous, piece of legislation than Clause 2 of this Bill, with the possible exception of Clauses 3 and 4 of this Bill'.[62] The main objection to the Act is that it adds nothing to the existing law: the common law requires the claimant to prove that the defendant acted unreasonably, having regard to all the circumstances. That means that the factors set out in the 2014 Act may be taken into account under the common law, rendering the Act redundant.

ANALYSING THE LAW

Was Lord Pannick right? Consider how the courts have taken all the circumstances into account in cases such as *Watt v Hertfordshire County Council* and *The Oropesa*. Is the Social Action, Responsibility and Heroism Act 2014 redundant?

SPORTS

Injuries are common in sports, and they are often caused by other players' carelessness. However, the standard expected from, for example, a driver in a Grand Prix race is the standard which 'the sport permits or involves'.[63] This is, of course, quite different from the standard expected of a driver on an ordinary road. Players do owe a duty of care to other players, and to spectators, but that duty is only breached if the player deliberately injures another player or spectator, or if he or she shows a 'reckless disregard' for their safety.[64]

In *Condon v Basi*,[65] a football player was injured by a foul tackle. The defendant had tackled the other player 'without thought of the consequences'. This was held to be a breach of the expected standard, in that by being careless of the consequences of his act, the defendant had acted with 'reckless disregard' for the claimant's injury. Likewise, a rugby player who 'closed her eyes' to the 'clear and obvious risk'[66] which she posed to the claimant when tackling her was held liable for the serious injury caused.

The Court of Appeal also held, in *Condon v Basi*, that the standard required was objective, but dependent on the circumstances. Professional footballers would be held to a higher standard than players in a local league match.[67] This is consistent with the approach to professionals or anyone who holds themselves out as having a particular skill, as opposed to a person with no particular skill.[68]

62 HL Deb 15 Dec 2014 Vol 758 Col 16.

63 *Wooldridge v Sumner* [1963] 2 QB 43 (CA) 57 (Sellers LJ).

64 Ibid, (CA) 72 (Diplock LJ).

65 [1985] 1 WLR 866 (CA).

66 *Czernuszka v King* [2023] EWHC 380 (KB), [2023] 4 WLR 26 [58] (Martin Spencer J).

67 *Condon v Basi* [1985] 1 WLR 866, (CA) 868 (Sir John Donaldson MR).

68 *Wells v Cooper* [1958] 2 QB 265 (CA).

Referees and other game officials also owe a duty of care to players. If they allow foul play or dangerous breaches of the rules to continue, then they are held to the standard of a reasonable referee.[69] Where, however, a volunteer from the spectators agrees to referee in the absence of a qualified referee, they would not be required to show the same skill, or 'even to be fully conversant with the laws of the game'.[70]

MISTAKES

The question of whether mistakes made when the defendant was carrying out a repetitive task was considered in *Penney v East Kent Health Authority*.[71] A cervical smear was examined by a trained screener, who failed to notice abnormalities. As a result, the claimant's diagnosis was delayed. It was acknowledged that even the best-trained and most diligent screener would, on occasion, make a mistake, and it was argued by the defendant that this sort of error was 'excusable': it was an error that did not reach the level of a breach of duty. This argument was not accepted: the question was whether a reasonable screener, exercising reasonable care, would have spotted the abnormality. As the answer to that question was yes, the claimants succeeded.

ANALYSING THE LAW

Even the most careful and conscientious person may make a mistake. For example, if a person undertakes to deliver a single, correctly addressed, package, but delivers it to the wrong house, it is reasonable to conclude that they did not take reasonable care. However, even the most diligent and conscientious postal delivery worker, delivering 1,500 letters a day, is certain sometimes to make a mistake. Should such a mistake be regarded as negligent?

3.9 STANDARD OF CARE OWED TO PARTICULAR CLAIMANTS

Although the court does not, with the exception of the allowance made for children, take into account the particular attributes of the defendant, the defendant is expected to take into account any specific attributes or vulnerabilities of the claimant. If a defendant is aware, or should be aware, that a particular group of potential claimants are more at risk of injury than a reasonable person, of average physical and intellectual capabilities, then the defendant should bear those potential claimants in mind.

69 *Vowles v Evans* [2003] 1 WLR 1607, [2003] EWCA Civ 318; *Smoldon v Whitworth* [1997] PIQR P 133 (CA).

70 *Vowles v Evans* [2003] 1 WLR 1607, [2003] EWCA Civ 318, [28] (Lord Phillips MR).

71 (1999) 55 BMLR 63 (CA).

KEY LEARNING POINT

The defendant should take particular care when children or vulnerable adults may be affected by his or her acts.

CHILDREN

In particular, defendants should be aware that children may be affected by their acts or omissions. The standard of care necessary to protect an adult may well not be sufficient to protect a child: as Lord Hoffman noted in *Jolley v Sutton London Borough Council*,[72] children's 'ingenuity in finding unexpected ways of doing mischief to themselves and others should never be underestimated'.[73]

KEY CASE

In *Taylor v Glasgow Corp* [1922] 1 AC 44 (HL), a 7-year-old boy died after eating deadly nightshade berries in Glasgow's Botanic Gardens. The plant was in a fenced part of the garden, but there was a gate which could be opened by a child. There were no notices to warn children, or their parents, that the berries were poisonous.

The House of Lords noted that the berries were as tempting to a child as grapes or cherries, and held that the defendants should have been aware of the danger to children in the gardens. Where the defendant knew or anticipated that young or disabled people were within the 'scope and hazard of their operations', they would be held to an appropriate standard that reflected the additional risk to those persons.

So, if the defendant knows, or should know, that children may be affected by their acts, they should bear them in mind when carrying out their acts. This means that the standard of care is higher where children are involved.

VULNERABLE CLAIMANTS

Similarly to children, where the claimant may be particularly vulnerable, owing to disability or another factor, the defendant should take that into account. The vulnerability may make the claimant more likely to suffer injury, or it may make the risk unacceptable.

In *Haley v London Electricity Board*,[74] the defendant had dug a hole in the pavement, leaving a long-handled hammer leaning across to warn pedestrians. The claimant, who was blind, did not detect the hammer with his white stick, and fell. The House of Lords held that it was foreseeable that people with visual impairments would be using the pavement, so the

72 [2000] 1 WLR 1082 (HL).

73 Ibid, 1093.

74 [1965] AC 778 (HL).

defendant should have considered their safety, as well as the safety of sighted pedestrians. In another House of Lords case, *Paris v Stepney Borough Council*,[75] the claimant worked as a garage hand. He was blind in his left eye, as a result of war injuries. This was known to his employers,[76] but they had not provided any additional protection for him, such as protective goggles. The claimant was injured in his right eye, causing complete blindness. The House of Lords held that the defendant was in breach of their duty of care: as they knew of the claimant's loss of sight, they should have taken that into account when considering the safety of their workers.

3.10 HISTORIC CASES

Although the test of reasonableness has not changed since the nineteenth century,[77] what the courts regard as reasonable has changed markedly since that time. In earlier times, occupational diseases and injuries were regarded as inevitable consequences of working in particular jobs. What would have been regarded as reasonable in the 1950s would, nowadays, be regarded as reckless indifference to the safety of workers. For example, in *Bonnington Castings v Wardlaw*,[78] a worker was exposed to silica dust, from which he contracted pneumoconiosis. Part of the exposure was due to the employer's failure to provide proper ventilation, which was a breach of his duty of care, and the worker was able to recover damages. However, the court accepted that there was a level of exposure which could not have been prevented, even with proper ventilation, and which contributed to the severity of the disease, and that the employer was not negligent in exposing their employees to this. Likewise, the doctor who administered ECT without anaesthesia or a muscle relaxant in *Bolam* would nowadays be regarded as negligent.

In the 1962 case of *McWilliams v Sir William Arrol & Co Ltd*,[79] a worker was killed when he fell from scaffolding. The House of Lords held that the employer had not been negligent. Although they had not provided a safety harness, there was no evidence that the worker would have used a harness if one had been available. The House of Lords warned against imposing a duty on employers to require or encourage workers to use safety equipment. Such an attitude would not be regarded as reasonable by a modern court.[80]

75 [1951] AC 367 (HL).

76 The Council had carried out a medical examination of Mr Paris, with the aim of offering him a permanent position. When they found that he was blind in one eye, and had other injuries, the Council refused him a permanent job and gave him two weeks' notice of dismissal. Mr Paris was working out his notice when the injury happened.

77 *Blyth v Birmingham Waterworks Co* (1856) 11 Ex 780.

78 [1956] AC 613 (HL).

79 [1962] 1 WLR 295 (HL).

80 Under the Personal Protective Equipment at Work Regulations 1992, employers have a statutory duty to provide personal protective equipment, to train employees in its use, and to take reasonable steps to ensure that it is used. Employees are also obliged, under s.10 of the Regulations, to use any equipment provided.

Some forms of industrial injury, caused by long exposure to dangerous chemicals, vibration, or noise, may take many years to develop: mesothelioma, for example, is a disease caused by exposure to asbestos which may take 40 years for symptoms to appear.[81] In such cases, the question is whether the employer's conduct was reasonable by the standards at the time of the breach, taking into account the state of knowledge of the effect of any exposure. In *Baker v Quantum Clothing Group*,[82] the claimants had suffered hearing loss as a result of exposure to noise over a period from the 1960s up until 1990, when new legislation controlling noise in workplaces was introduced. In determining whether the defendants had breached their duty to take reasonable care, the Supreme Court referred to guidance on noise in the workplace from 1970, which had set out good practice in industry. By that standard, the defendants had acted as reasonable employers.

3.11 THE BURDEN OF PROOF AND *RES IPSA LOQUITUR*

Although the burden of proof of breach always lies on the claimant, sometimes the circumstances are such that the damage cannot easily be explained unless the defendant has failed to use reasonable care. In such a case, the claimant can plead *res ipsa loquitur* ('the matter speaks for itself'). In *Scott v London and St Katherine Docks*,[83] the claimant was outside a warehouse when he was hit by six bags of sugar falling from above. Although the claimant was unable to show how the defendant had breached the duty of care, the court held that, where the thing causing the injury was under the control of the defendant, and the accident was of a type that would not normally occur when the defendant was using proper care, there was evidence of negligence, unless the defendant could provide an alternative explanation. This formulation was applied by the Privy Council in the case of *Airport Authority v Western Air Ltd (The Bahamas)*[84] when accepting that the theft of an airplane, under the control of the defendant, could not, in the absence of any alternative explanation, have taken place without negligence.

In *Ng Chun Pui v Lee Chuen Tat*,[85] a bus crossed a central reservation and collided with another bus on the opposite carriageway. The High Court of Hong Kong accepted that, as the bus was under the control of the defendant, and the accident would not normally have occurred without negligence on the part of the defendant, *res ipsa loquitor* had been established. This was interpreted as meaning that the formal burden of proof was reversed, and the defendant had to prove that they had not been negligent. The defendant claimed that another car had cut in suddenly in front of the bus. The court held that the defendant had not proved that they had not been negligent and gave judgment for the claimant.

81 See Chapter 4, Section 4.6.

82 [2011] UKSC 17, [2011] 1 WLR 1003.

83 (1865) 159 ER 665.

84 [2020] UKPC 29.

85 [1988] RTR 298 (PC).

The Privy Council overruled this judgment. Establishing *res ipsa loquitor* did not reverse the formal burden of proof. It was merely a way of describing a state of evidence from which negligence could be inferred, without requiring the claimant to establish the exact way in which the accident was caused.

POINTS TO REVIEW

- The duty of care is a duty to take reasonable care to prevent foreseeable harm.
- The test of reasonableness is an objective standard, measured by reference to an ordinary person.
- Children are expected to exercise less care than adults.
- Professionals are judged by the standard of an ordinary member of the profession.
- A person carrying out a role which requires professional expertise is not negligent if he or she acts in accordance with a practice accepted as proper by a responsible body of professional opinion.
- The defendant should take into account any foreseeable vulnerability or disability of the claimants.
- The law takes all the circumstances into account.

TAKING IT FURTHER

Nolan, D. 'Varying the Standard of Care in Negligence' (2013) 72(3) Cambridge LJ 651–688
A consideration of the objective standard applied in English law, which examines the case for varying the standard in some circumstances. The author argues that this could be an alternative to using the duty of care as a control mechanism.

Goudkamp, J. and Ihuoma, M. 'A Tour of the Tort of Negligence' (2016) 32 J Professional Negligence 137–152
This considers the objective standard of care applied in negligence, and whether it should be applied in the cases of adults who are suffering from mental disorders, such as the defendant in *Dunnage v Randall*. The authors argue that the judgment in Dunnage was inconsistent with the judgment in *Mansfield v Weetabix;* and that the Court of Appeal should have considered whether there should be an insanity defence in negligence.

Cave E. and Milo C. 'Informing Patients: The *Bolam* Legacy' (2020) 20 Medical Law International 103–130
Considers the effect of *Montgomery* in the context of the doctor's duty of care to patients and how this areas of law may develop to enhance patient-centred care.

4

CHAPTER 4
NEGLIGENCE: CAUSATION

4.1 INTRODUCTION

In this chapter, we consider the third element of the tort of negligence. Once it is established that the defendant owed a duty of care and that the defendant breached that duty, the next step in a successful claim in negligence is to show that the breach of duty caused the claimant to suffer damage.

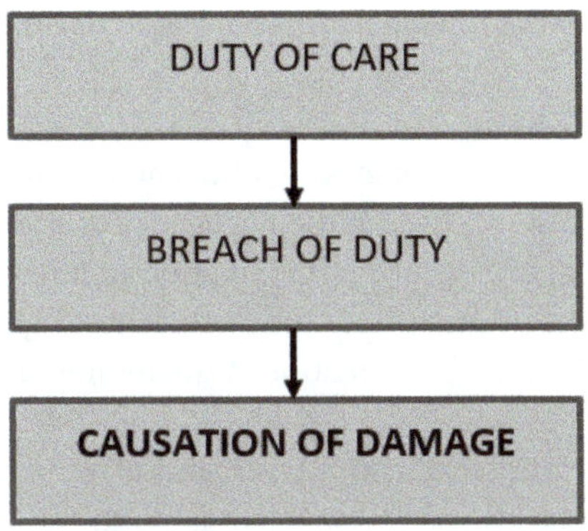

Figure 4.1 The elements of negligence: causation

In most cases, causation is relatively straightforward: the claimant has to show that the damage would not have happened if the defendant had not acted in breach of his or her duty of care. For example, a driver goes through a red traffic light and there is a collision with another car, which has the right of way. In this case, it seems obvious that the collision would not have happened if the first driver had not breached his or her duty to take reasonable care to avoid injuring other road users, and that is what a court would conclude.

If the claimant can show that the damage would not have happened if the defendant had not breached his or her duty of care, they will have established causation as a fact. However, the claimant also has to show that the consequences of the breach were not too remote from the breach itself, and that there was no intervening act, between the breach of duty and the damage happening, that 'broke the chain' of causation: this is known as establishing causation in law.

AS YOU READ

- Understand the 'but for' test for causation in fact.
- Understand the approaches used in cases of multiple causation.

DOI: 10.4324/9781003480051-04

- Understand the tests for causation in law.
- Identify where there are inconsistencies in the approach taken by courts.
- Consider whether these inconsistencies are justifiable.

Causation can, as we shall see, be a complex and contested area of the law. Particularly in the field of industrial diseases caused by asbestos, the courts have struggled to find a clear and consistent approach, and there remain inconsistencies in the way in which the court considers the issue.

The primary test applied by the courts in determining causation as a fact is the 'but for' test: the claimant has to show that, **but for** the breach, the damage would not have occurred. So, if the defendant is able to show that the damage would have occurred anyway, the claimant will not succeed.[1]

Meeting the 'but for' test is, however, not always sufficient: the claimant also has to show 'causation in law' or legal causation. Even if the negligent act clearly caused the damage, it will not be held, as a matter of law, to have been the causation unless the claimant can show that the damage was a foreseeable consequence of the defendant's negligence and that there was no intervening act that 'broke the chain' of causation. Causation is, therefore, a two-part test:

- Did the breach, as a matter of fact, cause the damage?
- Does the law regard the breach as causing the damage?

These are usually referred to as **causation in fact** and **causation in law**.

4.2 CAUSATION IN FACT: THE 'BUT FOR' TEST

To establish causation in fact, the claimant has to meet the 'but for' test. That is, to show that it is more likely than not that the damage would not have occurred, **but for** the negligence of the defendant.

KEY CASE

In *Barnett v Chelsea and Kensington HMC* [1969] 1 QB 428 (QB), three night-watchmen were suffering from stomach pains and vomiting. They went to the casualty department of the local hospital during the night. A nurse telephoned the on-call doctor, who advised the three men to see their own doctors in the morning. One of the men died later the same day. It was found that the cause of death was arsenic poisoning: tea which all three men had drunk had been poisoned and an inquest recorded a verdict of murder.

1 *Barnett v Chelsea and Kensington HMC* [1969] 1 QB 428 (QB).

The victim's widow brought a claim against the hospital for failing to admit and treat her husband when he first went to the casualty department. However, the court found, on evidence from expert witnesses, that even if the victim had been admitted when he first went to the casualty department, the poisoning would not have been diagnosed in time for him to be treated. The claimant had failed to prove that, but for the negligence of the on-call doctor, the victim would not have died.

This shows that even where the defendant fails to take reasonable care, they will not be liable for any damage unless the claimant can show that the damage would not have happened if the defendant had taken reasonable care. In this case, the damage would have happened, even if the defendant had taken reasonable care, so the claim failed.

This test is a simple and straightforward one, which works well in most circumstances: in the majority of cases, courts determine causation on the basis of common sense and no issues will arise.

4.3 THE BALANCE OF PROBABILITY AND THE LOSS OF CHANCE

KEY LEARNING POINTS

- In negligence claims, facts are determined on the balance of probability.
- A claimant cannot be compensated for a loss of a chance of avoiding physical injury.

As a civil claim, any facts in negligence have to be proved to the civil standard, which is the balance of probability: more likely to have happened than not to have happened. Facts which are more than 50% likely are held to be true, while those with a less than 50% chance are held not to be true.

The 'facts' determined by a court may refer to historic facts, which are things that did or did not happen. When determining historic facts, courts will consider evidence such as the testimony of the people involved, documentary evidence, and physical evidence. In a road traffic accident, for example, it may be important to determine whether a car was travelling too fast for the conditions. The court will take all the evidence – from the driver, other road users, and physical evidence, such as the damage to vehicles – into account and decide whether it was more likely than not that the car was travelling too fast.

Courts also, however, have to determine what might have happened if events had taken a different course. In particular, courts have to determine what would have happened if the defendant had not been negligent. This is the question at the centre of causation – what would have happened but for the defendant's negligence – and it is, by its nature, not a historic, objective fact. In some circumstances, what would have happened is virtually certain;

in other circumstances, it is unknowable and all that can be done is to balance the likelihood of different alternatives.

Take the example of a doctor who fails to spot the early signs of cancer. There are cancers for which treatment is 99–100% effective if the cancer is detected early enough. If the undiagnosed patient later dies from the cancer, it is possible to say that, but for the doctor's failure to diagnose at the earliest opportunity, the patient would not have died. However, if it is a less treatable form of cancer, the chances of the patient dying even if the cancer is spotted at the earliest opportunity may be much lower, and it is impossible to say with certainty that the patient would not have died but for the doctor's failure to spot the cancer. In these cases, the courts accept the most probable outcome, given the facts known to the court, is what would have happened.

This approach was adopted in two House of Lords cases: *Hotson v East Berkshire Area Health Authority*[2] and *Gregg v Scott*.[3] In *Hotson*, a hospital was sued for an injury suffered by a child falling out of a tree. The hospital failed to diagnose damage to the child's blood vessels, which could have been treated if it had been diagnosed at the time. By the time it was spotted, it was too late and the child suffered from a permanent disability. Unlike *Barnett*, where it was certain that the claimant would have died anyway, in *Hotson*, there was a 25% chance that treatment of the injury would have been successful, if the hospital had spotted it at the first opportunity. However, applying the balance of probability standard, the permanent injury would not have been prevented. The court held that the claimant had not proved that the failure to diagnose had caused the permanent disability and the claimant did not succeed.

In *Gregg v Scott*, the House of Lords followed the same approach as in *Hotson*: as in that case, there was a failure to diagnose which meant that the claimant lost the opportunity of timely treatment. In *Gregg*, the defendant GP negligently failed to diagnose the claimant's cancer, causing a nine-month delay in the claimant receiving treatment. The probability of the claimant surviving, had the cancer been diagnosed at the first opportunity, was 42%. By the time the cancer was diagnosed, the survival probability had dropped to 25%. Under the balance of probability approach, an event with a probability of more than 50% is regarded as having definitely happened, if referring to a past event, or as certain to happen, if referring to a future event. A probability of less than 50% is regarded as having definitely not happened in the past, or certain not to happen if referring to a future event. The probability of Mr Gregg, the claimant, dying of cancer – even if he had been diagnosed at the earlier opportunity – was 58%: in the eyes of the law, this was the most probable outcome, so was what would have happened.[4] That the probability of his dying increased to 75% by the time he was diagnosed did not change that. Accordingly, since the law regarded him as always certain to die, the GP's failure had not caused Mr Gregg any legally recognised damage.

2 [1987] AC 750 (HL).

3 [2005] UKHL 2, [2005] 2 AC 176.

4 In the event, Mr Gregg was still alive at the time of the House of Lords case in 2005, some nine years after his GP misdiagnosed his tumour.

ANALYSING THE LAW

In *Gregg v Scott*, Lord Nicholls, in a strong dissenting judgment, argued that the loss of an opportunity was real damage for which the claimant should have been compensated. Mr Gregg's chances of recovery had been significantly reduced by his GP's negligence. This was a lost opportunity which the law of negligence should recognise and compensate.

Do you agree? Should claimants be able to recover for loss of opportunities? If your job application was lost by someone's carelessness, and your application was never even considered, shouldn't you be compensated even if you were not able to prove that you were probably going to get the job?

In *Perry v Raleys Solicitors*,[5] however, the Supreme Court recognised that a loss of opportunity to bring a claim was a compensable loss. The claimant had been wrongly advised by the defendant firm of solicitors and accepted a lower sum in settlement of an industrial injury than he might have received. The claimant did not have to show that he was more likely than not to have received the additional compensation had he been properly advised: it was sufficient that he lost the opportunity to make the claim.[6]

4.4 MULTIPLE CAUSATION

Difficulties arise when there is more than one possible cause of the damage, particularly where the evidence is insufficient to determine whether any one of the causes is more likely than not to have caused the damage.

This is an area of law where the courts have accepted that there is some inconsistency. In some cases, particularly in the cases of industrial diseases caused by exposure to asbestos and other forms of harmful dust, the courts have not followed the traditional 'but for' approach. However, in other cases where there are multiple possible causes, the courts have held that the 'but for' test should continue to be applied.

There are three different scenarios:

1 The defendant's breach is just one of possible independent causes.
2 The defendant's breach contributes to the damage.
3 The defendant's breach contributes to the risk of damage.

5 [2019] UKSC 5, [2020] AC 532.

6 See also *Kitchen v Royal Airforce Association* [1958] 1 WLR 563 (CA) and *Allied Maples Group Ltd v Simmons & Simmons* [1995] 1 WLR 1602 (CA) for cases in which the claimant was able to recover damages for loss of an opportunity without having to prove that the opportunity would have resulted in success.

ANALYSING THE LAW

THE TWO HUNTERS PROBLEM

A problem which has been used as an example to think about issues of multiple causation is the 'two hunters problem'. In one variant of this scenario, two hunters are out hunting when both of them think they see a deer. Both raise their rifles and fire at the deer, more or less at the same time. To their horror, when they go over to see whether they have hit the deer, they see that they have shot a person. One of the shots hit the victim in the heart, while the other missed. The bullet passed through the victim, so it is impossible to say who fired the fatal shot.

The burden of proof lies on the claimant to show it was more likely than not that either the first or the second hunter fired the fatal shot. In this case, it is equally likely that either the first or second hunter fired the fatal shot, which is not sufficient to meet the burden of proof. Using traditional principles of causation, neither of the hunters will be held liable.

Do you think that is satisfactory? Can you think of another approach that would give a better result?

The criminal law has developed the doctrine of 'joint enterprise' to deal with this sort of case. Where two or more people are jointly engaged on a criminal enterprise, all the participants may be guilty of any crime committed during the joint enterprise, without the prosecution having to prove which of them carried out the criminal act. Could such an approach be used to allocate liability for negligence? Would it make a difference if the two hunters were hunting together, or if they were hunting on their own and just happened to be close to each other at the time they shot at the victim?

4.5 MULTIPLE INDEPENDENT CAUSES

KEY LEARNING POINT

Where the damage might have been caused by one of a number of independent causes, the claimant still has to show that, but for the defendant's negligence, the damage would probably not have occurred.

Where the defendant's breach is just one of several possible independent causes, the 'but for' principle still applies. The claimant still has to show, on the balance of probability, that 'but for the defendant's breach', the damage would not have occurred: in other words, that the other possible causes were not responsible for the damage.

KEY CASES

In *Wilsher v Essex Area Health Authority* [1988] AC 1074 (HL), a doctor negligently failed to place a blood oxygen level monitor correctly, with the result that too much oxygen was administered to a premature baby. The baby later suffered from damage to his eyes. While excess oxygen is a well-known cause of blindness in premature babies, the hospital was able to show that there were four other potential causes of blindness, which had not been excluded by the medical evidence.

The House of Lords held that the claimant had failed to prove that the excess oxygen was more likely to have caused the damage than any of four other possible causes and ordered a re-trial.

Wilsher confirmed that the 'but for' test applies to cases where there were a number of different, unrelated possible causes of the damage. It also confirmed that, if the defendant is able to identify another possible non-negligent cause or causes for the damage, the claimant has to prove that the defendant's breach caused the damage. In medical cases, such as *Wilsher*, this can prove a difficult hurdle for the claimant to cross.

4.6 EXPOSURE TO MULTIPLE SOURCES OF A SINGLE CAUSE

A large number of cases involving industrial diseases caused by long-term exposure to harmful substances have come before the courts since the 1980s. In particular, cases of diseases caused by exposure to asbestos continue to be heard. Although it has been known since the 1920s that some forms of asbestos are harmful,[7] employers continued to expose workers in the United Kingdom to asbestos until the end of the twentieth century. The most harmful forms – brown and blue asbestos – were banned in 1985 and the last type to be banned remained in use until 1999. Asbestos-related diseases may take many years to develop. For one of the diseases, mesothelioma, the time between exposure and first symptoms may be 40 years,[8] so a person who was exposed during the 1980s might still develop the disease. In fact, deaths from mesothelioma reached a maximum in the years from 2012 to 2020 and, although the number of deaths is now falling, over 2,200 people still die from mesothelioma every year.[9]

Claimants suffering from the two main asbestos-related diseases, asbestosis and mesothelioma, have faced formidable barriers to their claims. In many cases where the exposure took place decades before the illness developed, the company responsible is no longer in existence and

7 Cooke, W. E. 'Fibrosis of the Lungs Due to the Inhalation of Asbestos Dust' (1924) 2(3317) BMJ 147.

8 Sen, D. 'Working with Asbestos and the Possible Health Risks' (2015) 65(6) Occupational Medicine 6–14.

9 Health and Safety Executive, 'Mesothelioma Statistics for Great Britain, 2024' (HSE, July 2024).

therefore no one is in a position to pay compensation. Furthermore, many of the claimants had worked for a number of different employers: negligent exposure to asbestos was very widespread in some industries and occupations. This will make it difficult or impossible to prove that any specific employer had, on the balance of probability, caused the disease.

As a result of this, a different approach to causation has been taken where the causes are not independent and unrelated. Where the claimant has been exposed to a single harmful substance from different sources, the defendant is liable if the exposure that they were responsible for materially contributed to the severity of the damage caused or, in some cases, if the exposure increased the risk of the damage. Most of the cases concerned have arisen from exposure in the workplace, where the employer failed to take reasonable care to protect the workers.

KEY LEARNING POINT

DIVISIBLE AND INDIVISIBLE INJURIES

- Courts have distinguished between 'divisible' and 'indivisible' injuries when considering causation.
- A divisible injury is an injury or illness in which the severity of the injury is related to the degree of exposure to the cause. An example of a divisible injury is asbestosis: the more asbestos that the victim has been exposed to, the worse the condition gets.
- An indivisible injury is an injury or illness in which the severity is not related to the degree of exposure to the cause. An example of an indivisible injury is lung cancer: the severity of lung cancer does not depend on whether the sufferer was a smoker, but the chance of suffering from lung cancer does depend on whether he or she smoked.

4.7 MATERIAL CONTRIBUTION TO DAMAGE

In the case of divisible injuries – those in which the severity depends upon the amount of exposure – the claimant will be able to recover damages from a defendant if they can show that the defendant's negligence 'materially contributed' to the severity of the condition.

KEY CASE

In *Bonnington Castings Ltd v Wardlaw* [1956] AC 613 (HL), the claimant worked in a factory, where his job was to grind the irregularities off cast-steel machine parts. This involved the creation of large amounts of silica dust from the grinding wheels and hammers used in the process. It was accepted that it was impossible, given the filters available at the time, to remove all the dust from the air in the workshop, so the defendant was not liable for some of the exposure to the dust. However, the defendant was in breach of its duty to ventilate the workshop properly, so the claimant was exposed to much more of the dust than he should have been. The claimant contracted pneumoconiosis, a lung disease.

The defendant argued that, to succeed, the claimant would have to show, on the balance of probability, that the additional, negligent exposure to the dust, rather than the acceptable level of dust, caused the disease.

The House of Lords rejected this: the claimant would succeed if he could prove that the negligent exposure to dust either caused the disease, or if the negligent exposure materially contributed to the disease.

The principle established in *Bonnington Castings* applies where:

- a defendant has negligently exposed a claimant to some harmful substance, such as asbestos;
- the claimant has been exposed to the same substance in circumstances for which the defendant is not liable; and
- the exposure for which the defendant is liable has contributed to the severity of the harm.

The additional exposure may be due to another person's negligence or the claimant's own negligence, or it may be due to circumstances for which no one is liable.

In this case, the claimant does not have to show that, but for the defendant's breach of duty, he would not have suffered any injury. Rather, all that the claimant has to show is that, but for the defendant's breach, the injury would have been less severe. Obviously, if the claimant can show that the injury would not have happened at all, causation will also be established.

The 'material contribution to the injury' principle has been applied mainly in the context of industrial diseases caused by exposure to harmful materials such as asbestos, silica dust, and other potentially harmful materials, but it has also been recently applied in the case of exposure to infection from a ruptured appendix[10] and where a delay in medical treatment contributed to the severity of brain damage.[11]

10 *Williams v Bermuda Hospitals Board* [2016] UKPC 4, [2016] AC 888.

11 *John v Central Manchester & Manchester Children's University Hospitals NHS Foundation Trust* [2016] EWHC 407 (QB).

4.8 MATERIAL INCREASE IN RISK

The material contribution to the disease principle established in *Bonnington Castings* was reconsidered by the House of Lords in the case of *McGhee v National Coal Board*.[12] As in *Bonnington Castings*, the claimant in *McGhee* was exposed to harmful dust at work: his job was to clean out brick kilns, which exposed him to large amounts of brick dust. This caused a skin condition, and the claimant sued his employer in negligence.

As in *Bonnington Castings*, the House of Lords noted that the exposure could be divided into negligent and non-negligent exposure. They accepted that the defendant was not negligent in exposing the claimant to brick dust while he was at work. However, the court found that it was a breach of duty for the defendant not to provide showers, which would have allowed the claimant to clean off the brick dust after finishing work. As a result, the claimant continued to be exposed to brick dust while cycling home, which was held to be a breach of the duty of care owed by the defendant.

If the claimant had been able to show that the additional, negligent exposure had caused his skin condition or made it worse, then the principle in *Bonnington Castings* would have allowed him to succeed in his claim. However, there was some uncertainty in the medical evidence as to whether the increased exposure to the brick dust made the condition worse (which would have allowed the claimant to succeed on the basis of *Bonnington Castings*) or if it only increased the risk of suffering from the skin condition. The medical expert witnesses were willing to say that the increased exposure increased the risk of the skin condition, but were unwilling to say whether or not it increased the severity of the condition.

The House of Lords were willing to overlook or bridge this absence of evidence, and hold that, in the circumstances of the case, there was no difference between increasing the severity of a condition and increasing the risk of the condition.

The case of *McGhee* was considered by the House of Lords in the later case of *Wilsher*. In that case, it was held that *McGhee* did not change the law and that the House of Lords had legitimately inferred from the facts that the defendant had materially contributed to the severity of the claimant's injury.

This interpretation was later challenged by the House of Lords in *Fairchild v Glenhaven Funeral Services*.[13] In that case, the House of Lords held that *McGhee* did establish that a defendant who had contributed to the risk of an indivisible condition should be liable.

12 [1973] 1 WLR 1 (HL).
13 [2002] UKHL 22, [2003] 1 AC 32.

KEY CASES

Fairchild v Glenhaven Funeral Services Ltd [2002] UKHL 22, [2003] 1 AC 32 is another case concerning exposure to harmful dust at work. In this case, there were three workers, each of whom had been exposed to asbestos over their working lives, while working for several different employers. They had all developed mesothelioma, a lung disease caused by exposure to asbestos. Two of them had died from the condition.

Unlike *McGhee*, in which the medical expert witnesses were not willing to say whether exposure to the brick dust had made the condition worse or increased the risk of the condition, in this case the Court of Appeal held that mesothelioma was caused by a single fibre of asbestos: in other words, it was an indivisible injury.

That created a problem for the claimants. Since the House of Lords had stated, in *Wilsher*, that *McGhee* did not change the law, the Court of Appeal applied the 'but for' test, as applied in *Wilsher*. They treated the negligent exposure by each employer as a separate cause. Since the claimants could not prove which of the employers had been responsible for the single fibre which had caused the mesothelioma, their claims failed.

The claimants' appeal to the House of Lords succeeded. Recognising that it would be impossible for the claimants to be compensated if the 'but for' test was strictly applied, they created an exception to the rule: this is known as the 'Fairchild exception'. They stated that, where the state of medical knowledge meant that it was impossible to determine which of a number of defendants was responsible for the exposure that caused the injury, a claimant would succeed if he or she could show that the defendant's negligence materially increased the risk of the disease.

The Fairchild exception is based on considerations of justice and policy, rather than strict legal principles. As a result, the House of Lords did make it clear that it should not be allowed to undermine those principles in other circumstances.

The 'Fairchild Exception' applies when:

- the claimant suffers from mesothelioma or a very similar, indivisible condition;
- the claimant worked for a number of employers who negligently exposed the claimant to asbestos or other single harmful substance;
- the employers all materially increased the risk that the claimant would contract mesothelioma or other indivisible injury; and
- the state of medical or scientific knowledge is such that it is not possible to determine which of the defendants was responsible for the exposure to the single fibre of asbestos or harmful substance which actually caused the injury.

ANALYSING THE LAW

In both *Wilsher* and *Fairchild*, it was not possible to say, on the balance of probability, whether the defendant's breach had caused the damage.

In the case of *Wilsher*, the breach was one of five possible causes, which were distinct and independent. The claimants had to show that the damage suffered was caused by one of those causes, as opposed to the four others, to succeed.

In *Fairchild*, there had been separate negligent acts by each of the defendants – although all the negligent acts had been of the same type: exposure to asbestos. For each defendant, it was not possible to say that they were responsible for the exposure to the single fibre (out of the countless billions to which the defendant had been negligently exposed) that caused the mesothelioma.

Is it possible to justify the differing approaches taken in *Wilsher* and *Fairchild*? In *Wilsher*, the exposure to excess oxygen increased the probability of the child's sight being damaged, as did the other non-negligent causes. Where the possible causes of the damage are independent, rather than being of the same type, why should a different rule apply?

4.9 APPORTIONING DAMAGES: *BARKER V CORUS* AND THE COMPENSATION ACT 2006

While *Bonnington Castings* and *Fairchild* had established that a claimant could recover damages from any defendant who had materially contributed to the severity of a divisible injury, or materially increased the risk of an indivisible injury, neither case had considered expressly the extent of the defendant's liability. The orthodox approach, in the case of defendants who had materially contributed to damage, was to make each of the defendants jointly liable. Joint liability means that a claimant can recover all the damages from any one of the defendants. Clearly, this was a significant advantage for a claimant who would be suing employers from many years earlier: potential defendants might well have become insolvent during the intervening time. The joint liability rule meant that, as long as a claimant could identify one former employer who was in a position to pay damages, they could recover the full amount.

In *Holtby v Brigham & Cowan (Hull)*,[14] the Court of Appeal held that a claimant who was awarded damages under the principle in *Bonnington Castings*, for material contribution to the

14 [2000] EWCA Civ 111, [2000] 3 All ER 421. See also *Carder v University of Exeter* [2016] EWCA Civ 790.

injury, should only be awarded damages proportionate to the exposure that the defendant was responsible for.

In *Barker v Corus*,[15] the House of Lords considered the same issue for claimants who relied on the Fairchild exception. Was it fair, under the Fairchild exception, to hold a defendant liable for the full extent of the damage, where their contribution to the risk, while significant, might have been much less than other employers? The House of Lords agreed that, since *Fairchild* was itself an exception to the orthodox approach, there was no reason to apply the orthodox principle of joint liability. The Fairchild exception existed because it could not be proved that the defendant had contributed to the damage at all, let alone materially. In those circumstances, it would not be just to hold the defendant liable for the full extent of the damage. The House of Lords awarded damages against the defendant proportional to the amount of exposure for which the defendant was liable.

Barker v Corus provoked an immediate response from the government. A late amendment was introduced to the Compensation Bill, which was then progressing through Parliament, which had the effect of reversing the judgment. Section 3 of the Compensation Act 2006 provides that in cases of mesothelioma, where a defendant is liable in tort for having exposed a person to asbestos, that defendant is jointly and severally liable for the whole of the damage caused. The Act, at section 16(3), also provided that section 3 should be treated as having always had effect: in other words, the provision was retrospective and the claimants in *Barker v Corus* were able to recover full damages.

4.10 THE SCOPE OF THE FAIRCHILD EXCEPTION

The scope of the Fairchild exception and the meaning of the Compensation Act were considered by the Supreme Court in the case of *Sienkiewicz v Greif*.[16] In this case, the victim's exposure at work had been relatively minor, compared to the amount of asbestos in the atmosphere. The court held that the Act applied whenever the defendant had negligently exposed the claimant to any material risk[17] of mesothelioma, whatever other exposure the claimant might have been exposed to. This meant that the claimant was awarded full compensation for her mother's death.

In *Jones v Secretary of State for Energy and Climate Change*,[18] the claimants had been exposed to a combination of harmful chemicals, at their workplace, in the environment in the form of pollution, and from smoking. They had suffered from a variety of cancers, including skin, lung, and bladder cancers. It was accepted that all the harmful chemicals to which they had been exposed had played a part in the development of their cancers. The High Court held

15 [2006] UKHL 20, [2006] 2 AC 572.

16 [2011] UKSC 10, [2011] 2 AC 229.

17 'Material' may be as low as 2.3% of the total exposure: see *Carder v University of Exeter* [2016] EWCA Civ 790.

18 [2012] EWHC 2936 (QB).

that neither the principle from *Bonnington Castings*, nor the Fairchild exception, could be applied. Instead, it was held that, in order to succeed, the claimants would have to show that the defendant's negligent exposure to harmful chemicals doubled the risk of cancer. This would mean that it was more likely than not that the defendant caused the cancer. However, the claimants were unable to prove this and their claim failed.

Likewise, in *AB v Ministry of Defence*,[19] the Court of Appeal considered a claim brought by former servicemen who had been exposed to radiation fallout while witnessing nuclear weapons tests in the 1950s and who had subsequently developed cancer. The claims were struck out on the grounds of limitation, but the Court of Appeal also noted that, on the evidence available, the claimants would have been unable to prove that the exposure to radiation doubled their risk of developing cancer.[20]

The case of *Henegham v Manchester Dry Docks*[21] approved the approach in *Jones* when they considered the scope of the Fairchild exception, in the context of indivisible, asbestos-related diseases other than mesothelioma. In this case, the claim was brought on behalf of a person who had worked for six different employers, all of whom had negligently exposed him to asbestos. In addition, he was a smoker. The victim died from lung cancer: both his smoking and the asbestos had contributed to the risk of his contracting the cancer. The Court of Appeal held that the Fairchild exception could be extended to the lung cancer, which was indivisible and sufficiently similar to mesothelioma (which is a cancer of the lining of the lung or other organs), for the principle to apply. However, the Compensation Act could not be applied, as that Act was specific to cases of mesothelioma. The claimant received damages proportional to the exposure for which the defendant was liable.

4.11 MATERIAL CONTRIBUTION TO INDIVISIBLE INJURY

Some illnesses, such as asbestosis or mesothelioma, have relatively straightforward causes: they are caused by exposure to a single causative agent. However, many illnesses are multifactorial: they are caused by a combination of factors, such as genetic factors and environmental factors.

Where there are pre-existing factors that contribute to a condition, such as a genetic pre-disposition, or physical injury, then the defendant may be liable for either a divisible or indivisible condition if their breach of duty 'materially contributed' to the development of the condition, even if the claimant is unable to show that, but for the defendant's breach of duty, the damage would not have happened.

19 [2010] EWCA Civ 1317, 117 BMLR 101.

20 Ibid, [153]–[154]. This was described as 'plainly correct' by Lord Phillips JSC in the Supreme Court: see *AB v Ministry of Defence* [2012] UKSC 9, [2013] 1 AC 78, [157].

21 [2016] EWCA Civ 86.

This principle was recently examined by the Court of Appeal in the case of *Holmes v Poeton Holdings Ltd.*[22]

KEY CASES

In *Holmes v Poeton Holdings Ltd* [2023] EWCA Civ 1377, [2024] KB 521, the claimant had worked for the defendant for 15 years, during which he was negligently exposed to an industrial solvent, trichloroethylene (TCE), which was used to clean components. He subsequently developed Parkinson's disease, which is an indivisible condition. The High Court accepted the medical evidence of a link between exposure to TCE and Parkinson's disease and allowed the claim, on the grounds that the exposure had 'materially contributed' to the development of the claimant's illness. The defendant appealed on the grounds that the claimant had failed to prove that he would not have developed Parkinson's disease but for the negligent exposure to TCE.

The Court of Appeal noted that there was nothing in *Bonnington Castings*[23] or subsequent House of Lords or Supreme Court judgments[24] that restricted the application of the 'material contribution' principle to divisible injuries. In those cases, the courts had held that, when the principle applied, the claimant only needed to show that the defendant's breach materially contributed to the injury in order to receive full compensation. There was no need to show that the injury would not have occurred but for the breach. However, the scientific evidence of a relationship between exposure to TCE and Parkinson's disease was not sufficient to establish a material contribution, so the appeal was allowed.[25]

The aetiology of Parkinson's disease is not fully understood, but it seems clear that genetics and environmental factors, including exposure to industrial chemicals, both play a role. Without a fuller understanding, it is difficult to apply orthodox principles of causation. There are a number of different possibilities, including:

- a person with a genetic predisposition will not develop the disease unless they are also exposed to triggering environmental factors, including industrial chemicals; or
- a person with a genetic predisposition may develop the condition but are more likely to do so if they are exposed to environmental factors.

22 [2023] EWCA Civ 1377, [2024] KB 521.

23 [1956] AC 613 (HL).

24 Including *Nicholson v Atlas Steel Foundry and Engineering Co Ltd* [1957] 1 WLR 613 (HL); *McGhee v National Coal Board* [1973] 1 WLR 1 (HL); *Simmons v British Steel plc* [2004] UKHL 20; *Barker v Corus UK Ltd* [2004] UKHL 20, [2006] 2 AC 572; and *Sienkiewicz v Grief* [2011] UKSC 10, [2011] 2 AC 229.

25 See Patricia de Moraes Paisani Matthey Claudet, '*Michael Holmes v Poeton Holdings Ltd* [2023] EWCA Civ 1377: A Necessary Clarification for a Non 'De Minimis' Discussion in Causation' (2024) Med Law Rev 32(3) 410 for a case commentary.

In the first case above, the claim would be analogous to a 'thin skull' claim[26] and the claimant would be entitled to full compensation. They have a pre-existing vulnerability, but the injury was caused by the defendant's negligence. In those circumstances, the court does not consider whether the claimant would have suffered the injury anyway.[27]

The alternative, that the negligent exposure to environmental factors materially increases the risk of developing the indivisible injury, is a situation which the courts have previously considered, as discussed above: where there is a single causative agent, then any defendant who has negligently exposed the claimant is liable proportionately.[28] However, where there are multiple causative factors, previous cases have applied the 'doubling the risk' approach.[29]

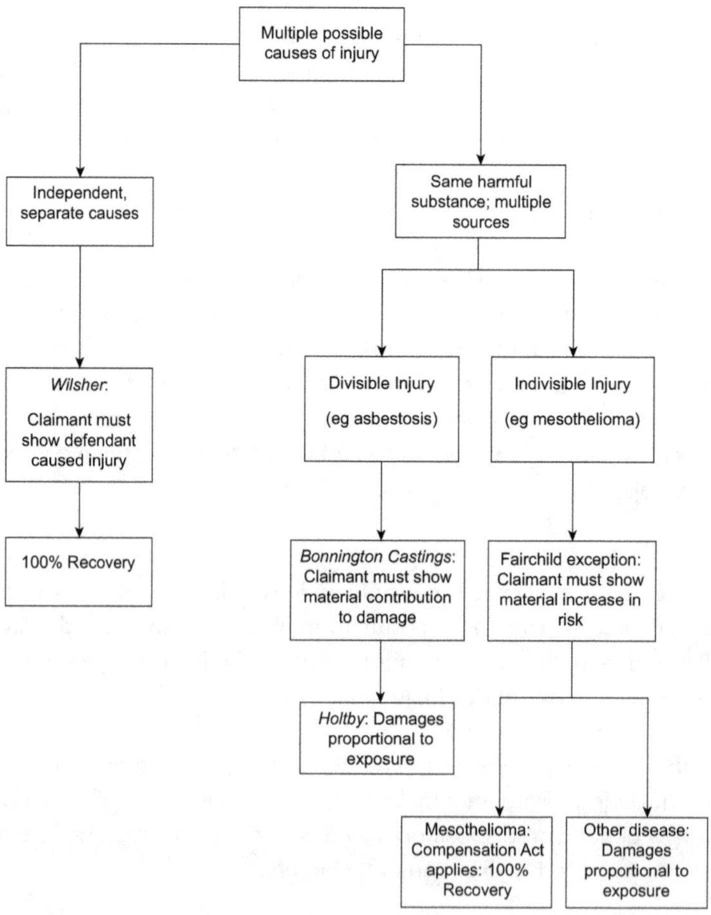

Figure 4.2 Multiple causation

26 See section 4.15 below.

27 See *Smith v Leech Brain* [1962] 2 QB 405 (QB), 413, where the court acknowledged that the victim might well have developed cancer without the negligence of the defendant.

28 See *Barker v Corus UK Ltd* [2004] UKHL 20, [2006] 2 AC 572, subject to the provisions of s.3 of the Compensation Act 2006; *Carder v University of Exeter* [2016] EWCA Civ 790.

29 *Jones v Secretary of State for Energy and Climate Change* [2012] EWHC 2936 (QB).

4.12 CONCLUSIONS ON MULTIPLE CAUSATION

It is reasonable to conclude that the rules on multiple causation in the asbestos cases are both confusing and confused. An unfortunate combination of factors, including inadequate medical evidence, the long latency period of the injuries concerned (with the result that many of the defendants are no longer in a position to pay compensation), the desire of the courts to do justice to victims suffering from painful and often fatal conditions, and a lack of clarity in some of the key judgments have meant that the development of the law in this area has not been as smooth as it might have been. To an extent, the search for an overriding principle is unlikely to be a fruitful exercise. In practice, it is probably better to consider it as an area of law with its own rules, which the courts must apply to new circumstances as best they can.

4.13 CAUSATION IN LAW

KEY LEARNING POINTS

- The claimant must establish causation in law, as well as meeting the 'but for' test for causation in fact.
- Damage which is not of a foreseeable type is regarded as too 'remote' and the defendant will not be liable for it.
- If the damage is of a foreseeable type, the defendant is liable for the full damage.
- There must be a direct chain of events between the defendant's negligent act and the claimant's injury.

One problem with the 'but for' test is that it may give too many 'false positives'. In other words, the application of the test may lead to the conclusion that a defendant is liable in circumstances where most people would not regard the damage as the defendant's fault.

For example, consider a case where a lorry driver, by mistake, drops off a load of gravel in front of the wrong house. If the claimant is unable to take her car out of her drive to get to work (because the gravel is in the way), should the lorry driver be liable if she is injured when the bus she takes instead is involved in an accident? It is certainly true that, 'but for' the lorry driver's mistake, the claimant would not have been on the bus and would not have been injured. But most people would think that, while it might be fair to compensate the claimant for the additional expense and inconvenience of having to go by bus, it would not be fair to hold the lorry driver liable for the injuries sustained in the unforeseen accident. It is also likely that the accident in which the bus was involved was the result of someone else's negligence: wouldn't it be fairer to hold that person liable for the claimant's injuries?

In fact, as the law stands, the lorry driver would not be liable: the 'but for' test is just one part of establishing causation. The claimant must also prove causation in law. That means that the damage was of a foreseeable type, and that there was an unbroken chain of causation from the negligent act to the damage suffered.

In the case of the lorry driver, it would not be regarded as foreseeable that leaving a load of gravel in front of a person's house would injure her. Furthermore, there would have to have been many different actions that had to be taken, by the claimant and other people, between the negligent act of the lorry driver and the injury suffered. Any of these different actions might 'break the chain' of causation.

Meeting these additional tests of causation – remoteness[30] and no breaking of the chain – are referred to as establishing 'causation in law'.

4.14 FORESEEABILITY AND REMOTENESS

KEY LEARNING POINTS

- The defendant is not liable for damage that is of an unforeseeable type.
- The defendant is, however, liable for all the damage of a foreseeable type, even if the extent of the damage is unforeseeable.

Defendants are only liable for damage of a type that is foreseeable. Where the defendant's acts cause harm of an unforeseeable type, then the damage is referred to as being too remote to hold the defendant liable. This should not be confused with a chain of events that result in harm being caused by an unforeseeable mechanism: as long as the chain is unbroken, and the type of harm is foreseeable, the defendant will be liable.

KEY CASE

In *The Wagon Mound (No 1)* [1961] AC 388 (PC), the defendant negligently discharged fuel oil from a ship in Sydney harbour. The fuel oil drifted and accumulated under a wharf belonging to the claimant. During welding operations carried out by the claimant, the fuel oil was set alight by a spark of hot metal and the ensuing fire caused serious damage to the wharf. The Privy Council heard, and accepted, expert evidence that it was virtually impossible to ignite fuel oil on water and that, therefore, damage by fire was of a type that was unforeseeable.

The Privy Council held that the defendant was not liable: the defendant was only liable for types of damage that were foreseeable.

30 Some commentators categorise remoteness as a separate issue to causation.

ANALYSING THE LAW

In the case of *Re Polemis and Furness Withy* [1921] 3 KB 560 (CA), a ship exploded when a stevedore dropped a plank into a hold containing petrol. The court held that the defendant was liable for all the damage caused directly by the negligence. This case was doubted by the *Wagon Mound (No 1)*, which held that the defendant should only be liable for foreseeable types of harm.

Is this reasonable? Shouldn't the defendant be liable for damage that they directly cause?

However, if the type of harm is foreseeable, then it does not affect the defendant's liability if the way in which it happened was not foreseeable. If a driver drives too fast, in breach of their duty of care to other road users, then there are many ways in which he or she may cause physical injury. Some of these are entirely predictable. Others might fairly be described as unforeseeable or freak accidents. However, the driver will be liable for any physical injury caused, no matter how it happens.

One example of a freak accident, in which the defendant tried to claim that the injury was unforeseeable, was the case of *Hughes v Lord Advocate*.[31] In this case, the defendant left a manhole open and unguarded. A child, playing with an oil lamp that had been left to mark the manhole, dropped the lamp into the hole. There was an explosion, which badly injured the child. The House of Lords acknowledged that the explosion was so unlikely as to be unforeseeable. However, they held that it was not material that the exact means by which the accident was caused was unforeseeable, as long as it was foreseeable that the defendant's negligence might cause physical injury by some means.

Likewise, in *Bradford v Robinson Rentals*,[32] the defendant argued that it was unforeseeable that the claimant would suffer frostbite when driving an unheated van during a very cold period. The court held that, while frostbite was unusual in England, it was foreseeable that the claimant would suffer injury from the prolonged exposure to the cold.

In *Tremain v Pike*,[33] on the other hand, a farm worker who caught Weil's disease from rats' urine did not succeed in a claim against the farmer. The court held that, while injuries and disease from rats' bites or contamination of food would have been foreseeable, Weil's disease was so rare as to make the claimant's damage unforeseeable.

31 [1963] AC 837 (HL).

32 [1967] 1 WLR 337 (Assizes).

33 [1969] 1 WLR 1556 (Assizes).

4.15 THE THIN SKULL RULE

As well as not applying to injuries of a foreseeable type which occur by an unforeseeable mechanism, the principle of remoteness also does not apply to injuries of a foreseeable type where the extent of the damage is unforeseeable. The so-called thin skull rule, first articulated in the case of *Dulieu v White*,[34] states that it is not a defence in a claim for negligent injury to say that the victim 'would have suffered less injury, or no injury at all, if he had not had an unusually thin skull'. In other words, the defendant must take the victim as he finds him, with the victim's particular vulnerabilities.

The thin skull rule is broader than only physical vulnerability: it has been applied in cases where the claimant was particularly vulnerable to psychiatric injury[35] or, in the phrase used in the case, had an 'eggshell personality'.[36] Where a claimant suffers greater financial loss, because they are financially vulnerable – such as the claimant who had to enter into a credit agreement because he could not afford to hire a car[37] – the defendant has to pay the full costs.

KEY CASE

In *Smith v Leech Brain* [1962] 2 QB 405 (QB), the claimant's husband worked in a factory where his job involved lowering articles into a tank of molten metal. As a result of his employer not providing adequate protection, he was injured when molten metal splashed onto his lower lip. At first, he thought nothing of the burn, but the wound did not heal and began to ulcerate. It was found that the burn had landed on a precancerous site on the claimant's lip and had triggered the development of cancer, which the claimant's husband later died of.

The employer argued that it was not foreseeable that the relatively minor injury, for which the claimant had not even sought medical treatment, would lead to a serious illness and the death of the claimant. The court held that the principle of *The Wagon Mound (No 1)* applied to the type of damage being unforeseeable, not the extent of the damage. The defendant should take the victim as he found him, and since it was foreseeable that their failure to provide adequate protection would cause a physical injury, they were liable for the full extent of the physical injury.

34 [1901] 2 KB 669 (KB).

35 *Page v Smith* [1996] AC 155 (HL).

36 Ibid, at 182 (Lord Browne-Wilkinson).

37 *Lagden v O'Connor* [2003] UKHL 64, [2004] 1 AC 1067.

4.16 BREAKING THE CHAIN

Damage often occurs as a result of a chain of events: for example, a claimant may be negligently injured by one defendant, and an opportunity to treat the injury may be lost by medical negligence. An intervening act between the original negligence and the final damage may 'break the chain' of causation.

It is possible to construct chains of events which have been set off by the defendant and result in damage to the claimant. In the case of *Sparrow v Andre*,[38] for example, the defendant collided with the claimant's car, causing minor damage. The claimant got out of his car to inspect the damage, forgetting to put the handbrake on. As he was inspecting his car, it started to roll down a slight slope. The claimant tried to stop the car by holding it back with his hands, but the car pushed him back and crushed his leg against a post. In those circumstances, should the defendant be liable for the injury, or did the claimant, in getting out of his car without putting the handbrake on, 'break the chain' of causation? In fact, the court found that the chain of causation was not broken, but that the claimant's negligence had contributed to the damage.[39]

Once the chain is broken, the defendant's liability ends: it is a complete defence against any claim for damage or injury which arises after the intervening event. However, the defendant remains liable for all damage caused by the original tort, up to the time at which the chain is broken.

Significant events which may affect the damage caused in a chain of events, following the original tort, include:

- a natural event;
- an act by the claimant him- or herself;
- a second tort committed by a third party; and
- a non-tortious act of a third party.

4.17 NATURAL EVENTS

In general, a natural event – such as a lightning strike or the claimant's illness – will break the chain of causation, if it causes further damage. The defendant will remain liable for the damage caused up to the point that the chain is broken, but no further. Natural events are regarded as one of the vicissitudes of life: the blameless events which any person may have to bear the consequences of.

38 [2016] EWHC 739 (QB).

39 See section 9.2 on contributory negligence.

In *Carslogie Steamship Co v Royal Norwegian Government*,[40] a House of Lords case, the claimant's ship was damaged by a collision with the defendant's ship. Following temporary repairs, the ship sailed to the United States so that permanent repairs could be carried out. On the voyage, the ship encountered a severe storm, which caused further more serious damage. It was held that the storm broke the chain of causation, and the claimant could only recover the repair costs for the original damage.

A naturally occurring illness will also break the chain of causation. Where the damage caused by the defendant is superseded by a naturally occurring illness, the defendant's liability will end at the point of the supervening illness. In *Jobling v Associated Dairies*,[41] the claimant injured his back at work. Three years later, before his claim had come to trial, he found that he was suffering from a naturally occurring condition which caused damage to his back, causing him permanent disability. The House of Lords held that he was only entitled to damages for the original injury up to the point where the naturally occurring condition became the primary cause of his disability. They held that the claimant should be compensated for the damage that would not have occurred 'but for' the defendant's negligence, but the claimant should not be left in a better position than he would otherwise have been in.

4.18 ACTS OF THE CLAIMANT

Where the claimant has, by his or her own voluntary act, made the damage or injury worse, the question of whether the defendant is liable for the subsequent damage depends upon whether the claimant was acting reasonably in all the circumstances.

KEY CASE

In *McKew v Holland & Hannen & Cubitts (Scotland) Ltd* [1969] 3 All ER 1621 (HL), the defendant had negligently injured the claimant's back and hips. It was not a serious injury, but it did mean that, on occasion, the claimant's leg would give way under him. When descending a steep stairway, without a handrail, the claimant felt his leg starting to give way and, scared that he would fall head first, jumped down the stairs. This jump caused a serious fracture of his ankle.

The House of Lords found that the claimant had acted unreasonably by descending the stairway, without assistance or a handrail. And where the claimant made his injury worse by his own unreasonable acts, that would be regarded as a *novus actus interveniens* (new and intervening act), which would break the chain of causation. The defendant remained liable for the original injury, but not the broken ankle.

40 [1952] AC 292 (HL).

41 [1982] AC 794 (HL).

By contrast, in *Wieland v Cyril Lord Carpets*,[42] in similar circumstances, the claimant's own act did not break the chain. The claimant was wearing a neck brace, as a result of an injury caused by the defendant's negligence. This meant that she was unable to tilt her head so as to see properly through her bifocal glasses. When she was descending some steps, assisted by her son, she slipped and fell, injuring her ankle. The court held that her acts did not break the chain and the first defendant was also liable for the leg injury.

In *Corr v IBC Vehicles Ltd*,[43] the claimant's husband suffered from depression following a serious head injury caused by the defendant's negligence, and later committed suicide. The defendant argued that this was an unreasonable act by the victim, which should break the chain of causation. However, the House of Lords recognised that the victim was suffering from a serious mental illness and held that the act was not voluntary. The victim's depression, which was caused by the defendant, meant that the suicide was not a voluntary and informed decision.

4.19 SUBSEQUENT TORTS

There is no hard and fast rule on whether a subsequent tort by a third party will break the chain of causation. In practice, the court considers the extent to which the original defendant and the third party should each be held liable and will apportion damages according to the degree of fault on the part of each defendant. In general, the more extreme or unusual a subsequent tort is, the more likely it is to break the chain.

KEY CASE

In *Rahman v Arearose* [2001] QB 351 (CA), the claimant was a manager of a fast food outlet. His eye was injured when he was attacked by two men in his workplace. The failure to protect him from the assault was a breach of his employer's duty of care. The claimant was taken to hospital where his eye was operated on. The operation was carried out negligently, and the claimant lost the sight in his right eye. As a result of the attack, the claimant also suffered serious mental health problems, including post-traumatic stress disorder and severe depression, which meant that he was unable to work.

The claimant's employers, who were liable for the original tort, argued that the later tort by the hospital extinguished their liability for the later damage, including the loss of sight and the psychiatric illness. However, the Court of Appeal found that there was no binding rule. Each defendant should compensate the claimant for the proportion of the injury damage caused which they should, in justice, be held responsible for. On that basis, it was held that the claimant's employers were also partly liable for the psychiatric injury.

42 [1969] 3 All ER 1006 (QB).
43 [2008] UKHL 13, [2008] 1 AC 884.

In *Wright v Cambridge Medical Group*,[44] a GP's negligent delay in sending a baby to hospital was followed by further negligence at the hospital. As a result, an infection of the baby's hip was not properly treated and the baby suffered permanent damage. The Court of Appeal followed *Rahman* and found that the hospital's negligence did not extinguish the GP's liability. In *Jenkinson v Hertfordshire City Council*,[45] the High Court rejected the argument that medical treatment of the original injury had to be 'grossly negligent' to break the chain of causation. The extent to which the original and subsequent tortfeasors should be held liable should be based on a consideration of all the circumstances.[46]

Where a second tort does not create any additional damage, the first defendant remains liable. This may be unfortunate for the claimant if the first defendant does not pay the damages. In *Performance Cars v Abraham*,[47] the claimant's Rolls Royce was negligently damaged, and damages were awarded which included £75 to respray the car. However, the defendant had not paid the damages, nor had the car been resprayed, when it was involved in a second accident, which caused similar damage. The claimant tried to recover the costs of the respray from the person responsible for the second accident. The Court of Appeal held that the claimant had not suffered any additional loss, and refused to hold the second defendant liable.

4.20 SUBSEQUENT NON-TORTIOUS ACTS

A subsequent act of a third party which increases the damage is unlikely to break the chain, unless it is a tort. In *The Oropesa*,[48] a ship was badly damaged in a collision at sea. The master of the damaged ship went, with some of his crew, to the other ship by lifeboat. The lifeboat capsized in heavy seas, resulting in the death of nine members of the crew. The family of one crew member brought a claim against the other ship owner as having caused the original collision. The defendant argued that the act of the master of the damaged ship broke the chain of causation, because his ship was not in immediate danger of sinking and he could have waited for safer conditions for the transfer to the other ship. However, the court held that his decision was not unreasonable in the circumstances, so the chain of causation was not broken. If the act had been unreasonable, it would have been a tort, and capable of breaking the chain of causation.

KEY CASES

In *Robinson v Post Office* [1974] 1 WLR 1176 (CA), the claimant was injured by his employer's negligence. The doctor treating him gave him a tetanus injection. The

44 [2011] EWCA Civ 669, [2013] QB 312.

45 [2023] EWHC 872 (KB), [2024] 2 All ER 514.

46 Ibid, [40] (Andrew Baker J).

47 [1962] 1 QB 33 (CA).

48 *Lord v Pacific Steam Navigation Co Ltd, The Oropesa* [1942] P 140 (P).

claimant was allergic to the injection and suffered a severe reaction, causing brain damage and permanent disability. The first defendant argued that the doctor, by giving the tetanus injection without testing the claimant for an allergic reaction, had been negligent and broken the chain of causation.

The court found that it was a breach of duty by the doctor not to test the patient for an allergic reaction to the tetanus injection. However, it also found that, even if the doctor had tested the patient, the test would not have shown that the patient was allergic. So, as in *Barnett v Chelsea and Kensington HMC* [1969] 1 QB 428 (QB), the doctor's breach of duty had not caused the damage. Since the doctor was not negligent, the chain of causation was not broken and the claimant's employer was liable for all the damage that was caused by the original negligence.

The same principle would apply in cases where a person might have intervened to prevent damage. Take the example of a road accident which takes place outside a GP's surgery. If one of the witnesses to the accident runs into the surgery, and asks one of the doctors to come and help, the doctor is under no obligation to do so:[49] a doctor does not owe a duty of care to a person until they accept them as a patient.[50] As the doctor would not be negligent if they did not intervene, their failure to do so cannot break the chain of causation. The person liable for the road accident would be liable for all the damage suffered, even if that damage could easily have been prevented by prompt medical attention.

POINTS TO REVIEW

- The claimant must show, on the balance of probability, that the defendant's breach of duty caused the damage.
- The general test for causation in fact is the 'but for' test.
- Causation in fact may also be established by showing that the defendant materially contributed to the damage or materially contributed to the risk of an indivisible injury.
- The claimant must show that the type of damage was not too remote.
- The claimant must show that the chain of causation was not broken by a natural event, their own acts or a tort committed by a third party.

TAKING IT FURTHER

Stapleton, J. 'Cause in Fact and the Scope of Liability for Consequences' (2003) 119(3) LQR 388–425

The author argues for a new approach to causation: rather than using causation in law and remoteness, she argues that a new and clearer language is needed. Causation in fact

49 See Chapter 7 on duty to rescue in English law.

50 *Barnett v Chelsea and Kensington HMC* [1969] 1 QB 428 (QB).

should be recast as 'historic involvement' in the claimant suffering damage. Remoteness should be reconceptualised as part of the scope of the duty of care.

Steel, S. and Ibbetson, D. 'More Grief on Uncertain Causation in Tort' (2011) 70 CLJ 451–468

The authors analyse the development of the Fairchild exception and consider the judgment in *Sienkiewicz v Greif*. They assess the current legal position and conclude that the law is now in an unprincipled position.

Bailey, S. H. 'Causation in Negligence: What Is a Material Contribution?' (2010) 30(2) Legal Studies 167–185

The author considers the 'but for' test in the context of the principle of *Bonnington Castings* and concludes that the principle established in that case is consistent with the 'but for' test, not an exception to it. He further argues that exceptions to the 'but for' test should be clearly identified as such and require a strong policy justification, as in *Fairchild*.

Stauch, M. 'Risk and Remoteness of Damage in Negligence' (2001) 64(2) MLR 191–214

The author considers the remoteness concept, addressing the issue of whether it is justified by legal principle or by policy. He concludes that the remoteness concept is justified by principle in the majority of cases.

Lam, C. M. 'Revisiting Loss of Chance in Medical Negligence: Employing Public Policy Positively as Justification' (2020) 3 Journal of Professional Negligence 105–132

Considers the approach to loss of chance in other common law jurisdictions, with reference to medical negligence, and analyses the policy reasons behind the approaches taken.

5

CHAPTER 5
NEGLIGENCE: ECONOMIC LOSS

5.1 INTRODUCTION

Where the defendant has negligently caused damage to a person or to property, the defendant must compensate the claimant for the financial loss caused. This will include the direct costs, such as the medical costs or costs of repairing or replacing the property damaged, and any financial costs or losses flowing directly from the damage. So a claim for damages for personal injury will include loss of earnings during the period that the claimant cannot work because of his or her injury. In cases of property damage, the claim could include the cost of hiring replacement property while the damage is repaired or the property is replaced. In a claim for a road accident, for example, the claimant's schedule of damages will often include the cost of hiring a replacement vehicle until the damaged vehicle is repaired or replaced.

This type of economic loss is referred to as consequential economic loss: those financial losses suffered by the claimant as a direct consequence of the defendant's liability. As a general rule, claimants will be able to recover the consequential economic losses caused by the defendant's negligence, subject to the foreseeability of the losses.

A second type of economic loss is commonly referred to as 'pure economic loss'. This is where the claim is only for financial or economic damage, not related to personal injury or property damage. Such a claim might be caused, for example, by negligent advice or misrepresentation: if a company accountant provides figures on the company's profitability, and an investor buys shares relying on those figures, the investor may suffer loss if the accountant negligently overstates the profits made by the company.[1]

AS YOU READ

- Understand the difference between consequential and pure economic loss.
- Understand the circumstances in which claimants can recover pure economic loss.

The distinction between consequential and pure economic loss is illustrated by the case of *Spartan Steel & Alloys Ltd v Martin & Co (Contractors) Ltd*.[2] In this case, the defendant's employees negligently damaged a power cable when digging up the road, cutting off the electricity supply to the claimant's foundry. At the time, the claimant was processing a batch of steel in its furnace and, when the supply was cut, the batch was damaged. The supply was

1 See, for example, *Caparo Industries plc v Dickman* [1990] 2 AC 605 (HL).

2 [1973] QB 27 (CA).

DOI: 10.4324/9781003480051-05

not restored for another 14 hours, during which time the claimant would have been able to process another four batches.

The claim was made up of three elements: the value of the damaged batch, the lost profit on the damaged batch, and the lost profits on the four batches that the factory was unable to process while there was no power. The first two claims, for the property damage and the economic loss caused directly by the property damage, succeeded; the third claim, for pure economic loss, failed.

ANALYSING THE LAW

It has been pointed out that if, in *Spartan Steels*, the property damaged by the workmen had belonged to the claimant, the loss of production would have been consequential economic loss, rather than pure economic loss, and the claimant would have received damages.

Should this matter? Should the claimant's chances of recovery depend on whether they own the damaged property, in which case they can recover for the losses arising from the damage to the property?

In another case, *Weller v Foot and Mouth Disease Research Institute*,[3] an auctioneer claimed against a research facility which they alleged was responsible for an outbreak of foot and mouth disease. During the outbreak, the cattle markets in the area had been closed to prevent the spread of the disease, which meant that the claimant had been unable to auction cattle and had lost money. The court held that a farmer whose cattle had contracted the disease would be able to claim against the defendant if they were able to show that they were responsible for the outbreak,[4] as this was a form of damage to property. However, the auctioneer had not suffered any damage to their property, and could not recover.

In *Muirhead v Industrial Tank Specialities*,[5] lobsters being held in a tank died when the pumps supplying the tanks with oxygenated water failed: the Court of Appeal held that the claimant could recover damages from the manufacturer of the pumps 'not in respect of the whole economic loss suffered by him, but only in respect of the physical damage caused to his stock of lobsters, and of course any financial loss suffered by the plaintiff in consequence of that physical damage'.[6]

Where property is damaged by negligence, it is only the owner of the property, or someone with a right to possess the property, that can claim for the physical damage and the consequential economic loss. This principle was established in *Cattle v Stockton Waterworks*

3 [1966] 1 QB 569 (QB).
4 Ibid, 587 (Widgery J).
5 [1986] QB 507 (CA).
6 Ibid, 533 (Goff LJ).

Company:[7] in that case, the claimant had contracted with a landowner to dig a tunnel through an embankment. The defendant had previously laid a water pipe under the same embankment, which was leaking. The claimant had to deal with the flooding, which caused him additional expense. It was held that the claimant could not recover for economic loss caused by damage to property which did not belong to him. Likewise, in *Leigh and Sillavan v Aliakmon Shipping*,[8] the buyer of a consignment of steel which was damaged in transit was unable to recover when the steel was damaged by the shipping company in transit: the House of Lords held that, as the buyers were not the legal owners of the property, they could not recover any damages from the shipping company.

Pure economic loss can only be compensated in specific circumstances: usually, where the defendant has assumed responsibility and has a duty to protect the claimant from economic loss.

> KEY LEARNING POINT
>
> Consequential economic loss is financial loss which is caused by personal injury or damage to property. If foreseeable, it can be recovered as damages in a personal injury or damage to property claim in negligence.
>
> Pure economic loss is loss not caused by personal injury or damage to the claimant's property. It can only be recovered in particular circumstances.

5.2 PURE ECONOMIC LOSS

It is possible to recover damages to compensate for pure economic loss, but courts have been cautious in expanding the circumstances in which it is allowed. The principal reason for the courts' caution is that claims for pure economic loss can give rise to 'liability in an indeterminate amount for an indeterminate time to an indeterminate class'.[9] Where a road user causes an accident, he or she is liable for the personal injury and the damage to other vehicles that are caused by his or her negligence. But road traffic accidents may also cause economic loss to other road users: the company that employs the delivery driver who is stuck in a resulting tail-back will have to pay his or her wages while he or she is delayed.

Likewise, if an accountant negligently published accounts that did not reflect the actual position of the company, people that might lose money might include people who bought shares on the basis of the false accounts and trade creditors who extended credit to the company on the understanding

7 (1875) LR 10 QB 453 (QB).

8 [1986] AC 785 (HL).

9 *Ultramares Corp v Touche* (1931) 174 NE 441, 444 (Cardozo CJ), cited in *Caparo Industries plc v Dickman* [1990] 2 AC 605 (HL) 621 (Lord Bridge). It is interesting to note that one of the defendants in *Caparo*, Touche Ross, was the successor organisation of the defendant in *Ultramares*, Touche Niven.

that the company was able to pay its debts. The potential liability that the accountant would face would be indeterminate and potentially enormous. In the United States, the courts refer to 'crushing liability':[10] an indeterminate liability which the defendant would have no means of meeting. The indeterminate liability that a defendant would face if anyone who suffered economic loss as a direct result of his or her negligence is a strong policy reason for restricting claims.

5.3 *HEDLEY BYRNE* AND THE ASSUMPTION OF RESPONSIBILITY

The first case to establish that, in some circumstances, a duty to take reasonable care to prevent another person from suffering pure economic loss would arise was *Hedley Byrne v Heller and Partners.*[11] The case held that a duty would arise if the defendant 'assumed responsibility' for the claimant.

KEY CASE

The House of Lords case of *Hedley Byrne v Heller and Partners* [1964] AC 465 (HL) concerned an advertising agency, Hedley Byrne, which was working on a television and newspaper advertising campaign for an electrical appliance manufacturer, Easipower Ltd. The practice at the time was for the advertising agency to book the advertising space from the television companies and the newspapers, and the agency was liable for payment. As the advertising agency was concerned about the creditworthiness of their client, they asked their bank for a reference. The reference, from the bank Heller and Partners, was favourable, but was expressed as being provided 'without liability' on the part of the bank.

In fact, Easipower was in financial difficulty, and within three months went into liquidation, leaving their debt to Hedley Byrne unpaid. The advertising agency sued the bank for negligence, claiming that they had not used reasonable care before assuring the advertising agency that their client would be able to pay their debts.

The House of Lords found that there was no negligence: the bank had provided the reference 'without liability'. However, they also held that, had the bank not disclaimed liability, it would have been negligent. Where a person with particular knowledge or skill provided advice, and the person receiving that advice relied upon it, a 'special relationship' was created between the parties, which would give rise to a duty to take reasonable care in giving the advice.

10 'Crushing liability' has not been adopted as a term by English courts but courts do recognise that liability may be disproportionate to the breach of duty.

11 [1964] AC 465 (HL).

One of the cases considered in *Hedley Byrne v Heller and Partners*[12] was *Candler v Crane Christmas*.[13] In this case, an investor wanted to invest £2,000 in a tin mine. He asked the company for their accounts, so that he could decide whether it was a good investment. The company showed him the accounts, which included assets which did not, in fact, belong to the company. As a result of relying on the accounts, the investor lost his money. He sued the accountants, but the Court of Appeal found that they did not owe him a duty of care. The case is notable for Denning LJ's dissent, which was approved by the House of Lords in *Hedley Byrne*.

Hedley Byrne established both a new mechanism by which a duty of care could arise and that defendants might become liable for pure economic loss. Like *Donoghue v Stevenson*, it established a principle that expanded the scope of negligence into new areas. The doctrine of assumption of responsibility is now the main way by which a duty to protect the claimant from pure economic loss is established.

> KEY LEARNING POINT
>
> Liability for pure economic loss arises when the defendant has assumed responsibility for the claimant's economic well-being.

Assumption of responsibility requires:

- a skilled or professional defendant
- providing advice, information or other service within his or her area of expertise
- to a known recipient for a specific purpose
- and the claimant reasonably relies on the advice or information.

The assumption is determined objectively: as Lord Steyn stated in *Williams v Natural Life Health Foods Ltd*, the determinative factor is not the state of mind of the defendant, but what the defendant said or did in his or her dealings with the claimant.[14]

There are two main ways in which the defendant may cause economic loss: by something he or she said – a negligent statement – or by something he or she did or failed to do – a negligent act or omission. Assumption of responsibility was developed in the context of negligent statements, and this remains one of the commonest contexts in which liability will arise. Liability can also, however, arise when the defendant causes economic loss by his or her acts or omissions.

12 Ibid.

13 [1951] 2 KB 164 (CA).

14 [1998] 1 WLR 830 (HL) 835 (Lord Steyn).

5.4 NEGLIGENT STATEMENTS

The extent of liability under the doctrine of assumption of responsibility was considered by the House of Lords in *Caparo Industries plc v Dickman.*[15] While this case is best known for Lord Bridge's dictum on the establishment of a duty of care under the three-stage test, the claim was made by a company which had relied upon accounts, which had been prepared for a second company by a firm of accountants in compliance with the requirements of the Companies Act 1985. The claimant company had launched a successful takeover bid, on the basis of the accounts. They later found that the second company's profits were significantly lower than the projections in the published accounts.

The claim failed: in order to bring the claim within the Hedley Byrne principle, the statement or representation had to be made directly to a known recipient, for a specific purpose which the defendant was aware of, and the defendant also knew that the claimant would be relying on the statement. In this case, the accountants and the company had not provided the accounts directly to the claimant.[16]

The Hedley Byrne principle was applied in the case of *Spring v Guardian Assurance:*[17] this was a claim arising from a reference provided to the claimant by a former employer, which made a number of damaging statements about the claimant's conduct and honesty. The House of Lords held that there was a duty to take reasonable care in providing the reference.

KEY CASE

In *Spring v Guardian Assurance plc* [1995] 2 AC 296, the claimant had been dismissed by the defendant, a life assurance company, when they found that he was planning to start working for one of their competitors. Under the regulations in force in the life assurance sector, when employees moved from one company to another, the new employer was obliged to seek, and the former employer obliged to provide, a reference of character and experience. The claimant's new employees therefore asked the defendants, as his former employers, for a reference. The reference made damaging allegations about the claimant's honesty and integrity. As a result, the new employer withdrew their offer of employment to the claimant.

The claimant was unable to bring claims in defamation or malicious falsehood, as either would have required him to show that the defendant made the statement knowing them to be untrue or reckless as to its truth or falsity. He claimed in negligence, arguing that the defendant owed him a duty to take reasonable care when providing the reference.

15 [1990] 2 AC 605 (HL).

16 Compare this with *Candler v Crane Christmas* [1951] 2 KB 164 (CA), where the accounts in question had been provided directly to the claimant for the purpose of helping him to decide whether to invest in the company.

17 [1995] 2 AC 296 (HL).

The House of Lords held that the former employer did owe the claimant a duty to take reasonable care when providing the reference: they found that the defendant had been in possession of 'special knowledge', and that the claimant had been relying on the defendant exercising reasonable care when preparing the reference.

Not all transactions between employer and employee will, however, result in a duty to protect the employee from economic loss. For example, in *Crossley v Faithful & Gould Holdings Ltd*,[18] an employee lost benefits under the company disability insurance scheme when he took early retirement on health grounds. When he realised that he had lost the benefits, he claimed against the company for failing to warn him. The Court of Appeal held that an employer's duty of care to its employees extended to their health and safety, not to their economic well-being, and that the company had not assumed responsibility for the claimant.

KEY CASE

In *Steel v NRAM Ltd* [2018] UKSC 13, a solicitor was acting for a company which owned three units in a business park, which it had used to secure loans from the claimant bank. As the company wished to sell one of the units, the solicitor negotiated the discharge of the security on that unit. A sum was agreed. At that point, the solicitor sent an email which stated that the agreed sum was to discharge the security on all three units and sent the company deeds of discharge for the company to execute. This was not what had been agreed, but apparently assuming that the solicitor knew what she was doing, the bank accepted the agreed sum and executed the discharge deeds for the securities on all three units. The company continued to pay interest on the outstanding loan, until it became insolvent three years later. At that point, the bank, seeking to recover the money owed, discovered that their securities had been discharged, and that they were unable to take possession of the units. The bank sued the solicitor, arguing that she had, by negligently making the statement about the agreement to discharge the security on one unit, assumed responsibility.

The Supreme Court found that the solicitor did not owe the bank a duty of care. The most basic precautions would have disclosed that the solicitor had made a mistake, and it was not reasonable of the bank to rely upon the solicitor. Furthermore, the bank had negotiated the agreement with the solicitor, and its knowledge of the agreed terms was the same as the solicitor's. There was no case in which a defendant had assumed liability to a claimant in carelessly misrepresenting facts which were known to the claimant.

18 [2004] EWCA Civ 293, [2004] 4 All ER 447.

In *Steel v NRAM Ltd*,[19] the Supreme Court confirmed that assumption of responsibility 'remains the foundation of the liability' for pure economic loss.[20] In conjunction with *Robinson v Chief Constable of West Yorkshire Police*,[21] it now appears that new duties to avoid causing the claimant economic loss will only arise under the established doctrine of assumption of responsibility, although 'it may require cautious incremental development in order to fit cases to which it does not readily apply'.[22]

The most recent case in which the Supreme Court has considered pure economic loss is *Manchester Building Society v Grant Thornton*.[23] In this case, a firm of accountants had provided financial advice to the claimant building society on how it could manage risk by the use of hedge accounting. As a result of relying on the advice, the building society suffered serious economic loss. The Supreme Court noted that, although the relationship between the parties was contractual, the claim was based on a breach of duty in negligence. The key issue was whether the economic loss was caused by a breach within the scope of the duty of care. As the purpose was to advise the claimant on whether it could use hedge accounting in the regulatory environment, the loss was within the scope of the defendant's duty and they were liable.

5.5 THE SKILL OR KNOWLEDGE OF THE DEFENDANT

Part of the rationale for the doctrine of assumption of responsibility is that the defendant is exercising some form of skill or expertise, or has some 'special knowledge',[24] which the claimant is reasonably relying upon. Merely asking another person for their advice, when the issue is outside that person's particular skill, will not create a duty of care by assumption of responsibility.

It was held, in *Steel v NRAM Ltd*,[25] that assumption of responsibility cannot arise when the claimant knows, or has access to, the information provided by the defendant: 'special knowledge' must be something known to the defendant, but not the claimant.

In *Chaudhry v Prabhakar*,[26] the claimant asked a friend of hers, who had no particular expertise other than some experience of buying and selling cars, to find a car for her. The friend found a car which he thought was a good buy and recommended it to her. It was later discovered that the car had been involved in a serious accident and has been so badly repaired that it was

19 Ibid.

20 Ibid, [24].

21 [2018] UKSC 4, [2018] 2 WLR 595. See also Chapter 2.

22 *Steel v NRAM Ltd* [2018] UKSC 13, [24] (Lord Wilson, with whom Lady Hale, Lord Reed, Lord Hodge, and Lady Black agreed).

23 [2021] UKSC 20, [2022] AC 783.

24 *Spring v Guardian Assurance plc* [1995] 2 AC 296 (HL) 318 (Lord Goff).

25 Ibid.

26 [1989] 1 WLR 29 (CA).

unroadworthy. The claimant sued her friend, who conceded that he owed her a duty of care. However, in the Court of Appeal, May LJ doubted whether the concession had been rightly made: the defendant had no particular skill and knowledge, other than a general interest in cars, and such a duty should not be imposed when a person was acting as a friend, rather than in a commercial context.[27]

KEY LEARNING POINT

The assumption of responsibility requires the defendant to be exercising a particular skill or expertise or to be in possession of 'special knowledge'.

5.6 NEGLIGENT ACTS AND OMISSIONS

The Hedley Byrne principle was developed in the context of negligent statements or advice, and this remains one of the main areas in which it is significant: negligent statements – for example, from a tax adviser or valuer – are clearly capable of causing pure economic loss. However, the principle is not confined to statements or advice: a negligent act, or a failure to carry out an act which the defendant had undertaken to do, might also cause economic loss.[28]

Assumption of responsibility was applied by the courts in the case of *Henderson v Merrett Syndicates*:[29] this was a claim arising from heavy losses in the London insurance market. Lloyds, an insurance provider, provided capital to back their insurance by recruiting wealthy individuals, known as 'names', to become members of insurance syndicates. On becoming a name, the individual agreed to make their entire personal wealth available to meet any losses suffered by the insurance syndicate. In return, the name was entitled to a percentage of the profits made by his or her syndicate.[30] Some Lloyds syndicates suffered heavy losses in the late 1980 and early 1990s, and the names were called upon to meet their guarantees: some were bankrupted by the claims.

In *Henderson*, the House of Lords considered whether the managing agents owed the names a duty of care in tort, despite there being no contract between the names and the managing

27 [1989] 1 WLR 29 (CA) 39 (May LJ). See also the comments of Lord Diplock on advice given in a social context in *Mutual Life and Citizens' Assurance v Evatt* [1971] AC 793 (PC) 806.

28 See, for example, *White v Jones* [1995] 2 AC 207 (HL).

29 [1995] 2 AC 145 (HL).

30 Although being a 'name' at Lloyds did expose the name to unlimited liability and potential bankruptcy, the possibility of this happening was regarded as remote. Furthermore, becoming a name did not require the person to actually provide any money: the promise to meet the syndicate's debts was sufficient. In return, the name received an annual payment. Many wealthy individuals regarded being a name at Lloyds as a risk-free source of free money.

agents. This is not a case of a negligent statement: the managing agents were not advising the names, but carrying on the business of insurance on behalf of the syndicate and its names.

The House of Lords, applying *Hedley Byrne*,[31] held that the elements of assumption of responsibility had been established,[32] and there was a duty to take reasonable care not to cause economic loss to the names. They held that such a duty would arise independently of any contractual duty owed to the claimant by the defendant, and the claimant was free, if a contractual duty also existed, to pursue his or her claim in contract or in tort. The House of Lords also confirmed that a professional adviser who was voluntarily providing advice could disclaim liability, as the defendant had done in *Hedley Byrne*.

In *Customs & Excise Commissioners v Barclays Bank plc*,[33] the claimant had been granted a freezing injunction, which they had served on the defendant bank. The injunction ordered the bank to freeze the accounts of two companies which had substantial arrears in their VAT payments. By an administrative error, the bank failed to freeze the accounts, and large sums of money were withdrawn, resulting in the Customs & Excise Commissioners being unable to recover the amount owed. The House of Lords held that there had been no assumption of responsibility: the doctrine required the claimant to act voluntarily, but in this case, the duty was imposed on the bank by law.

KEY LEARNING POINT

A duty not to cause economic loss by acts or omissions, as well as by advice, may arise if the defendant assumes responsibility for the claimant.

5.7 DUTIES TO THIRD PARTIES

In the cases considered so far, the statement or act causing economic loss has been made by the defendant to the claimant, or in the context of a relationship between claimant and defendant. However, it is possible that advice or a service provided to one person, whether given voluntarily or under a contract, may cause economic loss to another person.

Where a defendant owes a duty to one person, in contract or in tort, then there is no duty, in normal circumstances, to any third party: a person who is not party to that relationship. So, in the example above, of an accountant preparing company accounts, there is a contractual duty owed by the accountant to the company. However, there is no duty to the shareholders or

31 [1964] AC 465 (HL).

32 [1995] 2 AC 145 (HL) 182 (Lord Goff).

33 [2007] 1 AC 181 (HL).

other persons, such as trade creditors, who may be relying on the company's accounts when deciding to invest in the company or to extend the company's credit.[34]

However, in some circumstances, a duty may arise to an individual if the professional providing a service to one party assumes responsibility for another party. This was seen in the House of Lords case of *Smith v Eric S Bush*.[35] This involved two conjoined cases: in both, a property surveyor was employed by a mortgage lender to survey and value a residential property; and in both cases, the surveyor failed to notice significant structural problems with the properties, which meant that, in one case, the buyer was faced with a large repair bill, and, in the other, the house was worth very much less than the buyer paid.

The surveyors were working for, and owed a contractual duty to, the mortgage lenders, not the buyers of the property. However, it was the buyers who suffered the economic loss. The House of Lords held that the surveyors were providing specialist knowledge and that they were aware that the buyers were not providing their own survey, so would be relying on the mortgage lenders' surveys. Accordingly, the surveyors had assumed responsibility for the buyers. The House of Lords also held that, as in *Hedley Byrne*, a defendant could avoid assuming responsibility by a disclaimer. However, the disclaimer which the surveyors had included in their agreement with the mortgage lenders was void, under the Unfair Contract Terms Act 1977.

Smith v Eric S Bush was not followed in the case of *Scullion v Bank of Scotland plc (trading as Colleys)*.[36] As in *Smith*, the purchaser relied upon a valuation report produced for the mortgage lender when purchasing a property. However, in this case the purchaser was buying the property as a rental property, and in those circumstances it would not be foreseeable that the claimant would rely upon the report prepared by the defendant. *Smith* had been decided on the basis of a 'modest' property bought as a home, rather than in a commercial context.

A limit on liability to third parties was placed by the Court of Appeal in the case of *West Bromwich Albion Football Club v El-Safty*.[37] This case arose from a knee operation carried out by the defendant, an orthopaedic surgeon, on Michael Appleton, a premier league footballer who played for West Bromwich Albion. The operation was unsuccessful, and Appleton successfully sued the surgeon for the loss of his earnings as a premier league footballer, as consequential economic loss caused directly by the unsuccessful operation.[38] West Bromwich Albion also sued the surgeon for their pure economic loss, in the form of the wages that they had paid Appleton while he was unable to play. The claim did not succeed: the Court of Appeal held that the surgeon had not assumed responsibility for the football club's financial loss. Furthermore, there was no 'fundamental community'[39] between the physical injury caused by the defendant's negligence and the economic loss suffered by the football club.

34 *Caparo Industries plc v Dickman* [1990] 2 AC 605 (HL).

35 [1990] 1 AC 831 (HL).

36 [2011] EWCA Civ 693, [2011] 1 WLR 3212.

37 [2006] EWCA Civ 1299, 92 BMLR 179.

38 *Appleton v El-Safty* [2007] EWHC 631 (QB).

39 Ibid, [59] (Rix LJ).

West Bromwich Albion Football Club v El-Safty establishes that, where the defendant is providing advice or a service to one person, another person cannot claim for damage, even where the defendant knows or should know that the third party will suffer damage, unless there is a 'fundamental community' between the type of damage that the defendant has a duty to protect the primary party from.

5.8 ASSUMPTION OF RESPONSIBILITY WITHOUT RELIANCE

In the case of *Smith v Eric S Bush*, the claimants knew that the house that they were hoping to buy was being surveyed; and they were relying on the outcome of the survey. In *Hedley Byrne*,[40] that the advertising agency had relied upon the bank's financial reference when extending credit was a key reason that the House of Lords held that the bank should be liable to the advertising agency. 'Reliance' is usually held to be a key element of assumption of responsibility.[41]

In some cases, however, liability has been imposed where the claimant did not know that the advice or service was being provided, so could not have been relying on it. This is a significant development of the assumption of responsibility doctrine, which has been described by Witting as the 'extended Hedley-Byrne principle'.[42]

The case of *White v Jones*[43] was the first application of the extended principle. In this case, a father had fallen out with his two daughters. Following the argument, the father had made a will, leaving his daughters nothing. However, shortly before the father's death, there had been a reconciliation, and he decided to make a new will, leaving his daughters £9,000 each, which was approximately one-third of his estate. The father instructed a solicitor to draft the new will, but, owing to the negligence of the solicitor, the new will had not been signed before the father died. The daughters, who had lost their inheritance because of the solicitor's negligence, claimed against the solicitor.

The House of Lords allowed the claim, despite the claimants having been unaware that the defendant had been instructed to prepare a new will, so could not be said to have been relying on the defendant's professional skill and expertise. In an earlier High Court judgment, *Ross v Caunters*,[44] in which a solicitor who negligently allowed a beneficiary's husband to witness a will, causing loss to the beneficiary when the gift to her was held void under the Wills Act 1837, the solicitor had been held to owe a duty to the disappointed beneficiary. That

40 [1964] AC 465.

41 See, for example, *Henderson v Merrett Syndicates Ltd* [1995] 2 AC 145 (HL) 181 (Lord Goff).

42 C. Witting, 'Duty of Care: An Analytical Approach' (2005) 25(1) OJLS 33–63. The same term ('Extended Hedley Byrne principle') has also been used judicially to describe the extension of *Hedley Byrne* to circumstances where the breach was caused other than by negligent statements: *Williams v Natural Life Health Foods Ltd* [1998] 1 WLR 830 (HL) 834 (Lord Steyn).

43 [1995] 2 AC 207.

44 [1980] Ch 297 (Ch).

judgment had, however, been reached on the basis of the test in *Anns v Merton London Borough Council*,[45] which had since been overruled.[46]

The House of Lords applied the assumption of responsibility doctrine. On the issue of reliance, Lord Browne-Wilkinson held that:

> What is important is not that A knows that B is consciously relying on A, but A knows that B's economic wellbeing is dependent upon A's careful conduct of B's affairs.[47]

One of the significant factors was, in the words of Lord Goff, the 'impulse to do practical justice'.[48] If the claim failed, the only person who would have a valid claim – the testator – would have suffered no loss. This would result in a 'lacuna in the law'.[49]

Gorham v British Telecom[50] saw an application of the same principle: a widow sued her husband's employer and pension provider for giving her husband negligent advice on his pension arrangements, which had left her and their children substantially worse off than they might have been. Following *White v Jones*,[51] the claim succeeded. And in the recent case of *Ashraf v Lester Dominic Solicitors*,[52] *White v Jones* was also applied when a firm of solicitors registered an incorrectly completed document with the Land Registry, causing loss to the owner of the property concerned, even though the owner was not the solicitor's client.

Witting has set out the required elements of the extended Hedley Byrne principle as:

- comparative skill or expertise;
- actual knowledge;
- conscious decision to accept responsibility for their acts or advice to the primary party; and
- tight causal connection.[53]

Applying these principles, a duty to prevent economic loss to a third party will arise where a professional assumes responsibility for a primary party; that the defendant knows that breach will cause economic loss to a third party; and there is no conflict between the interests of the primary and third parties.[54] This, coupled with a direct causal link between the professional's statement or act and the economic loss, creates a duty of care.

45 [1978] AC 728 (HL).
46 *Murphy v Brentwood District Council* [1991] 1 AC 398 (HL).
47 *White v Jones* [1995] 2 AC 207 (HL) 272 (Lord Browne-Wilkinson).
48 Ibid, 259.
49 Ibid, 260.
50 [2000] 1 WLR 2129 (CA).
51 [1995] 2 AC 207 (HL).
52 [2023] EWCA Civ 4.
53 C. Witting, 'Duty of Care: An Analytical Approach' (2005) 25(1) OJLS 33, 59–60.
54 See *McLeod v Crawford* [2011] SCLR 133, where a claim based on *White v Jones* failed on lack of fundamental community, as the defendant's client had different interests from the claimant; and *Caliendo v Mishcon de Reya* [2016] EWHC 150 (Ch), [725]: the solicitors' duty to a third party extended as far as the third party's interests were aligned with the solicitors' clients' interests.

5.9 LIABILITY FOR DEFECTIVE PRODUCTS

Another way in which economic loss may be caused is where a product is defective: loss may arise because the product itself is devalued by the defect, or because the claimant is unable to use the product. In general, the provider of the product will only be liable in contract,[55] but in some circumstances, the claimant will seek to recover either the value of the defective product or the economic loss caused by the defect from a third party, such as the building inspector who should have noticed that the foundations of a house were inadequate.[56] Other examples include the liability of subcontractors for work of poor quality, which required money to make good.[57]

This is a complex area of law, which is now largely of historic importance only. Following the Court of Appeal's decision in *Dutton v Bognor Regis District Council*,[58] the House of Lords held, in *Anns v Merton London Borough Council*,[59] that a householder could recover damages for the loss of value of their property against the local authority building inspectors for failing to ensure that the foundations of their property were adequate. During the period, following *Anns*, when the House of Lords had expanded the scope of negligence, a number of related cases were heard, in which householders were able to recover for damage to their property which had either reduced the value of the property or which had cost money to repair.[60]

However, by 1990, the direction of tort law had changed, and in *Murphy v Brentwood District Council*,[61] the House of Lords overruled *Anns*.[62]

KEY CASE

Murphy v Brentwood District Council [1991] 1 AC 398 (HL) was a claim by a property owner against the local authority. In 1969, the council had approved plans for a house, relying on a report by consulting engineers. The consulting engineers had not noticed an error in the design of the foundations of the house, which resulted in the foundations being inadequate. Some 12 years later, in 1981, the then owner of the house noticed a crack in one of the interior walls. Inspection by a consulting engineer showed extensive

55 The provider of the defective product will be liable in negligence for any personal injury or property damage caused by the product – see *Donoghue v Stevenson* [1932] AC 562 (HL) and the Consumer Protection Act 1987 – but not for pure economic loss.

56 *Dutton v Bognor Regis District Council* [1972] 1 QB 373 (CA).

57 *Junior Books v Veitchi* [1983] 1 AC 520 (HL).

58 [1972] 1 QB 373 (CA).

59 [1978] AC 728 (HL).

60 See, for example, *Junior Books v Veitchi* [1983] 1 AC 520 (HL); *Batty v Metropolitan Property Realisations* [1978] QB 554 (CA); and *Dennis v Charnwood Borough Council* [1983] QB 409 (CA).

61 [1991] 1 AC 398 (HL).

62 See Chapter 2 for a discussion of 'the retreat from Anns'.

damage to the house. The house was subsequently sold for around half the price it would have been worth in sound condition. Following *Anns v Merton London Borough Council* [1978] AC 728 (HL), the Court of Appeal awarded damages of £35,000, as the amount that the claimant had lost in selling the house in its damaged condition.

The House of Lords overturned the Court of Appeal's judgment, and used the 1966 Practice Statement to depart from the decision in *Anns*. Lord Keith noted that *Anns* had

> introduced a new species of liability governed by a principle indeterminate in character but having the potentiality of covering a wide range of situations, involving chattels as well as real property, in which it had never hitherto been thought that the law of negligence had any proper place.

The House of Lords concluded that the claim was for pure economic loss, rather than damage to property: such a claim could only be made on the basis of the established Hedley Byrne principle.

Murphy v Brentwood District Council resolved a number of issues, such as whether it was necessary for the property to be dangerous to those living there, as had been held in *Anns*, and clarified that the 'complex structure'[63] theory, which had been discussed as a potential justification for recovery in *D & F Estates v Church Commissioners*,[64] could not be used as a basis for allowing claims in economic loss caused by defective products or premises.

Following *Murphy*, it is not possible to recover in negligence for pure economic loss caused by defective products, unless the claimant can establish that the defendant assumed responsibility for the claimant's economic well-being.

5.10 CONCLUSION

Liability for economic loss is an area of negligence, like psychiatric injury, which has developed its own particular rules. These rules have evolved since the case of *Hedley Byrne v Heller*[65] and now appear to be fairly well settled.

A claimant can recover for economic loss which has not been directly caused by personal injury or damage to property only if the defendant has assumed responsibility for the claimant.

63 The complex structure theory applies where the property in question is regarded as being made up of a number of different components. If damage is caused by a defect in one of the components, such as damage to a car caused by a failure in the brakes, or damage to a house caused by the failure of its foundations, the theory allows the claimant to recover on the basis that the defective component has caused property damage, as opposed to pure economic loss.

64 [1989] AC 177 (HL) 206–207 (Lord Bridge).

65 [1964] AC 465 (HL).

This requires the defendant to provide, voluntarily, a statement or service, within his or her own particular professional expertise or special knowledge, upon which the claimant has reasonably relied[66] or which the defendant knows[67] will affect the claimant's economic well-being.

While courts have previously applied a principled test,[68] such as the Caparo tripartite test, in economic loss cases, this approach has been overruled in the case of *Robinson v Chief Constable of West Yorkshire Police*,[69] and a duty to avoid causing economic loss in new circumstances can only arise where the defendant has assumed responsibility.

POINTS TO REVIEW

- Negligence distinguishes between 'consequential' economic loss, which is the result of personal injury or damage to property, and 'pure' economic loss, caused by negligent statements or acts.
- Damages awarded in negligence claims for personal injury or damage to property will include any financial damages (special damages) caused by the personal injury or property damage, such as loss of earnings while the claimant recovers or the costs of repairing or replacing the damaged property.
- Claimants can only recover for pure economic loss if the defendant has assumed responsibility for the claimant's economic well-being.
- The defendant may be liable for negligent statements, or negligent acts or omissions.
- Assumption of responsibility requires the defendant to be exercising a particular skill or be in the possession of special knowledge, and voluntarily to provide that knowledge or exercise that skill for the benefit of the claimant.
- It is not necessary that the claimant knows that the defendant is providing the information or a service, as long as the defendant knows that his or her acts will affect the claimant's economic well-being.
- Liability for economic loss caused by defective products is no longer recoverable from third parties, unless the third party has assumed responsibility for the claimant's economic well-being.

TAKING IT FURTHER

Witting, C. 'Duty of Care: An Analytical Approach' (2005) 25(1) OJLS 33
Considers approach taken by the courts to liability, in the case of negligent misstatement. There is a detailed analysis of *Hedley Byrne* and the doctrine of

66 Ibid.

67 *White v Jones* [1995] 2 AC 207 (HL).

68 See Chapter 2 for a discussion of the distinction between the principled approach and the incremental approach to establishing new duties of care.

69 [2018] UKSC 4, [2018] 2 WLR 595, [21] (Lord Reed).

assumption of responsibility and the basis of liability in *White v Jones*, where there was no reliance by the claimant.

Witting, C. 'Justifying Liability to Third Parties for Negligent Misstatements' (2000) 20(4) OJLS 615
An analysis of *White v Jones*, and the circumstances in which liability to third parties for pure economic loss may be justified.

Stapleton, J. 'Duty of Care and Economic Loss: A Wider Agenda' (1991) 107 LQR 249–297
Written in the period following *Caparo v Dickman*, this criticises the House of Lords' approach to economic loss and the dependence on concerns about 'floodgates'.

6

CHAPTER 6
NEGLIGENCE: PSYCHIATRIC INJURY

6.1 INTRODUCTION

Psychiatric injury, in the form of a recognised psychiatric illness such as depression or post-traumatic stress disorder, is recognised as recoverable damage in negligence. However, unlike physical injury, there is no overarching principle, such as the neighbour principle, that imposes a duty not to cause psychiatric injury to others. A duty of care, such as the duty of an employer to an employee, may include a duty not to cause psychiatric injury by, for example, exposing the employee to stress.[1]

However, where there is no pre-existing duty of care between the defendant and claimant, the duty will only arise in specific circumstances.

The law distinguishes between people who suffer psychiatric illness as a result of being exposed to physical danger, and those whose illness is caused by other types of trauma.

The rules governing whether the defendant owes the claimant a duty not to cause psychiatric injury have been acknowledged by the courts as being illogical and inconsistent.[2] The main area of criticism relates to 'secondary victims': these are people who suffer from psychiatric illness, through witnessing an accident, resulting in the death of a family member, caused by the negligence of the defendant.

Following a series of cases in the 1990s, the Law Commission recommended reform of the law,[3] but Parliament took no action. A more recent private member's bill failed for lack of Parliamentary time.

AS YOU READ

- Understand the requirement that the claimant has suffered from a recognised psychiatric illness.
- Distinguish between primary and secondary victims.
- Know the requirements for secondary victim claims and understand how they are applied.

1 *Barber v Somerset County Council* [2004] 2 All ER 385, [2004] UKHL 13.

2 *Alcock v Chief Constable of South Yorkshire Police* [1992] 1 AC 312, 418 (Lord Oliver).

3 The Law Commission, Liability for Psychiatric Illness (1998) Law Com No 249.

DOI: 10.4324/9781003480051-06

- Understand the requirements for a rescuer claim.
- Know what an 'unwilling participant' is and how they may claim.

6.2 RECOGNISED PSYCHIATRIC ILLNESS

KEY LEARNING POINT

The claimant must show that he or she is suffering from a recognised psychiatric illness, and not just emotional distress, to bring a successful claim.

In all negligence claims, the claimant must show that they have suffered damage, in the form of loss or injury, which is caused by the defendant's breach of duty. A mental, as opposed to a physical, injury is only recognised as damage if it is in the form of a recognised psychiatric illness. Emotional distress is not, by itself, regarded as damage for the purposes of a claim.[4] So, it does not matter how serious the breach was or how upset or distressed the claimant was: if there is no psychiatric illness caused by the breach, the claimant cannot recover damages.

In *Hicks v Chief Constable of South Yorkshire Police*,[5] a claim was brought on behalf of two of the victims of the Hillsborough disaster, in which 96 people were killed by crushing at a football match. The claim was for the mental suffering of the victims during the time between their starting to experience the crushing and their loss of consciousness. The House of Lords, in dismissing the appeal of the parents, held that it was 'perfectly clear law that fear by itself, of whatever degree, is a normal human emotion for which no damages can be awarded'.[6]

Any damage suffered by a claimant is likely to distress him or her, whether the damage is physical injury, damage to property, or economic loss. In the case of physical injury, this is recognised by the inclusion of suffering as contributing to the financial award made to compensate for 'pain, suffering and loss of amenity'.[7] For other claims, however, the damages do not reflect the distress caused by the defendant's negligence.

Courts will rely upon expert evidence to determine whether the damage caused reaches the level of seriousness required. Psychiatrists will usually refer to one of the two internationally recognised classifications of psychiatric illness: the *Diagnostic and Statistical Manual*, 5th edition ('DSM-5') and the *International Classification of Diseases*, 11th edition ('ICD-11'). These set out the recognised psychiatric illnesses and their diagnostic criteria, and are accepted as authoritative.

4 *Hicks v Chief Constable of South Yorkshire Police* [1992] 2 All ER 65, 69 (Lord Bridge).

5 [1992] 2 All ER 65.

6 Ibid, 69 (Lord Bridge, giving the only judgment).

7 See Chapter 9.

The two main psychiatric illnesses that are recognised as being caused by trauma or shock are post-traumatic stress disorder and depression, which may take a number of forms.[8] However, it has been accepted that other psychiatric illnesses may be caused by shock or other trauma.[9]

6.3 NERVOUS SHOCK

The current law on psychiatric injury evolved from the doctrine of 'nervous shock'. At the start of the twentieth century, when understanding of psychiatric illness was less developed than it is nowadays, it was accepted that a sudden shock could result in physical symptoms, which were recognised as physical injuries and thus giving rise to a claim in negligence. The earliest cases refer to the claimant being able to recover for the 'bodily injury'[10] caused by the shock, rather than psychiatric illness, as it is now understood. The types of bodily injuries caused could be specific, such as death,[11] miscarriage,[12] or the claimant's hair turning white,[13] or non-specific, resulting in the claimant suffering from 'delicate health'.[14]

However, by 1925, claims could also be made for 'mental' injury, as well as for physical injury, where the mental, or psychiatric, injury was caused by a shock.[15] Such a shock might be caused by fear for one's own safety, fear for a loved one, or by another traumatic event.

The first successful psychiatric injury claims were for what are now called 'primary victims': people who suffered from injury as a result of fear for their own safety. In the Privy Council case of *Victorian Railway Commissioners v Coultas*,[16] a woman was travelling in a carriage, which was crossing a railway line. The gate keeper opened the gates and allowed the carriage to cross, not realising that a train was approaching, which narrowly missed the carriage. The claimant 'received a severe shock, and suffered personal injuries, and still suffered from delicate health and impaired memory and eyesight'.[17] The Privy Council allowed an appeal by the defendant railway company, holding that there was no liability for injuries caused by shock.

8 In particular, depression caused by loss of a loved one, where that is more severe than the normal bereavement reaction, is recognised as a psychiatric disorder.

9 In *A v Bishop of Birmingham* [2005] EWHC 1361 (QB), it was held that the childhood sexual abuse suffered by the claimant caused schizophrenia. See [73] of the judgment.

10 *Dulieu v White* [1901] 2 KB 669.

11 *Hambrook v Stoke Brothers* [1925] 1 KB 141.

12 *Bourhill v Young* [1943] AC 92.

13 *Wilkinson v Downton* [1897] 2 QB 57. Although this was not a claim in negligence, as the act causing the shock was intentional rather than negligent, it was claimed that the shock of being told that her husband had been seriously injured had caused the claimant's hair to turn white.

14 *Victorian Railway Commissioners v Coultas* (1887) 13 App Cas 222. 'Delicate health' might well be diagnosed as acute stress disorder or another psychiatric illness today.

15 *Hambrook v Stoke Brothers* [1925] 1 KB 141, 154 (Atkin LJ).

16 (1887) 13 App Cas 222.

17 Ibid, 223 (Sir Richard Crouch).

However, the English High Court did not follow *Coultas* in the case of *Dulieu v White*,[18] in which the landlady of a pub suffered from nervous shock when a horse-drawn van crashed into the pub: she was pregnant at the time and, as a result of the shock, the child was born prematurely and disabled. The court held that the driver of the van owed her a duty of care, and that he had negligently caused her injury.

> KEY LEARNING POINT
>
> A person who suffers from a psychiatric illness, caused by reasonable fear for their own safety, is a primary victim.

The case of *Hambrook v Stokes Brothers*[19] was the first to accept that 'nervous shock' could be caused by factors other than the claimant's fear for his or her own safety: in this case, a mother saw a runaway lorry heading down the street where she knew her children were walking. The defendant was held liable for the injury caused by the shock of seeing the threat to her children and later seeing her daughter's injuries. This was the first case in which a person who was not placed in danger by the defendant's negligence was able to recover damages.

> KEY LEARNING POINT
>
> A person who suffers from a psychiatric illness, caused by witnessing the death or serious injury of a person close to them, is a secondary victim.

A further way in which a claimant might suffer nervous shock was established in the case of *Dooley v Cammell Laird*.[20] In this case, a crane's cable snapped, dropping the load into the hold of a ship where dock workers were unloading a cargo. Although no one was injured, the crane driver suffered from psychiatric illness, caused by the belief that he might have been responsible for the death of one of his fellow workers. Such claimants are referred to as 'unwilling participants'.

> KEY LEARNING POINT
>
> A person who suffers from a psychiatric illness, caused by witnessing a death or serious injury for which they reasonably believe they are responsible, is an 'unwilling participant'.

The fourth category of claimant was established in the case of *Chadwick v British Railways Board*.[21] The victim lived close to a railway line and, hearing that there had been an accident, went to the scene to do what he could to help. The accident was very serious: two trains had

18 [1901] 2 KB 669.
19 [1925] 1 KB 141.
20 [1951] 1 Lloyd's Rep 271.
21 [1967] 1 WLR 912.

collided, and over 90 people were killed. Mr Chadwick spent the night bringing aid and comfort to the injured passengers and, as a result, suffered a recurrence of a depressive illness. The High Court allowed his claim for psychiatric injury, finding that it was foreseeable that a person who witnessed the horrific scenes of injured, dead, and dying passengers would suffer from psychiatric illness.

KEY LEARNING POINT

A person who suffers from a psychiatric illness, caused by their participation in the rescue of victims of an incident, is a 'rescuer'. The claimant must also show that they placed themselves in physical danger.

6.4 THE DUTY OF CARE

In all these types of claim – primary, secondary, involuntary participants, and rescuers – the principal question which the court has considered is whether the defendant's duty not to cause physical injury also included a duty not to cause psychiatric injury, either to the victim him- or herself, or to others who might be psychologically affected by the incident. If there is no such duty, then there can be no claim.

A duty not to cause personal injury comprises a duty not to cause physical or psychiatric injury.[22] In the case of primary victims, the defendant has breached the duty and either physically injured the claimant, or caused the claimant reasonably to fear physical injury, and the defendant is liable for all the injury caused, whether physical or psychiatric. So a person who suffers physical injury which causes psychiatric illness may claim for both the physical injury and the psychiatric injury.[23] A person who reasonably fears for his or her personal safety, but who does not actually suffer physical injury, can claim for any psychiatric injury caused by his or her reasonable fear.

In cases where the claimant was not at risk of physical injury, but suffered psychiatric injury as a result of witnessing the injury or participating in the rescue, courts formerly applied the Caparo test[24] to determine whether the defendant owed a duty not to cause psychiatric injury. The Caparo test is the three-stage test of foreseeability, proximity, and whether it is fair, just, and reasonable to impose a duty of care. The courts used the test as a control mechanism, particularly in cases other than primary victims, to limit claims and to keep the tort within reasonable bounds. Courts only found a duty where it was foreseeable that a person of ordinary fortitude would suffer psychiatric injury, and there was sufficient proximity between

22 *Page v Smith* [1996] AC 155, 190 (Lord Lloyd).

23 *Malcolm v Broadhurst* [1970] 3 All ER 508.

24 The Tripartite or Caparo test was the primary mechanism for determining whether a duty of care existed until the 2018 case of *Robinson v Chief Constable of West Yorkshire Police* [2018] UKSC 4, [2018] AC 736. See Chapter 2.

the defendant and the claimant. In addition, courts took into account policy considerations, including, in particular, the potential number of claims that might arise if the criteria were relaxed.[25]

6.5 PRIMARY VICTIMS

Dulieu v White established the doctrine of primary victims: a person who suffers shock as a result of reasonable fear for their own safety, caused by the negligence of the defendant, can recover for any injury caused by the shock: as stated by Kennedy J in that case, the 'shock, where it operates through the mind, must be a shock which arises from a reasonable fear of immediate personal injury to oneself'.[26]

In *Page v Smith*,[27] a motorist was involved in a traffic accident, described as a 'collision of moderate severity'. Although he was not physically injured, the claimant did suffer a shock. He later suffered a recurrence of his existing condition of chronic fatigue syndrome which, before the accident, had been in remission. Medical evidence that the shock of being involved in the accident had caused the recurrence was accepted, and the claimant succeeded in the High Court.

The House of Lords held that the driver liable for the accident was also liable for the injury caused by the shock: if the defendant had a duty not to cause injury, then that duty included a duty not to cause psychiatric injury as well as physical injury. As long as the claimant could establish that the defendant's breach caused the psychiatric injury, they would be able to recover.[28] There was no need for the claimant to show that the psychiatric injury, as opposed to the potential physical injury, was foreseeable.

The formulation in *Page v Smith* is wider than in *Dulieu*: there is, strictly speaking, no need for the claimant to show that his or her psychiatric injury was caused by a reasonable fear of physical injury. However, the claimant does need to show that the defendant's breach might have caused physical injury and did cause psychiatric injury. For the breach to cause psychiatric injury, some form of intense fear or trauma would be required.

In *White v Chief Constable of South Yorkshire Police*, the House of Lords referred to primary victims as those who suffer 'an apprehension of physical harm' or those within the range of 'foreseeable physical injury'.[29] If such a person suffered psychiatric injury, he or she would be able to succeed in a claim.

25 For a discussion of the importance of policy considerations in psychiatric injury claims, see Lord Steyn's speech in *White v Chief Constable of South Yorkshire Police* [1999] 2 AC 455, 492ff.

26 [1901] 2 KB 669, 675 (Kennedy J).

27 [1996] AC 155.

28 Ibid, 190 (Lord Lloyd, with whom Lords Ackner and Browne-Wilkinson agreed).

29 [1999] 2 AC 455, 504.

A person who witnesses an injury at close hand, but who is outside the range of foreseeable physical injury, is a 'bystander': as such, they cannot claim as a primary victim and would have to show that it was foreseeable that a person of ordinary fortitude would suffer psychiatric injury. In the case of *Robertson v Forth Road Bridge Joint Board*,[30] a workman sitting on a metal sheet in the back of a pick-up truck was killed when a strong gust of wind picked up the sheet and him and blew him over the side of the Forth Road Bridge. The driver of the pick-up and another worker suffered from psychiatric illness, caused by the shock of seeing the sudden death of their friend and colleague. However, the court held that the claimants were not in danger, and there was no close tie of love and affection between them and the victim, so there was no duty of care owed.

> KEY LEARNING POINT
>
> A person who witnesses a person being killed or seriously injured, but who is not in the area of physical danger, will not be able to recover unless he or she can show that they meet the criteria for secondary victims or unwilling participants.

The case of *Young v Charles Church (Southern) Ltd*[31] also involved a claimant who had seen a colleague killed at close quarters: in this case, the claimant had handed a scaffolding pole to another worker. The worker took the pole, and raised it to the vertical, where it touched an overhead power line: he was killed instantly. As in *Robertson*, witnessing the sudden death of a colleague caused the claimant to suffer psychiatric illness. However, in this case, the Court of Appeal held that the claimant was in physical danger himself, so was able to claim as a primary victim.

6.6 SECONDARY VICTIMS

A secondary victim is a person who is not in any physical danger themselves, but who suffers shock from witnessing an accident, resulting in witnessing a loved one killed or seriously injured. The first 'secondary victim' case was *Hambrook v Stokes Brothers*.[32] In this case, the defendant had left a lorry unattended at the top of a steep street: the brakes failed and the lorry started down the street where the victim's children were on their way to school. The victim had walked part of the way to school with her children and had just left them when she saw the runaway lorry heading towards the corner, knowing that her children were just around the corner. When she reached the scene of the accident, she found that her daughter was missing, and was told that a girl matching her description had been injured and taken to hospital. The victim went to the hospital, where she found her daughter, who had been seriously injured. As a result, the victim suffered from nervous shock, which resulted in her

30 [1995] IRLR 251.
31 (1997) 39 BMLR 146.
32 [1925] 1 KB 141.

death some 11 weeks later. The Court of Appeal held that the duty of care owed by the defendant not to cause physical injury directly included a duty not to cause injury by nervous shock, and that the victim's husband should be able to recover damages for his loss.

Hambrook v Stokes Brothers was relied upon by the claimant in the next important case in the development of the doctrine of secondary victims: *Bourhill v Young.*[33] In this case, a pregnant woman heard a motorcycle accident, which happened on the other side of the tram from which she had just alighted. She later saw the motorcyclist's blood on the road. As a result of the nervous shock, her child was stillborn. The House of Lords held that it was not foreseeable that the negligence of the motorcyclist would cause nervous shock to the claimant and that he had not, therefore, owed the claimant a duty of care. The House of Lords did not overrule *Hambrook*: rather they held that it was not necessary to decide whether that case was correct, as the facts were sufficiently distinguishable.

6.7 THE AFTERMATH DOCTRINE

The next significant development for secondary victims was the case of *McLoughlin v O'Brian.*[34] In this case, a woman's child was killed and other members of her family were injured in a road accident. Unlike *Hambrook*, the mother was not present at the time: she was informed by a friend of the family who had witnessed the accident and went to the hospital, arriving about two hours after the accident. At the hospital, she was told that her youngest child had been killed and saw her husband and two other children, all of whom had been injured and who were covered in dirt and oil from the accident. She later suffered from psychiatric illness. She brought a claim against the driver whose negligence had caused the accident.

The House of Lords recognised that there was no previous case in which a claimant had succeeded where he or she had not witnessed the injury to the near relative. In *Hambrook*, the Court of Appeal had made a clear distinction between shock caused by witnessing the injury and shock caused by hearing about the injury. However, it had been accepted in both Australia and in Canada that shock could be caused by witnessing the immediate aftermath of an injury.[35] The House of Lords held that the logical development of the law of psychiatric injury meant that the claimant should succeed in her claim. However, it was also held that the case was 'upon the margin' of what the development of the law should allow.

To recover for psychiatric injury caused by seeing a person killed or seriously injured, the claimant would have to show that the injury was foreseeable, and that there was sufficient proximity to the incident. It was held it was not foreseeable that ordinary members of the public of 'sufficient fortitude' would suffer psychiatric illness on seeing someone killed, but it was foreseeable that a person who bore a 'close tie of love and affection' to the victim might suffer

33 [1943] AC 92.

34 [1983] 1 AC 410.

35 *Benson v Lee* [1972] VR 879; *Marshall v Lionel Enterprises Inc* [1972] 2 OR 177.

psychiatric illness. A close tie of love and affection could be presumed where the claimant was the parent of, or married to, the victim, but other claims should be 'very carefully scrutinised'.[36]

The claimant would also have to show proximity to the incident: this meant that they were close in time and space. This could be by actually being present at the time, or seeing the aftermath of the incident within a short period. Claimants who were not present, or who heard about the incident indirectly, would not be able to meet this criterion.

The relaxation of the rule that the claimant had to be present at the incident was a significant expansion of the doctrine established in *Hambrook* and previous cases,[37] where the claimant's shock had been caused by seeing the actual incident in which their loved one had been killed or injured. *McLoughlin* established that it was not necessary that the claimant should witness the actual event in order to claim. If what the claimant witnessed was closely related to the damage caused by the defendant's negligence, such as the immediate aftermath of a road accident or the victim of the accident bearing the signs of the accident, then there was sufficient proximity, and the defendant would be liable.

McLoughlin also established that where the claimant was the victim's spouse or parent, it was foreseeable that they would suffer psychiatric illness as result of seeing them killed or seriously injured, and the law would accept that there was a close tie of love and affection. In other cases, the claimant would have to prove a close tie of love and affection.

KEY CASE

Alcock v Chief Constable of South Yorkshire Police [1992] 1 AC 310 was a claim arising from the Hillsborough disaster. This had happened at a football match, when the police had negligently opened the exit gates to the ground, allowing a large number of fans to enter into a confined space: this caused overcrowding. Ninety-five people were killed by crushing.

There were ten claimants, nine of whom had lost a relative, including children, brothers, and a grandson. The tenth had lost her fiancé. Two of the claimants had been at the match, and knew that their relative was in the Leppings Lane part of the ground, where the deaths occurred. The others had seen the match on television or had heard of the death of their relatives from a third party. All of them suffered from psychiatric illness, caused by the shock of the death of their loved one.

The claimants argued that the police owed them a duty of care, in that it was foreseeable that they would suffer psychiatric illness, caused by the shock of seeing or hearing about the death of their relative.

36 [1983] 1 AC 410, 422 (Lord Wilberforce).

37 *Hinz v Berry* [1970] 2 QB 40.

The House of Lords followed *McLoughlin v O'Brian*. They declined to relax either of the requirements of 'the closest of family ties' between victim and claimant, or the proximity in both time and space to the accident or its immediate aftermath. Applying *McLoughlin*, it was held that none of the relatives was owed a duty of care: either their relationship to the victim was not close enough that it was foreseeable that they would suffer psychiatric illness, or they were insufficiently proximate in time and space to the shocking incident.

6.8 THE *ALCOCK* ELEMENTS APPLIED AND CLARIFIED

Until January 2024, *Alcock* remained the most recent House of Lords or Supreme Court case concerning secondary victims. Subsequent cases before the High Court or Court of Appeal saw all the elements of the Alcock criteria applied strictly. Some of the elements were clarified by the Supreme Court in *Paul v Royal Wolverhampton NHS Trust*.[38]

6.9 EVENT OR ACCIDENT

In *Alcock*, Lord Ackner noted the need for the 'sign or sound of a horrifying event, which violently agitates the mind'.[39] Cases since have considered the application of this and later whether this was needed.

In the case of *Sion v Hampstead Health Authority*,[40] a parent suffered from psychiatric illness after spending two weeks at his son's bedside as he died. The Court of Appeal held that there was no shocking or horrifying event, as required in *Alcock*: the events causing the claimant's illness unfolded over time and the son's death was not unexpected. The claim failed. Further cases also highlighted no relaxation on behalf of the courts.[41]

However, in the case of *Walters v North Glamorgan NHS Trust*,[42] the Court of Appeal held that the death of a child, starting with the child having a fit and ending, some 36 hours later, with the child dying in his mother's arms, was a sudden shock to the mother, rather than a gradual realisation. The court noted that there was no requirement, in *Alcock* or in other cases, that the shock be limited in duration, and the whole 36-hour experience of the mother should be regarded as a single event.

38 [2024] UKSC 1.

39 [1992] 1 AC 310, 410.

40 [1994] 5 Med LR 170.

41 *Liverpool Women's Hospital NHS Foundation Trust v Ronayne* [2015] EWCA Civ 588, (2015) 145 BMLR 110.

42 [2002] EWCA Civ 1792.

KEY CASE

The *Walters* case, however, was revisited by the Supreme Court in *Paul v Royal Wolverhampton NHS Trust.*[43] This case involved joined appeals, all involving the claims for psychiatric injury after witnessing the death of loved ones from medical negligence. The joined appeals were rejected by a majority in the Supreme Court.[44]

The Supreme Court focused particularly on the need for there to be an accident (or its aftermath) witnessed by the secondary victim. The accident, said the Supreme Court, need not be horrifying.[45] An accident was defined as 'external event which causes, or has the potential to cause, injury: it is not the injury, if there is one, caused by that event'.[46] Rather than being an accident, the Supreme Court noted that the death or suffering of a loved one from illness was a 'medical crisis'.[47] In terms of previous cases, the Supreme Court in *Paul* stated that the 36 hours in *Walters* could not be regarded as an accident. Furthermore, while the correct outcome was reached in *Sion*, the case was decided on the wrong basis as there was no accident.[48]

The Supreme Court further noted:

> We are not able to accept that the responsibilities of a medical practitioner, and the purposes for which care is provided, extend to protecting members of the patient's close family from exposure to the traumatic experience of witnessing the death or manifestation of disease or injury in their relative.[49]

This is an interesting point to make: should the family members of the victim be in the mind of the medical practitioner when making decisions?

There are clearly very substantial restrictions from the *Paul v Royal Wolverhampton NHS Trust* case, in terms of claims by secondary victims in relation to medical negligence. Indeed, Lord Burrows in his dissenting judgment noted that 'subject to possible rare exceptions' this would mean 'recovery for negligently caused psychiatric illness by secondary victims will be closed off in medical negligence cases'.[50]

43 [2024] UKSC 1.

44 Appeal from *Royal Wolverhampton NHS Trust, Polmear v Royal Cornwall Hospital NHS Trust, Purchase v Ahmed* [2022] EWCA Civ 12.

45 [2024] UKSC 1, [75].

46 [2024] UKSC 1, [105].

47 [2024] UKSC 1, [53].

48 The Supreme Court noted this see e.g. paragraph 71 about the *Ronayne* case (cited above in fn 41).

49 [2024] UKSC 1.

50 Ibid, [250].

6.10 PROXIMITY IN TIME AND SPACE

If an accident is found, the requirement of proximity in space to means that the claimant must be present at the accident or its aftermath and witness it with their own unaided senses: seeing accidents on television or being told about them will not meet this condition. In *Alcock* itself, those relatives who heard about the disaster on the television or radio were not successful.

It seems to be accepted that proximity in time means that the claimant sees the incident, or its aftermath, within around two hours: this was the time between the accident in *McLoughlin* and the mother seeing her family, bearing the obvious signs of the accident, in hospital. In *Alcock*, the earliest that one of the claimants saw the body of the victim was some eight hours after the disaster. This was held not to be sufficiently proximate.

Proximity in time was slightly extended in the case of *Galli-Atkinson v Seghal*,[51] where two-and-a-quarter hours elapsed between the accident and the victim's mother seeing the aftermath, in the form of her daughter's body, which bore the visible signs of the accident. Although the claimant had been first informed of the accident by telephone, which might have excluded her claim, the Court of Appeal held that, as in *Walters*, the whole sequence of events was a single event.

The case was revisited in *Paul v Royal Wolverhampton NHS Foundation Trust*, with the Supreme Court deciding, as in *Walters*, that the approach in *Galli-Atkinson* 'should also not be followed',[52] a whole sequence of events should not be classed as a single event or accident. It is evident that witnessing the *immediate aftermath* as in *McLoughlin* could continue to allow a claim.

6.11 A CLOSE TIE OF LOVE AND AFFECTION

A secondary victim must also show that they had a close tie of love and affection with the victim. It is presumed that a parent has a close tie to his or her children, and that a husband and wife have close ties to each other. In all other cases, the claimant must prove that there is such a tie. In the case of *Alcock*, five of the ten claimants had lost brothers, and it was held in these cases that the relationship was not close enough.

The onus is on the claimant, in cases where the victim was not his or her spouse or child, to show that there was a close tie of love and affection. This was proved in *McCarthy v Chief Constable of South Yorkshire Police*,[53] another Hillsborough claim. In this case, the claimant was at the ground, and witnessed the crushing at close hand. He was able to show, on evidence from

51 [2003] EWCA Civ 697.

52 [2024] UKSC 1, [122].

53 Unreported, 11 December 1996.

family members, that the relationship between himself and the victim was particularly close, so as to make it a close tie of love and affection. In *Shorter v Surrey and Sussex Healthcare NHS Trust*, the claimant was also able to prove a close tie of love and affection with her sister,[54] although that claim failed as the claimant was unable to show sufficient proximity in time and space.

ANALYSING THE LAW

The 'Alcock criteria' have been widely criticised as being unfair, arbitrary and restrictive. This has even been acknowledged by the House of Lords, in *White v Chief Constable of South Yorkshire Police*, where Lord Steyn described the law as a 'patchwork quilt of distinctions which are difficult to justify'.[55]

The Law Commission's report of 1998, which followed *Alcock*, recommended reform of the law, by removing the requirement for proximity in time and space and widening the class of people who would be presumed to have a close tie to the victim. However, the government did not implement these proposals. More recently, the Negligence and Damages Bill 2015, a private member's bill which made similar provisions, failed for lack of Parliamentary time.

In *Paul v Royal Wolverhampton NHS Trust* the Supreme Court stated that the requirement to claim for secondary victims was

> to restrict the class of eligible claimants to those who are most closely and directly connected to the accident which the defendant has negligently caused and to apply restrictions which are reasonably straightforward, certain and comprehensible to the ordinary person.[56]

Do you agree with the current approach to compensation of secondary victims?

6.12 BYSTANDERS

A 'bystander' is a person who witnesses a shocking event, which causes them to suffer from a diagnosed psychiatric illness. Where such a person is unable to establish a close tie of love and affection, or that he or she reasonably believed that they contributed to the incident, they will be unable to recover. However, in *Alcock*, the House of Lords left open the possibility that a person who witnessed a particularly horrific incident might recover. Lord Ackner referred to a petrol tanker crashing into a school and bursting into flames as an example of a sight so

54 [2015] EWHC 614 (QB), 144 BMLR 136, [18]–[22] (Swift J).

55 *White v Chief Constable of South Yorkshire Police* [1999] 2 AC 455.

56 *Paul v Royal Wolverhampton NHS Trust* [2024] UKSC 1, [141].

horrific that it would be foreseeable that a person of ordinary fortitude witnessing the event would suffer psychiatric illness.[57]

The case of *McFarlane v EE Caledonia*,[58] however, did involve a bystander who witnessed particularly horrifying sights at close hand. The claimant was on board a support ship at the time of the Piper Alpha disaster, in which a North Sea oil platform caught fire. One hundred and sixty-seven people were killed in the fire and explosions. The claimant's ship participated in the rescue operation. The claimant witnessed three major explosions, burning men trying to escape by jumping into the sea, and another vessel being destroyed, with all the members of its crew killed, when it was engulfed by a fireball. The Court of Appeal referred to the references to possible claims by bystanders in the judgments in *Alcock*, but did not accept that the claimant should succeed as a bystander: there was no close tie of love and affection between him and the men he saw killed, and he was not so close to the danger that it would be foreseeable that a person of ordinary fortitude would suffer psychiatric illness.

The accounts of the Piper Alpha disaster make it clear that the scenes on that night were particularly horrific, and it would require unusual circumstances for a person to have a stronger bystander claim than in *McFarlane*. Despite the observations of the House of Lords in *Alcock*, it seems unlikely that a bystander claim would succeed.

6.13 RESCUERS

Historically, courts have been sympathetic to the claim of the 'rescuer': that is, a person who voluntarily goes to the rescue of another person in danger. If the rescuer suffers physical injury, the person who is liable for the injury to the person being rescued is also liable for the rescuer's injuries.

It is well established that the doctrine of *volenti*[59] – that persons who willingly risk injury cannot claim if they are injured – does not apply to rescuers.[60] A rescuer is regarded as being compelled to intervene to save lives, rather than being a volunteer.[61]

In the case of *Chadwick v British Railways Board*,[62] the rescuer suffered from psychiatric, rather than physical, injury. The claimant lived close to a railway line and, when he heard that there had been a major rail accident, went to the scene to see if he could help. As he was 'a fairly small man', he was able to get to parts of the wreckage that were inaccessible to other rescuers, and he spent the night helping the injured passengers. He later suffered from psychiatric

57 [1992] 1 AC 310, 403 (Lord Ackner).
58 [1994] 2 All ER 1.
59 See Chapter 9.
60 *Haynes v Harwood* [1935] 1 KB 146.
61 *Ward v TE Hopkins & Son Ltd; Baker v TE Hopkins & Son Ltd* [1959] 1 WLR 966.
62 [1967] 1 WLR 912.

illness and was admitted to a mental hospital. The court acknowledged that the claimant had placed himself in danger by going into the wreckage, but held that he was entitled to on the basis that his psychiatric illness had been caused by the 'horror of the whole experience'.

KEY CASE

White v Chief Constable of South Yorkshire Police [1999] 2 AC 455 was, like *Alcock*, a claim for psychiatric injury arising from the Hillsborough disaster. In this case, rather than the relatives of those killed, the claimants were police officers who had attended the disaster and who had seen the injured, dead, and dying spectators. A large number of them had suffered from psychiatric injury, caused by the trauma of witnessing the large-scale injury and loss of life.

In *Alcock*, the claims of the relatives had not succeeded. However, the police officers' claims had succeeded before the Court of Appeal, which had caused considerable public anger: it was the police force's negligence that had caused the death of 95 spectators.

The claimants relied upon *Chadwick*, in which a rescuer had been able to recover for his psychiatric illness, caused by the horror of witnessing death and injury at a major railway accident. They claimed that, as rescuers, they should be regarded as being akin to secondary victims, even though there was no 'close tie of love and affection' between the claimants and the persons killed and injured.

The House of Lords did not accept this argument. They held *Chadwick* did not show that rescuers who had not been in any physical danger could recover for psychiatric illness. The rescue cases showed that a person who owed the duty not to cause harm to the victims of the incident also owed a duty not to physically harm any person who came to rescue the victims. If the rescuers were not in physical danger, then the person liable for the incident was not in breach of his or her duty to the rescuers. However, if the defendant did breach their duty to the rescuers, by placing them in physical danger, they would be liable for the foreseeable injuries to them, both physical and psychiatric.

This means that a person claiming as a rescuer must show that he or she placed themselves in physical danger, although they do not need to show that the physical danger caused the psychiatric illness. If there is no physical danger, then rescuers are in the same position as bystanders and unable to claim.

Two members of the House – Lord Goff and Lord Griffiths – dissented. Lord Goff held that in some circumstances, including the rail crash in *Chadwick* and the Hillsborough disaster itself, what the rescuers witnessed was so horrific that it was foreseeable that a person of ordinary fortitude would suffer psychiatric injury.

White restricted the rescuer's claim to cases where the claimant had been in physical danger as a result of the defendant's negligence. However, the rescuer does not need to show that the psychical danger caused the psychiatric injury. It is sufficient that the defendant breached his or her duty not only not to endanger the victim, but also not to endanger any person who came to rescue the victim.

ANALYSING THE LAW

One of the issues in *White* was that the claimants were police officers, who are required, as emergency workers, to attend accidents and other incidents where they are likely to be in physical danger and to see horrifying sights.

In some jurisdictions, particularly in the United States, the 'fireman's rule' applies. This rule is that anyone who has chosen to become an emergency worker knows that he or she will face the risks of the job, and cannot claim in negligence for any physical or psychiatric injury caused by them.

However, in *Ogwo v Taylor* [1988] AC 431, the House of Lords considered the 'fireman's rule' and held that it was not part of English law. An emergency worker who is injured while doing his or her job can claim on the same basis as any other person. In *White*, the House of Lords confirmed that this applied to psychiatric injury as well as physical injury.

Do you think this is fair? When it comes to psychiatric injury, shouldn't the law be more ready to compensate members of the public who volunteer than police officers?

A rescuer who is not in danger, but who does have a close tie of love and affection to the person being rescued, can also bring a claim as a secondary victim. It is rare for rescuers to have a close relationship with those whom they are rescuing, but such a claim was brought in *Greatorex v Greatorex*.[63] The claimant was a fire officer who attended a car accident, caused by the defendant overtaking on the brow of a hill. The defendant was the claimant's son, and the claimant was later diagnosed with post-traumatic stress disorder, caused by the shock of seeing his injured son trapped in his car.

Although the claimant did meet all the Alcock criteria, in that he had a diagnosed psychiatric injury, caused by the shock of seeing, with his own eyes, the serious injury of his son, his claim failed. It was held that, as a matter of policy, a secondary victim cannot bring a claim where the person killed or injured is responsible for their own death or injury. The reasons given were that to allow such a claim would cause family 'strife' and inhibit the defendant's freedom of action.

63 [2000] 1 WLR 1970.

6.14 UNWILLING PARTICIPANTS

The fourth class of claimant is the 'unwilling participant': this is a person who reasonably believes that they have participated in causing the death or serious injury of another person. Involuntary participants may be able to claim for any psychiatric illness suffered as a result of witnessing the incident.

The case which established the doctrine is *Dooley v Cammell Laird*.[64] In this case, the claimant was a crane driver, who was raising cargo from the hold of a ship. The crane's sling broke, and the load fell into the hold. The crane driver succeeded in a claim for psychiatric illness caused by the trauma of thinking that he might have played a part in the injury or death of the men working in the hold, although no one was actually injured.

KEY CASE

In *Hunter v British Coal Corp* [1999] QB 140, a claim was made by a worker who was driving a vehicle along a roadway in a coal mine. The roadway was narrower than the regulations required, and there was no lighting. The claimant clipped a high pressure water hydrant with the edge of his vehicle, causing it to leak. He tried to stop the leak, with two other workers helping him. He then set off to look for a hose. When he was about 30 yards from the hydrant, he heard an 'almighty bang', caused by the head of the hydrant blowing off under the water pressure. One of the workers who had been trying to control the leak was killed. The claimant was prevented by fellow workers from returning to the scene of the accident, and did not see the body of the victim. He was later diagnosed with a psychiatric illness.

The court held that the victim's death was caused by the negligence of the mine's operator, as they had failed to provide a wide enough roadway. However, the claimant could not claim as a primary victim, as he had not been in physical danger, or as a secondary victim, as he had not witnessed the death or its aftermath. An appeal was dismissed by the Court of Appeal: to succeed as an 'unwilling participant', the claimant would have to show that they were sufficiently proximate in time and space to the event. In the same way as a secondary victim could not recover unless he or she had seen the incident, or its immediate aftermath, with their own sight and hearing, an unwilling participant who had not been present at the incident, or soon afterwards, could not recover. In this case, the claimant was told about the death, rather than seeing it for himself, so was unable to meet this requirement.

Hunter established that an unwilling participant must meet the Alcock criteria, with the exception that, instead of showing a close tie of love and affection to the victim, the claimant

64 [1951] 1 Lloyd's Rep 271.

has to establish that he or she reasonably believed that they were responsible for the victim's death or serious injury. The other requirements, including a shocking incident and proximity in time and space to the incident, are the same.

6.15 SHOCK FROM OTHER CAUSES

All the claims considered above have been based on a shock caused by physical danger to a person or personal injury, whether the danger or injury causes shock directly, as in primary victims, or indirectly, as in secondary victims or unwilling participants.

However, other causes may also give rise to a claim. In *Attia v British Gas plc*,[65] the nervous shock suffered by the claimant was seeing her home extensively damaged by a fire caused by the defendant's negligence. The High Court struck out the claim, as damages for psychiatric illness could only be recovered if caused by physical injury, either to the claimant or to a person with whom the claimant had a close tie. However, the Court of Appeal allowed the claim to proceed, holding that it was foreseeable that a person who saw their home and possessions destroyed would suffer from a psychiatric illness.[66]

6.16 OTHER CLAIMS FOR PSYCHIATRIC INJURY

The issue in the above cases has been whether the defendant owed a duty to the claimant not to cause psychiatric illness by nervous shock, whether owed to the claimant as part of their duty not to cause physical injury, or to secondary victims foreseeably affected.

However, where there is a pre-existing relationship between the claimant and defendant, such as between employee and employer, then that relationship may give rise to a duty not to cause psychiatric injury by means other than by nervous shock.

6.17 EMPLOYERS AND EMPLOYEES

Stress in the workplace is recognised as a major cause of psychiatric illness, for which the employer may be liable. Stress is not a psychiatric condition as such: rather, it refers to the emotional and physical response to adverse or pressured circumstances, such as when an employee is placed under pressure by managers or colleagues. This can cause depression or related psychiatric illnesses.

65 [1988] QB 304.

66 For an unusual claim for psychiatric injury caused by damage to 'property', see *Yearworth v North Bristol NHS Trust* [2010] QB 1.

KEY CASE

In *Hatton v Sutherland* [2002] EWCA Civ 76, [2002] 2 All ER 1, the Court of Appeal heard conjoined appeals by four employers who had been found liable for their employees' psychiatric illnesses caused by stress at work.

Hale LJ set out a number of principles to guide courts in determining whether an employer should be liable for psychiatric illness caused by stress in the workplace. These included:

- an employer's duty of care applied to psychiatric injury caused by stress in the same way as it applied to physical injury;
- no job or profession is inherently stressful, so as to make employees more likely to suffer psychiatric illness;
- employers are generally entitled to assume that employees are not suffering from stress unless the employee discloses that he or she has a problem or the problem would be obvious to a reasonable employer; and
- an employer that provides a free and confidential counselling service is likely to have taken reasonable care.

Applying those principles, the Court of Appeal found that three of the four employer defendants had acted reasonably and were not liable for the employees' psychiatric illness.

The House of Lords allowed an appeal by one of the claimant employees in the case of *Barber v Somerset County Council* [2004] UKHL 13, [2004] 2 All ER 385, but described Hale LJ's principles as a 'valuable contribution to the development of the law', although it warned against regarding them as having statutory force.

The issue in cases of psychiatric illness caused by stress in the workplace is whether, taking into account the principles set out in *Hatton*, it was foreseeable that the employee would suffer from psychiatric injury. If the injury is not foreseeable, the employer is not liable. However, once it is established that the psychiatric illness was foreseeable, the claimant still has to show that the employer did not take reasonable care. An employer who knows that an employee is under stress and is at particular risk of psychiatric illness might fulfil their duty by, for example, giving the employee time off, moving them to a different role, or providing additional support, in the form of counselling or providing other assistance. Whether the steps taken by the employer were reasonable would depend upon all the circumstances, including the resources available.[67]

67 *Hatton v Sutherland* [2002] EWCA Civ 76, [2002] 2 All ER 1, [32]–[34] (Hale LJ).

6.18 SOLDIERS

Members of the armed forces are, when on active service, likely to be exposed to physical danger, which may cause psychiatric illness. Post-traumatic stress disorder was, in fact, first recognised in American veterans of the Vietnam War, although previous conflicts had recognised that the stress of exposure to combat caused psychiatric illness.[68] As such, it is foreseeable that a serving member of the armed forces may suffer from psychiatric illness if exposed to combat conditions.

The liability of the government was considered in *Multiple Claimants v Ministry of Defence*.[69] This was a group litigation, brought by former service personnel who had served in various conflicts between 1969 and 1996, including in Northern Ireland, the Falklands, and the First Gulf War. The claimants were all suffering from psychiatric illness, mainly post-traumatic stress disorder.

It was accepted that the Ministry of Defence owes a duty of care to members of the armed forces, analogous to an employer's duty of care.[70]

For the claims before 1987, the government was able to rely on statutory immunity under section 10 of the Crown Proceedings Act 1947, which provided that no claim against the government could be brought by a member of the armed forces for any injury suffered while on active duty. However, the statutory immunity had been repealed in 1987. For the claims following repeal, it was accepted that the principle of 'combat immunity' applied: the duty of care did not apply in battlefield conditions. The claimants, however, argued that the Ministry of Defence had failed in its duty of care by not providing adequate psychological support to soldiers following exposure to trauma on the battlefield. However, it was found that the Ministry of Defence had acted as a reasonable employer.

6.19 THE 'WORRIED WELL'

In a 'worried well' claim, the claim is brought by a person who has been told that they are at a specific risk of a serious illness, caused by the negligence of another person, and who develops psychiatric illness as a result.

In the *Creutzfeldt-Jakob Disease Litigation*,[71] the claimants had received injections of human growth hormone (HGH) as participants in a clinical trial. The HGH used had been

68 'Shell shock' in World War I and 'battle fatigue' in World War II were recognised as psychiatric conditions.

69 [2003] EWHC 1134 (QB).

70 Ibid, [2.A.1]–[2.A.4] (Owen J). *Jebson v Ministry of Defence* [2000] 1 WLR 2055; *Radclyffe v Ministry of Defence* [2009] EWCA Civ 635.

71 *The Creutzfeldt-Jakob Disease Litigation; Group B Plaintiffs v Medical Research Council* (1997) 41 BMLR 157.

contaminated with Creutzfeldt-Jakob disease, a fatal degenerative illness. The claimants had found out that they had received contaminated HGH and that they were at risk of developing the disease. This had caused them to suffer from psychiatric illness. It was held that the proximity of the relationship between the researchers and the participants in the clinical trial, and the foreseeability of the participants developing psychiatric injury, meant that there was a duty not to cause psychiatric injury.

The claimants in *Rothwell v Chemical & Insulating Co Ltd*[72] had been negligently exposed by their employers to asbestos, and had developed a form of scarring on their lungs, known as pleural plaques. While pleural plaques did not cause any symptoms, they were a sign that the person had been exposed to asbestos and might later develop asbestosis, a fatal condition.

One of the claimants in *Rothwell*, Mr Grieves, had developed psychiatric illness as a result of worrying about the possibility of developing asbestosis. The House of Lords held that, as they did not cause any symptoms, pleural plaques were not a physical injury. Unlike the claimant in *Page v Smith*,[73] Mr Grieves had not suffered physical injury or been at risk of immediate physical injury, so could not claim as a primary victim. As it was not foreseeable that a person of reasonable fortitude would suffer from psychiatric illness, the claim failed.

POINTS TO REVIEW

- Claims may only be brought if the claimant has suffered from a diagnosed psychiatric illness, as opposed to mental distress.
- If there is no relationship giving rise to a duty not to cause psychiatric illness, the claimant can only recover if the psychiatric illness is caused by nervous shock.
- If the claimant is in physical danger, they can claim as a primary victim.
- If the claimant witnesses the death or injury, they can claim as a secondary victim if they meet the criteria from *Alcock*.
- If the claimant reasonably believes that they are liable for the death, they can claim if they were sufficiently proximate to the accident.
- Other relationships, such as employer–employee, may give rise to a duty to take reasonable care not to cause psychiatric harm.

TAKING IT FURTHER

Law Commission, Liability for Psychiatric Illness (Law Com No 249, 1998)
The Law Commission's report was issued following the Hillsborough disaster and the case of *Alcock*. The report recommended the removal of the shock requirement, and expansion of the presumption of a close tie of love and affection to include parents, siblings, and co-habitants.

72 [2008] 1 AC 281, [2007] UKHL 39.
73 [1996] AC 155.

Mulheron, R. 'Rewriting the Requirement for a "Recognized Psychiatric Injury" in Negligence Claims' (2012) 32(1) OJLS 77

This article looks at the requirement for a recognised psychiatric injury, and argues that this has led to inconsistencies and distortions in the law. The author argues for reform of the law.

Ahuja, J. 'Liability for Psychological and Psychiatric Harm: The Road to Recovery' (2015) 23(1) Med Law Rev 27

This examines the requirement for a diagnosed psychiatric illness and argues that the current approach should be reconsidered, in light of current psychological research. The author argues that the current rules are based on a misunderstanding of mental illness and trauma, and that the reframing of the law would allow a more rational and coherent approach.

Dove, E. S. 'Psychiatric Illness and Clinical Negligence: When Can "Secondary Victims" Successfully Claim for Damages? Recent Developments from the United Kingdom' (2024) 21 Journal of Bioethical Enquiry 217–224

This article considers updates to the law on negligently caused psychiatric injury, particularly focusing on *Paul v Royal Wolverhampton NHS Trust* [2024] UKSC 1. The author considers the majority and minority judgments in the case. The author also makes some interesting points in relation to recent case law surrounding medical negligence (e.g. the author discusses *Meadows v Khan* [2021] UKSC 21 and *McCulloch v Forth Valley Health Board* [2023] UKSC 26). In relation to *Paul*, the author further notes, for example, the difficulty with the need for an 'accident'.

7

CHAPTER 7
NEGLIGENCE: LIABILITY FOR OMISSIONS

7.1 INTRODUCTION

In negligence, there is a distinction between harm caused by the defendant and harm which might have been prevented or mitigated by the defendant. The latter are referred to as 'pure omissions' or, in the term now preferred by the courts,'failing to confer a benefit'. Liability for omissions refers to the circumstances where the defendant did not take action to prevent the claimant from suffering harm from a cause such as illness, natural events, acts of third parties or even acts of the claimant him- or herself. In such a case, the defendant is not the primary cause of the harm and is not liable in negligence, other than in particular circumstances.

As a general rule, there is a duty in negligence to take reasonable care not to directly cause harm or damage to any other person, but there is no general duty to take any action to prevent another person from suffering harm from another cause. However, a pre-existing duty of care may include a duty to confer a benefit by protecting the claimant from harm. There are also other circumstances, such as when the defendant has assumed responsibility for the claimant, where the defendant is under a duty to take positive action to protect the claimant from harm.

AS YOU READ

- Understand the distinction between acts and 'pure omissions'.
- Understand the reasons that there is no general liability for damage caused by pure omissions.
- Know the circumstances in which a duty to take action will arise.

KEY LEARNING POINT

- English law does not, as a general rule, require any person to take positive steps to prevent harm to another person who is suffering or who might suffer harm, unless there is a prior duty of care to that person.

DOI: 10.4324/9781003480051-07

7.2 WHAT IS AN OMISSION?

Many cases in negligence can be seen as omissions: something that the defendant did not do, rather than something he or she did. In *Donoghue v Stevenson*,[1] there was no positive act on the part of the drinks manufacturer that led to the claimant's illness: the manufacturer did not actually put the snail in the bottle. Rather, they failed to act: they omitted to check the bottles before filling to make sure that the bottle was free from any contaminants. Similarly, a road traffic accident may be caused by the failure of a driver to apply his or her brakes at the right time, or physical harm may be caused by the failure of a doctor to carry out the appropriate diagnostic test.

This can lead to some confusion as to what constitutes an omission in negligence. In *Smith v Littlewoods Organisation*,[2] Lord Goff referred to 'pure omissions'.[3] These are failures to take actions that would have prevented the harm from occurring, where the primary cause of the harm is not the defendant's fault. More recently, courts have started to refer to 'pure omissions' as 'failures to confer a benefit',[4] which is a clearer description of what is meant by omission in this context.

The term 'pure omission' or 'failure to confer a benefit' refers to where the defendant might have acted to prevent or mitigate harm or damage which was not directly caused by the defendant. The primary cause might be an act by a third party, a natural occurrence, illness or an act by the claimant him- or herself.

The starting point for the law on omissions is that English law does not impose any duty on a person to take positive steps to rescue or protect any person who is suffering or who might suffer harm, unless there is an existing duty of care to that person.

This is sometimes expressed in the example of an adult standing by as a toddler drowns in a few inches of water. As Lord Nicholls noted in the case of *Stovin v Wise*, the recognised legal position is that the adult does not owe the drowning child a duty.[5] Despite the fact that it might be the 'simplest exertion'[6] to lift the child out of the water, English law does not impose any obligation on the bystander to rescue the child.[7]

In the same passage, Lord Nicholls also noted that there is no duty to warn another person of danger. Even if you see a person about to step into the path of an oncoming car, or to walk over a cliff,[8] there is no requirement to warn the person.

1 [1932] AC 562 (HL).

2 [1987] AC 241 (HL).

3 Ibid, 271.

4 *N v Poole Borough Council* [2019] UKSC 25, [2020] AC 780 [31] (Lord Reed). See also *Stovin v Wise* [1996] AC 923 (HL), 949 (Lord Hoffmann).

5 *Stovin v Wise* [1996] AC 923 (HL), 931 (Lord Nicholls).

6 Ibid.

7 This principle does not apply where the adult in question is responsible for the child, as its parent, babysitter, school teacher or other adult who has assumed responsibility or who has a duty of care to the child: *Woodland v Essex County Council* [2013] UKSC 66, [2014] AC 537.

8 *Yuen Kin Yeu v Attorney General of Hong Kong* [1988] AC 175 (PC) 192 (Lord Keith).

Another type of pure omission is where a person might have prevented the danger by taking action to protect the injured party, in particular from acts of third parties or natural events. For example, a person who sees, from a window in his or her own home, a burglar breaking into the house next door has no legal obligation to call the police or take any other action, even though a quick phone call might protect his neighbour from loss and damage to his or her property.[9]

> KEY LEARNING POINT
>
> English law does not impose a general duty to rescue or protect any person to whom the defendant does not owe a prior duty of care.

7.3 TYPES OF PURE OMISSION

Pure omissions may be divided into:

- failure to rescue; and
- failure to protect.

In general, neither will give rise to civil liability on the part of any person who might have taken effective action but failed to do so, unless there is an existing duty of care.

FAILURE TO RESCUE

A duty to rescue may arise when a person is aware that another person is suffering harm or is in danger of immediate harm, and the circumstances mean that the first person is required to take steps to prevent or reduce the harm.

Failure to rescue cases are rare in English law, perhaps because the existence of such a duty has been clearly denied by the House of Lords and in other cases. In *Dorset Yacht v Home Office*,[10] Lord Reid referred to the biblical parable of the Good Samaritan.[11] This was the tale of a man who was robbed and beaten and left by the roadside. Two men passed by, without taking the time to help the victim: a priest and a Levite. In the words of Lord Reid, the two men 'would have incurred no civil liability in English law'[12] for their failure to rescue or assist the victim.

A duty to rescue may arise as part of a prior duty of care: in *Davis v Stena Line*,[13] a passenger fell from a ferry crossing from Ireland to Wales. The master of a ship owes a duty of care

9 'There is no general duty upon a householder that he should act as a watchdog . . . to protect his neighbour's house'. *Smith v Littlewoods Organisation* [1987] AC 241 (HL) 271 (Lord Goff).

10 [1970] AC 1004 (HL).

11 *The Bible*, Luke 10:25–10:37.

12 [1970] AC 1004 (HL) 1060.

13 [2005] EWHC 420 (QB).

to his or her passengers and, if a passenger does fall overboard, there is a duty to rescue the passenger. In *Davis*, the rescue operation was negligently carried out and the passenger drowned. The captain of the ship and the ferry company were both held to have been negligent. But there was no possibility of the other vessel on the scene being liable, even though it was within 100 yards of the man in the water and was capable of rescuing him.

In *Watson v British Boxing Board of Control*,[14] the claimant was a boxer, who had suffered a serious head injury during a bout, which was licensed and regulated by the defendant. He was treated by a doctor at the scene, and later transferred to hospital, but suffered permanent brain damage. It was found that the medical provision at the scene was inadequate, and the brain damage could have been avoided had he received immediate resuscitation. The Court of Appeal held that the defendant, which had been in complete control of the bout, had assumed responsibility for the claimant's physical safety. When the claimant suffered the injury, the defendant had a duty to provide medical treatment.

Davis and *Watson* are examples of a pre-existing duty to take reasonable care for the physical safety of the claimant, which included a duty to rescue.

A duty to rescue may also arise where the defendant assumes responsibility. In *Barrett v Ministry of Defence*,[15] a naval airman, while off-duty, had drunk to excess and had passed out. He was carried back to his bunk by other servicemen and placed in the recovery position but died from inhaling vomit later the same night. The High Court found that the defendant had a duty to take reasonable steps to prevent him from drinking to excess. On appeal, it was held that the defendant did not have a duty to prevent him from drinking, but, from the time that the defendant assumed responsibility by taking the victim to his bunk, there was a duty to take reasonable care.[16]

In *Bishara v Sheffield Teaching Hospitals NHS Trust*,[17] a woman who had just concluded a stressful meeting suffered from a migraine attack. Her claim stated that she asked the person she had been meeting, who was a doctor, to call an ambulance. The other person did not respond to her request, with the result that the claimant did not receive any medical attention for four hours. The claim was struck out, as it was held that there was no duty of care. However, on appeal, it was accepted that a duty of care might have arisen, if the defendant had assumed responsibility for the claimant.

Most of the rescue cases that have been considered are those in which the defendant is a public authority, such as the fire and rescue authority, which has a statutory duty to protect life and property in the event of a fire.[18] The liability of public authorities is considered in detail in Chapter 8, but the general principle has been established that breach of a statutory

14 [2001] QB 1134 (CA).
15 [1995] 1 WLR 1217 (CA).
16 Ibid, 1225 (Beldam LJ, with whom Neill and Saville LJJ agreed).
17 [2007] EWCA Civ 353.
18 Fire and Rescue Services Act 2004 s.7.

duty does not generally give rise to a claim in negligence by any person affected by the breach of statutory duty.[19] It was also held, in *Capital and Counties plc v Hampshire County Council*,[20] that even where the public authority does undertake a rescue, no duty will arise other than a duty not to make things worse than they would otherwise have been. The Court of Appeal also stated:

> It is not clear why a rescuer who is not under an obligation to attempt a rescue should assume a duty to be careful in effecting the rescue merely by undertaking the attempt. It would be strange if such a person were liable to the dependants of a drowning man who but for his carelessness he would have saved, but without the attempt would have drowned anyway.[21]

In *Kent v Griffiths*,[22] the claimant called 999, and was told that an ambulance would be dispatched. The ambulance took 40 minutes to reach the claimant, which was significantly longer than should have been taken. Although the ambulance service argued that their duty was only not to make things worse, the Court of Appeal held that *Capital and Counties* should not be followed. The ambulance service, as part of the NHS, should be treated in the same way as a doctor, and that a duty of care arose as soon as the ambulance had accepted the call, in the same way that a doctor owes a duty to any person whom he or she accepts as a patient.[23] Similarly, in a claim in negligence against the St John's Ambulance Brigade, who had assisted a boy involved in a motorcycle accident,[24] the court did not question that the first aider owed a duty of care.

This raises the question of whether a duty to rescue arises when a person starts to help: *Capital and Counties* makes it clear that a rescuer owes no duty other than not to make things worse than they would otherwise have been; on the other hand, *Barrett* states that a duty to confer a benefit arose as soon as the defendant assumed responsibility for the victim by carrying him to his bunk, and the appeal in *Bishara* was allowed on the basis that a duty to rescue could arise from an assumption of responsibility. *Kent v Griffiths*[25] held that, where the defendant is part of the NHS, a doctor–patient type duty arises as soon as the defendant accepts the claimant as a patient and the defendant may be liable for failing to provide reasonable care. Similarly, in *Hedley Byrne v Heller and Partners*, Lord Morris held that, if a doctor started to treat an unconscious person who was not one of his or her patients, the doctor would be under a duty to exercise reasonable skill and care.[26]

19 *X (minors) v Bedfordshire County Council* [1995] 2 AC 633 (HL).

20 [1997] QB 1004.

21 Ibid, 1037 (Stuart-Smith LJ, giving the judgment of the court).

22 [2001] QB 36.

23 *Barnett v Chelsea and Kensington Hospital Management Committee* [1969] 1 QB 428 (QB) 435 (Nield J).

24 *Cattley v St John's Ambulance Brigade* (Unreported, 25 November 1988).

25 [2001] QB 36 (CA).

26 [1964] AC 465 (HL) 495. See also Lord Atkinson's dictum to the same effect in *Banbury v Bank of Montreal* [1918] AC 626, 689. In *Capital and Counties Bank v Hampshire County Council* [1997] QB 1004 (CA), however, the Court of Appeal held that a doctor's 'only duty as a matter of law is not to make the victim's condition worse' (at 1035).

It is difficult to draw a firm rule from these cases, but the distinction seems to be between those who assume responsibility for a person's physical well-being and those who are preventing other forms of damage, such as property damage.

APPLYING THE LAW

Edward Hyde is an actor, who has just been cast as the lead role in a major film. As it is a physically demanding role, the production company instruct Dr Jekyll to carry out a medical examination of Edward to make sure he is fit enough for the role.

During the examination, Edward suffers a heart attack and collapses. Dr Jekyll has read Edward's medical notes, and knows that Edward suffers from epilepsy, so assumes that Edward is having a seizure. He cushions Edward's head and places him in the recovery position. Edward dies. Medical evidence shows that prompt CPR would have saved his life.

Is Dr Jekyll liable? Did a duty of care arise and, if so, when: when Dr Jekyll started the examination or when he started to treat Edward for the misdiagnosed seizure? And what was the scope of the duty?

FAILURE TO PROTECT

A duty to protect is a duty to take action to prevent another person from suffering injury or damage, where the primary cause of the injury is an act of a third party, a natural event or even the act of the claimant him- or herself, rather than the defendant. A duty to protect may be discharged by taking positive action, such as stopping someone from harming the claimant, or by warning the claimant, so that he or she can take the necessary action to avoid harm.

As with the duty to rescue, the law does not impose a general duty to protect a person from damage caused by an accident, a third party or a natural event, whether by taking action or by warning the potential victim. As Lord Sumner held in the case of *Weld-Blundell v Stephens*, 'even though A is in fault, he is not responsible for injury to C which B, a stranger to him, deliberately chooses to do'.[27] In the case of *Deyong v Shenburn*, an actor claimed that a theatre had a duty to protect his property from theft: the court held that there 'was not a shred of authority that any such duty exists or ever has existed'.[28]

FAILURE TO WARN

One form of the failure to protect is a failure to warn. This refers to a situation where one person has information relating to another person, which that other person is not aware of

27 [1920] AC 956, 986.
28 [1946] KB 227, 233 (du Parcq LJ).

and which might allow that person to take steps to avoid damage or harm. A duty to warn is a duty to take reasonable steps to make the other person aware of the information and is a particular form of the duty to protect.

A duty to warn may well be part of an existing duty of care, such as the duty that an occupier owes to visitors,[29] but does not usually arise in other circumstances. So, as seen above, a person who sees a pedestrian about to step into the path of an oncoming vehicle has no obligation to shout a warning.

Duties to warn do arise from contract and may be part of a non-contractual duty of care. A doctor has a duty to warn his or her patients of any health issues that he or she is aware of, and it has been stated: 'If a dentist is asked to treat a patient's tooth and, on looking into the latter's mouth, he notices that an adjacent tooth is in need of treatment, it is his duty to warn the patient accordingly'.[30]

That the defendant knows of a danger and can foresee that another might be harmed is not sufficient to create a duty to warn. In *Stagecoach South Western Trains v Hind*,[31] a railway company sued a tree surgeon when a tree fell onto the tracks and damaged a train. The claim against the tree surgeon was based on the fact that he had worked on the tree and that he knew, or should have known, that it was rotten and likely to fall. It was foreseeable that it might fall onto the railway tracks. In those circumstances, it was argued that the tree surgeon owed the railway company a duty to warn them of the danger. The court found that there was no such duty: there was no contractual or other prior relationship between the tree surgeon and the railway company which gave rise to a duty to warn, and there were no reported cases in which such a duty had been held to exist.[32] And in *Mitchell v Glasgow City Council*,[33] the House of Lords considered a claim that the Council should have warned a murder victim that his neighbour might wish to harm him. The House of Lords held that there was no general duty to warn a person that he or she was at risk of harm from the acts of a third party. As Lord Hope expressed it,

> I would also hold, as a general rule, that a duty to warn another person that he is at risk of loss, injury or damage as the result of the criminal act of a third party will arise only where the person who is said to be under that duty has by his words or conduct assumed responsibility for the safety of the person who is at risk.[34]

Mitchell v Glasgow City Council[35] was considered by the Court of Appeal in *Selwood v Durham County Council*.[36] This was a case in which the claimant, a social worker, had been injured

29 See Occupiers Liability Act 1957 s.2(4).

30 *Credit Lyonnais SA v Russell Jones & Walker (a firm)* [2002] EWHC 1310 (Ch), [28] (Laddie J).

31 [2014] EWHC 1891 (TCC).

32 Ibid, [100] (Coulson J).

33 [2009] UKHL 11, [2009] AC 874.

34 Ibid, [29].

35 [2009] UKHL 11, [2009] AC 874.

36 [2012] EWCA Civ 979.

by a mental patient who had been discharged from hospital. The claimant argued that the hospital should have foreseen the risk of her being attacked and had a duty to warn her that the patient had been discharged. The claim was struck out by the High Court, but the Court of Appeal held that, in the particular circumstances of the case, which included that the social worker's employer and the defendant hospital worked closely together on the management of the mental health patient, it was arguable that the defendant had assumed responsibility for the claimant.

DUTY OF DOCTORS TO WARN NON-PATIENTS

A particular form of the duty to warn is where a doctor is aware of information that might affect a third party who is not one of his or her patients. This might be where the patient is suffering from an infectious disease which could harm those living with or in a relationship with the patient.[37] Another example is where the patient has a genetic condition, in which case there is a possibility that his or her relations have the same genetic condition.[38] A further example, which has been considered in the United States, is where a patient has expressed an intention to harm a third party.[39]

KEY CASE

In *ABC v St George's Healthcare NHS Trust* [2017] EWCA Civ 336, the claimant was the daughter of a patient, who was being treated by the defendant. The patient himself had killed the claimant's mother and had been convicted of manslaughter and detained in hospital under the Mental Health Act 1983. While in hospital, he started to show symptoms which were later diagnosed as Huntington's disease, a serious genetic disorder. The doctors asked the claimant's father whether they should inform his family that he was suffering from the condition, so that they could be tested for the gene. The claimant's father refused his consent to disclosure of his genetic condition, and the doctors accepted his decision.

At the time that the doctors became aware that the claimant's father had Huntington's disease, the claimant herself was pregnant. The claimant sued the doctors, arguing that they had a duty to warn her that her foetus might carry the gene for Huntington's disease.

The High Court originally struck out the claim as showing no reasonably arguable cause of action, but an appeal was allowed and the case went to trial.

37 *Evans v Mayor of Liverpool* [1906] 1 KB 160 (KB). Doctors have a statutory duty to inform public health authorities about patients with certain infectious diseases, under the Health Protection (Notification) Regulations 2010, but this duty does not create a duty to warn others who may be affected.

38 *ABC v St George's Healthcare NHS Trust* [2017] EWCA Civ 336; *Smith v University of Leicester NHS Trust* [2016] EWHC 817 (QB).

39 *Tarasoff v Regents of the University of California* (1976) 551 P.2d 334.

At trial, the High Court held that, in the particular circumstances of the case, including that the claimant was also being treated by the defendants, there was a duty to the claimant. However, in balancing the father's wish that his daughter not be informed with their duty to the claimant, the defendants had acted in accordance with professional guidance, so the claim failed.[40]

ABC v St George's Healthcare[41] does not establish that all doctors owe a duty to warn non-patients if they are aware of information that is relevant to that person's health. The case involved particular circumstances which established the necessary degree of proximity between the doctors and the claimant. In other circumstances, where there is no proximity between doctor and claimant, there would be no duty to warn.

A duty to warn has been found in other jurisdictions where there was no proximity to the claimant: the US cases of *Tarasoff v Regents of the University of California*[42] and *Safer v Pack*[43] were both cited by the Court of Appeal in *ABC*.[44] In both of these cases, a medical professional had come into possession of information, which they did not disclose to a third party who was directly affected by the information. In *Tarasoff*, the information was that one of a psychologist's patients was planning to attack a young woman. In *Safer*, the doctor did not disclose details of a genetic condition to a patient's daughter, with the result that the daughter did not have the opportunity to seek early treatment. And, in both cases, the US court had found the defendant liable for breach of their duty to warn the person affected.

7.4 CIRCUMSTANCES CREATING A DUTY TO CONFER A BENEFIT

There are limited circumstances in which a person does have a duty to confer a benefit by rescuing or protecting another from damage. These are usually where the defendant has assumed responsibility for the claimant or where the defendant has contributed to the damage by introducing or having control over the source of harm.

In *Smith v Littlewoods Organisation*,[45] Lord Goff set out four circumstances where a duty to confer a benefit would arise: these were where a landowner was aware that something on his or her land might damage neighbouring land;[46] where the defendant caused or permitted the

40 [2020] EWHC 455 (QB).

41 [2017] EWCA Civ 336.

42 (1976) 551 P.2d 334.

43 (1996) 291 N.J. Sup. 619, 677 A.2d 1188.

44 [2017] EWCA Civ 336 [50]ff and [57]ff.

45 [1987] AC 241 (HL).

46 See *Goldman v Hargrave* [1967] 1 AC 645 (PC), where a landowner was liable for failing to prevent fire, caused by a lightning strike, from spreading to the neighbour's land.

source of the damage; where the defendant assumed responsibility for the claimant; and where there was a 'special relationship' between the defendant and the person who caused the damage.

More recent cases have, however, preferred a different summary of the circumstances in which the defendant will be under a duty to confer a benefit by protecting the claimant.

KEY CASE

Great Lakes Reinsurance (UK) plc v RAV Bahamas Ltd [2024] UKPC 11 was a claim brought by the insurers of a motor yacht against the owners of the marina from which it was stolen. A man, claiming to be the owner of the yacht, asked a porter at the marina to prepare the yacht for departure. The following day, two men paid the porter and a cleaner that he had hired to help with the preparation, then went aboard the yacht and sailed her away. The porter working for the marina did not check the men's identity and did not do anything to prevent them from taking the vessel away. The insurance company sought to recover the payment of $580,000 made to the owner, arguing that the marina owed a duty to protect the yacht's owner from theft.

The Privy Council held that the claim involved an omission, or failure to confer a benefit, on the part of the defendant. The insurance company argued that, as the marina provided security for the boats moored in the marina, the owner of the yacht had reasonably expected the defendant to protect his vessel from theft. However, the Privy Council did not agree that there was an assumption of responsibility. Unlike *Stansbie v Trotman* [1948] 2 KB 48, the marina was not in control of the vessel and had not been entrusted with its keys.

The Privy Council noted Lord Goff's judgment from *Smith v Littlewoods Organisation* [1987] AC 241 (HL), and approved (at [21]) a summary of the position relating to liability for failures to confer a benefit from Stelios Tofaris and Sandy Steel in their article 'Negligence Liability for Omissions and the Police' (2016) 75 CLJ 128:

> In the tort of negligence, a person A is not under a duty to take care to prevent harm occurring to person B through a source of danger not created by A unless (i) A has assumed a responsibility to protect B from that danger, (ii) A has done something which prevents another from protecting B from that danger, (iii) A has a special level of control over that source of danger, or (iv) A's status creates an obligation to protect B from that danger.

This statement of the principles of liability for omissions or failure to confer benefits was also approved by the Supreme Court in the cases of *Robinson v Chief Constable of West Yorkshire Police* [2018] UKSC 4, [2018] AC 736; *N v Poole Borough Council* [2019] UKSC 25, [2020] AC 780; *HXA v Surrey County Council* [2023] UKSC 52, [2024] 1 WLR 335; and *Tindall v Chief Constable of Thames Valley Police* [2024] UKSC 33.[47]

47 See also Chapter 8 on the liability of public authorities.

Tofaris and Steel's statement of the circumstances in which a defendant will be liable for a failure to conder a benefit has now been approved by the Supreme Court on four occasions and by the Privy Council. The circumstances in which the defendant will be liable for failing to prevent harm happening to the claimant are:

- where the defendant assumed responsibility to protect the claimant from that type of danger;
- where the defendant had done something to prevent another person from protecting the claimant from the danger;
- where the defendant had a special level of control over the source of the danger; and
- where the defendant's status creates a duty to protect the claimant from the danger.[48]

These categories differ from those set out in *Smith v Littlewoods Organisation.*[49] In particular, they do not refer to a landowner's duty to the owners of neighbouring land as a specific category. Lord Goff's separate categories of introducing the danger and a 'special relationship' between the defendant and the person causing the damage are combined into a single category of 'special control' over the source of the danger. And Tofaris and Steel introduce two new circumstances which do not readily correspond with Lord Goff's categories: where the defendant has prevented another person from protecting the claimant and where the defendant's status creates an obligation to protect the claimant.

LANDOWNERS

The liability of landowners for damage caused to neighbouring land is considered in Chapter 12. Where a landowner is aware of something that might cause damage on his or her land, even if the danger was not caused by the landowner, they are under a duty to prevent the danger from causing damage to neighbouring land. However, the liability of landowners for failing to protect their neighbour's land from physical damage is a duty arising in the context of the well-established duty of a landowner to take reasonable care not to damage neighbouring land, so is not a true example of a failure to confer a benefit.

ASSUMPTION OF RESPONSIBILITY

> KEY LEARNING POINT
>
> A duty to take reasonable steps to protect a person from injury or damage may arise if the defendant has assumed responsibility for the claimant's well-being or the safety of their property.

The most common way in which a duty to confer a benefit arises is when the defendant has assumed responsibility for the claimant.

48 S. Tofaris and S. Steel, 'Negligence Liability for Omissions and the Police' (2016) 75 CLJ 128

49 [1987] AC 241 (HL).

In *Stansbie v Trotman*,[50] a decorator was liable to the householder when he left the house unlocked and the house was burgled. This case was cited in *Smith v Littlewoods Organisation*[51] as an example of a duty arising from assumption of responsibility, but Lord Goff's judgment did not set out the elements of the principle in this context.

The doctrine of assumption of responsibility established by *Hedley Byrne v Heller and Partners*[52] requires representation by a skilled or professional defendant and reliance by the defendant:[53] in *Marc Rich v Bishop Rock Marine*,[54] the argument that the defendant had assumed responsibility for the claimant was rejected because the claimant was not aware of the defendant's role and could not be said to be relying on the defendant.[55]

However, in the context of a duty to protect from physical injury, assumption of responsibility does not require any particular skill or reliance on the part of the claimant. In *Barrett v Ministry of Defence*,[56] for example, the defendant was held to have assumed responsibility for the claimant when they started to take care of him: this finding was despite the claimant being unaware of the defendant's actions, as he was unconscious at the time. And the persons who assumed responsibility were not medically trained or exercising a particular skill: they were service personnel who intervened to look after the claimant.

This was confirmed in *HXA v Surrey County Council*,[57] when considering the liability of a social services authority for failing to protect children from abuse by their parents. In that case, the Supreme Court distinguished between assumption of responsibility in economic loss cases,[58] where the claimant's reliance on the defendant was 'central' to the principle, and other forms of damage, such as personal injury, where reliance appeared 'not to be a necessary requirement'.[59] In these cases, a person may be held to have assumed responsibility for the safety of the claimant even though the claimant was not aware of their actions.

In *Selwood v Durham County Council*,[60] a social worker who was seriously assaulted by a mental patient sued the hospital for failing to warn her that the patient had been discharged. In *Palmer v Tees Health Authority*,[61] a similar claim brought by a person injured by a mental patient who had not been detained or treated, failed. On the basis of this, and other failure to protect cases, the claim was struck out in the High Court, but the Court of Appeal allowed

50 [1948] 2 KB 48 (CA).
51 [1987] AC 241 (HL) 272 (Lord Goff).
52 [1964] AC 465 (HL).
53 *Henderson v Merrett Syndicates Ltd* [1995] 2 AC 145 (HL) 180 (Lord Goff). See Chapter 5 for a full discussion of assumption of responsibility in economic loss cases.
54 [1996] AC 211 (HL).
55 Ibid, 238 (Lord Steyn).
56 [1995] 1 WLR 1217 (CA).
57 [2023] UKSC 52, [2024] 1 WLR 335.
58 See Chapter 5.
59 [2023] UKSC 52, [2024] 1 WLR 335, [90] (Lord Burrows and Lord Stephens).
60 [2012] EWCA Civ 979.
61 [1999] Lloyds Law Rep Med 351 (CA).

an appeal: it was possible that the claimant would be able to establish that the defendant had assumed responsibility for the social worker.

Calvert v William Hill Credit[62] is an unusual case, as it is one in which the claim was for harm caused by the claimant's own voluntary and informed actions. The claimant, a problem gambler, had entered into a 'self-exclusion' agreement with a bookmaker: the bookmaker promised him that they would not accept any of his bets. The gambler later lost over £2 million in bets that the bookmaker had agreed not to accept. It was found that the defendant had assumed responsibility to protect the claimant from his own actions. However, the court found that the breach had not caused the loss, as the claimant would have been free to make the same bets with any of the defendant's competitors and would, on the balance of probability, have done so.

THE INTERFERENCE PRINCIPLE

The second circumstance in the Tofaris and Steel categories which creates a duty to rescue or protect the claimant arises where the defendant has done something which prevented another person from protecting the claimant from harm. Tofaris and Steel do not provide any examples of this being applied in practice, but the principle was explained and approved by the Supreme Court in *Tindall v Chief Constable of Thames Valley Police.*[63] Previously, it had been argued that it provides an alternative source of the duty to rescue in *Kent v Griffith.*[64] In this case, an ambulance took 40 minutes to arrive, during which time the claimant suffered a cardiac arrest. The Court of Appeal noted that the doctor attending the patient testified that, if he had known that the ambulance would be delayed, he would have taken the patient to hospital in his own car, but this was not the basis on which the court found a duty of care.

The Supreme Court explained the principle, which they referred to as the 'interference principle', in *Tindall v Chief Constable of Thames Valley Police.*[65] In this case, Mr Kendall had skidded on a patch of black ice while driving. He called the police and, while he was waiting, stood by the side of the road warning passing cars of the danger. When the police arrived, Mr Kendall stopped warning the passing cars and left the scene in an ambulance. The police placed a 'Police Slow' warning notice while they were clearing the scene, but when they left, the police took the warning notice away with them. Shortly afterwards, a motorist was killed in a second accident caused by the black ice.

It was argued that the police, by taking control over the scene of the first accident, had prevented Mr Kendall from protecting other road users and should therefore owe a duty to confer a benefit on road users on that stretch of road by warning them of the dangerous conditions.

62 [2008] EWCA Civ 1427, [2009] Ch 330.
63 [2024] UKSC 33.
64 [2001] QB 36 (CA).
65 [2024] UKSC 33.

The Supreme Court confirmed that a duty of care would arise when the defendant prevented another person from conferring a benefit on the claimant, but this duty would only arise if it was foreseeable that the defendant's acts would have that effect. It was well established that the police were under no obligation to confer a benefit but would be liable for making things worse, as established in *Capital & Counties plc v Hampshire County Council.*[66] So where the defendant's acts made things worse by preventing another person from conferring a benefit, the defendant would owe a duty of care. However, this was subject to the defendant knowing that his or her interference would prevent another from rescuing or protecting the claimant. The Supreme Court approved the formulation of the principle set out by Nicholas McBride and Roderick Bagshawe:

> [I]f A knows or ought to know that B is in need of help to avoid some harm, and A knows or ought to know that he has done something to put off or prevent someone else helping B, then A will owe B a duty to take reasonable steps to give B the help she needs.[67]

On the facts of *Tindall*, however, the police did not know or ought to have known that their arrival would prevent Mr Kendall from continuing to warn passing motorists of the dangerous conditions. Accordingly, the interference principle, as formulated by McBride and Bagshawe, did not apply to the facts and the police did not owe a duty of care to motorists using that stretch of road after their departure from the scene.

Tindall does, however, overrule *OLL Ltd v Secretary of State for Transport.*[68] In this case, the coastguard had taken control of a rescue operation at sea and directed a Royal Navy helicopter to search in the wrong area. The High Court did not accept that the coastguard was liable even though, by misdirecting the helicopter, it had prevented another party from rescuing the group. The Supreme Court held that the interference principle should have been applied as the misdirection by the coastguard had made the claimants worse off and it was foreseeable that it would have that effect.

APPLYING THE LAW

Quint is fishing from a pier when he slips and falls into the water. Quint cannot swim and is in obvious difficulty, so Hooper, who is a strong swimmer, takes off her coat ready to jump in to rescue Quint. However, Brody, an off-duty police officer, restrains Hooper, telling her that it is too dangerous and that she should wait for the lifeguard. By the time the lifeguard arrives, Quint has drowned.

Does Brody owe a duty to confer a benefit on Quint, arising from his preventing Hooper from rescuing him?

66 [1997] QB 1004 (CA).

67 See Nicholas McBride and Roderick Bagshaw, *Tort Law* (6th edn Pearson, London 2018) 213–217, cited in *Tindall* at [2024] UKSC 33 [50]ff.

68 [1997] 3 All ER 897 (QB).

'A SPECIAL LEVEL OF CONTROL'

KEY LEARNING POINT

A duty to confer a benefit can arise where the defendant has 'a special level of control' over the source of danger.

A duty to protect the claimant, or to confer a benefit may arise where the defendant has a special level of control over a potential source of danger or the persons who cause the harm to the claimant.

In the case of *Haynes v Harwood*,[69] the defendant had left his two-horse van unattended in the street while he made a delivery. A boy threw a stone at the horses, which caused them to bolt, and the claimant was injured while trying to stop the horses. The case was used by Lord Goff, in *Smith v Littlewoods Organisation*,[70] as an example of a duty to protect from damage caused by a third party where the defendant caused or permitted the potential danger. Alternatively, as the source of the danger – the horse – was under the control of the defendant, it can be viewed as a case where the defendant had a special level of control over the danger, under the Tofaris and Steel categorisation approved by the Supreme Court in *Robinson v Chief Constable of West Yorkshire Police*[71] and other cases.

Home Office v Dorset Yacht[72] concerned a group of young offenders who had been taken to Brownsea Island for a trip, under the care of prison officers working for the defendant. The boys absconded during the night and damaged a boat belonging to the claimant while trying to escape to the mainland. It was held that there was a 'special relationship' between the defendant and the boys, who were the primary cause of the damage: the young offenders were, or should have been, under the control of the prison officers. And in *Carmarthenshire County Council v Lewis*,[73] the council were liable for the acts of a small child who wandered away from a school into the road, where a lorry driver was killed when he swerved to avoid the child, as the school was in control of the child.

The same principle was seen in *Attorney General of the British Virgin Islands v Hartwell*.[74] In this case, the person who caused the damage was a police officer who was stalking a former partner. He had, without authority, taken a firearm from the police station and set off to look for her. Finding her with another man, he shot at her and the other man, wounding the claimant, a bystander. The Privy Council found that the government, as the police officer's employer, was not vicariously liable: the police officer was not acting in the course of his employment.[75] However, the government was liable on its own account. In allowing a person

69 [1935] 1 KB 146 (KB).
70 [1987] AC 241 (HL), 272–273.
71 [2018] UKSC 4, [2018] AC 736.
72 [1970] AC 1004 (HL).
73 [1955] AC 549 (HL).
74 [2004] UKPC 12, [2004] 1 WLR 1273.
75 See Chapter 10. This case might be compared with *Bernard v Attorney General* [2004] UKPC 47, considered in the same year by the Privy Council: this was another police shooting, in which the employer was vicariously liable.

access to firearms, the government had caused a danger, and thereby came under a duty to ensure that the person was suitable to be entrusted with them.

These cases show that, where the defendant has control of a potential danger, such as an untended horse or a firearm,[76] the defendant may have a duty to protect those who may be foreseeably harmed by the danger.

THE 'STATUS' OF THE DEFENDANT

The final circumstances, in the Tofaris and Steel classification, is where the defendant's 'status' creates an obligation to confer a benefit. In particular, the authors identify the police as having a special status, arising from the legal powers conferred on police constables and the public resources provided to police forces. This should, in their view, impose a duty to confer a benefit on members of the public by rescuing them or protecting them from harm.

However, in the case of *Michael v Chief Constable of South Wales Police*,[77] the Supreme Court did consider Tofaris and Steel's arguments[78] but did not accept them. In *Robinson v Chief Constable of West Yorkshire*,[79] the Supreme Court again considered the Tofaris and Steel arguments. While the Tofaris and Steel classification of the circumstances in which a person may be under a duty to rescue or protect a person from danger caused by an external factor was approved, the Supreme Court emphasised that public authorities, including the police, are in principle subject to the same duties of care as any other person or body.[80] In other words, their status as public bodies exercising statutory powers and in receipt of public funds was not capable, in itself, of creating a duty to confer a benefit on members of the public.

The public authority, which has been held to have a duty to protect members of the public, and is arguably based on their status as a provider of health services, is the National Health Service. This is discussed in more depth in Chapter 8.

ANALYSING THE LAW

The courts have been firm in denying that there is a general duty to rescue, warn, or protect people from injury and damage, even when a simple act might have prevented serious harm. Other jurisdictions do impose positive duties on members of the public, and on others, such as the emergency services, to rescue, warn, and protect. For example, the law of France requires a person to assist persons in danger, with criminal

76 See also *Burfitt v A and E Kille* [1939] 2 KB 743 (KB), in which a shopkeeper was liable for the injury caused by a blank firing pistol, which he had sold to a 12-year-old boy.

77 [2015] UKSC 2, [2015] AC 1732.

78 Although the Tofaris and Steel article cited above was not published until 2016, after the judgment in Michael, an earlier research paper, which included the principal arguments, was cited to the court and was referred to by Lord Kerr and by Lady Hale, who both dissented from the majority.

79 [2018] UKSC 4, [2018] AC 736.

80 Ibid, [31]ff (Lord Reed).

sanctions for those who fail in this duty. In the United States, health professionals may be under a duty to warn non-patients of any matters that affect their health or safety.

In the case of *Stovin v Wise* [1996] AC 923 (HL), Lord Hoffman outlined what he described as the 'why pick on me?' argument (p. 944). Where a person is in danger, there may be a large number of people who might be able to do something. But why should one be liable rather than another?

Are you convinced by this argument? Shouldn't people have a duty to take reasonable steps to help or protect anyone who they can see is in danger?

7.5 CONCLUSION

The law has generally maintained a firm line in denying liability where a person might have rescued another already in danger or protected a person from harm caused by third parties, natural events, or their own actions. However, there are exceptions, of which the most common are where the defendant assumed responsibility for the claimant's well-being and where the defendant had control over the source of the injury or damage to the claimant.

POINTS TO REVIEW

- There is no general duty to confer a benefit on a claimant by rescuing or protecting him or her from harm caused by a third party, natural event, or that person's own acts, unless there is a prior duty of care whose scope includes such a duty, other than in specific circumstances.
- A duty to intervene to rescue or protect may arise if the defendant has assumed responsibility for the claimant.
- A duty to rescue or protect may arise where the defendant has a special level of control over the source of the harm.
- A duty to rescue or protect may arise where the defendant has prevented another person from rescuing or protecting the claimant and the defendant is, or should be, aware that their actions have had that effect.
- A duty to rescue or protect the claimant may arise from the status of the defendant, although this does not mean that there is a general duty on public authorities to rescue or protect.

TAKING IT FURTHER

Nolan, D. 'Assumption of Responsibility: Four Questions' (2019) 72(1) Current Legal Problems 123

A discussion of the assumption of responsibility doctrine in the context of liability for failure to confer a benefit which identifies and discusses some of the issues around the way in which courts have used this concept and how it is defined.

Tofaris, S. and Steel, S. 'Negligence Liability for Omissions and the Police' (2016) 75(1) Cambridge Law Journal 128–157

Sets out the circumstances in which a person will have a duty to rescue or protect another person from harm and argues that the particular status of the police should make them liable to protect victims of crime in particular circumstances.

Williams, K. 'Medical Samaritans: Is There a Duty to Treat?' (2001) 21(3) Oxford J Legal Studies 393–413

Argues that doctors should have a duty to rescue where they are aware of a nearby person in need of urgent attention. Analyses the Australian case of *Lowns v Woods*, in which a doctor was held liable when he refused to go to the aid of a nearby child who had suffered an epileptic seizure.

8

CHAPTER 8
NEGLIGENCE: PUBLIC AUTHORITIES

This chapter considers the liability of public authorities for harm suffered by members of the public, which was either caused by or might have been prevented by the public authority.

8.1 INTRODUCTION

A public authority is a body, funded by the government and usually part of central or local government, which provides a service to members of the public, in the exercise of a statutory duty to provide that service. Public authorities are also granted powers to enable them to carry out their duty. They include the emergency services, including the police, fire service, ambulance service and the coastguard, services managed by central government, such as the prison service and the NHS, and local authorities, who provide services such as education, social services, social housing, and maintenance of roads.[1]

AS YOU READ

- Understand the different types of claim that can be made against public authorities.
- Understand the liability of public authorities for breaches of statutory duty.
- Understand when a public authority will owe a duty of care in negligence.
- Understand when public authorities will be liable for failing to protect a person's human rights.
- Understand the scope of the duty of care owed by public authorities to the general public and to people using their services.

The question is whether a public authority should be liable to any member of the public if he or she suffers damage caused by, or which might have been prevented by, a public authority.

1 Duties to provide local services, such as education, social services, highways, housing, etc are usually conferred by statute on to 'the local education authority', 'local social services authority', etc: the authority in question will be the local council responsible for that function in that area. So, for example, the local education authority in the county of Essex is Essex County Council; the local planning authority in Manchester is Manchester City Council.

DOI: 10.4324/9781003480051-08

For example, the police have a duty to investigate crime. If they carry out this duty negligently and fail to catch a particular offender, then it is foreseeable that the offender will carry out more crimes. If a burglar is still able to commit crimes because the police have negligently failed to arrest him or her, should any person who is burgled be able to sue the police?

The extent of public authority liability has been regularly considered by the House of Lords and the Supreme Court. The case of *Robinson v Chief Constable of West Yorkshire Police*[2] and subsequent cases have brought some clarity to this area of law by confirming the principle that a public authority's liability in negligence is, generally, the same as a private individual: they are liable for directly caused harm and to those to whom they owe a pre-existing duty of care, but are under no general obligation to confer a benefit on a claimant by rescuing or protecting him or her from harm caused by a third party or external factor.[3]

8.2 TYPES OF CLAIM

There are three potential claims that a claimant can make against a public authority. The first two are common law torts, and the third is a claim under the Human Rights Act 1998:

- breach of statutory duty;
- common law negligence;
- breach of human rights.

These are separate causes of action, with different criteria. In English law,[4] there is nothing to prevent a claimant from making claims in all three on the same facts:[5] an act of a public authority can simultaneously be a breach of statutory duty, common law negligence, and an interference with the claimant's human rights.

8.3 BREACH OF STATUTORY DUTY

If a duty is imposed on a public authority by statute, and the authority fails to carry out the duty, the authority has acted unlawfully. And if the breach causes harm to a member of the

2 [2018] UKSC 4, [2018] AC 736.

3 *Robinson v Chief Constable of West Yorkshire Police* [2018] UKSC 4, [2018] AC 736 [69] (Lord Reed); *N v Poole Borough Council* [2019] UKSC 25, [2020] AC 780 [64]–[65] (Lord Reed); *HXA v Surrey County Council* [2023] UKSC 52, [2024] 1 WLR 335 [48]ff, [87] (Lord Burrows and Lord Stephens); *Tindall v Chief Constable of Thames Valley Police* [2024] UKSC 33 [1] (Lord Leggatt and Lord Burrows).

4 This is not the case in other jurisdictions, such as France, where the claimant must decide which cause of action to pursue.

5 See, for example, *Michael v Chief Constable of South Wales Police* [2015] UKSC 2, [2015] AC 1732, in which the negligence claim was struck out, but the human rights claim was allowed to proceed.

public, it might seem reasonable that the person should be able to claim compensation from the public authority.

> KEY LEARNING POINTS
>
> - Breach of statutory duty is a separate tort to negligence, although a claim in negligence will often arise on the same facts.
> - Breach of statutory duty will not give rise to a right to compensation, unless the claimant can show that it was Parliament's intention to create such a right.

As an example, a local fire and rescue authority has a statutory duty to provide a water supply for fighting fires.[6] In *Church of Jesus Christ of Latter-Day Saints v West Yorkshire Fire and Civil Defence Authority*,[7] the claimant sued the local authority when there was no water available to tackle a fire in its property. The claim was not successful: the statutory duty did not create a right to compensation for anyone damaged by a breach of the duty.[8]

As well as duties, public authorities have the powers necessary for them to be able to carry out those duties: for example, local social services authorities have the duty to protect children, and to carry out that duty, they can apply to court for orders to assist them in the duty, such as an order to permit the child to be assessed by a doctor or social worker.[9]

A number of House of Lords cases, including *X (minors) v Bedfordshire County Council*,[10] *Phelps v Hillingdon London Borough Council*,[11] and *Stovin v Wise*,[12] have considered the liability of public authorities when carrying out their statutory duties and exercising their powers. A number of principles have been established:

- A claim can be made if damage is caused by a public authority's breach of statutory duty, but the burden is on the claimant to show that Parliament intended that he or she should have a right to sue the public authority for the damage caused.
- There is no tort, equivalent to breach of statutory duty, of failing to exercise or negligently exercising a statutory power.
- Policy decisions made under statutory powers are not justiciable and cannot give rise to a claim in negligence.
- A claim in common law negligence may be brought in respect of the way in which a duty has been performed or a power has been exercised, on the usual principles of negligence.

6 Fire and Rescue Services Act 2004 s.38(1) (re-enacting the Fire Services Act 1947 s.13).

7 *Church of Jesus Christ of Latter-Day Saints (Great Britain) v West Yorkshire Fire and Civil Defence Authority* (reported as *Capital & Counties v Hampshire County Council*) [1997] QB 1004 (CA).

8 *X (minors) v Bedfordshire County Council* [1995] 2 AC 633 (HL) 730–731 (Lord Browne-Wilkinson).

9 The Children Act 1989 s.43.

10 [1995] 2 AC 633 (HL).

11 [2001] 2 AC 619 (HL).

12 [1996] AC 923 (HL).

To succeed in a claim for breach of statutory duty, the claimant must show that Parliament intended, when imposing the duty on the public authority, to create a right for him or her to be compensated for any damage caused by a breach of the duty.[13]

In determining whether a statutory duty creates a right to sue for damages caused by its breach, the court will consider what the purpose of the act was: if the aim was to protect a specific and limited class of members of the public, then it is more likely that the right to sue will be found. On the other hand, if the act is for the benefit of the public as a whole, then it is less likely that a right to sue for damages will apply.[14]

Applying these principles, the courts have found that industrial health and safety legislation is intended to protect workers, so Parliament intended that those affected should be able to claim for breach of statutory duty.[15] Other than in health and safety legislation, the courts have found in most cases that the statutory duty does not create a right to sue the authority for breach.

8.4 FAILURE TO EXERCISE A POWER

Where the statute gives powers to the authority, which might have been, but were not, exercised to protect the claimant from damage from an external cause, there is no specific tort of failure to exercise a statutory power. In *Stovin v Wise*,[16] for example, the local highway authority had the power to remove hazards to road users, such as visual obstructions, from land next to a road.[17] The House of Lords held that no claim for failure to exercise a power could arise, unless the failure to exercise the power was irrational and there were exceptional circumstances which gave rise to a duty of care to the claimant.

As a general rule, a failure to exercise a power is a failure to confer a benefit, and liability for such failures will only arise if the defendant has a duty to rescue or protect the claimant from harm caused by a third party or natural event.[18] Public authorities are, in principle, liable on the same basis as private individuals[19] and no duty will arise, other than under the established circumstances, such as assumption of responsibility.[20]

13 *X (minors) v Bedfordshire County Council* [1995] 2 AC 633 (HL).

14 Ibid, 732 (Lord Browne-Wilkinson).

15 *Groves v Lord Wimborne* [1898] 2 QB 402 (CA). Note that the extent of civil liability may be expressly provided for under health and safety legislation: see Health and Safety at Work Act 1974 s.47.

16 [1996] AC 923 (HL).

17 Highways Act 1980 s.154.

18 See Chapter 7.

19 *Robinson v Chief Constable of West Yorkshire Police* [2018] UKSC 4, [2018] AC 736, [33]–[35] (Lord Reed).

20 See Chapter 7 for the circumstances in which a duty to confer a benefit will arise.

8.5 POLICY DECISIONS

Some decisions made by public authorities are regarded as policy decisions, which are based on factors such as the public authority's strategic aims and management of resources. Examples include a decision by a police force to prioritise the investigation of knife crime over burglaries, a decision by an NHS Clinical Commissioning Group not to make a specific drug available to NHS patients in their area, or the example given in *X (minors)*, a decision by a local education authority to close a school.[21] Members of the public who are affected by these decisions – such as the householders whose homes are burgled or the patients denied the drug that could have cured them – might reasonably blame the local authority for the harm caused. However, decisions taken at this level cannot give rise to a claim in tort. Where the public authority has been given the power to make policy decisions, as long as it exercises that power lawfully, there is no remedy for any person affected by the decision. The decision may be challenged and reversed by judicial review proceedings,[22] but those proceedings do not give rise to a claim in damages for the person affected.

8.6 CLAIMS IN NEGLIGENCE

If there is no claim for breach of statutory duty, then the claimant must rely upon a common law claim in negligence. As with any claim in negligence, the first issue that has to be considered is whether the defendant owed a duty of care to the claimant. If there is no duty of care, the claim fails at the first hurdle and the defendant, whether a public authority or a private person, is not liable for the damage suffered by the claimant.

KEY LEARNING POINT

Claims against public authorities fall into four main categories, depending on the activity of the authority and its relationship with the claimant:

- where a prior relationship between the authority and the claimant arises from the authority carrying out its statutory functions;
- where a prior relationship between the authority and the claimant arises from the authority carrying out activities ancillary to its functions;
- where there is no prior relationship between the authority and the claimant, but damage is directly caused by an act or omission of the authority;
- where there is no prior relationship and the authority fails to rescue, warn, or protect the claimant from damage caused by a natural event or third party.

21 *X (minors) v Bedfordshire County Council* [1995] 2 AC 633 (HL) 735 (Lord Browne-Wilkinson).

22 See, for example, *R v Cambridge Health Authority, ex p B* [1995] 1 WLR 898 (CA).

The first category, of claimants with a prior relationship with the public authority arising from the authority carrying out its functions, includes NHS patients, clients of social services, users of highways maintained by the authority, and tenants of publicly owned housing. It also includes people in the care or custody of a public authority, including prisoners,[23] people detained under the Mental Health Act,[24] children at schools managed by the local authority,[25] people in residential care, and looked-after children.[26] In these cases, there will, in many cases, be a duty of care owed to the person concerned, the scope of which is determined by the nature of the relationship. For example, where the local authority is responsible for providing education, it owes a duty of care to the children at its schools.[27]

The second category is where there is a relationship arising from the public authority carrying out activities incidental to its public functions. Like other organisations, public authorities employ people and occupy land: in such cases, the public authority is liable in the same way as any other employer to their employees or occupier of land to visitors. Public authority employees, acting in the course of their employment, carry out such activities as driving vehicles, and the employees owe the usual duty of care to other road users. As the employer, the authority will be vicariously liable for any damage caused by their employees' negligence.[28] So, if a person driving a vehicle, such as a fire engine,[29] on behalf of a public authority negligently causes injury to another road user, the public authority will be vicariously liable.

The third category is those who are directly harmed by the acts of a public authority, but where there is no prior relationship. In these cases, a duty will arise on conventional principles of negligence: either on the basis of precedent or, in the absence of precedent, on the incremental development of the law on the basis of existing duties.[30] In claims for directly caused personal injury[31] and property damage,[32] it is likely that there will be a duty of care.

The fourth category is where there is no prior relationship between the claimant and the public authority, and the public authority has failed to confer a benefit by rescuing or protecting a person from self-inflicted harm or harm caused by an external cause, such as a natural event or the acts of a third party, which may be criminal or negligent. Claims under this heading include claims brought by the families of murder victims[33] and owners of premises damaged by fire.[34] As discussed in Chapter 7, duties to confer a benefit will only arise

23 *Reeves v Commissioner of Police of the Metropolis* [2000] 1 AC 360 (HL).

24 *Rabone v Pennine Care NHS Foundation Trust* [2012] UKSC 2, [2012] 2 AC 72.

25 *Woodland v Essex County Council* [2013] UKSC 66, [2014] AC 537.

26 *Barrett v Enfield London Borough Council* [2001] 2 AC 550 (HL).

27 *Woodland v Essex County Council* [2013] UKSC 66, [2014] AC 537.

28 Police constables are office holders, rather than employees. However, the Police Act 1996 s.88 provides that the Chief Constable for a police area is liable for wrongful acts of constables under his or her direction.

29 See, for example, *Purdue v Devon Fire and Rescue Service* [2002] EWCA Civ 1538.

30 See Chapter 2.

31 *Robinson v Chief Constable of West Yorkshire Police* [2018] UKSC 4, [2018] AC 736.

32 *Rigby v Chief Constable of Northamptonshire* [1985] 1 WLR 1242 (QB).

33 *Hill v Chief Constable of West Yorkshire Police* [1989] AC 53 (HL); *Michael v Chief Constable of South Wales Police* [2015] UKSC 2, [2015] AC 1732.

34 *Capital & Counties plc v Hampshire County Council* [1997] QB 1004 (CA).

in limited circumstances, and, in principle, the same approach is applied to public authorities as to private individuals.[35] It is this category which has been responsible for much of the litigation. In addition, the principles developed in this category have been misapplied to other categories of claim,[36] which had caused some confusion in the law.

8.7 TYPES OF CLAIM

LIABILITY OF PUBLIC AUTHORITIES TO 'SERVICE USERS'

As outlined above, the first category to consider is where there is a prior relationship between the claimant and the public authority, which arises from the public authority carrying out its functions. Public authorities carry out a huge range of activities, from making laws to providing street lighting. Some, such as the prison service and the NHS, are run by central government. Others, such as schools and social services, are run by local authorities. Some of these services, such as schools and the NHS, are provided directly to specific members of the public, who can be regarded as 'service users': this term covers a wide range of potential claimants, including prisoners, NHS patients, road users, social services clients, looked-after children, school pupils, tenants of publicly provided housing, and residents in care.

Where the claimant is a user of a service provided by a public authority, there will be proximity between the claimant and the authority. This will, in many circumstances, mean that the public authority has a duty to take reasonable care to prevent the claimant from suffering foreseeable harm. So schools have a duty to their pupils to protect them from physical injury,[37] hospitals have a duty to their patients,[38] police to people in their custody,[39] prisons to prisoners,[40] and local authorities have a duty to children in their care.[41]

Other relationships may also give rise to a duty of care: in *Swinney v Chief Constable of Northumbria Police*,[42] the claimant had provided information to the police about the identity of the driver of a vehicle which had killed a police officer. The police negligently allowed the informant's name and address to fall into the hands of the suspect. The Court of Appeal refused to strike out the claim.[43]

35 *Robinson v Chief Constable of West Yorkshire Police* [2018] UKSC 4, [2018] AC 736 [34]–[35], *Tindall and another v Chief Constable of Thames Valley Police* [2024] UKSC 33 [1].

36 In, for example, the Court of Appeal judgment in *Robinson v Chief Constable of West Yorkshire Police* [2014] EWCA Civ 15.

37 *Woodland v Essex County Council* [2013] UKSC 66, [2014] AC 537.

38 *Cassidy v Ministry of Health* [1951] 2 KB 343 (CA).

39 *Reeves v Metropolitan Police Commissioner* [2000] 1 AC 360 (HL).

40 *Ellis v Home Office* [1953] 2 QB 135 (CA).

41 *Barrett v Enfield London Borough Council* [2001] 2 AC 550 (HL); *Surtees v Kingston-upon-Thames Borough Council* [1991] 2 FLR 559 (CA).

42 [1997] QB 464 (CA).

43 See also *An Informer v A Chief Constable* [2012] EWCA Civ 197, [2013] QB 579.

Physical injury is, of course, not the only sort of damage that service users may suffer: they may suffer from psychiatric injury or economic loss,[44] in which case the principles developed for those types of claim would normally apply.

The exact nature and scope of the duty owed to persons with a prior relationship with the public authority will depend upon the nature of the relationship. Where the person is in the custody or under the control of a public authority, there will be a duty to take reasonable care to protect the person from personal injury, including that caused by other persons or by self-inflicted injury or suicide if it is foreseeable.[45] The authority may be liable for releasing a person from custody or not taking reasonable care to keep him or her in custody, if he or she is in a vulnerable state and likely to suffer harm or to harm him- or herself, whether deliberately or accidentally.[46]

Other 'service users' may have a more remote relationship, in which case the scope of the duty is more limited. For example, the police owe no specific duty to victims, suspects, or witnesses of crime when interviewing them as part of a criminal investigation,[47] other than the usual duty owed to anyone, not directly to cause personal injury. If a suspect is taken into custody, a more extensive duty of care arises, which includes a duty to take reasonable care to protect the suspect from foreseeable harm.[48] Likewise, local social services authorities owe a more extensive duty to looked-after children than they do to children to whom they are providing support at home, whom they do not have a duty to rescue or protect from harm.[49]

NON-DELEGABLE DUTIES

In some circumstances, a public authority will owe a 'non-delegable' duty to persons who are under their care or control. This is a duty which continues when the person is in the custody of, or being looked after by, another person or organisation. The issue was considered by the Supreme Court in the case of *Woodland v Essex County Council*.[50] In this case, a child got into difficulties during a swimming lesson and suffered a serious brain injury, caused by oxygen starvation. The swimming lesson was being run by an independent provider, but the claimant sued the local education authority, arguing that the duty to protect pupils from harm could not be delegated to any other person. The Supreme Court agreed. The duty of a school to its pupils was non-delegable and continued even when the child was being supervised by other people. There were five factors which supported this conclusion: the claimant was a child or vulnerable

44 In *Lambert v West Devon Borough Council* (1997) 96 LGR 45 (QB), a council employee was held liable for the loss caused by negligent misstatement relating to planning permission.

45 *Savage v South Essex Partnership NHS Trust* [2008] UKHL 74, [2009] AC 681.

46 *Rabone v Pennine Care NHS Trust* [2012] UKSC 2, [2012] 2 AC 72: this was a human rights claim, but the defendant accepted liability in negligence.

47 *Brooks v Commissioner of Police of the Metropolis* [2005] UKHL 24, [2005] 1 WLR 1495; *Vellino v Chief Constable of Greater Manchester* [2001] EWCA Civ 1249, [2002] 1 WLR 218.

48 *Reeves v Commissioner of Police of the Metropolis* [2000] 1 AC 360 (HL). The police, as occupiers of the police station, will also owe an occupier's duty of care to anyone who is on the premises, including witnesses, etc.

49 *X (Minors) v Bedfordshire County Council* [1995] 2 AC 633 (HL); *Barrett v Enfield London Borough Council* [2001] 2 AC 550 (HL); *HXA v Surrey County Council* [2023] UKSC 52, [2024] 3 All ER 341.

50 [2013] UKSC 66, [2014] AC 537.

person; there was a prior relationship, in which the claimant was in the care or custody of the defendant; the claimant had no control over how the defendant performed their duties; the delegated person was performing some function which was integral to the defendant's role and was exercising care or control over the claimant; and the delegated person was negligent in his or her performance of the very function which had been delegated to him or her.

The same issue arose in a more recent Supreme Court case, *Armes v Nottinghamshire County Council*.[51] In this case, a child had been taken into care and placed with foster parents, who abused the child. The child sued the local social services authority, claiming that the duty of the authority to looked-after children was non-delegable, in the same way as the duty of schools to their pupils. The Supreme Court held that the duty of local social services authorities to protect looked-after children was not a non-delegable duty. However, the relationship between the authority and the foster parents, although not an employer–employee relationship, was sufficiently akin to an employment relationship as to make the authority vicariously liable for the abuse.[52]

Other non-delegable duties include the duty of hospitals to patients, and of employers to employees. Where the service being provided is one that is also provided by private sector providers, there will be no difference, in principle, between the public sector provider's liability and the private sector provider's liability. There is no difference between the liability of a publicly run school to its pupils and the liability of a private school, or between the liability of NHS doctors and private healthcare providers.

LIABILITY OF PUBLIC AUTHORITIES FOR ANCILLARY ACTIVITIES

Where there is a prior relationship between the claimant and the public authority, which arises not from the authority carrying out its core functions, but from ancillary activities, there is no difference, either in principle or in practice, between the duty owed by the public authority and any other defendant. This is true whether the ancillary activity is necessary to the carrying out of the function or incidental to it.

The police operate motor vehicles, which may be used in a way that is necessary for their core function of preventing and investigating crime or in a way that is incidental. A police car may be travelling in pursuit of another vehicle for the purpose of arresting the driver, or it may be being driven to a garage for maintenance. In either case, the driver owes other road users a duty of care. In *McLeod v Commissioner of Police of the Metropolis*,[53] for example, a cyclist was injured by a police car which was responding to an emergency. There was no question that, as a road user, the police driver owed the claimant, as another road user, a duty to take reasonable care not to cause personal injury. The law does make allowance for emergency situations, but this is an issue considered at the breach stage of negligence.[54]

51 [2017] UKSC 60, [2018] AC 355.

52 See Chapter 10 for a discussion of the circumstances where a person will be vicariously liable on the basis of a relationship 'akin to employment'.

53 [2015] EWCA Civ 688.

54 *Watt v Hertfordshire County Council* [1954] 1 WLR 835 (CA). See Chapter 3.

The commonest circumstances in which the prior relationship arises is when the public authority is occupying land and employing people. In such cases, the public authority's liability is the standard duty of an occupier to visitors[55] and of a landowner to neighbouring landowners,[56] and the standard liability of an employer to an employee.[57] The other main circumstance is where a public authority's employee is driving a vehicle on behalf of the authority. In these circumstances, the employee is liable as a road user, and the authority is vicariously liable on the same basis as any other employer.[58]

LIABILITY OF PUBLIC AUTHORITIES FOR DIRECTLY CAUSED HARM

Where there is no prior relationship between the authority and the claimant, liability in negligence for directly caused harm will arise on the established principles of negligence. So, if a police officer injures a member of the public while making an arrest, the police officer is liable, on the neighbour principle, for any physical injury caused.

Where the harm caused is personal injury or property damage, there will usually be a duty of care. In *Robinson v Chief Constable of West Yorkshire Police*,[59] the injury to the claimant was caused directly by the acts of the police officers, who cannoned into her while arresting a suspected drug dealer; in *Knightley v Johns*,[60] the claimant police officer was injured when ordered by a police inspector to ride his motorcycle down a road tunnel against the flow of traffic. In both cases, the physical injury was directly caused by the negligence of the public authority, so the authority was liable.

Other examples of the police being liable for directly caused harm were in the claims arising from the Hillsborough disaster, in which 96 people were killed by crushing at a football match. The principal cause of the disaster was the decision of the police officer in charge of controlling the crowd to allow a large number of people to enter the ground through an exit gate.[61]

In the case of *Rigby v Chief Constable of Northamptonshire*,[62] the police fired a CS canister into a shop when attempting to arrest a suspect. The canister started a fire, which caused extensive damage to the shop and its contents. In this case, the primary cause of the fire was the firing of the CS canister, so the harm was caused directly by the police, who were held to be liable in negligence for failing to take reasonable care in the circumstances.

LIABILITY OF PUBLIC AUTHORITIES FOR 'OMISSIONS'

As discussed in Chapter 7, a defendant is only liable for 'pure omissions' or failures to confer a benefit in specific circumstances. In other words, a duty to rescue or protect a person from

55 *Jolley v Sutton London Borough Council* [2000] 1 WLR 1082 (HL).

56 *Delaware Mansions v Westminster County Council* [2001] UKHL 55, [2002] 1 AC 321.

57 *Watt v Hertfordshire County Council* [1954] 1 WLR 835 (CA).

58 See Chapter 10 for vicarious liability.

59 [2018] UKSC 4, [2018] AC 736.

60 [1982] 1 WLR 349 (CA).

61 The police accepted liability in negligence for the people who were killed or physically injured in the disaster: see *Alcock v Chief Constable of South Yorkshire Police* [1992] 1 AC 310 (HL) 392 (Lord Keith).

62 [1985] 1 WLR 1242 (QB).

harm caused by a third party or natural event will only arise in particular circumstances: where there is a prior relationship between claimant and defendant, where the defendant has assumed responsibility for the claimant, where the defendant has done something to prevent another person from rescuing or protecting the claimant, where the defendant has a special level of control over the source of the harm and where the defendant's status creates a duty to protect the claimant.[63] These principles apply to all defendants, including public authorities.[64]

Many of the omission cases concern the liability of public authorities. As discussed above, if there is a prior relationship between the claimant and defendant, then the question is whether the failure to rescue, warn, or protect was within the scope of the duty of care arising from the relationship.

In cases where the claimant is a member of the general public with nothing to distinguish him or her from any other member of the public, there is no prior relationship with the public authority, nor will the authority have assumed responsibility for the claimant. There will be no proximity between claimant and defendant, and it was on this ground that the House of Lords held that the police do not owe a duty to take reasonable care to protect members of the public by catching criminals.[65] In these cases, it will also be difficult, if not impossible, to argue that the public authority has assumed responsibility for the claimant, as a member of the public.

Public authorities have been held liable in negligence where they had a special level of control over the source of danger: for example, in *Dorset Yacht v Home Office*,[66] the House of Lords referred to the 'special relation' between the prison officers and the young offenders who had damaged the claimant's yacht, arising from the control that the defendants exercised over the young offenders.[67] Likewise in *Attorney General of the British Virgin Islands v Hartwell*,[68] the Government of the British Virgin Islands had control over the weapon used by an off-duty police officer to shoot a tourist.

Public authorities may also be liable on the 'interference principle'. This is one of the Tofaris and Steel categories[69] where a person is liable for failing to confer a benefit, where that person 'has done something which prevents another from protecting B from that danger'.[70] The

63 S. Tofaris and S. Steel, 'Negligence Liability for Omissions and the Police' (2016) 75 CLJ 128. See also *Robinson v Chief Constable of West Yorkshire Police* [2018] UKSC 4, [2018] AC 736 [34] (Lord Reed).

64 'These general principles have been worked out for the most part in cases involving private litigants, but they are equally applicable where [the defendant] is a public body'. *Michael v Chief Constable of South Wales Police* [2015] UKSC 2, [2015] AC 1732, [101] (Lord Toulson). See also *Stovin v Wise* [1996] AC 923 (HL) 946 (Lord Hoffmann).

65 *Hill v Chief Constable of West Yorkshire Police* [1989] AC 53 (HL). See section 8.8.

66 [1970] AC 1004 (HL).

67 Ibid, 1039 (Lord Morris).

68 [2004] UKPC 12, [2004] 1 WLR 1273.

69 See Chapter 7.

70 S. Tofaris and S. Steel, 'Negligence Liability for Omissions and the Police' (2016) 75 CLJ 128, cited in *Tindall v Chief Constable of Thames Valley Police* [2024] UKSC 33 [42] (Lord Leggatt and Lord Burrows).

application of this principle was recently explained by the Supreme Court in *Tindall v Chief Constable of Thames Valley Police*,[71] which held that

> if A knows or ought to know that B is in need of help to avoid some harm, and A knows or ought to know that he has done something to put off or prevent someone else helping B, then A will owe B a duty to take reasonable steps to give B the help she needs.[72]

On this basis, the Supreme Court overruled the case of *OLL v Secretary of State for Transport*,[73] in which the coastguard had misdirected a Royal Navy helicopter carrying out a search and rescue mission. In that case, the coastguard knew that the missing person were in need of help and their act, by directing the Royal Navy helicopter to search in the wrong area, had prevented the Royal Navy from rescuing the missing persons. In the original case, the High Court held, correctly, that the coastguard did not owe a duty to the missing persons. However, the High Court also held that the misdirection of the Royal Navy helicopter did not create a duty, and it is on this issue that the Supreme Court overruled *OLL*.[74]

In most cases the courts have found that the public authority does not owe a duty of care to members of the public who have been harmed by their failure to take action to rescue or protect them from harm caused by third parties or natural events, if there is no prior relationship between the claimant and the authority. This approach has been confirmed by the Supreme Court in *Robinson v Chief Constable of West Yorkshire Police*:[75] the liability of public authorities in negligence, where the authority has failed to confer a benefit by rescuing or protecting the claimant, is based on the same principles as private individuals. If the claim does not fall within one of the established exceptions from the general principle, there will be no duty of care.

KEY CASES

HXA v Surrey County Council [2023] UKSC 52, [2024] 1 WLR 335 was a claim brought against social services authorities which had failed to protect children from harm caused by, in this case, their parents or their parents' partners. The issue of whether social services authorities have a duty to protect children and vulnerable adults from crime or abuse, whether within the family or from outside the home, had been considered by the House of Lords and Supreme Court previously. Both *X (Minors) v Bedfordshire County Council* [1995] 2 AC 633 and *N v Poole Borough Council* [2019] UKSC 25, [2020] AC 780 had held that the social services authority was not under a general duty to confer a benefit on its clients, even where it might have acted to protect the claimants from harm.

71 [2024] UKSC 33.

72 Ibid, [50] (Lord Leggatt and Lord Burrow) citing Nicholas McBride and Roderick Bagshaw, *Tort Law* (6th edn Pearson, London 2018) 213–217.

73 [1997] 3 All ER 897 (QB).

74 *Tindall v Chief Constable of Thames Valley Police* [2024] UKSC 33 [57] (Lord Leggatt and Lord Burrows).

75 [2018] UKSC 4, [2018] AC 736 [32]–[33] (Lord Reed).

As in previous cases, the Supreme Court held that social services authorities did not have a general duty to protect the children from harm, although such a duty could arise where the authority assumed responsibility for the children's well-being. In this case, however, although the social services authority was aware that the abuse was occurring and had, in one case, decided to start the process of taking the children into care, they had not assumed responsibility and did not owe a duty to confer a benefit on the children. The Supreme Court noted that the essential facts were indistinguishable from *N v Poole Borough Council*, where the Supreme Court had held that the social services authority being aware of and monitoring a situation did not amount to the provision of a service or benefit capable of giving rise to an assumption of responsibility (see [101]).

8.8 SPECIFIC DUTIES OF CARE

THE EMERGENCY SERVICES

The emergency services are the police, fire and rescue service, and the ambulance service. In addition, the coastguard is responsible for coordinating rescues at sea.

The police, fire and rescue services, and the coastguard do not have a duty to rescue, warn, or protect members of the general public from harm caused by criminals, other third parties, the claimant's own acts, or natural events. Where they do attend an emergency, they are under no obligation to rescue any people involved and do not owe a duty to the victims of the emergency. Their only duty is not to cause damage that would not otherwise have been caused or 'make matters worse'. So, in in *Michael v Chief Constable of South Wales Police*,[76] there was no duty to protect a woman whose former partner had said that he was coming to harm her. In *Alexandrou v Oxford*,[77] the police responded to a burglar alarm at the claimant's shop, but did not check the rear of the premises, where there had been a break-in. The court held that the police did not owe the claimant a duty to protect him from the loss caused by the burglary.

In the case of *Tindall v Thames Valley Police*,[78] the Supreme Court confirmed that this is the extent of the emergency services liability. In that case, the Supreme Court also held that, if the police did something to prevent another person from protecting the claimant, they would be liable under the 'interference principle' if they knew or should have known that their acts had that effect. This is an aspect of the duty of the police not to make things worse.[79]

76 [2015] UKSC 2, [2015] AC 1732.

77 [1993] 4 All ER 328 (CA).

78 [2024] UKSC 33.

79 See section 7.4 for a full discussion of the interference principle as explained by *Tindall*.

Likewise, the fire and rescue service is not obliged to attend a fire when called, and if they do attend, they are only liable if their actions create additional damage. In *Capital and Counties v Hampshire County Council*,[80] the fire and rescue service was liable in one case, where the fire officer in charge ordered the sprinkler system to be turned off, thus making the damage worse, but not in two other cases, where the fire and rescue service had not used reasonable care to protect the premises from fire damage.

KEY LEARNING POINTS

- The police, fire and rescue service, and the coastguard do not owe a duty to rescue members of the public from harm caused by another cause, such as criminal acts or natural causes.
- The ambulance service is part of the NHS and does owe a duty to patients in the same way as doctors and nurses. The duty arises when the ambulance service accepts a call.

The case of *OLL Ltd v Secretary of State for Transport*[81] involved the liability of the coastguard for rescuing people at sea. In that case, it was held that there was no duty to rescue the eight children and their teacher, who had got into difficulty when canoeing at sea. That part of the judgment remains correct: if the coastguard is the only party involved, then it is not liable for failing to rescue people at sea. However, the High Court also held that the coastguard was not liable on the grounds that it had prevented another party from rescuing the missing children and the teacher. This was overruled by the Supreme Court in *Tindall v Chief Constable of Thames Valley Police*, as discussed above and in section 7.4.

The ambulance service, however, does owe patients a duty to rescue them. In *Kent v Griffiths*,[82] the claimant suffered an asthma attack, and her doctor called for an ambulance, which did not arrive within a reasonable time. The Court of Appeal held that, when the ambulance service accepted the call, a relationship akin to a doctor–patient relationship arose, which meant that the ambulance service did owe the claimant a duty to take reasonable care.

ANALYSING THE LAW

In their paper, 'Negligence Liability for Omissions and the Police' (2016) 75 CLJ 128–157, Tofaris and Steel say that a duty to prevent harm from occurring to a claimant will arise when the defendant's 'status' creates an obligation to protect the claimant. The authors argue that the status of the police as the body responsible for protecting society from criminal activity, and the extensive powers and resources that they are

80 [1997] QB 1004 (CA).
81 [1997] 3 All ER 897 (QB).
82 [2001] QB 36 (CA).

granted to help them perform this duty, gives them a special status which means that they should be under a duty to take reasonable care to protect members of the public.

Do you agree? Should the police be liable for failing to rescue or protect members of the public, if they knew that the member of the public was at risk? What about other emergency services?

THE LIABILITY OF THE POLICE

As well as responding to emergencies, the police have a duty to keep the peace by investigating and preventing crime. However, they are not liable to members of the public from harm caused by their failure to carry out those duties. So, in *Hill v Chief Constable of West Yorkshire Police*,[83] the police owed no duty to protect the victims of a serial murderer, and in *Michael v Chief Constable of South Wales Police*,[84] there was no duty to protect a woman whose former partner had said that he was coming to harm her. In *Alexandrou v Oxford*,[85] the police responded to a burglar alarm at the claimant's shop, but did not check the rear of the premises, where there had been a break-in. The court held that the police did not owe the claimant a duty to protect him from the loss caused by the burglary.

In the case of *Hill*,[86] the House of Lords held that the police did not owe a duty of care to a member of the public who had been the final victim of a serial murderer or, more generally, a duty to protect members of the public from harm caused by the criminal acts of a third party other than in specific circumstances, such as an assumption of responsibility. That rule of law has never been doubted by the courts and was reaffirmed by the Supreme Court in the cases of *Michael v Chief Constable of South Wales Police*[87] and *Commissioner of Police of the Metropolis v DSD*.[88] In *Hill*, the rule was explained by lack of proximity between the victim and the police force, as there was no prior relationship between them. This conclusion was reinforced by policy considerations.

The rule of law set out in *Hill* has, however, been expressed by courts in wider and more general terms, as a form of immunity from civil liability conferred specifically upon the police when investigating crime.[89] Lord Neuberger, for example, stated that the rule was 'when investigating crime, the police owe no duty of care in tort to individual citizens'.[90] This statement of the law needs qualification to be a true statement of the rule set out in *Hill*, and some courts have been misled by wider statements of the rule. When *Robinson v Chief Constable*

83 [1989] AC 53 (HL).

84 [2015] UKSC 2, [2015] AC 1732.

85 [1993] 4 All ER 328 (CA).

86 [1989] AC 53 (HL).

87 [2015] UKSC 2, [2015] AC 1732.

88 [2018] UKSC 11, [2018] 2 WLR 895, [67] (Lord Kerr), [97] (Lord Neuberger), [130] (Lord Hughes).

89 It is, perhaps, unfortunate that Lord Keith referred to the police being 'immune from an action of this kind' in *Hill v Chief Constable of West Yorkshire Police* [1989] AC 53 (HL) 64.

90 *Commissioner of Police of the Metropolis v DSD* [2018] UKSC 11, [2018] 2 WLR 895, [97] (Lord Neuberger).

of West Yorkshire Police[91] was heard by the Court of Appeal, the court held that the police had 'immunity' from liability for harm caused by the police when they were investigating crime. As the claimant's injury was caused during the arrest of a suspected drug dealer, it was covered by the immunity, and the police were not liable under the Hill principle.[92]

The Supreme Court allowed an appeal in *Robinson* and clarified the nature and extent of the Hill principle. The police were, as a matter of principle, liable for their acts and omissions on the same basis as any private individual. That meant that they were under no duty to rescue or protect members of the public from harm caused by third parties or natural events, unless there were special circumstances, such as the assumption of responsibility.[93] However, the police were liable for any harm that they directly caused, whether while investigating crime or otherwise.

The police do owe a duty of care to prisoners being detained, which includes a duty to confer a benefit by protecting them from harm. There are other circumstances in which the police have a duty to confer a benefit on other persons with whom they have a prior relationship. So in *Reeves v Commissioner of Police of the Metropolis*,[94] the police did owe a duty to protect a vulnerable prisoner from suicide[95] and, in *An Informer v A Chief Constable*,[96] the police had assumed responsibility for a person providing confidential intelligence.

Woodcock v Chief Constable of Northamptonshire Police,[97] similarly to *Michael v Chief Constable of South Wales Police*,[98] concerned a woman who was attacked by a former partner. In *Woodcock*, there had been a series of incidents involving the former partner and the police, and they were aware of the risk. The judgment makes it clear that awareness of a risk to a particular member of the public is not sufficient to create an assumption of responsibility, even where the police had previously responded to the risk.[99] In this case, however, the police had taken further steps to protect the victim, including placing a police car outsider her house. In those circumstances, the High Court held that the police had assumed responsibility and were liable when they failed to confer a benefit on the claimant by warning her that her attacker had been seen close to her home.

THE NATIONAL HEALTH SERVICE

The NHS, as well as running the ambulance services, provides a comprehensive health service. While hospitals and doctors are not obliged to accept any person as a patient,[100] once a patient

91 [2014] EWCA Civ 15.

92 Ibid, [47] (Hallett LJ) and [65] (Arnold LJ).

93 [2018] UKSC 4, [2018] AC 736, [70] (Lord Reed).

94 [2000] 1 AC 360 (HL).

95 See also *Lukes v Kent and Medway NHS and Social Care Partnership Trust* [2024] EWHC 753 (KB) which accepted that, while the claimant was in police custody, the police had a duty to protect him from his own actions.

96 [2012] EWCA Civ 197, [2013] 2 WLR 694. See *also Swinney v Chief Constable of Northumbria Police Force* [1997] QB 464 (CA).

97 [2023] EWHC 1062 (KB), [2024] 1 All ER 157.

98 [2015] UKSC 2, [2015] AC 1732.

99 See [47], citing *Tindall v Chief Constable of Thames Valley* Police [2022] EWCA Civ 25, [2022] 4 All ER 372.

100 *Barnett v Chelsea and Kensington Hospital Management Committee* [1969] 1 QB 428 (QB), 435 (Nield J).

has been accepted for treatment, the hospital or doctor does owe a duty to take reasonable care to diagnose and treat the patient in accordance with recognised medical practice. The hospital also owes a duty to take reasonable care to protect patients from injuring themselves, either deliberately or by accident.[101]

Policy decisions, however, are not justiciable: if an NHS body decides, as a matter of policy, not to make a particular drug available as part of its role of managing resources, a patient affected by the decision cannot bring a claim in negligence.[102] There may be a public law claim, but courts will only overrule resource decisions made by health authorities on specific grounds, such as Wednesbury unreasonableness.

The NHS is not usually liable to members of the public where there is no doctor–patient relationship. A hospital or doctor is not liable, for example, if a patient is discharged while suffering from an infectious disease and harms members of his or her family by infecting them.[103] Nor is the NHS liable to a member of the public if it fails to detain a person with a mental disorder who later injures a member of the public.[104]

However, in the case of *Griffiths v Chief Constable of Suffolk Police*,[105] the court accepted, without coming to a firm conclusion, that there might be a duty of care to a detained mental patient's former partner, as the relationship between the former partner and the patient was capable of providing the necessary proximity and foreseeability, and the patient was under the control of the defendant, as were the young offenders in *Dorset Yacht v Home Office*.[106]

SCHOOLS AND LOCAL EDUCATION AUTHORITIES

Schools and teachers owe a non-delegable duty to take reasonable care for the health and safety of their pupils. The local education authority, as the employer, will be vicariously liable. Even where school activities are provided by an independent contractor, the duty is non-delegable and the school remains liable. In the case of *Woodland v Essex County Council*,[107] the local education authority was liable for the injury suffered by a child during a swimming lesson supervised by an independent provider.

Historically, teachers have been held to the same standard as a reasonable parent,[108] although this may be difficult when a teacher is responsible for a much larger group of children than any parent would be looking after. This includes a duty to protect children at school from

101 *Spearman v Royal United Bath Hospitals NHS Foundation Trust* [2017] EWHC 3027 (QB).

102 *R v Cambridge Health Authority, ex p B (a minor)* [1995] 1 WLR 898 (CA).

103 In *Evans v Mayor of Liverpool* [1906] 1 KB 160 (KB), the court did appear to accept that a doctor did owe such a duty. However, there is no support for such a duty in more recent case law.

104 *Palmer v Tees Health Authority* [1999] Lloyd's Rep. Med. 351 (CA).

105 [2018] EWHC 2538 (QB).

106 [1970] AC 1004 (HL).

107 [2013] UKSC 66, [2014] AC 537.

108 *Williams v Eady* (1893), 10 TLR 41 (QB) 42 (Lord Esher MR); *Rich v London County Council* [1953] 1 WLR 895 (CA) 900 (Singleton LJ).

harm caused by the child to him- or herself, as well as harm caused by other pupils. A teacher is obliged to take reasonable care, but courts have recognised the difficulty in supervising all pupils at all times in determining whether the school and its staff have acted reasonably.

Schools may also be liable for failing to provide a proper education, and teachers, like doctors and other professionals, owe a common law duty to exercise the skill and care of a reasonable teacher, as do specialists in education, such as educational psychologists.[109]

Local education authorities have also been held liable to third parties: in *Carmarthenshire County Council v Lewis*,[110] a lorry driver was killed when he swerved to avoid a 4-year-old child who had wandered into the road from the school he was attending. The school was held to be liable.

HIGHWAY AUTHORITIES

Highway authorities have a statutory duty to maintain the highway, which includes roads and pavements.[111] A breach of this duty will give rise to a claim, so highway authorities are liable to drivers and pedestrians in breach of statutory duty if the road surface is dangerous.[112] Personal injury claims may be made against the highway authority for trips caused by poorly maintained footpaths, as may claims by road users where an accident is caused by a poorly maintained road surface.[113]

Two House of Lords cases, *Stovin v Wise*[114] and *Gorringe v Calderdale Metropolitan Borough Council*,[115] considered the extent of the liability of the local highway authority for failing to ensure that a road was reasonably safe. In *Stovin*, the highway authority was aware of a bank of earth which blocked the view of drivers turning from a side road onto a main road and had asked the landowner for permission to enter the land to remove the bank, but nothing had been done at the time of the accident. The claimant was seriously injured when a car emerged from the side road. In *Gorringe*, the highway authority had not repainted a 'slow' sign on the road which had previously warned drivers of a dangerous crest and bend. The claimant was injured when she skidded on the bend.

In *Stovin*, the House of Lords held that the highway authority was not liable, either for breach of statutory duty or in negligence. There was no breach of the statutory duty under section 41 of the Highways Act 1980, as the accident was not caused by the state of the road surface. With regard to the negligence claim, the highway authority had not exercised its

109 *X (minors) v Bedfordshire County Council* [1995] 2 AC 633 (HL), 766 (Lord Browne-Wilkinson); *Phelps v London Borough of Hillingdon* [2001] 2 AC 619 (HL).

110 [1955] AC 549 (HL).

111 The Highways Act 1980 s.41.

112 *Goodes v East Sussex County Council* [2000] 1 WLR 1356 (HL).

113 *Thomas v Warwickshire County Council* [2011] EWHC 772 (QB). The injury must be caused by the road surface itself, as opposed to anything on the surface, such as snow or ice.

114 [1996] AC 923 (HL).

115 [2004] UKHL 15, [2004] 1 WLR 1057.

power to require the removal of the obstruction, but failure to exercise a statutory power would only create a common law duty of care in exceptional circumstances.[116]

In *Gorringe*, the failure to provide a warning sign was also held to be outside the scope of section 41. The claimant argued that section 39 of the Road Traffic Act 1988, which imposed a duty to provide warning signs, gave rise to a breach of statutory duty claim, but this was rejected. There was also no common law duty to take reasonable care to prevent accidents by providing warning signs.

LOCAL SOCIAL SERVICES AUTHORITIES

Local social services authorities provide services to children and adults. In the case of children, they have a statutory duty to 'safeguard and promote the welfare' of children living in their area.[117] To help them to carry out this duty, local authorities have a number of statutory powers. Ultimately, the local authority may remove children from the family, and place them in residential care, with foster parents or arrange for the child to be adopted. Failure to exercise these powers properly can result in a child remaining in an abusive environment when he or she might have been removed, or in a child being wrongly removed when he or she was not suffering harm or was not at risk of harm. Failure to remove a child can cause harm, in the form of abuse or neglect, while wrongful removal can also cause emotional and psychological harm to both the child and to the child's mother and father.

A number of claims for failure to remove from an abusive family environment and wrongful removal were considered in *X (minors) v Bedfordshire County Council*.[118] The House of Lords held that no claim for breach of statutory duty could be brought in respect of the local authority's duties, either by the children who had not been taken into care and who had suffered from abuse or neglect, or by parents whose children had been wrongly removed. The aim of the legislation was to protect children, and to allow claims for breach of statutory duty would impede the local authority in carrying out this aim.

In *X (minors)*, the House of Lords also held that, for policy reasons, no common law negligence claim could be brought in respect of the failure to remove and the wrongful removal of the children. Lord Browne-Wilkinson held that it would not be fair, just, and reasonable to 'superimpose a common law duty of care on the local authority in relation to the performance of its statutory duties to protect children'.[119] To impose such a duty would conflict with the aims of the legislation and encourage social services authorities to adopt a 'more cautious and defensive'[120] approach.

X (minors) was appealed to the European Court of Human Rights as *Z v United Kingdom*,[121] which held that the state was in breach of its duty to protect members of the public from

116 [1996] AC 923 (HL) 953 (Lord Hoffmann).
117 The Children Act 1989 s.17(1)(a).
118 [1995] 2 AC 633 (HL).
119 Ibid, 749 (Lord Browne-Wilkinson).
120 [1995] 2 AC 633 (HL) 750 (Lord Browne-Wilkinson).
121 [2001] ECHR 29392/95.

infringement of their article 3 (prevention of torture and inhuman and degrading treatment) rights and awarded compensation to the children who had not been removed from the abusive family environment.

Following this case, in *D v East Berkshire Community Health Trust*,[122] the House of Lords held that claims by children who had been failed by the social services authority could no longer be excluded.[123]

Where a child has been taken into care a duty of care will exist, and there is a duty on the social services authority not to cause the claimant foreseeable harm.[124] It is probable that this extends to a duty to protect the claimant from harm caused by third parties. In addition, the local authority will owe a duty of care as an occupier to people being looked after in residential care run by the authority and be liable for harm caused directly by its employees. This applies to looked-after children and adults in residential care.

Where a looked-after child is placed with foster parents, the local authority's duty is to make sure that the foster parents are properly selected and trained, but the authority is not directly liable for harm caused by the foster parents. However, the authority is vicariously liable for any harm caused directly by the foster parents.[125]

Where the client is not in the care of the local social services authority, but is being supported in his or her own home or provided with other services, there is no duty to rescue or protect the client from harm caused by an external cause. In *X v Hounslow London Borough Council*,[126] the claimants were clients of the local social services authority, which had failed to protect them from criminal acts carried out by third parties, even though the harm was foreseeable. The Court of Appeal held that there was no duty to protect the claimants.

This was confirmed by the most recent Supreme Court cases involving social services authorities, *N v Poole Borough Council*[127] and *HXA v Surrey County Council*.[128] These cases both concerned children who were being supported by social services in their homes and who suffered harm from third parties: in *N*, the children were subject to physical and verbal abuse from neighbours, while in *HXA*, the children were subjected to abuse at the hands of their parents and their partners. Although in both cases, the social services were aware that the abuse was happening, the Supreme Court held that in neither case had the social services assumed responsibility to protect the children from that harm.

122 [2005] UKHL 23, [2005] 2 AC 373.

123 Ibid, [30] (Lord Bingham) and [82] (Lord Nicholls).

124 *Barrett v Enfield London Borough Council* [2001] 2 AC 550 (HL).

125 *Armes v Nottinghamshire County Council* [2017] UKSC 60, [2018] AC 355.

126 [2009] EWCA Civ 286, [2009] 2 FLR 262.

127 [2019] UKSC 25, [2020] AC 780.

128 [2023] UKSC 52, [2024] 1 WLR 335.

REGULATORY BODIES

One particular type of public authority is the regulatory body. This is a body, usually created by statute, that has the power to regulate a particular profession, type of service provider, or other body. The two principal aspects of regulation are maintaining a register of regulated persons or bodies, and ensuring that the person or body is meeting the requirements of the profession, service or other function. As Lord Toulson observed in *Michael v Chief Constable of South Wales Police*:[129]

> [I]t is a feature of our system of government that many areas of life are subject to forms of state controlled licensing, regulation, inspection, intervention and assistance aimed at protecting the general public from physical or economic harm caused by the activities of other members of society.[130]

For example, Companies House maintains a register of limited companies, and ensures that companies submit the information required by the Companies Act 2006; the Charity Commission registers charities and ensures that they meet the requirements of the Charities Act 2011; and the General Medical Council maintains a register of medical practitioners and ensures that they are fit to practise. The regulator has the power to apply sanctions to any person or body that does not meet the requirements, and may remove a person or body from the register. This may mean that the person or body concerned will no longer be able to operate as, for example, a doctor or charity.

If the regulatory body does not take reasonable care in maintaining its register and removes a regulated person or body by mistake, it is foreseeable that this will cause economic loss to the person or body removed. On the other hand, if the regulatory body registers a person or body that does not meet the requirements for registration, then a person who does business with the regulated person or body may suffer loss, in the form of personal injury or economic loss.

However, as Lord Toulson went on to say, that the aim of the regulatory body is to protect the general public from injury or economic loss does not mean that a member of the public should be compensated by the body for any harm caused by a failure to take reasonable care in regulating an activity. Imposing such liability would be contrary to the ordinary principles of the common law.[131]

There have been a number of claims. In *Jain v Trent Strategic Health Authority*,[132] the claimants were the owners of a nursing home, which was regulated under the Registered Homes Act 1984.[133] The Act provided that it was an offence to operate an unregistered residential care home, and gave the Secretary of State the power to remove a residential care home from the

129 [2015] UKSC 2, [2015] AC 1732.

130 Ibid, [113].

131 [2015] UKSC 2, [2015] AC 1732, [114] (Lord Toulson).

132 [2009] UKHL 4, [2009] AC 853.

133 Since repealed.

register if it was satisfied that the person running it was not a fit person or if the home itself was not fit to be used as a residential care home. Using powers delegated by the Secretary of State, the health authority applied to a magistrate for the emergency removal of the claimant's nursing home from the register, which had the effect of causing irrevocable damage to the claimant's business. Although the claimant successfully appealed the decision to close the nursing home, this was too late to save the business. The claimant sued the health authority in negligence, arguing that they owed a common law duty to take reasonable care not to cause economic loss to the registrants.

The House of Lords held that there was no such duty: where a public authority was exercising a power 'designed for the benefit or protection of a particular class of persons, a tortious duty of care will not be held to be owed by the State authority to others whose interests may be adversely affected by an exercise of the statutory power'.[134] In this case, the aim of registration under the Act was to protect the residents of registered homes, and to hold that the regulatory body owed a duty to the owners of the homes that would be affected would conflict with the statutory aim.

However, successful claims have been made against regulatory bodies: in *Sebry v Companies House*,[135] the regulatory body made a mistake by including in a company's entry that the company was in liquidation. In fact, the company was solvent: the regulatory body had confused the claimant's company with another company with a very similar name.[136] The inclusion of the wrong information led to the claimant's company being refused credit by its suppliers and further loans by its bank, which caused the company to go into administration. The court held that Companies House did owe a duty to the companies it regulated, to use reasonable care not to cause economic loss when maintaining the register of companies.

The other type of claim that can be made is by a person who relies on the regulatory body and who suffers loss as a result of a mistake made by the body. For example, in *Schubert Murphy v Law Society*,[137] the claimant firm of solicitors was acting for the buyer of a house. The solicitor for the seller was a firm called Acorn Solicitors. As recommended by the Law Society as a protection against fraud, the claimant checked the Law Society's online database of solicitors, which confirmed that Acorn Solicitors was a genuine firm of solicitors. The claimant then transferred the purchase money to Acorn Solicitors in return for an undertaking that the outstanding mortgage loan on the house would be repaid. The purchase money was not used to pay the mortgage, which meant that the new owner was liable to the mortgage lender. It was discovered that Acorn Solicitors was not a legitimate firm, but that a fraudster had stolen the identity of a retired solicitor and used it to register Acorn Solicitors. The new owner sued his solicitors and was compensated for his loss. The solicitors then sued the Law Society in negligence, arguing that it owed a duty to take reasonable care when maintaining the database of solicitors not to cause users of the database economic loss. The

134 [2009] UKHL 4, [2009] AC 853, [28] (Lord Scott).

135 [2015] EWHC 115 (QB), [2015] 4 All ER 681.

136 The claimant's company was called 'Taylor and Sons Ltd'; the insolvent company was called 'Taylor and Son Ltd'.

137 [2017] EWCA Civ 1295, [2017] 4 WLR 200.

Law Society applied to have the claim struck out, but the Court of Appeal refused to do so: although it recognised that the claimant faced 'undoubted difficulties' in establishing that the regulatory body owed a duty of care to the regulated persons or to the public,[138] it could not be said that the claim had no realistic prospect of success.

8.9 THE HUMAN RIGHTS CLAIM

The European Convention on Human Rights and Fundamental Freedoms (ECHR) sets out a number of human rights, which include the rights to life, to freedom from torture or inhuman and degrading treatment, to a fair trial, to privacy, and to other rights. Where the state, or a public authority such as the police force, interferes directly with a person's human rights, the Human Rights Act 1998 provides that the person has a claim against the state or public authority.

In many cases, claims on human rights grounds may be brought on the same facts as claims in tort. Where the state deprives a person of his or her liberty unlawfully, the person will have a claim in the common law tort of false imprisonment and a claim for breach of article 5 (right to liberty and security). In *ZH v Commissioner of Police of the Metropolis*,[139] for example, claims against the police for breach of articles 3 (prohibition of torture) and 5 (right to liberty and security) succeeded, as did claims in the common law torts of battery and false imprisonment and a claim in discrimination.

While claims for harm caused directly by a public authority are relatively straightforward, claims for failure to rescue, warn, or protect the claimant may also arise under the Human Rights Act. The ECHR imposes a positive duty on the state 'to secure to everyone within their jurisdiction the rights and freedoms' defined in the Convention.[140] In some circumstances, the state is obliged to take positive actions to prevent a person from having their human rights interfered with by a third party, by warning or protecting the person.

KEY CASE

Osman v United Kingdom (1998) 29 EHRR 245, [1999] 1 FLR 193 was a claim under the ECHR for breach of article 2 (right to life), brought by the family of a murder victim. The murderer was a school teacher called Paget-Lewis, who had formed an attachment to one of his pupils, a 15-year-old boy. Over a period of over a year, Paget-Lewis carried out a series of acts targeting the boy and his family: these included damaging the family car on several occasions and vandalising the boy's home. The family contacted

138 [2017] EWCA Civ 1295, [2017] 4 WLR 200, [6] (Beatson LJ).

139 [2013] EWCA Civ 69, [2013] 1 WLR 3021.

140 European Convention on Human Rights and Fundamental Freedoms, article 1: 'The High Contracting Parties shall secure to everyone within their jurisdiction the rights and freedoms defined in Section I of this Convention'. Article 1, however, was not included in the Human Rights Act 1998, Sch. 1.

the police, who were aware of all the acts of vandalism, and that Paget-Lewis was responsible for them. The police did not, however, arrest Paget-Lewis. Some weeks later, Paget-Lewis stole a shotgun and went to the family home, where he shot and killed the boy's father.

The family brought a claim in negligence against the police (*Osman v Ferguson* [1993] 4 All ER 344). They argued that the police owed a duty to protect the victim from his murderer. They argued that the case could be distinguished from *Hill v Chief Constable of West Yorkshire Police* because in that case, the victim was unknown to the police so there was no proximity; in *Osman*, the police were aware that the boy and his family were at risk from the actions of Paget-Lewis. The claim did not succeed: the Court of Appeal applied *Hill*, holding that although it was arguable that there was sufficient proximity between the police and the victims, it would be against public policy for the police to owe a duty of care to victims of crime.

The family appealed to the European Court of Human Rights (ECtHR). The ECtHR rejected the claim that the state had failed to protect the victim's article 2 right (right to life), as it was not foreseeable that Paget-Lewis's campaign against the family would escalate from relatively minor acts of criminal damage to lethal violence.

While the Osman family's claim at the ECtHR failed, the court did hold that, in other circumstances, there would be a positive duty on the state to protect a person's life. If the authorities knew, or should have been aware of, a real and immediate risk to a person's life, the ECHR required the state to take action that would reasonably be expected to avoid the risk.

KEY LEARNING POINT

The state will be liable to the victim under Osman Principles for failing to protect their human rights if:

- the authorities knew or should have been aware that there was a real and immediate risk to a particular person's rights under article 2 (right to life), article 3 (prohibition of torture), article 4 (prohibition of slavery and forced labour), or article 5 (right to liberty and security) or that their rights under articles 3, 4, or 5 were being infringed;
- the state failed to take action which could reasonably be expected to avoid the risk or end the infringement; and
- the victim's rights under articles 2, 3, 4, or 5 were infringed.

The scope of the Osman principle, and its relation with negligence, was considered by the House of Lords in the case of *van Colle v Chief Constable of the Hertfordshire Police*.[141] In this case, the claimant's son was due to give evidence in a criminal trial for theft. The accused

141 [2008] UKHL 50, [2009] AC 225.

had approached the claimant's son and had made aggressive phone calls. Shortly before the criminal trial, the claimant's son was shot dead by the accused. The claim was brought against the police for failing to secure the victim's human rights under the ECHR. The claim did not succeed: as in *Osman*, there was no reason to believe that the low-level acts of aggression against the victim would escalate to lethal force. The accused had no history of violence and was being tried for a minor offence of theft. Furthermore, the phone calls had not included any specific threat to kill.[142]

In *van Colle*, the House of Lords also considered whether the common law of negligence should be adapted to make it compatible with the ECHR. This would mean excluding the general principle of *Hill*,[143] that the police owed no duty of care to future victims of crime, in circumstances where the Osman Principles applied. The House of Lords decided that the human rights claim should remain separate from the common law claim.[144]

The human rights claim is, therefore, a separate cause of action: the liability of the police in negligence is unaffected by *Osman* and subsequent cases. In *Michael v Chief Constable of South Wales Police*,[145] there were claims in negligence and in human rights on the same facts. The negligence claim was struck out, but the human rights claim was allowed to proceed to trial.

The human rights claim against the police will only apply where there has been a breach of an ECHR right which is also a criminal offence which the police have a duty to investigate or prevent. This would usually restrict claims to cases of infringements of articles 2, 3, 4, and 5. A successful article 4 claim was brought in the case of *OOO v Commissioner of Police of the Metropolis*:[146] in this case, the police had taken no action, despite having clear evidence that the claimants were being used as domestic slaves. An article 5 claim could be brought if the police knew of a person being deprived of his or her liberty but did not take action capable of ending the deprivation of liberty,[147] although it does not appear that such a claim has been brought in England and Wales.

Not all crimes involve breaches of the victim's human rights: while murder will infringe the victim's right to life, an assault must be serious to infringe the article 3 prohibition of torture or inhuman and degrading treatment. In *Commissioner of Police of the Metropolis v DSD*, the Supreme Court held that article 3 would be breached by an assault equivalent to the criminal offence of causing actual bodily harm, and would include sexual assault.[148] Article 3 may also be breached by degrading treatment which would not be a tort, such as where a person

142 An application to the ECtHR did not succeed: see *van Colle v United Kingdom* [2012] ECHR 7678/09.

143 *Hill v Chief Constable of West Yorkshire Police* [1989] AC 53 (HL).

144 Lord Hope (with whom Lord Carswell agreed) and Lord Brown both held that it was unnecessary to develop the common law to reflect the ECHR jurisprudence: see [2008] UKHL 50, [2009] AC 225, [82] and [136]–[139]. Lord Bingham thought that the common law should develop in line with the ECHR jurisprudence: see [58].

145 [2015] UKSC 2, [2015] AC 1732.

146 [2011] EWHC 1246 (QB).

147 See *Rantsev v Cyprus and Russia* [2010] ECHR 25965/04, an ECtHR case which allowed an article 5 claim.

148 See *Commissioner of Police of the Metropolis v DSD* [2018] UKSC 11, [2018] 2 WLR 895, [128] (Lord Neuberger).

is forced to strip.[149] However, in the case of *AB v Worcestershire County Council*,[150] the court found that a series of incidents of physical abuse of a child including smacking were not sufficiently serious to engage article 3.

As well as the obligation to prevent current or imminent breaches of a person's rights by a third party, the ECHR also imposes a duty on the state to investigate breaches of human rights which it could not have prevented. Where a person's article 2 or article 3 rights have been infringed by a third party, the state is obliged to take action to investigate the breach, with the aim of preventing or reducing further breaches.[151] Failure to investigate gives the victim of the breach a right to compensation. In the case of *DSD v Commissioner of Police of the Metropolis*,[152] a woman who had been raped by a taxi driver reported the crime to the police. However, the police did not investigate the crime effectively. A claim by the woman succeeded, as the police were in breach of their obligations to investigate the breach of the victim's article 3 rights.

POINTS TO REVIEW

- Claims may be brought against public authorities for breach of statutory duty, in common law negligence, or for failure to protect the claimant's human rights.
- A public authority is only liable for harm caused by a breach of its statutory duty if the claimant can show that it was the intention of Parliament to give a remedy for people harmed by the breach.
- A public authority cannot be liable in negligence for policy decisions taken under a power or discretion created by statute.
- Public authorities are, in principle, liable in negligence on the same principles as any private individual.
- Public authorities do owe a duty of care to those members of the public to whom they provide services, and the scope of the duty depends upon the nature of the service and the relationship between the authority and the member of the public.
- Public authorities, when occupying land, employing people, or carrying out other ancillary activities, owe exactly the same duties as any other person carrying out the same activity.
- Public authorities are liable for directly caused harm on the same basis as any other person.
- Public authorities do not owe a duty to rescue, warn, or protect members of the public, unless there is a prior relationship or they fall within one of the exceptions set out in *Smith v Littlewoods*.

---

149 See *Wainwright v United Kingdom* (App no 12350/04) – [2006] ECHR 12350/04, [41]–[42].

150 [2022] EWHC 115 (QB).

151 It is possible that the obligation to investigate breaches of other rights might arise, but the question has not received detailed consideration: *Commissioner of Police of the Metropolis v DSD* [2018] UKSC 11, [2018] 2 WLR 895, [129] (Lord Neuberger).

152 [2018] UKSC 11, [2018] 2 WLR 895.

- If a public authority is aware, or should be aware, of an imminent risk to a person's human rights under articles 2, 3, 4, or 5 of the European Convention on Human Rights, the public authority is obliged to take action capable of avoiding the risk and is liable to the victim if it fails to do so and the victim's rights are infringed.

TAKING IT FURTHER

Tofaris, S. and Steel, S. 'Negligence Liability for Omissions and the Police' (2016) 75 CLJ 128–157

The authors argue that the police should be liable for failing to rescue, warn, or protect members of the public from harm caused by third parties when they are aware that a member of the public is at risk. This is based on the status of the police, and the powers and resources that society gives them.

Nolan, D. 'The Liability of Public Authorities for Failing to Confer Benefits' (2011) 127 LQR 260–287

Reframes liability for omissions as a failure to confer a benefit on the claimant. Criticises the law, particularly in relation to *Gorringe v Calderdale*, which is regarded as overly restrictive with regard to harm which might have been prevented by the exercise of a statutory power.

DuBois, F. 'Human Rights and the Tort Liability of Public Authorities' (2011) 127 LQR 589–609

Considers the relationship between a claim in negligence and the human rights claim on the Osman Principles. The author notes that the human rights claim gives rise to a claim against public authorities specifically, and welcomes the decision, in *van Colle*, to develop this area separately from the common law.

9

CHAPTER 9
NEGLIGENCE: DEFENCES AND REMEDIES

This chapter considers specific defences to claims in negligence, and looks at the remedies that the court can award a successful claimant.

9.1 INTRODUCTION

In this chapter, we look at the specific defences that may be pleaded by the defendant in negligence. In practice, most defendants will defend a claim against them by contesting the claimant's version of the facts or on the issues of breach and causation. However, there are three specific defences that the defendant can argue in claims in negligence. These are:

- contributory negligence;
- voluntary assumption of risk; and
- illegality.

Contributory negligence is a partial defence. The claim succeeds, but the damages awarded are reduced by a percentage. Voluntary assumption of risk and illegality are complete defences: if they succeed, then the claim fails.

The second part of this chapter looks at the remedies available in negligence. Historically, the only remedy which a common law court could award was damages, and this remains the main remedy. Awarding compensation for the harm caused requires, in the case of personal injury, the court to put a price on the value of an injury, and this chapter sets out how the court determines what is a fair amount for the defendant to pay if he or she has, for example, caused a serious head injury or a broken leg. Claimants can also recover any financial costs caused by the personal injury, such as the loss of earnings and future care costs.

Other remedies include court orders, or injunctions, to make the defendant do something or to prevent him or her from doing something. These are rarely used in negligence, but are commonly granted in other torts, such as trespass to land.

AS YOU READ

- Understand the defences of contributory negligence, voluntary assumption of risk, and illegality, and the circumstances in which they apply.

DOI: 10.4324/9781003480051-09

- Understand the remedies available in negligence, and the principles on which they are awarded.

9.2 CONTRIBUTORY NEGLIGENCE

Contributory negligence can be pleaded by the defendant where the claimant's own actions have contributed to the harm caused: where the claimant has failed to take reasonable care for his or her own well-being, and that lack of care is one of the factors that has caused the damage, the claimant is contributorily negligent. The claimant's lack of care may contribute to the incident causing the damage, or it may make the damage more severe.

> KEY LEARNING POINT
>
> Contributory negligence is a defence where the claimant's failure to take reasonable care for his or her own safety:
>
> - was one of the factors causing the incident; or
> - did not cause the incident, but did contribute to the severity of the injury.

Contributory negligence was, until 1945, a complete defence. If the claimant was partially responsible for the injury that he or she suffered, then the defendant was not liable for causing the injury. This was particularly significant in industrial injuries, where an employer, by showing that the worker had not taken reasonable care for his or her own safety and had substantially contributed[1] to the harm caused, could completely avoid any obligation to compensate the worker. In *Lewis v Denye*,[2] for example, a worker suffered injuries to his hand when working on a circular saw. The court found that both parties were negligent: the employer for not fitting proper guards to the saw, and the employee for putting his hand too close to the saw blade rather than using the push stick provided. As the employee's negligence had contributed to the injury, the claim was not allowed.

In 1945, the Law Reform (Contributory Negligence) Act was passed. This allowed courts to allocate liability to both parties, and to award damages 'reduced to such extent as the court thinks just and equitable having regard to the claimant's share in the responsibility for the damage'.[3] The Act changed contributory negligence from a complete defence to a partial defence, which may be pleaded where the defendant admits liability, but is seeking to reduce the damages payable.

An example of where the incident might have been avoided altogether might be the case of a pedestrian walking into the road without looking.[4] If a car is speeding, so that it does not have

1 *Swadling v Cooper* [1931] AC 1, 6 (Viscount Hailsham).

2 [1939] 1 KB 540.

3 Law Reform (Contributory Negligence) Act 1945 s.1.

4 *Jackson v Murray* [2015] UKSC 5, [2015] 2 All ER 805.

time to stop before hitting the pedestrian, then both parties might reasonably argue that, but for the other party's failure to take reasonable care, the damage would not have occurred. It is true that both parties' failure caused the accident, in that but for the failure of both parties to take reasonable care, the accident would not have happened. In such cases, the court can allocate liability based on each party's fault and contribution to the damage caused.

In other cases, the claimant's own conduct does not cause the accident, but contributes to the injury or the severity of the injury. A good example is not wearing a seat belt. Wearing a seat belt does not prevent accidents, but it is well established that it does prevent or reduce the injury suffered in a road accident. So if a claimant is injured in an accident caused by the negligence of another road user, and his or her injuries are worse than they would have been if he or she had been wearing a seat belt, the defendant is entitled to argue that the claimant's injuries are, at least partly, the claimant's own fault.

9.3 APPORTIONMENT

The 1945 Act does not specify how damages should be apportioned, other than as the 'court thinks just and equitable', taking into account each party's 'responsibility' for the damage. This means that courts have a wide degree of discretion in coming up with an actual figure. In *Eagle v Chambers*,[5] for example, the court had to determine the relative responsibility of a pedestrian who was walking along the middle of a straight, well-lit road in a seaside resort and a motorist who had a significant, but legal, level of alcohol in his blood and who was driving above the speed limit. The trial court found that the pedestrian bore most of the responsibility and she should bear 60% of the damages. The Court of Appeal thought that the motorist should bear most of the responsibility and set the level of contributory negligence at 40%.

KEY CASE

Jackson v Murray [2015] UKSC 5, [2015] 2 All ER 805 was a claim brought by a pedestrian who was knocked down by a speeding car. The claimant was a 13-year-old schoolgirl, who walked out from behind a school minibus into the path of the defendant's car. The trial court found that the defendant was speeding, was not keeping a proper lookout, and had failed to anticipate that a child might step out from behind the school bus, which was clearly marked and which was showing its hazard lights. The court held that the claimant, who had not looked before crossing, was contributorily negligent, and held that she was 90% at fault. This figure was reduced to 70% on appeal.

The Supreme Court allowed an appeal, holding that the claimant's contribution to her injury should be quantified at 50%.

5 [2003] EWCA Civ 1107.

In *Jackson v Murray*,[6] the Supreme Court recognised the difficulties in apportioning the damages between claimant and defendant and held that it was 'not possible to arrive at an apportionment which is demonstrably correct'.[7] The factors that the court should take into account were not capable of being measured precisely, and there was an asymmetry between claimant and defendant: the defendant's fault lay in his or her breach of a legal duty owed to the claimant, while the claimant's 'fault' was not to look after his or her own interests. Apportionment was inevitably a 'rough and ready exercise', and it was possible for different judges legitimately to take different views.[8]

The Supreme Court did set out the two factors that the court should consider when determining the extent to which each party should be held to have contributed to the damage. These factors are:

- 'blameworthiness'; and
- causative potency.

Blameworthiness is a measure of each party's legal or moral fault. Causative potency relates to the contribution that each party's acts made to the damage.

While it is possible to take an objective approach to the causative potency of each party's acts, blameworthiness requires the court to take a more subjective approach, and to consider the blame that should be attached. Blame does not mean the same as fault, in a legal sense: blame implies a consideration of moral issues. Most people would regard driving while drunk as reprehensible, and attach a great deal of blame to the driver. They may attach less blame to a driver who was not paying sufficient attention, even though the end result – the injury or death of another road user – may be the same. So a court might regard an inattentive driver as less blameworthy than a drunk driver. The causative potency, however, is the same whether the accident is caused by the driver's inattention or because his or her reaction times are affected by alcohol.

9.4 ROAD USERS

Failing to wear a seat belt is, perhaps, the clearest example of a person failing to take reasonable care for his or her own safety, and is a recognised form of contributory negligence.[9] In the case of motorcyclists, failing to wear a helmet is also well established as contributory negligence,[10] as is failing to secure the chinstrap of the helmet.[11]

6 [2015] UKSC 5, [2015] 2 All ER 805.
7 Ibid, [27] (Lord Reed).
8 [2015] UKSC 5, [2015] 2 All ER 805, [28] (Lord Reed).
9 *Froom v Butcher* [1976] QB 286.
10 *O'Connell v Jackson* [1972] 1 QB 270.
11 *Capps v Miller* [1989] 1 WLR 839.

In the case of cyclists, the evidence that failure to wear a helmet increases the risk of injury is less clear-cut than in motorcyclists. In *Smith v Finch*,[12] the court found that the claimant's injuries would not have been prevented or reduced by wearing a helmet, as cyclists' helmets are only designed to protect the head in low-speed impacts. However, in *Reynolds v Strutt & Parker LLP*,[13] where there was a low-speed impact, the court did find the claimant contributorily negligent.

In principle, a person who voluntarily travels in a car driven by a person whom the passenger knows is drunk has not taken reasonable care for his or her own safety. This was confirmed in *Owens v Brimmell*.[14] In this case, the claimant and the defendant had spent the evening drinking together, and both were drunk. The claimant accepted a lift home from the defendant. There was an accident, and the claimant suffered serious head injuries. The court held that, by accepting the lift when he knew that the driver was drunk, the claimant had contributed to his injuries and reduced damages by 20%.[15]

9.5 VOLUNTARY ASSUMPTION OF RISK

If the claimant has voluntarily accepted[16] the risk of a particular activity, then he or she cannot claim if he or she is injured. This principle, historically referred to as *volenti non fit injuria*[17] or *volenti*, is a defence to a claim in negligence. If it succeeds, it is a complete defence, and the claim will fail.

The defendant needs to show that the claimant not only knew of the risk, but that he or she voluntarily accepted it. If the claimant has no choice but to accept the risk, then the defence does not apply.

KEY LEARNING POINT

Where the claimant knows of a risk and voluntarily accepts it, he or she cannot claim in negligence if he or she is injured as a result.

Morris v Murray[18] shows how the defence is applied. The claimant and defendant had been drinking together, with the defendant consuming quantities of alcohol equivalent to a bottle of whisky. The claimant had also been drinking heavily. After some hours' drinking, the

12 [2009] EWHC 53 (QB).

13 [2011] EWHC 2740 (QB), [45] (HHJ Oliver-Jones QC).

14 [1977] QB 859.

15 See also *Campbell v Advantage Insurance Co Ltd* [2021] EWCA Civ 1698.

16 Although the defence is referred to as 'voluntary assumption of risk', courts refer to the claimant 'accepting the risk' interchangeably with 'assuming the risk'.

17 The literal translation from the Latin is 'to a willing person, harm is not done': this means that the law does not recognise the injury as harm, so no claim can be brought in negligence.

18 [1991] 2 QB 6.

defendant, who held a private pilot's licence, asked the claimant if he would like to go on a flight with him. The claimant agreed, and the two men drove to the airfield, where the claimant and defendant took off for a 'short and chaotic'[19] flight, which ended in a matter of minutes when the aircraft crashed. The pilot was killed and the claimant seriously injured. The Court of Appeal allowed an appeal by the defendant. The claimant was not so drunk as to be incapable of making a decision and he had known of, and voluntarily accepted, the risks of flying with a pilot who was very drunk.

9.6 RISKS IN THE WORKPLACE

KEY CASE

In *Smith v Baker & Sons* [1891] AC 325, the claimant was working for a construction company which was making a cutting through rock. The claimant's job was to make holes in the rock for explosive charges. At the same time, rocks were being cleared from the site by a crane, which carried the rocks in a sling, at times passing over the claimant's head. A stone fell from the sling and injured the claimant. The claimant brought a claim in negligence. At trial, the claimant accepted that he was aware that rocks were being carried over where he was working, and that he was aware that there was a risk that rocks might fall on him. The court held that the claimant had voluntarily accepted the risk and found for the defendant.

The claimant appealed to the House of Lords, who allowed the appeal. Knowledge of a risk was not the same as acceptance of a risk, so the claimant could not be said to have voluntarily accepted the risk. In this case, the claimant had, whenever he had warning, got out of the way of the sling carrying the rocks. On the occasion when he was injured, he had been focusing on his job, so was unaware that the sling was passing over his head. Although he knew of the risks, he had not voluntarily accepted them.

Smith v Baker & Sons[20] established that employers could not rely on the defence of voluntary assumption of risks in the workplace merely because a worker had continued to do his or her job knowing that there was a risk. It also establishes, as a principle, that knowledge of a risk is not the same as voluntary acceptance of a risk.

That does not mean that employees are never considered to have voluntarily accepted a risk. If an employee carries out a task in a dangerous way, despite having the opportunity

19 [1991] 2 QB 6, 10 (Fox LJ).
20 [1891] AC 325.

to carry it out safely, then the employee may be held to have accepted the risk. In *Imperial Chemical Industries v Shatwell*,[21] a worker was injured when a co-worker breached the statutory regulations on testing explosives. The injured worker was himself a qualified and experienced shot-firer, who had agreed to the breach of the regulations. The House of Lords held that he had voluntarily assumed the risk of injury and the company was not liable for his injuries.

Shatwell was applied in the case of *McMullen v National Coal Board*.[22] In this case, the claimant jumped off a moving vehicle and was injured. The employer had repeatedly warned employees against the practice and had fined employees for breach of their instructions. The court held that the claimant had voluntarily accepted the risk when he decided to jump. In *Roles v Nathan*,[23] two chimney sweeps were called in to clean a boiler's chimney. An independent expert was also called in, who declared that the boiler room was dangerous, and ordered the two men to leave. The men returned during the night to complete the job, and were overcome by fumes and killed. The claim by their widows failed, as it was held that they had voluntarily assumed the risk.

> KEY LEARNING POINT
>
> Employees do not voluntarily assume the risks of their job, unless they do something, of their own initiative, which is not required by the job.

9.7 RESCUERS

A rescuer who puts him- or herself in danger is not regarded as voluntarily taking on the risk. In *Baker v TE Hopkins*,[24] a doctor was lowered on a rope into a well shaft to rescue two workers who had been overcome by carbon monoxide. The doctor was himself overcome by the gas and was killed. The defendant claimed that the doctor knew of the risks, and was under no obligation to undertake the rescue attempt, so should be regarded as having voluntarily assumed the risk. The court disagreed: a person who was engaged in rescuing another person was not voluntarily assuming the risk, but was 'prompted by the finest instincts of humanity'.[25] In support, the court quoted a dictum from the US case of *Wagner v International Railway*, which had considered the same point. In that case, Cardozo J had held that: 'Danger invites rescue. The cry of distress is a summons to relief'.[26]

21 [1965] AC 656.

22 [1982] ICR 148.

23 [1963] 1 WLR 1117.

24 [1959] 1 WLR 966. See also *Haynes v Harwood* [1935] 1 KB 146.

25 [1959] 1 WLR 966, 971 (Morris LJ).

26 (1921) 232 NY Rep 176, 180.

KEY LEARNING POINT

Rescuers, who are motivated by a desire to help another person, are also not regarded as making a free and informed decision to accept the risk.

THE 'FIREMAN'S RULE'

Some jobs have well-known risks, which any person who takes on the job will be aware of. In some jurisdictions, the decision to become, for example, a firefighter means that the person has voluntarily accepted all the usual risks of the job, and cannot claim in negligence if he or she is injured. This is known as the 'fireman's rule'.[27]

The fireman's rule is not part of English law: a firefighter does not voluntarily accept the risks associated with his or her job and can claim for injuries suffered when fighting a fire against any person whose negligence caused the fire. The issue was considered in the House of Lords case of *Ogwo v Taylor*.[28] In this case, the defendant had negligently caused the fire when using a blowtorch to remove paint from the outside of his house. The claimant suffered serious burns when tackling the fire. The House of Lords held that they had 'no doubt that the American "fireman's rule" has no place in English law'.[29]

ROAD USERS

Where a car is being used on a 'road [or other public place]',[30] the defence of voluntary assumption of risk is excluded by statute under section 149 of the Road Traffic Act 1988. In the case of passengers who accept a lift, knowing that the driver is drunk, for example, the defendant cannot plead voluntary assumption of risk. However, the defence of contributory negligence can be pleaded.[31]

SPORTS PARTICIPANTS

It is well established that a person playing or watching sport cannot claim in negligence if he or she is injured during the usual course of the sport.[32] One potential reason for this rule might be that participants and spectators have voluntarily accepted the risk of injury. The courts, however, have usually taken a different approach to reach the same conclusion.[33] Any person playing the game, taking into account that players are trying hard to win and may,

27 In California, for example, a firefighter injured when fighting a fire cannot claim in negligence against any person whose negligence caused the fire: see *Walters v Sloan* (1977) 20 Cal 3d 199. The same rule applies to other emergency workers.

28 [1988] AC 431.

29 Ibid, 449 (Lord Bridge, giving the only judgment).

30 This is where insurance is compulsory (s.143(1)(a) Road Traffic Act 1988).

31 *Owens v Brimmell* [1977] QB 859.

32 *Wooldridge v Sumner* [1963] 2 QB 43.

33 In some cases, such as *O'Dowd v Frazer-Nash* [1951] WN 173, courts have held participants to have voluntarily accepted the risk.

in the heat of the moment, make mistakes, is not in breach of duty unless he or she shows a 'reckless disregard'[34] for the safety of other participants or spectators.[35]

9.8 ILLEGALITY

As a general rule, a claimant cannot bring any type of civil claim for any damage which arises directly from his or her own illegal acts. This applies to negligence, as well as other torts. The doctrine was formerly referred to as *ex turpi causa*.[36] Illegality is a complete defence, like voluntary assumption of risk.

The defendant needs to show that the harm arose directly from the illegal activity. It is not enough to show that the claimant was breaking the law at the time of the incident. In *Delaney v Pickett*,[37] the claimant and defendant were both travelling in a car to carry out a drugs deal when the car was in an accident caused by the defendant's negligence. The passenger's claim against the driver was dismissed by the High Court on the grounds of illegality. The Court of Appeal held that the criminal activity was incidental to the accident, and the defence did not apply.

In *Joyce v O'Brien*,[38] the claimant was also injured as a passenger in a vehicle while he and the driver were engaged in a crime. In this case, however, 'the accident occurred in the course of the two men making a speedy getaway from the scene of the crime',[39] and the defence succeeded.

The defence may be applied wherever the injury arises from the claimant's own criminal conduct. This may be where only the claimant is acting illegally, or in the course of a joint criminal activity with the defendant.

In *Patel v Mirza*,[40] the Supreme Court considered the defence of illegality in the context of unjust enrichment. They also considered the defence more widely. They confirmed that the approach to application of the illegality should be based on policy considerations rather than allowing or denying the defence by applying a more formal approach. Moreover, the court should consider whether upholding the defence would be a proportionate response to the illegality.

34 *Condon v Basi* [1985] 1 WLR 866.

35 *Wooldridge v Sumner* [1963] 2 QB 43; *Caldwell v Maguire* [2001] EWCA Civ 1054; *Blake v Galloway* [2004] EWCA Civ 814, [2004] 1 WLR 2844.

36 '*Ex turpi causa*' is short for the Latin phrase '*ex turpi causa non oritur actio*': from a criminal cause, no action shall arise.

37 [2011] EWCA Civ 1532, [2012] 1 WLR 2149.

38 [2013] EWCA Civ 546, [2014] 1 WLR 70.

39 Ibid, [35] (Elias LJ).

40 [2016] UKSC 42, [2017] AC 467.

Later cases have confirmed and applied the approach taken *Patel v Mirza*, such as *Stoffel v Grondona*.[41] In this case the claimant sued her solicitors in negligence for failure to register her title on a property. The solicitors argued that the defence of illegality should apply, as the claimant had engaged in mortgage fraud. The Supreme Court noted that the 'law should condemn mortgage frauds which are serious criminal offences',[42] although it further noted that the failure to compensate would not be contemplated by those committing mortgage fraud.[43] In terms of solicitors, the Supreme Court noted the need for solicitors to 'perform their duties to their clients diligently and without negligence and that, in the event of a negligent breach of duty, those who use their services should be entitled to seek a civil remedy'.[44] In relation to proportionality, it would not be proportionate to deny a remedy to the claimants, especially as the fraud committed by the claimants was 'conceptually entirely separate' to the negligence of the defendant solicitors.[45]

KEY LEARNING POINT

The court will consider policy reasons and proportionality when determining whether the illegality defence will apply. The policy reasons will invariably depend on the case, and these will be balanced.

KEY CASE

Gray v Thames Trains Ltd [2009] UKHL 33, [2009] AC 1339 was a claim brought by a man who was involved in a major train crash, in which 31 people were killed. The claimant suffered from post-traumatic stress disorder, caused by the trauma of being in the crash. Two years after the crash, the claimant was involved in an argument with a drunken pedestrian. He obtained a knife, then returned to the area, where he found the pedestrian and stabbed him to death. At trial, it was accepted by the prosecution that the killing was, in part, caused by the claimant's mental disorder, and they accepted a plea of guilty to manslaughter on the grounds of diminished responsibility caused by post-traumatic stress disorder. The claimant was detained under the Mental Health Act 1983.

The claimant sued the train company for the psychiatric illness caused by the accident, his loss of earnings as a result of his illness and his detention, for his loss of liberty, and for feelings of guilt and remorse.

The House of Lords did not allow the claimant to recover for any of the damage caused by the killing, including the loss of earnings while detained, the loss of liberty,

41 [2020] UKSC 42.

42 Ibid, [29] (Lord Lloyd-Jones).

43 Ibid.

44 [2020] UKSC 42, [32] (Lord Lloyd-Jones).

45 [2020] UKSC 42, [43] (Lord Lloyd-Jones).

or for the feelings of guilt and remorse. This was based on the rule of public policy that prevents a criminal from profiting or being compensated for harm caused by his or her criminal acts.

9.9 CLAIMANT ONLY ACTING ILLEGALLY

In *Gray v Thames Trains Ltd*,[46] the House of Lords referred to two versions of the illegality rule: the wider rule is that a criminal should not be compensated for loss caused by his or her own criminal behaviour. The narrower rule states that a criminal cannot be compensated for any loss caused by the imposition of a sentence lawfully imposed by a court. Both rules – the wide and narrow – were upheld in *Gray*, but it is the wide version that is most applied in negligence. The principle does not mean, however, that any harm done to a person who is committing a crime cannot be compensated. The harm must arise directly from the criminality: as expressed by Lord Hoffmann in *Gray*, it must be the case that 'although the damage would not have happened but for the tortious conduct of the defendant, it was caused by the criminal act of the claimant'.[47] If 'although the damage would not have happened without the criminal act of the claimant, it was caused by the tortious act of the defendant',[48] the defence will not succeed.

The distinction found in *Gray* may be seen in two cases: *Vellino v Chief Constable of Manchester Police*[49] and *Revill v Newbery*.[50] In the former case, the claimant injured himself jumping from a balcony to escape from police custody, so the defence succeeded: the damages were caused by the claimant's own criminal act of escaping from police custody. In the latter case, the defendant shot through a door to frighten a burglar, wounding the claimant. The cause of the injury was the defendant's tortious act in firing his shotgun, so the defence did not apply. The claimant's damages were reduced, however, on the basis of his contributory negligence.

Whether the approach in *Gray* could be applied post *Patel v Mirza* was explored by the Supreme Court in *Henderson v Dorset Healthcare*.[51] Here the claimant, who suffered with paranoid schizophrenia, killed her mother while suffering from a schizophrenic episode and agreed a plea of manslaughter by reason of diminished responsibility. Dorset Healthcare Trust admitted liability in negligence after failing to ensure that the claimant was in hospital during the schizophrenic episode which would have prevented the killing of her mother. The Supreme Court allowed the defence of illegality based on the rule in *Gray* and noted that

46 [2009] UKHL 33, [2009] AC 1339.

47 [2009] UKHL 33, [2009] AC 1339, [54] (Lord Hoffmann).

48 Ibid.

49 [2001] EWCA Civ 1249, [2002] 1 WLR 218.

50 [1996] QB 567.

51 [2020] UKSC 43.

the approach in *Gray* was consistent with the judgment in Patel. Consequently, the approach taken in *Gray* can continue to be used in future similar cases.

In *Ranwell v G4S Health Services*,[52] the claimant, suffering from schizophrenia and during a serious episode, killed three people. He was found not guilty by reason of insanity; this is different to the *Gray* and *Henderson* cases where the claimant was found guilty of manslaughter by reason of diminished responsibility. In *Ranwell*, the claimant sued the local health services, NHS, Devon County Council, and the police for negligence (and under section 7 of the Human Rights Act 1998) after failing to detain him and prevent him from killing. A majority in the Court of Appeal held that the defence would fail; Lord Justice Underhill explored several policy factors, such as in relation to consistency in the law, public conscience and costs to the NHS, and stated that the defence of illegality could not be used in this case. There is a clear distinction here from the Court of Appeal in terms of being guilty by reason of diminished responsibility and not guilty by reason of insanity, in the latter there is no 'moral culpability'.[53] This case is currently subject to an appeal to the Supreme Court.

9.10 JOINT CRIMINAL ENTERPRISE

KEY CASE

In *Pitts v Hunt* [1991] 1 QB 24, the claimant was riding as the pillion passenger on a motorcycle driven by the defendant. The defendant was underage, drunk, unlicensed, and uninsured. The passenger was encouraging the driver to ride in a reckless and dangerous manner, which was a criminal offence. The motorcycle crashed, and the passenger sued the driver. The court held that both were engaged in a criminal activity and the claim was denied under the doctrine of *ex turpi causa*.

Where both the claimant and the defendant are participating in a crime at the time of the damage, there will be no liability for any injury caused by the negligence of the defendant, if the negligence is caused by the criminal act of the claimant or the defendant.

Pitts v Hunt[54] followed *Ashton v Turner*[55] and Australian case law[56] to find that there was no duty owed by participants in criminal enterprises to the other participants. As Ewbank J held:

52 [2024] EWCA Civ 138.

53 [2024] EWCA Civ 138, [104] (LJ Underhill).

54 [1991] 1 QB 24.

55 [1981] QB 137.

56 *Jackson v Harrison* (1978) 138 CLR 438.

> The law of England may in certain circumstances not recognise the existence of a duty of care owed by one participant in a crime to another participant in the same crime, in relation to an act done in connection with the commission of that crime.[57]

Cases since the House of Lords case of *Gray v Thames Trains Ltd* have taken a different approach, based on Lord Hoffman's explanation that the defence of illegality applied where the damage was caused by the criminal act of the claimant, rather than where the criminal act provided the circumstances in which the damage happened.

For joint enterprise cases, the defence applies where the damage was caused by the criminal act of the claimant or the other participant in the crime. So, where a criminal act, whether on the part of the claimant or the defendant, causes the damage, the defendant is not liable.

The distinction may be seen in the two Court of Appeal cases of *Delaney v Pickett*[58] and *Joyce v O'Brien*.[59] In both cases, the claimant was injured in a road traffic accident, caused by the negligence of the defendant; and in both cases, the claimant and defendant were travelling by car in the course of committing a crime. In *Delaney*, the purpose of the journey was to sell drugs; in *Joyce*, the car was being driven away from the scene of a theft. In *Delaney*, the criminal purpose was incidental to the defendant's breach of duty. In *Joyce*, the defendant was breaching his duty to his passenger and other road users because of the crime: he was driving too fast to get away from the crime scene as quickly as possible.

If two participants in a crime owe no duty of care to each other, then any claim in negligence can be brought by either party in respect of any injury suffered during the commission of the crime, however the damage was caused. The causation-based approach applied by the Court of Appeal, on the other hand, allows the courts to apply the principles set out in *Patel v Mirza*.[60] As the Court of Appeal held in *Revill v Newbery*,[61] criminals are not 'outlaws' who can be killed or injured without legal consequences.[62]

9.11 REMEDIES

INTRODUCTION

As Sir Thomas Bingham MR stated, 'the rule of public policy which has first claim on the loyalty of the law [is] that wrongs should be remedied'.[63] An ideal remedy will put the claimant back into the position he or she was in before the harm occurred and, in some cases,

57 *Ashton v Turner* [1981] QB 137, 146.
58 [2011] EWCA Civ 1532, [2012] 1 WLR 2149.
59 [2013] EWCA Civ 546, [2014] 1 WLR 70.
60 [2016] UKSC 42, [2017] AC 467.
61 [1996] QB 567, 579 (Evans LJ).
62 An 'outlaw' was regarded in law as a non-person: any crime or tort committed against an outlaw could not give rise to a prosecution or claim.
63 *X (minors) v Bedfordshire County Council* [1995] 2 AC 633, 663.

this may be possible. If the defendant's negligence causes economic loss, that may be repaired by a financial remedy. Where damage to property has been caused, the costs of repairing or replacing the property will put the claimant back to where he or she was before the negligence, although he or she will have suffered some inconvenience.

Where the damage is personal injury, whether physical or psychiatric, there is no prospect of undoing the harm or putting the claimant back to where he or she was, but the law still has to provide a remedy which compensates the claimant for his or her injury.

The main remedy in negligence is financial, in the form of damages. The other remedies available to the courts are injunctions, or orders, and declarations. These are more commonly granted in other torts, such as defamation, and in other areas of law.

> KEY LEARNING POINT
>
> The main remedy in negligence is damages, which compensate the claimant for the harm that he or she has suffered.

DAMAGES

Damages are a financial award which the court orders the defendant to pay the claimant. In addition, the defendant may be ordered to pay the claimant's legal costs. The general principle for the awarding of damages in negligence is to compensate the claimant for his or her loss.

Compensatory damages are based on a consideration of the claimant's position before and after the damage caused by the negligence, and determining a financial award which will compensate the claimant, both for the financial losses caused directly by the defendant's acts and omissions, and any non-financial harm, such as the pain and suffering that the claimant has suffered.

There are other principles on which damages can be awarded. If the defendant has made a financial gain from his or her wrongdoing, the court can award damages based on the defendant's gain, rather than the claimant's loss. Damages may be vindicatory, particularly where there is a recognition of a breach of the claimant's rights. Nominal damages are awarded where the claimant has suffered a legal wrong, but has not suffered personal injury or any form of economic loss. Courts can also award aggravated or exemplary damages, which reflect their disapproval of the defendant's conduct. Finally, courts will, on rare occasions, award derisory damages, of the minimum amount possible. However, it is rare for courts to award any form of damages other than compensatory damages in negligence.

COSTS

In addition to damages, a successful claimant will usually be awarded costs. Costs are the legal costs incurred by the litigant in preparing for and conducting the court case. They include the fees paid to the solicitors who are preparing the case, the barristers representing the litigant in court and any expert witness who is appearing for the litigant. Costs also include any money spent in preparing for the claim, such as medical reports, photographing the scene of the incident, reimbursing witnesses for their travel expenses, and other costs. In general, the successful party in any litigation will be awarded costs, which means that the losing party has to pay the successful party's costs, as well as his or her own costs.

Costs may be substantial, of a similar or greater amount than the damages sought. An award of costs against the claimant may mean that the claimant is financially worse off despite having won the case. The Civil Procedure Rules allow awards of costs to be used to encourage early settlement of claims before trial, by awarding costs against a claimant who has not accepted a reasonable offer in settlement of the claim.[64]

COMPENSATORY DAMAGES

Compensatory damages are based on a consideration of the claimant's position before and after the negligence, and compensating the claimant for any financial loss caused by the negligence and for any pain, suffering and loss of amenity caused by the negligence. Damages are divided into two categories:

- special damages; and
- general damages.

Special damages are the financial loss caused by the negligence up to the date of trial, including any property damage, loss of earnings, and the costs of medical treatment.

General damages are non-financial losses, both before and after the trial, and include compensation for the pain, suffering, and loss of amenity caused; compensation for a restriction in employability;[65] and compensation for the loss of congenial employment.[66]

The claimant may also recover damages for future financial losses, including loss of earnings and the costs of medical treatment and care. In the case of serious personal injury, these may be substantial, and it is this element of the award of damages that can run into millions of pounds.

Damages to compensate for pain, suffering, and loss of amenity are much lower. The maximum payable to compensate the claimant for the pain, suffering, and loss of amenity for a very serious injury resulting in severe brain damage or complete paralysis is about £493,000.[67]

64 The Part 36 procedure under the Civil Procedure Rules allows the court to award costs against a claimant if the claimant does not accept an offer of settlement and, at trial, fails to obtain a judgment more favourable than the offer. In other words, if the damages awarded are less than an offer that the claimant has refused, the claimant must pay the defendant's costs.

65 This is known as a *Smith v Manchester* award: *Smith v Manchester Corp* (1974) 17 KIR 1.

66 *Morris v Johnson Matthey* (1967) 112 Sol Jo 32.

67 The Judicial College, 'Guidelines for the Assessment of General Damages in Personal Injury Cases' (17th edn 2024).

SPECIAL DAMAGES

Any financial loss directly caused by the injury up to the date of trial is claimable as special damages. Where there is property damage, this includes the cost of repairing or replacing the damage, and, if appropriate, of hiring a replacement while the original property is being repaired.

Where the claimant is unable to work because of a personal injury, any loss of earnings can be claimed. Other commonly claimed special damages include the costs of medical treatment and any associated costs, such as transport to and from the hospital.

Claimants are obliged to act reasonably and to mitigate their losses where possible. If, for example, a claimant's work vehicle is damaged in a road traffic accident, the claimant cannot claim loss of earnings because he or she was no longer able to carry on his or her business: the claimant is expected to hire another vehicle. The costs of hiring a replacement vehicle can be claimed as special damages.

A claim for special damages must be accompanied by a complete schedule of each item claimed, with evidence, in the form of receipts, payslips, etc.

GENERAL DAMAGES

General damages are those damages which do not have an exact financial value: they may be non-financial damage, such as the pain and suffering caused by an injury, or they may be future financial costs whose exact value can only be estimated.

PAIN, SUFFERING, AND LOSS OF AMENITY

The award of damages for pain, suffering, and loss of amenity compensates the claimant for the personal injury. Other elements of damages, with the exception of loss of congenial employment awards, relate to financial consequences, such as the costs of care and loss of income.

Awards for pain, suffering, and loss of amenity are, perhaps, surprisingly low, particularly when multimillion-pound settlements for personal injury are reported. Awards are set on the basis of guidelines issued by the Judicial College. The guidelines issued in 2024, provide the following figures:

Amputation of both legs below the knee	£245,000 to £329,620
Loss of a hand	£117,360 to £133,810
Complete loss of vision	In the region of £327,940
Severe psychiatric illness	£66,920 to £141,240
Very severe brain damage	£344,150 to £493,000

The court will take a number of factors into account when determining how much, within the range indicated by the guidelines, the award should be. Long-term effects of the injury, including loss of function, continued need for medical treatment, and long-term pain, will push the injury to the top of the range.

LOSS OF CONGENIAL EMPLOYMENT

Loss of congenial employment means that the claimant has to give up work that he or she enjoys. The court will usually make such an award where there is evidence that the claimant derived particular pride, enjoyment, or satisfaction from his or her work. In *Appleton v El-Safty*,[68] a professional footballer was unable to continue playing football after reconstructive surgery on his knee was negligently carried out. The court awarded £25,000 for the loss of a career that was his 'passion'.[69] As the court acknowledged, this was in 'exceptional circumstances' and awards are usually lower.[70] Awards have been made to skilled tradesmen,[71] prison officers,[72] and, on one occasion, a person who had to give up his voluntary work as a motorcycle courier taking blood and tissue samples between hospitals.[73]

RESTRICTION OF FUTURE EMPLOYABILITY

In the case of *Smith v Manchester Corp*,[74] the claimant was awarded £1,000 for the 'existing and permanent reduction' in her earning capacity. An award for reduction in earning capacity is now known as a '*Smith v Manchester* award'. The award compensates the claimant where the long-term effects of the injury mean that, if the claimant loses his or her current job, he or she may have to take lower-paid employment.

LOSS OF FUTURE EARNINGS

Where the claimant is unable to work as a result of the damage caused by the defendant's negligence, any loss of earnings up to the date of trial can be accurately calculated and should form part of the claim for special damages. How much the claimant will lose in future earnings is less certain: it may be reasonable to assume that the claimant would continue to earn a comparable amount, taking into account increases in earnings as a result of wages growth, and that the claimant would have opportunities to increase his or her earnings by promotion within his or her chosen career, but these are assumptions rather than facts.

In *Appleton v El-Safty*,[75] the court considered the claimant's prospects and made a number of assumptions about the course of his career and his earnings as a footballer, potential earnings from media work, and taking into account the possibility of the player becoming a manager. The award took into account that the claimant's club had been promoted to the Premiership, and that the claimant would expect to be paid significantly more as a Premiership player.

68 [2007] EWHC 631 (QB).

69 Ibid, [84] (Sir Christopher Clarke J).

70 *Wilbye v Gibbons* [2003] EWCA Civ 372, [11] (Kennedy LJ).

71 *Seers v Creighton & Son Ltd* [2015] EWHC 959 (QB).

72 *Marsh v Ministry of Justice* [2017] EWHC 1040 (QB).

73 *Lowe v Firth-Campbell* (Unreported, Sheffield County Court, 26 October 2017).

74 (1974) 17 KIR 1.

75 [2007] EWHC 631 (QB).

Any figure for future earnings is, however, an estimate based on the most likely turn of events and reasonable assumptions, rather than an accurately calculable figure.

FUTURE MEDICAL AND CARE COSTS

A claim for general damages will include the expected future costs of medical treatment and care.[76]

Where a claimant suffers from a severe disability, where 24-hour care is required over the claimant's expected life, all costs are recoverable, including costs of equipment and adaptation of the claimant's home.

PROVISIONAL DAMAGES

In some cases, the court will make an award of provisional damages, which compensate for the known risk of additional medical conditions being caused by the injury. One such circumstance in which such awards are made is where the claimant has suffered a brain injury. In these cases, it is foreseeable that, in a significant number of cases, the claimant will suffer from epilepsy at some point in the future. A provisional award of damages compensates the claimant for the increased risk.[77]

FATAL ACCIDENTS

Where the negligence results in a death, a claim may be brought by his or her estate for the benefit of the victim's dependants. This is governed by the Fatal Accidents Act 1976. The dependants can claim for all damages that the victim could have recovered up to the point of their death, including damages for pain, suffering, and loss of amenity, and loss of earnings if the victim did not die during the incident.[78]

The claimants under the Fatal Accidents Act can also claim for bereavement, and loss of financial support and loss of services, such as care, where they were dependent on the victim.[79]

INJUNCTIONS

Injunctions are orders of the court, usually addressed to the defendant, ordering him or her to either do something or refrain from doing something. They may be interim injunctions, granted before trial, or final injunctions, granted as a remedy.

---

76 This can include as noted in the Supreme Court judgment in *Whittington Hospital NHS Trust v XX* [2020] UKSC 14, the claimant's commercial surrogacy treatment from outside of the UK (note that commercial surrogacy treatment is not permitted in the UK). There are limits, as noted by Lady Hale (at [53]) in terms of 'the costs involved must be reasonable'. Moreover, as noted by Lady Hale (at [53]) that 'the proposed programme of treatments must be reasonable' and further that (at [53]) 'it must be reasonable for the claimant to seek the foreign commercial arrangements proposed rather than to make arrangements within the UK'.

77 The Senior Courts Act 1981 s.32A.

78 Damages for pain and suffering while dying are not recoverable: *Hicks v Chief Constable of South Yorkshire Police* [1992] 2 All ER 65.

79 Fatal Accidents Act 1976 ss.1A, 3.

Where, for example, an activity carried on by the defendant is causing a nuisance to the owner of neighbouring land, the claimant's priority may be to stop the defendant's activity rather than being compensated for the nuisance.

Since an injunction is usually in the form of an order to the defendant to do something or to stop doing something, it is implicit in the granting of the injunction that the defendant is doing, or not doing, something intentionally.[80] That means that they are rarely appropriate in the case of negligence claims, where the harm is not caused intentionally, but by the failure of the defendant to take reasonable care.

DECLARATIONS

The High Court may, under its inherent jurisdiction, make a declaration. A declaration is a statement, by the court, that a certain state of affairs exists or that certain facts are established. In some cases, this may be the principal aim of the parties to the dispute, and no other remedy is required. For example, where two landowners are disputing the boundary between their lands, a declaration that the boundary follows a particular course will settle the argument. It is rarely applicable in negligence, although a finding by the court that the defendant failed to take reasonable care may be important to the claimant.

POINTS TO REVIEW

- Contributory negligence is a partial defence to a negligence claim that applies when the claimant's failure to take care for his or her own safety contributes to the damage suffered.
- If the court finds that the claimant's fault has contributed to the damage, it can reduce the damages by an amount that it considers just and equitable.
- In determining what is a just and equitable amount to reduce damages where there has been contributory negligence by the claimant, the court will consider the blameworthiness and causal potency of both parties' acts.
- If a claimant voluntarily assumes the risk of an activity, he or she cannot claim for any injury caused by that risk.
- Where a passenger accepts a lift from a drunk driver, the defence of voluntary assumption of risk is excluded by statute, but the defendant can plead contributory negligence.
- Employees do not voluntarily accept the risks of their employment, unless they are doing something dangerous, on their own initiative.
- Rescuers are not regarded as acting voluntarily.
- When determining whether the illegality defence applies, the courts will weigh up public policy and look at proportionality.

80 An exception to this may be where the defendant is allowing a nuisance on his or her land to continue, which causes damage to neighbouring land. In this case, a claim may be made in negligence or nuisance (there is no difference between the claims in these cases: *Delaware Mansions v Westminster City Council* [2001] UKHL 55, [2002] 1 AC 321, [31]) seeking an injunction to stop the defendant from continuing the nuisance.

- Where two or more people are engaged in a joint criminal activity, a claimant cannot sue in negligence for harm caused by the criminal activity, whether the harm is caused by the claimant or any of the other participants.
- The main remedy in negligence is compensatory damages.
- Compensatory damages are intended to put the claimant into the position he or she would have been in if the harm had never happened.
- Damages are recoverable for all financial losses caused by the negligence, including costs of repairing or replacing damaged property, loss of earnings, and future costs of medical treatment and care.
- Damages are recoverable for the pain, suffering, and loss of amenity caused by personal injuries.
- Damages are payable for a loss of future employability and loss of congenial enjoyment.
- Other remedies, such as injunctions, are rarely granted in negligence.

TAKING IT FURTHER

Gardner, J. 'Rethinking Risk Taking: The Death of Volenti?' (2023) 82(1) Cambridge Law Journal 110–137

Considers several issues with the defence of *volenti* and limitations. Considers that *volenti* should be abolished, with some cases dealt with through contributory negligence and others through another tort element.

10

CHAPTER 10
EMPLOYERS' LIABILITY

This chapter discusses employers' non-delegable duty of care, breach of statutory duty, and vicarious liability.

What happens if an employee at work trips down some badly lit stairs and injures their ankle? What if a worker on scaffolding drops a hammer on a pedestrian passing underneath? This chapter is about when the employer has to pay compensation for the injury. This occurs in two broad categories of case:

1. Where an employer is liable for harm done *to* its employees. In this context, we consider: (a) the employer's non-delegable duty of care; and (b) the tort of breach of statutory duty. In other words, this is where the employer itself is at fault, for example because there are unsafe working conditions (like the badly lit stairs).
2. Where an employer is liable for harm done by its employees. This is the concept of vicarious liability. It can extend beyond a strict employment relationship to encompass other relationships 'akin to employment'. In other words, this is where the employee is at fault (like dropping the hammer on the pedestrian), but the employer is made to pay compensation.

This chapter proceeds as follows. First, we consider an employer's non-delegable duty of care. Second, we discuss, more briefly, breach of statutory duty. Third, we discuss some defences potentially available to the employer. Finally, we address vicarious liability.

AS YOU READ

- Distinguish between an employer's liability *to* its employees, and an employer's liability for torts committed *by* its employees.
- Understand how these two regimes can also overlap.
- Be aware of how the facts might give rise to other causes of action in tort besides employers' liability.
- Be aware that the doctrine of vicarious liability is still evolving.
- Consider how the law might be simplified or improved.

DOI: 10.4324/9781003480051-10

10.1 NON-DELEGABLE DUTY OF CARE

KEY LEARNING POINT

An employer owes a non-delegable duty of care to its employees to provide a reasonably safe place and system of work, competent staff, and adequate equipment.

In this section, we will consider what is meant by 'non-delegable', before exploring what the requirements are for a safe system of work, competent staff, adequate equipment, and a safe place of work.

NON-DELEGABLE

An employer does not guarantee that there will be no accidents at work. The workplace does not have to be 100% safe. But it does have to be reasonably safe. An employer owes a duty of care to its employees to provide a reasonably safe workplace. This is called (perhaps unhelpfully) a non-delegable duty.[1] Really, what this means is that the employer will be liable if the workplace is not reasonably safe, no matter what steps the employer has otherwise taken. It is all about the outcome: is the workplace reasonably safe? If not, the employer is liable. It is no defence, for example, for the employer to say that they took reasonable care in delegating the task to someone else, or in appointing a specialist third party, whose job it was to ensure that the workplace was reasonably safe. If, despite everything else that has been done, the workplace is still not reasonably safe, then the employer is still liable.

EXPLAINING THE LAW

It is called a non-delegable duty of care. Note this distinction: the employer can delegate the task, but they cannot delegate (or shrug off) the legal duty of care. For example, at a factory, an employer might delegate to an employee to ensure that factory floor is free from obstacles. Nevertheless, if obstacles remain on the factory floor, then another employee who trips over an obstacle and suffers injury can still blame and sue the employer. It is no defence for the employer to say that this was the act of an employee.

Further, an employer is under a statutory duty, on pain of criminal liability, to obtain insurance to cover its liability for injury sustained by its employees in the course of their employment.[2] This seeks to ensure that if an employee does suffer injury, then an employer should always be able financially to meet any obligation to pay compensation.

1 *Wilson and Clyde Coal Co Ltd v English* [1938] AC 57 (HL).

2 Employers' Liability (Compulsory Insurance) Act 1969. While breach of this statutory duty may incur criminal liability, it does not incur civil liability: *Richardson v Pitt-Stanley* [1995] QB 123 (CA); *Campbell v Peter Gordon Joiners Ltd* [2016] UKSC 38.

It makes sense to impose the duty to insure on the party with the legal obligation to pay compensation. Thus, if the duty to insure is imposed on the employer, it is good policy to make certain that the legal obligation to pay compensation remains with the employer, and cannot be delegated or shrugged off to someone else (who themselves might not be insured). Ultimately, this is all about protecting employees, by holding an employer to account, legally and financially, for the safety of its employees. The law empowers the employee against the employer.

MAKING CONNECTIONS

An employer who fails to take reasonable care of its employees might also incur liability in negligence for any injury suffered.

Negligence asks: what steps has the employer taken to protect its employees? Were those steps reasonable? For example, an employer might engage a consultant with a specialism for safety at work to advise ways to make the workplace safer. That would be reasonable behaviour by the employer. In contrast, the non-delegable duty of care considers not what steps the employer has taken, but the end result. Thus, an employer might behave reasonably in appointing a consultant and following their advice, and so avoid liability in negligence, but if the end result is still an unreasonably dangerous workplace, then the employer remains liable to its employees after all for breach of its non-delegable duty.

If the unsafe workplace resulted from a failing by the consultant, then the employer might be able to sue the consultant, for example for breach of contract.

SAFE SYSTEM OF WORK

A system of work is how the work is carried out. For example, at a factory, there might be forklift trucks ferrying materials around, and people operating machinery. A safe system of work might have forklifts restricted to certain non-pedestrian zones, and the moving parts of machinery surrounded by protective fencing.

It is the employer's duty to ensure that the way in which the employee works is reasonably safe, rather than perilous of personal injury. For example, if someone is working on scaffolding, at height, they ought to be provided with a safety harness, securing them to the scaffolding, to catch them should they fall. A failure to provide a safety harness would likely make the employer liable. However, in *Cummings v Sir William Arrol & Co Ltd*,[3] the court said that, if the evidence proves that the employee would not have worn the harness anyway, the employer is

3 [1962] 1 All ER 623 (HL).

not liable after all. In other words, it was the employee's own choice not to wear the harness which was the sole cause of the accident.

ANALYSING THE LAW

The decision in *Cummings* must be questionable. There is a difference between, on the one hand, an employer providing safety equipment, which the employee secretly chooses not to wear – surely the employee bears the risk in such a situation; and on the other hand, where the employer knows that the employee is not wearing the safety equipment, as in *Cummings* itself. In the latter case, the correct approach is surely for the employer to discipline the employee, and replace them with someone prepared to work under proper conditions, rather than carry on regardless with a dangerous, even life-threatening, activity. (The employee in *Cummings* died from the fall.) What would you do with an employee who refused to act safely?

A safe system of work includes giving consideration to the mental health of the employee. In *Walker v Northumberland County Council*,[4] the claimant was a social services officer in an area which had a high proportion of childcare problems. He had a nervous breakdown because of the stress and pressures of work. He took time off work, and before returning was promised extra assistance. However, no assistance materialised, and the claimant even had to clear the backlog of work from his time off. When he suffered a second mental breakdown, the employer was liable.[5]

The court in *Walker* said that the first breakdown had not been reasonably foreseeable, but the second one had been (in light of the first one) – rendering the employer liable for the second one only. This does mean, however, that if an employee fails to speak up about the difficulties they are facing, it might not be reasonably foreseeable to an employer that the employee's health is at risk.[6]

The corollary is that an employer might need to take extra care of employees known to be at additional risk. For example, in *Paris v Stepney Borough Council*,[7] a workman in a garage had only one good eye. When he was working on a rusty vehicle, a chip flew into his good eye, causing serious injury. He had not been supplied with goggles. The court held the employer negligent. It said that, although the employee's disability did not increase the risk of an eye accident, it did increase the risk that any eye accident would be serious, and this was relevant in determining what precautions the employer should have taken.

4 [1995] 1 All ER 737 (QBD).

5 See too *Melville v Home Office* [2005] EWCA Civ 6, where a prison officer, charged with recovering the bodies of suicides, suffered psychiatric injury, which the employer foresaw, and yet failed to provide sufficient support.

6 *Barber v Somerset County Council* [2004] UKHL 13, [64] (a case about teachers suffering from stress).

7 [1951] AC 367 (HL).

COMPETENT STAFF

Many employees work in a team. It is the employer's duty to ensure that each member of the team is reasonably competent. This might involve ensuring that all staff have sufficient training in their tasks, and that they have a reasonable awareness of how to minimise the risk of accidents. It might also involve ensuring that staff behave in a responsible way.

For example, in *Hudson v Ridge Manufacturing Co Ltd*,[8] for four years an employee had larked about, tripping up fellow employees. He had been reprimanded by the foreman, but no further steps were taken to restrain his behaviour. One day he tripped the claimant, who suffered injury. Since the employer had known about this behaviour and failed to prevent it, the employer was liable to the claimant for failing to take proper care of his safety. In other words, the employer was liable for exposing the claimant to another employee who was a known risk.

In *Water v Commissioner of Police of the Metropolis*,[9] a police officer made a complaint about sexual assault against another officer. She was then bullied by other members of staff. Now, every police officer is a constable, regardless of rank, and the Office of Constable is, as it were, a stand-alone appointment, designed to ensure each police officer's independence from everyone, answerable only under the rule of law. Nevertheless, the court said that the defendant police commissioner owed duties of care towards the police officer analogous to those owed by an employer to an employee. The defendant could be liable, said the court, for mental harm caused by the bullying, where the defendant knew or might reasonably have foreseen that behaviour, yet did nothing to protect her.

MAKING CONNECTIONS

Bullying a co-worker might constitute the tort of harassment (see Chapter 13). That would make the bully both criminally and civilly liable. An employer can also be vicariously liable for harassment (see below).[10] Thus, a victim could sue both the bully for harassment and the employer for vicarious liability.

ADEQUATE EQUIPMENT

As for adequate equipment, if, for example, an employer provides a ladder for the use of its employees, the ladder must be safe to use. If, for some reason, the ladder is unsafe, then the employer will be liable for any harm done.[11]

8 [1957] 2 QB 348 (Manchester Assizes).

9 [2000] 1 WLR 1607 (HL).

10 *Majrowski v Guy's and St Thomas' NHS Trust* [2006] UKHL 34.

11 See *Wheeler v Copas* [1981] 3 All ER 405 (QBD), where a farmer negligently supplied a faulty ladder to independent contractors carrying out building work (discussed further in Chapter 11).

In addition to the non-delegable duty of care at common law, an employer might also incur statutory liability for defective equipment under the Employers' Liability (Defective Equipment) Act 1969, which provides as follows. Where an employee suffers personal injury, in the course of employment, in consequence of a defect in equipment provided by the employer for the purposes of its business, and the defect is attributable to the fault of a third party (like the manufacturer), the injury is deemed attributable to the negligence of the employer also.

MAKING CONNECTIONS

Where an employee suffers injury as a result of faulty equipment, the employee can sue the employer. If the employer bought that faulty equipment, then the employer might be able to sue the seller for breach of contract. The employer might even be able to sue a negligent manufacturer under the Civil Liability (Contribution) Act 1978.

If a ladder is otherwise safe, but is deliberately kicked away by another employee, the employer might not be liable. In *Horton v Taplin Contracts Ltd*,[12] an employee, through a deliberate and wanton act, deliberately pushed over what was otherwise safe scaffolding, because he was angry following an argument with the claimant on the scaffolding. The employer was held not liable for the claimant's injury following this violent and unpredictable act.

EXPLAINING THE LAW

In *Horton*, the court also used the language of causation: what caused the injury was not anything wrong with the scaffolding itself, nor any dereliction of duty by the employer, but the deliberate act of another disgruntled employee. Furthermore, said the court, such an act was not reasonably foreseeable. This stands in contrast to cases like *Water* (the bullied police officer) and *Hudson* (the prankster employee): if a co-worker persistently misbehaves, then the employer is likely to be in breach of its non-delegable duty to provide competent staff.

MAKING CONNECTIONS

In *Horton*, the scaffold was safe, so the employer was not in breach of its non-delegable duty to provide reasonably safe equipment. The one-off act of violence by the co-worker was not predictable, meaning that the employer was not in breach of its non-delegable duty to provide competent staff. But the employer might still be vicariously liable for the attack (there are several examples discussed below).

12 [2002] EWCA Civ 1604.

In deciding whether the equipment is defective, its purpose can be relevant. For example, a ladder may be appropriate for climbing up a wall, but unsuitable as a bridge across a ditch.

In *Fytche v Wincanton Logistics plc*,[13] an employee, who drove a milk tanker, was provided with steel-capped boots. While out on delivery, the employee's truck got stuck on an icy road. The protocol prescribed by the employer was to stay in the cab, and call for help. Nevertheless, the employee sought instead to dig out the truck. There was a hole in one boot, and the employee caught frostbite. The court held that the boot was *not* defective: it was meant to protect against impact injuries, like falling milk churns, not against the cold.

ANALYSING THE LAW

Lady Hale in *Fytche* thought that the boots were defective: they had a hole in them. After all, we might say, surely footwear has multiple functions. The steel caps are there to protect the toes from falling objects. However, shoes are also meant to protect the feet from other injury, like treading on something sharp. Anyone sent out into the cold can surely expect clothing from their employer which offers some protection from the weather too. The employee may have been to blame for not staying in the cab, but that is a separate question from whether the boots were defective. If an employee in England gets frostbite, is there not something wrong with their clothes?

SAFE PLACE OF WORK

An employer is under a duty to provide a reasonably safe place of work. This can involve ensuring against hazards which might entail personal injury. For example, floors should be clean, and free of obstacles to trip over, while machinery with sharp moving parts should be fenced in.

In *Latimer v AEC Ltd*,[14] a heavy rainstorm caused a factory floor to flood. The employer put down sawdust, but there was not enough to cover the whole floor. An employee slipped on a part of the floor left uncovered. The court held that the employer was not negligent, having done all that could be reasonably expected, bearing in mind the degree of risk involved.

MAKING CONNECTIONS

An occupier of premises (including an employer) owes a duty to take reasonable care to see that a visitor (including an employee) will be reasonably safe in using the

13 [2004] UKHL 31. In that case, the claim was framed as a breach of the Personal Protective Equipment at Work Regulations 1992 (SI 1992/2966). Now, however, breach of health and safety regulations rarely result in civil liability: Health and Safety at Work Act 1974 s.47 (discussed below). The court's approach in *Fytche* would still apply analogously to a claim for breach of the common law non-delegable duty to provide adequate equipment.

14 [1953] 2 All ER 449 (HL).

premises (see Chapter 11). An employee who suffers injury because of the condition of the workplace premises will often sue for breach of an employer's non-delegable duty of care, and under the Occupiers' Liability Act 1957. The standard of care owed under each is comparable.

ANALYSING THE LAW

This decision in *Latimer* seems questionable. (And it pre-dates the Occupiers' Liability Act 1957.) There is a difference, also acknowledged in occupiers' liability, between, on the one hand, a rainstorm causing a slippery floor which has happened so recently that no one has yet been able to clear it up, and on the other hand, a slippery floor which has been cleaned up, but not properly. While the former will not usually attract liability, since the occupier or employer has not had a reasonable chance to act, the latter should attract liability. The employer in *Latimer* knew that the factory floor was slippery, and that action had to be taken, hence the sawdust. It was simply that the employer ran out of sawdust. Should that be the employer's problem or the employee's problem?

An employer's duty to provide a safe place of work is strongest when the employee works on the employer's own premises. If the employee works abroad, it seems that different considerations might apply. In *Cook v Square D Ltd*,[15] an electronics employee was sent to install a computer system in Saudi Arabia. He tripped on a raised floor tile and injured his knee. The court said that it lacked reality to hold the employer liable for the daily events on a site in Saudi Arabia.

ANALYSING THE LAW

The duty of care to provide a reasonably safe place of work is non-delegable, as the court confirmed in *Cook* – so what difference does it make whether the employee is sent to work in Saudi or Swindon? In 'reality', the employer is unlikely to accompany the employee to either destination. If the employer decides to send an employee to another's premises, then the employer should surely bear the risk. Its duty of care is non-delegable. Why should the employee bear the risk, when they have to work where they are told?

In *Cook*, Farquharson LJ at least accepted that, where a number of employees work on a foreign site, or for a long period, an employer might after all be required to inspect

15 [1992] ICR 262 (CA).

the site for safety. But why is an inspection not needed for a solitary employee, or a shorter length of time?[16]

MAKING CONNECTIONS

If the employee is sent to work at another's premises in England and Wales, that other person will at least owe duties of care in negligence and under occupiers' liability. Below, we discuss how the law on vicarious liability has been prepared to recognise a notion of dual vicarious liability, that is, how one employee might have two employers. Perhaps, by analogy, an employee sent to work by employer 1 at the premises of employer 2 might argue that both employers owe them a non-delegable duty of care.

10.2 BREACH OF STATUTORY DUTY

Can a citizen ever bring a civil action against a party who fails to fulfil their statutory duty? The answer lies in construing the statute, to see whether there is a clear Parliamentary intention that breach of statute should provide an injured claimant with a civil right to sue. In that regard, it may be relevant whether the statute was passed to benefit or protect a limited class of person such as the claimant, and whether the statute provides for other consequences upon breach (instead of civil liability).[17]

In this section, however, we are concerned with the narrower question, whether an employee can sue their employer for failing to comply with the latter's statutory obligations.

There is plenty of legislation governing health and safety at work. For example, under section 2 of the Health and Safety at Work Act 1974, an employer is under a general duty to ensure the reasonable health, safety, and welfare of its employees, including such matters as safe machinery, an absence of dangerous substances, provision of proper training, and proper facilities at work. What happens if an employer fails to comply with these duties?

Under section 33 of the 1974 Act, the employer incurs criminal liability. However, pursuant to section 47, the employer incurs no civil liability. Further, section 47 provides that the employer does not incur civil liability for breach of any health and safety regulations, or for breach of any other health and safety statute, unless further regulations say so.

16 In *McDermid v Nash Dredging and Reclamation Co Ltd* [1987] AC 906 (HL), the claimant was a deckhand employed by the defendant. He was assigned to work on a tug operated by another company. When the claimant suffered injury because of an unsafe system of work, the defendant was liable – even though, we might add, the place of work was not the defendant's own workplace.

17 *Lonhro Ltd v Shell Petroleum Co Ltd (No 2)* [1982] AC 173 (HL); *X v Bedfordshire County Council* [1995] 2 AC 633 (HL).

Similarly, we noted earlier how an employer is under a statutory duty to obtain insurance to cover its liability for injury sustained by its employees in the course of their employment.[18] Failure to insure results in criminal liability for the company directors, but again the employee cannot bring a civil claim against the directors.[19]

However, there are a few regulations which do indeed provide for civil liability. For example, an employer can incur civil liability when they permit a woman to work during the compulsory period of maternity leave immediately following the birth of her child;[20] or where an employer fails to carry out a risk assessment for, or make alterations to the working conditions of, a new or expectant mother.[21]

Nevertheless, even if a regulation does not provide for civil liability, it still informs normative standards of reasonable behaviour. In other words, statutory duty aside, an employer will still owe common law duties, in negligence, or under the non-delegable duty of care, or under occupiers' liability, to take reasonable care of its employees. What counts as reasonable care? That would surely be informed by what standards Parliament has dictated in its own health and safety legislation.

EXPLAINING THE LAW

Parliament may think it desirable that employers behave in certain ways. If they do not behave, it need not follow automatically that an employee can sue in tort. A range of other responses might be a more appropriate way of ensuring that an employer complies with its duties – like imposing criminal liability on company directors.

10.3 DEFENCES

In this section, we discuss the following possible defences available to employers who find themselves in breach of their non-delegable or statutory duties of care: contributory negligence by the employee; *volenti* (that is, voluntary assumption of risk by the employee); and the employee's own illegal behaviour.

CONTRIBUTORY NEGLIGENCE

An employer must take reasonable care for the safety of its employees. At the same time, the employee is also expected to take reasonable care for their own safety. Indeed, the need for

18 Employers' Liability (Compulsory Insurance) Act 1969.

19 *Richardson v Pitt-Stanley* [1995] QB 123 (CA); *Campbell v Peter Gordon Joiners Ltd* [2016] UKSC 38.

20 Health and Safety at Work etc Act 1974 (Civil Liability) (Exceptions) Regulations 2013 (SI 2013/1667).

21 Management of Health and Safety at Work Regulations 1999 (SI 1999/3242), reg 22.

an employee to take reasonable care for their own safety, and to cooperate as their employer attempts to fulfil its statutory duties, is made explicit in section 7 of the Health and Safety at Work Act 1974.

If an employee is injured because they take unreasonable risks, that will likely reduce any compensation the employee receives on account of their own contributory negligence. If the employee's risk-taking is wholly to blame, then their own negligence will be the sole cause of the accident, and the employer will incur no liability at all (as we saw with *Cummings* and the scaffold worker who refused to wear the safety harness).

ASSUMPTION OF RISK

Just because an employee has turned up to work, that alone does not mean that the employee has voluntarily assumed the risk of injury at work. In particular, *volenti*, or voluntary assumption of risk, is *not* a defence when the employer is itself in breach of duty.

For example, in *Wheeler v New Merton Board Mills Ltd*,[22] the employer, in breach of statutory duty, failed to fence in a machine. The employee was allowed to use the machine. This did not mean that the employee had voluntarily assumed the risk of being injured by the machine. The court held that the employer could not raise the defence of *volenti*.

EXPLAINING THE LAW

If an employer is in breach of its non-delegable duty to provide a reasonably safe place of work, but directs the employee to continue working anyway, what should the employee do? The employee might protest, or refuse to follow the employer's orders, or even resign and find a new job. However, this puts a lot of pressure on the employee. Refusing to follow orders may cause strain in their relationship with the employer. Finding a new job might not be realistic if other jobs are not available, or not available soon enough to meet the daily financial needs of the employee. Rather, the decision in *Wheeler* in effect says that the employee can carry on working (if they are willing to run the risk, or have little practical choice), and the employer remains liable for any subsequent injury. In other words, *Wheeler* recognises that when an employee follows orders, this is not usually the sort of free choice which might characteristically give rise to a defence of *volenti*, but often no real choice at all.

Similarly, there was no defence of *volenti* in *Smith v Charles Baker & Sons*,[23] where an employee continued to work on a railroad, even though this exposed him to the known danger of a crane swinging stones overhead. (A stone fell and injured the employee.) Also, there was no

22 [1933] 2 KB 669 (CA).
23 [1891] AC 325 (HL).

defence of *volenti* in *Davies v Global Strategies Group (Hong Kong) Ltd*,[24] when the employee went to Iraq as a security officer, even though Iraq was obviously a risky place to work.

However, *volenti* can be a defence when the employer itself is not in breach of duty. In *ICI Ltd v Shatwell*,[25] two employees were carrying out explosions in a quarry. Statutory regulations, and the employer's orders, required the employees to be in a shelter at the time of the explosions, as they knew. Instead, they carried out the explosions in the open, and suffered injury. The court said that *volenti* was a complete defence for the employer.

MAKING CONNECTIONS

In *Cummings*, discussed above, a worker fell to his death from scaffolding when he should have been wearing a harness. The court said that any breach of duty by the employer had no causative effect, since the employee would have refused to wear the harness anyway. We might say, alternatively, that the employee in *Cummings* voluntarily took the risk of injury by refusing to wear a harness, like the employees in *Shatwell* not taking cover. Thus, we can see here a relationship between questions of causation, and the defence of *volenti*.

ANALYSING THE LAW

Note again the differences between *Cummings* and *Shatwell*. In *Cummings*, the employee chose not to wear the harness, and the employer knew about this general practice. In *Shatwell*, the employees chose not to abide by the safety rules, but this was contrary to their employer's directions, and there was nothing to suggest that the employer knew that the employees would behave that way. Hence, in *Shatwell*, it seems fair to excuse the employer. In contrast, why excuse the employer in *Cummings* who was complicit in the employee breaking the rules?

ILLEGALITY

Illegality might also be relevant. In *Hewison v Meridian Shipping Services Pte Ltd*,[26] a seafarer fraudulently concealed his epilepsy from his employer. Had he revealed his condition, he would not have been employed as a seafarer. He was injured at work and sued for compensation. The employer admitted liability for the accident, and on that basis had to pay compensation for the injury itself. However, the court said that the employer did not have to pay compensation for future loss of earnings from being a seafarer, because those earnings were dependent on continuing to defraud the employer.

24 [2009] EWHC 2342 (QB), [86].

25 [1965] AC 656 (HL).

26 [2002] EWCA Civ 1821.

ANALYSING THE LAW

The decision in *Hewison* is probably right, as far as it goes: an employee should not be able to sue for loss of future earnings from a job which the employee could not lawfully carry out. However, if the claimant was unable to work again, because of the accident, whether as a seafarer or anything else, one would have expected the claimant to argue, in the alternative, for compensation which reflected loss of future income from any other job he could lawfully have done instead. For example, if the claimant could lawfully have worked as a cashier in a bank, but now cannot work at all because of the accident, then he might have sued for loss of future earnings as a cashier.

10.4 VICARIOUS LIABILITY

A worker on scaffolding drops a hammer on a pedestrian passing underneath. It will usually be more attractive for the pedestrian to sue the worker's employer rather than the worker. As compared to the worker, the employer is more likely to have public liability insurance to pay for the injury and is anyway more likely to have greater assets should it need to fund any compensation out of its own pocket. Vicarious liability is the doctrine which makes the employer liable for the torts of its workers.

MAKING CONNECTIONS

Vicarious liability is not just about workers injuring third parties. Workers might also injure co-workers. For example, if one employee negligently harms another employee, the victim might be able to sue: the employer, for breach of the employer's non-delegable duty of care (for example, for not providing competent staff); the employer, as vicariously liable for the negligence of the employee who caused the harm; and the employee who caused the harm, for their own negligence.

Now, the law of vicarious liability is evolving. Traditionally, it is about an employer incurring liability for torts committed by its employees in the course of their employment. More recently, it has been extended, beyond employers, to those 'akin to employers', and to behaviour 'closely' connected to the employee's work.

KEY LEARNING POINT

An employer, or someone akin to an employer, is vicariously liable for harm inflicted by the tortious act of its worker where there is close connection to their work.

In this section, we consider the following questions. Which types of worker can cause vicarious liability to arise? Can more than one employer be vicariously liable for the torts of a single worker (the question of dual vicarious liability)? What does it mean for someone to be 'akin' to an employer? Which type of acts can cause vicarious liability to arise? We shall take each in turn.

WHICH WORKERS?

Not every type of worker attracts vicarious liability.

Traditionally, the contrast is between an employee and an independent contractor. An employee can attract vicarious liability, whereas an independent contractor cannot.[27]

Now consider this scenario. I am buying a house. The house is still under construction. I am viewing the house, when I get hit by a ladder, carried by a negligent carpenter. Whom can I sue? In particular, is the carpenter a one-person business, engaged by the developer as an independent contractor? Alternatively, is the carpenter employed by the developer, so that I can sue the developer as well or instead? This matters, depending on who has insurance or the financial means to meet my claim for compensation.

In *Ferguson v John Dawson & Partners (Contractors) Ltd*,[28] labourers on a building site were styled 'self-employed' by their contract, to avoid income tax and national insurance contributions being deducted from their weekly payments. However, when a labourer was injured, the court held them to be an employee: the defendant could dismiss them, move them to other sites, tell them what work to do, and provide tools.

According to Cooke J in *Market Investigations Ltd v Minister of Social Security*,[29] the fundamental question is whether the person providing the service is in business on their own account (in which case they are independent contractors).[30] In answering that question, he said, relevant considerations include: whether that person provides their own equipment, whether they can hire extra staff, what degree of financial risk they take in providing the service, what opportunity there is to earn profit, what degree of responsibility they have for management, and whether or not their work is subject to control by others.[31]

This traditional distinction, between an employee and an independent contractor, is still useful.[32] But now, other types of worker, beyond employees, can also attract vicarious liability.

27 Somewhat unhelpfully, it is sometimes expressed as the difference between a contract *of* service (employee) and a contract *for* services (independent contractor).

28 [1976] 1 WLR 1213 (CA).

29 [1969] 2 QB 173 (QBD).

30 The test adopted in *Lee Tin Sang v Chung Chi-Keung* [1990] 2 AC 374 (PC).

31 On this basis, even an employment agency can be an employer of workers on its books: *McMeechan v Secretary of State for Employment* [1997] IRLR 353 (CA).

32 As recently confirmed in *Kafagi v JBW Group Ltd* [2018] EWCA Civ 1157, where a bailiff was held to be an independent contractor, and the debt collection agency which used him was not vicariously liable for the assault he committed.

This has come about in two ways: (1) with the recognition of dual vicarious liability; and (2) in the context of relationships akin to employment. We shall take each in turn.

DUAL VICARIOUS LIABILITY

What happens when an employee is loaned by one employer to another?

Previously, only one person could be vicariously liable for a worker. For example, in *Mersey Docks and Harbour Board v Coggins & Griffith (Liverpool) Ltd*,[33] a harbour authority let a mobile crane, with driver, to a firm of stevedores, for loading a ship. The crane driver was negligent and injured another person. Although the firm of stevedores was directing what the crane was picking up and moving, it was held that the harbour authority alone remained vicariously liable for the driver. At the time, the driver was paid by, and could be dismissed by, the harbour authority. Further, the stevedores could not tell him how to drive the crane; that discretion was vested in him by the harbour authority. Further still, it made no difference that, as between the harbour authority and the stevedores, the contract of hire said that the crane driver would be the servant of the stevedores.

EXPLAINING THE LAW

How the parties view the arrangement, and so how they describe things in a contract, is relevant – but it is not conclusive, as cases like *Ferguson v John Dawson* and *Mersey Docks* demonstrate. After all, it is for the courts to decide the true state of affairs, and not for the parties to decide (and thereby oust the role of the courts).

Now, however, it has been accepted that more than one party can be vicariously liable for a worker. In *Viasystems (Tyneside) Ltd v Thermal Transfer (Northern) Ltd*,[34] there was a chain of subcontractors working on a site, when a worker's negligence caused a fracture in the fire sprinkler system, leading to flooding. It was held that more than one of the subcontractors was vicariously liable. Rix LJ said that the relevant question was whether the worker was so much part of the work, business, or organisation of both employers that it was just to make both employers answer for his negligence.[35]

We might put it this way: if what the worker does is a central part of fulfilling the responsibilities of multiple parties, all those parties should have to take the consequences of the worker's negligence.

33 [1947] AC 1 (HL).

34 [2005] EWCA Civ 1151.

35 Ibid [79], an approach endorsed in *Various Claimants v Catholic Child Welfare Society* [2012] UKSC 56, [45].

EXPLAINING THE LAW

In a case like *Viasystems*, the injured party could recover in full from either 'employer'. Thereafter, the employer who paid could recover a contribution from the other employer, under the Civil Liability (Contribution) Act 1978. That contribution would be a 50% share. As the court said in *Viasystems*, since the two employers vicariously liable were not personally at fault, it was equitable, when it came to assessing their respective contributions, that each would bear an equal share.

ANALYSING THE LAW

If a worker is an independent contractor, there is no vicarious liability. If the worker is an employee, there can be vicarious liability. However, what dual vicarious liability shows is how flexible, or non-technical, the concept of employee is. In a case like *Viasystems*, only one party will be paying the worker a wage and deducting income tax. The worker will only have signed a contract of employment with one party. Nevertheless, in *Viasystems*, there was more than one party which could control or supervise the work being done. Also, there was more than one party procuring that work, to fulfil their own obligations to get that work done. What a case like *Viasystems* shows is how policy-driven the notion of vicarious liability is. It is more about who should take responsibility for the worker, and less about who is the technical employer.

We might put it this way: if the work is central to a company, and the company is taking the benefit of the work, it should also shoulder the risk, and pay compensation to the victim of the worker's tort. Ultimately, dual vicarious liability seems to be about two things. First and foremost, ensuring that a victim can sue someone who can afford to pay compensation. This prospect increases the more (insured) employers are in the frame. Second, ensuring that everyone who directly benefits from the work takes their fair share of responsibility for it being properly carried out.

AKIN TO EMPLOYMENT

Vicarious liability is available outside of an employment relationship. For example, a partnership firm is liable for the wrongs of any partner.[36] Similarly, a chief officer of police is liable for the unlawful conduct of their constables.[37] However, these are specialist contexts. More recently, the court has recognised in general terms that a worker can give rise to vicarious liability in another party whose relationship to the worker is 'akin' to employment (but not actually employment).

36 Partnership Act 1890 s.10.

37 Police Act 1996 s.88.

In *E v English Province of Our Lady of Charity*,[38] the claimant alleged that she had been sexually abused at school by a priest appointed by the bishop. There is no employment contract between a bishop and a priest. Nevertheless, said the court, the relationship was sufficiently akin to employment that it was just and fair to impose vicarious liability on the bishop. After all, the bishop had a degree of control over the priest, and the priest played a role which was central to the objectives of the church, into whose structure the priest was integrated.

KEY CASES

In *Various Claimants v Catholic Child Welfare Society*,[39] the claimants were residents at a boys' Catholic school. The diocesan bodies responsible for managing the school left it to a charity to supply the teachers. The mission of the charity was providing a Catholic education to children, and the charity consisted of Catholic brethren who took vows to the charity. The claimants, who were previously boys at the school, made allegations of sexual assault against the brethren teachers. Although there was no employment contract between the charity and the brethren, the court held that the charity could be vicariously liable. The business and mission of the charity was the common business and mission of the brethren who were members of the charity. To further its mission, the charity had put the brethren in a position, as teachers at a residential school, which created or significantly enhanced the risk of victims suffering abuse. Overall, said the court, it was fair, just, and reasonable to impose vicarious liability on the charity.

When is a relationship akin to employment? In *Catholic Child Welfare Society*, the court listed five relevant factors: (1) whether the defendant, rather than the worker, is more able to compensate the victim; (2) whether the tort was committed by the worker in the course of activity taken on behalf of the defendant; (3) whether that activity is part of the defendant's 'business';[40] (4) whether the defendant, in using the worker, created the risk of the tort; and (5) to what extent the worker is under the control of the defendant.

Here are some further examples where vicarious liability was imposed despite the absence of an employment relationship. In *Cox v Ministry of Justice*,[41] the government was vicariously liable for a prisoner who negligently dropped a bag of rice on another person while working in the prison kitchen. In *Armes v Nottinghamshire County Council*,[42] a local authority was vicariously liable for abuse committed by foster parents with whom the authority had placed the claimant.

38 [2012] EWCA Civ 938.

39 [2012] UKSC 56.

40 It need not be a commercial enterprise. For example, *Catholic Child Welfare Society* was a charity.

41 [2016] UKSC 10.

42 [2017] UKSC 60.

KEY CASE

Barclays Bank v Various Claimants[43] involved a claim against Barclays Bank, after a doctor who performed medical checks on applicants for employment to the bank sexually assaulted them. The Supreme Court found that Barclays Bank were not vicariously liable. There were several patients of the doctor, the doctor would have carried his own insurance, and could refuse to perform medical checks if requested. The doctor was an independent contractor, rather than there being a relationship akin to employment. Further, Lady Hale stated that 'in doubtful cases' the five factors stated in *Catholic Child Welfare Society* 'may be helpful';[44] however, in clearer cases, they do not need to be considered. It is evident, consequently, that there continues to be a difference between a relationship 'akin to employment' and a contractor, the latter of which does not entail vicarious liability.

In *Trustees of the Barry Congregation v BXB*,[45] the claimant was a Jehovah's Witness who was raped by an elder while at the elder's house. The claimant sued the Trustees of Barry Congregation as well as the Watch Tower and Bible Tract Society of Pennsylvania (worldwide supporters of Jehovah's Witnesses). The Supreme Court found that the relationship between the elder and organisations was akin to employment with several factors present, such as that the defendant worked on behalf of the organisation and with duties to further the aims of the organisation, although found no vicarious liability due to the second stage of vicarious liability.

WHICH ACTS?

Not every type of act done by a worker attracts vicarious liability. Traditionally, the question is whether the act was done in the course of employment. For example, if a dentist performs dentistry work on someone at the dental practice, that work is done in the course of the dentist's employment. If the same dentist, while on a skiing holiday in France, bumps into someone when exiting the chair lift, that occurrence is not in the course of the dentist's employment.

It can still be in the course of employment, even though what the worker does is negligent. This must be so. For example, an employer orders all its employees not to be negligent. Nevertheless, one employee commits a negligent act. If the employer could turn around and say that the act was not in the course of employment, because the employer had prohibited negligence, that would sidestep the doctrine of vicarious liability. However, the very purpose of vicarious liability is to make an employer liable for the torts of its employees. Thus, when it comes to the course of employment, it matters more *what* the employee is doing, rather than *how* they are doing it.

Admittedly, it can sometimes be a fine line between, on the one hand, acting within the course of one's employment, but in a way which is grossly negligent, or even an abuse of one's position, and on the other hand, acting outside the course of one's employment. The best approach is to consider the case law, and get a feel, through the facts of specific cases, of where that line might lie.

43 [2020] UKSC 13.

44 Ibid, [27] (Lady Hale).

45 *Trustees of Barry Congregation v BXB* [2023] UKSC 15.

For example, an employer was vicariously liable when its employee, a tanker driver delivering petrol, took a cigarette break, and discarded the match, causing an explosion.[46] An employer can be vicariously liable when one member of staff harasses a colleague at work.[47] A nightclub owner was vicariously liable when its bouncer stabbed a patron, where the owner had previously encouraged the bouncer to use violence.[48] A firm of solicitors was liable when an employee, whose job it was to draft documents, took the opportunity to draft fraudulent documents.[49]

Traditionally, acting in the course of employment, which can attract vicarious liability, is contrasted with the worker being, to quote Parke B, 'on a frolic of their own'.[50] There is no vicarious liability for a 'frolic'.

For example, the government was not vicariously liable when a policeman left his post to go into a bar and shoot at his girlfriend in a fit of jealous rage.[51] The court described this as a 'vendetta of his own'. (But the government was liable in negligence for giving a gun to an unreliable person.)

Here are two pairs of cases which fall either side of the line:

> The first scenario: employee A is assaulted at work by employee B. Is the employer vicariously liable?

- In one case, the employer was liable, because the assault was there and then, an immediate if irrational reaction by B to an otherwise proper, work-related instruction given by A. It was perhaps a case of workplace frustrations boiling over.
- In another case, the employer was not liable. B was off-duty, at home and drunk, when they were called by A, asking if they might come to work to fill in for another member of staff who was ill. B was free to decline. Instead, he took offence at A's tone, and made a special trip by bicycle into work to carry out the attack. The court described it as an independent venture of his own.[52]

Table 10.1 Vicarious liability for assaults at work

Attack by fellow employee at work	
Vicarious liability	*No vicarious liability*
Face-to-face conversation, in the workplace, immediate reaction	Telephone conversation, attacker drunk and at home, special trip to work to carry out attack

46 *Century Insurance Co Ltd v NI Road Transport Board* [1942] AC 509 (HL).

47 *Majrowski v Guy's and St Thomas' NHS Trust* [2006] UKHL 34.

48 *Mattis v Pollock (t/a Flamingos Nightclub)* [2003] EWCA Civ 887.

49 *Dubai Aluminium Co Ltd v Salaam* [2002] UKHL 48. The partnership was vicariously liable, not for any tort committed by the employee, but for the equitable wrong of dishonest participation in breach of trust.

50 *Joel v Morison* (1834) 6 C & P 501, 172 ER 1338.

51 *Attorney-General of the British Virgin Islands v Hartwell* [2004] UKPC 12.

52 Both cases are addressed in the conjoined appeal in *Weddall v Barchester Healthcare Ltd* [2012] EWCA Civ 25.

The second scenario: the employee drives a vehicle. It is forbidden to carry any other people in that vehicle. But the employee does carry another person, who suffers injury because of the employee's negligence. Is the employer vicariously liable?

- In one case, the employer was not liable.[53] The employee was simply giving a lift to another colleague who happened to be travelling along the same route. The lift had nothing to do with the employee's delivery work.
- In another case, the employer was liable.[54] The person being carried was helping the employee carry out their delivery work.

Table 10.2 Vicarious liability when giving an unauthorised lift

Injured passenger carried in vehicle by employee contrary to instructions	
Vicarious liability	*No vicarious liability*
Passenger helping employee carry out their work	Passenger not doing any work, just getting a lift

And on the topic of travel: a commuter, travelling to their place of work, is acting on their own account. In contrast, when an employee is paid wages to travel from place to place as part of their work, that act of travel might be in the course of employment.[55] For example, it is part of the paid employment of a washing machine repair person that they travel to the homes of customers who bought the washing machine.

The traditional test, as we have seen, is whether the act was in the course of employment. More recently, an alternative test has been used, concerning whether there is a 'sufficient', or more recently, 'close' connection.

KEY CASES

In *Lister v Hesley Hall Ltd*,[56] the claimants were former residents of a school boarding house. They alleged that the house warden, employed by the school, had sexually abused them. The court held the school vicariously liable. Obviously, the warden was employed to care for the children, not abuse them. However, said the court, there was a 'sufficient connection' between what the warden had been employed to do and the acts of abuse to impose vicarious liability. After all, the warden had been employed to have close personal contact with the children, which itself involved inherent risks of abuse, and it was in that role that those risks materialised.

53 *Twine v Bean's Express Ltd* (1946) 175 LT 131 (CA).
54 *Rose v Plenty* [1976] 1 All ER 97 (CA).
55 *Smith v Stages* [1989] AC 928, 936–937 (HL).
56 [2001] UKHL 22.

In *Mohamud v Wm Morrison Supermarkets plc*,[57] there was a sufficient connection between the violent and racially motivated attack by an employee at a petrol station upon a customer who made an unwelcome inquiry, and the employee's job of attending to customers and responding to their inquiries, to make the supermarket vicariously liable. Lord Toulson noted that serving customers was in the employee's 'field of activities'.[58] Lord Toulson stated that 'I do not consider that it is right to regard him as having metaphorically taken off his uniform the moment he stepped from behind the counter';[59] what happened at the petrol station was an 'seamless episode' and an 'unbroken sequence of events'.[60]

In *Bellman v Northampton Recruitment Ltd*,[61] there was a sufficient connection to the company when a managing director made a violent attack on an employee at an after-party drinking session which followed the office Christmas party, because that attack happened during the managing director's drunken sermon on his power and authority within the company.

In contrast, a lack of sufficient connection to the employee's work meant that there was no vicarious liability when one garage employee, as a prank, set fire to another employee whose clothes had been splashed with flammable liquid.[62]

KEY CASE

The Supreme Court addressed the connection required in *Morrisons v Various Claimants*.[63] This involved the release of data of Morrison's employees purposely by another Morrison's employee, Skelton. The employee was employed to release data to a third party but instead released it on the internet. This, as noted by the Supreme Court, was different to other cases of vicarious liability, as in this case the intention of the employee was specifically to harm the employer. The Supreme Court found that the release of employee information on the internet was not an act which the employee was 'authorised to do'. There was therefore not a 'close' connection.

The High Court in *Morrisons v Various Claimants* noted (which was cited and affirmed by the Court of Appeal)[64] that the release of data was a 'seamless and continuous sequence of events'[65] from Skelton's employment. This was a misreading of the intention of Lord Toulson in *Morrisons v Mohamud*, said the Supreme Court in *Morrisons v Various Claimants*, who noted 'a temporal or

57 [2016] UKSC 11.

58 [2016] UKSC 11, [47] (Lord Toulson).

59 Ibid.

60 Ibid.

61 [2018] EWCA Civ 2214.

62 *Graham v Commercial Bodyworks Ltd* [2015] EWCA Civ 47.

63 [2020] UKSC 12.

64 [2018] EWCA Civ 2339, [73] (Sir Terence Etherton, Lord Justice Bean, Lord Justice Flaux).

65 [2017] EWHC 3113 (QB), [183] (Mr Justice Langstaff).

causal connection does not in itself satisfy the close connection test'.[66] Moreover, the employer in this case was not liable because the employee was pursuing a 'personal vendetta' rather than trying to enhance his employer's business.[67] This overall therefore highlights the Supreme Court trying to prevent a significant widening of vicarious liability.

Even though the Supreme Court in *Morrisons v Various Claimants* prevented a widening of vicarious liability, it did not overrule the previous *Northampton Recruitment v Bellman* case. As discussed above, this involved an assault by the director of a company to a worker outside of working hours and away from the office. The Supreme Court in *Morrisons v Various Claimants* stated that the assault in *Northampton Recruitment v Bellman*, despite not being on the work premises and outside of working hours, was closely connected. The managing director was 'purporting to act in the course of employment by asserting his authority'.[68] This therefore shows that while location and timing is a factor in determining whether there is 'close connection', a tort committed away from the working location and outside of working hours is not always indicative of an unsuccessful vicarious liability claim. It is evident that the application of *Northampton Recruitment v Bellman* is likely to be limited due to the specific nature of the facts, a managing director who assaulted an employee after a works staff party. However, should a company be liable for an employee's actions away from the workplace and outside of working hours?

The 'close connection test' was revisited by the Supreme Court in *Trustees of the Barry Congregation of Jehovah's Witnesses v BXB*[69] (discussed above in relation to 'akin to employment') involving the rape of the claimant by a former elder. Lord Burrows stated that the close connection test was not met and noted several factors.[70] Furthermore, this case could be contrasted with previous cases such as *Lister* and *Christian Brothers*, where the abuse was on institutional premises. The Supreme Court also stated in relation to both the employment/akin to employment test and close connection tests that 'the same two stages, and the same two tests, apply to cases of sexual abuse as they do to other cases on vicarious liability'.[71]

It is evident overall that vicarious liability and both stages of the test are very fact specific, and it will not always be clear on which side of the line a case will fall. Does the law currently provide enough clarity for claimants and employers? How could the law be clarified further?

66 [2020] UKSC 12, [31] (Lord Reed).
67 [2020] UKSC 12, [47] (Lord Reed).
68 [2020] UKSC 12, [46] (Lord Reed).
69 [2023] UKSC 15.
70 Ibid, [74].
71 [2023] UKSC 15, 24.

SUPPLEMENTARY MATTERS

There are three further points worth noting.

First, most claimants seeking to establish vicarious liability are wanting compensation for an injury which they have suffered. Thus, compensatory damages are the usual remedy. That said, aggravated and exemplary damages are also available against the vicariously liable party, even though they are not personally at fault. For example, a chief constable might still be the subject of exemplary damages for assault, false imprisonment, and malicious prosecution carried out by subordinates, albeit that these events occurred without the chief constable's personal involvement.[72]

Second, an employer who is vicariously liable for the tort of an employee might sue the employee for an indemnity. This might involve suing the employee for breach of an implied term of reasonable care and skill in their employment contract,[73] or under the Civil Liability (Contribution) Act 1978. However, this is rare. Other options might include giving the employee further training, disciplining the employee, or dismissing them.

Third, where a defendant engages an independent contractor, traditionally the defendant incurs no vicarious liability, as we have seen. However, that is not the end of the matter. The defendant might still incur *primary* liability, in one of two ways. (1) The defendant may be under a duty to take reasonable care in the selection of the independent contractor. If the defendant was negligent in selecting an incompetent contractor, and thereby exposed others to risk of harm, then the defendant might be liable in negligence. (2) The defendant might have a non-delegable duty of care. We have already seen how an employer is under a non-delegable duty to provide a reasonably safe place of work. Accordingly, if a defendant engages an independent contractor to inspect the workplace, and make it safe, but the independent contractor fails to make it safe after all, then the defendant remains liable under its non-delegable duty.

MAKING CONNECTIONS

It is not just employers who have non-delegable duties of care. In *Woodland v Essex County Council*,[74] a school took children to swimming lessons, where the swimming teacher and lifeguard were independent contractors. When a child suffered serious injury due to the negligence of the independent contractor, the court held that the school was also liable under its non-delegable duty to take care of the children. After all, said the court, the lessons were part of the school curriculum, and were held during school hours, at a time when the children had been entrusted to the school's care.

72 *Rowlands v Chief Constable of Merseyside Police* [2006] EWCA Civ 1773.

73 *Lister v Romford Ice and Cold Storage Co Ltd* [1957] AC 555 (HL).

74 [2013] UKSC 66.

APPLYING THE LAW

Bajul and Camilla work for The Devon Inn. Bajul is taking a bottle of wine into the dining room, but he is also trying to text on his mobile phone. He bumps into a chair and drops the bottle, which smashes on the floor. Camilla is also working in the dining room. About ten minutes later, as she leaves the dining room, she slips on the spilt wine. She injures her ankle, and cuts her wrist on the broken glass. Advise the parties.

Camilla will want to recover compensation for her injuries. She is most likely to sue The Devon Inn, rather than Bajul, because The Devon Inn will probably have insurance to cover this accident, or otherwise will be more likely to have sufficient money to pay her compensation.

First, she might sue The Devon Inn for breach of its duty to provide a reasonably safe workplace. The workplace was not safe: the spilt wine and remnants of broken glass were a danger. Now, it is not reasonable to expect spills to be cleaned up immediately. Nevertheless, ten minutes is probably an unreasonable delay, not just to leave a spillage on the floor, but especially when there is broken glass there too. It does not matter whether The Devon Inn told another employee to clean it up, or had a protocol for cleaning which was not followed; the duty is non-delegable, so the fact that the workplace was not reasonably safe is sufficient to incur liability.

Second, Camilla might sue The Devon Inn for its vicarious liability for the negligence of Bajul. When he dropped the bottle, Bajul was not taking reasonable care (he was texting on his phone). In short, he was negligent. He was an employee of The Devon Inn. And what he was doing – carrying a bottle of wine into the dining room, presumably for patrons there, he was acting in the course of his employment. There is little doubt that The Devon Inn will incur vicarious liability.

Since Camilla has to show that Bajul was negligent, that might provide The Devon Inn with the opportunity for them to seek an indemnity from Bajul (to cover their own liability to Camilla), either for his breach of an implied term of his employment contract to take reasonable care when working, or under the Civil Liability (Contribution) Act 1978. In terms of public relations, this might not be an attractive way for The Devon Inn to treat its employees. Also, it might be doubted whether Bajul has sufficient assets to make the effort in suing him worthwhile.

Additionally, Camilla might sue The Devon Inn under the Occupiers' Liability Act 1957 for failing to take reasonable care to see that she was reasonably safe while using the premises of The Devon Inn for the purposes of her work.

POINTS TO REVIEW

- At common law, an employer owes a non-delegable duty of care to its employees to provide a reasonably safe place and system of work, competent staff, and adequate equipment.
- An employer might not be liable for breach of duty, for example where an employee's own act is contributorily negligent or breaks the chain of causation, or where it amounts to a voluntary assumption of risk.
- An employer, or someone akin to an employer, is vicariously liable for harm inflicted by the tortious act of its worker, if there is a close connection to their work.

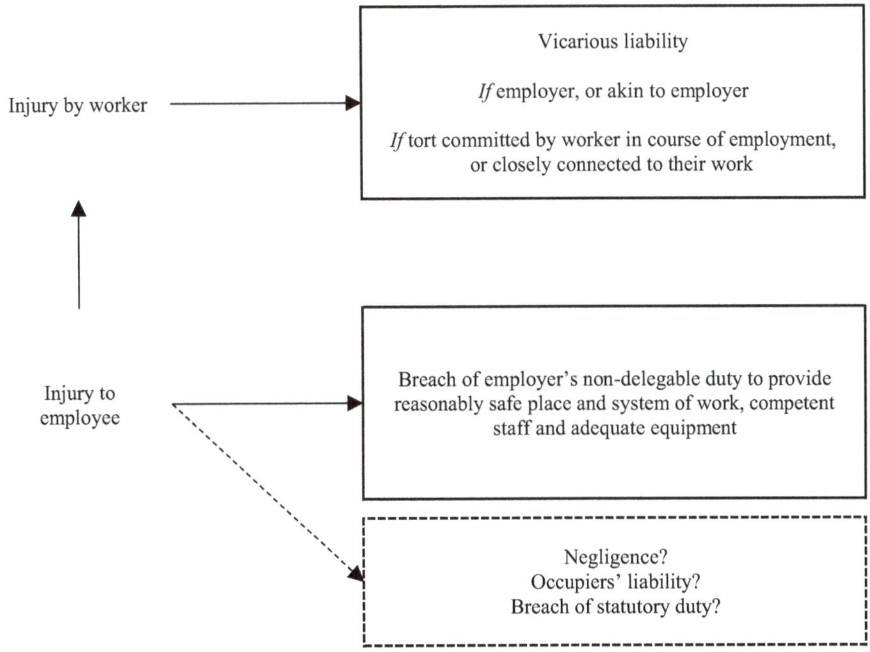

Figure 10.1 Vicarious liability: overview

TAKING IT FURTHER

Neyers, J. W. 'A Theory of Vicarious Liability' (2005) 43 Alberta L Rev 287
The author suggests that vicarious liability is not about the relationship between the employer and the tort victim, but the relationship between the worker and the employer. Specifically, vicarious liability is about the employer implicitly promising to indemnify the worker for any liability they incur in carrying out the work. One consequence, he says, is that an employer should not be able to sue their employee for an indemnity. We might ask, does this mean that an employer could explicitly refuse to indemnify an employee, and so avoid vicarious liability altogether?

Stevens, R. 'Vicarious Liability or Vicarious Action?' (2007) 123 LQR 30
The author argues that vicarious liability is a misnomer. It is not the employee's *liability* which is attributed to the employer. Rather, it is the employee's *acts* which are attributed to the employer. This is important, he says, because in some cases it can make a difference: just because an act done by one person is a tort, it does not follow that the same act done by (attributed to) another person is also a tort. We might still ask, *why* attribute one person's acts to another person? Is there a more persuasive reason to attribute acts rather than liability?

11

CHAPTER 11
OCCUPIERS' LIABILITY

This chapter discusses the duty of occupiers to take reasonable care of visitors under the Occupiers' Liability Act 1957, and of non-visitors under the Occupiers' Liability Act 1984.

If someone trips over a loose tile on the floor of a hotel lobby, can they sue for their injury? What if that person was trespassing? This chapter is about the duty of care owed by occupiers of 'premises' (typically land or buildings) to other people on those premises. The duty of care owed to *visitors* is governed by the Occupiers' Liability Act 1957. The duty of care owed to *non-visitors* (usually trespassers) is governed by the Occupiers' Liability Act 1984.

This chapter proceeds as follows. First, we shall consider some themes and concepts common to both Acts. Second, we shall discuss the duty of care owed to visitors. Third, we discuss the duty of care owed to non-visitors. Finally, we shall explore some common defences.

AS YOU READ

- Identify the differences between the regimes of the 1957 Act and the 1984 Act.
- Identify the common ground shared by the two Acts.
- Be aware of how the facts might give rise to other causes of action in tort besides occupiers' liability.
- Consider whether the law strikes a fair balance between the duties imposed on an occupier and the person injured on their premises.

11.1 COMMON THEMES

In this section, we explore how occupiers' liability is concerned with the condition of the premises, rather than activities performed on those premises. Then we turn to consider concepts like 'occupier' and 'premises' which are common to both the 1957 Act and the 1984 Act.

LIABILITY FOR CONDITION OF PREMISES

Although there remains some academic discussion of the point, the case law seems to suggest that occupiers' liability is concerned only with the condition of the premises, that is, whether the premises themselves are safe or not. It is not concerned with

DOI: 10.4324/9781003480051-11

the occupier's activities on the premises.[1] So, for example, if a visitor to a warehouse trips over an uneven floor, that might engage occupiers' liability. But if the floor is perfectly even, and the visitor is instead run over by a forklift truck, that does not engage occupiers' liability.

MAKING CONNECTIONS

Nevertheless, on the previous example, the forklift driver might be sued in negligence. And their employer might be vicariously liable (see Chapter 10). Further, harm caused by an occupier but suffered *off* premises – like an occupier who plays loud music which annoys a neighbour – might sound in nuisance (see Chapter 12).

In a similar vein, the danger must arise from the state of the premises rather than the claimant themselves doing something dangerous on those premises. In *Keown v Coventry Healthcare NHS Trust*,[2] a child was climbing up the underside of a fire escape, although he knew that he should not have been, and that it was dangerous. He fell and suffered serious injury. The court said that the occupier was not liable, since there was nothing unsafe about the fire escape itself.

EXPLAINING THE LAW

A contrary decision, said Lewison J in *Keown*, would mean that occupiers up and down the country would have to childproof their buildings just in case children tried to climb them.[3] And, we might add, the advent of the sport of free-running, which sees any structure as an opportunity for acrobatics, would otherwise pose yet more difficulties for occupiers. For example, a free-runner might run up a wall, just to perform a back-flip. How could we proof walls, fire escapes, indeed every facet of a building, against people wanting to create an opportunity for challenge?

Similarly, when a car veered off a road into a reservoir, causing the driver to drown, it was not the state of the reservoir which was the problem, but the driving.[4] In other words, just because an injury has occurred, it does not mean that the premises are to blame. All premises have some level of hazard, but exposure to that everyday hazard is not necessarily tortious. Thus, it might be a blameless accident when a shopper trips over the kerb in a car park;[5] or

1 *Revill v Newbery* [1996] QB 567 (CA); *Ogwo v Taylor* [1988] AC 431 (HL), 438; *Bottomley v Todmordern Cricket Club* [2003] EWCA Civ 1575, [31].

2 [2006] EWCA Civ 39.

3 [2006] EWCA Civ 39, [24]. In *Swain v Puri* [1996] PIQR P 442 (CA), it was suggested that the roof of an abandoned warehouse constituted an allurement to children (to explore and play there). McCowan LJ rejected that. Otherwise, he said, it meant that every householder could be said to be alluring children.

4 *Brown v South West Lakes Trust* [2022] EWCA Civ 18.

5 *Kanwarjit Singh Juj v John Lewis Partnership PLC* [2023] EWCA Civ 1507.

a passenger, struck by the normal functioning of a closing train door, falls from the carriage onto the platform;[6] or a participant falls while playing on an obstacle course.[7]

COMMON DEFINITIONS

The Occupiers' Liability Act 1984 (which applies to non-visitors) explicitly states that the terms 'occupier', 'premises', and 'visitor' have the same meaning as under the Occupiers' Liability Act 1957 (which applies to visitors).[8] We shall take those terms in order.

OCCUPIER

A duty of care is imposed upon occupiers of premises. There can be more than one occupier of the same premises, potentially with different expectations of each occupier depending on their respective levels of control.

KEY CASES

In *Wheat v Lacon & Co Ltd*,[9] a guest who was staying at a pub fell down some stairs in the night and died. The stairs were unlit because a lightbulb was missing. The wife of the guest sued the brewery who owned the pub. The brewery said that the real occupier was the publican. However, the court said that both the publican and the brewery were occupiers. The publican was resident at the pub, and thus an occupier. But the brewery, which had granted only a licence to the publican (and not a tenancy), also retained a right of access, which made them an occupier too. However, the brewery was held not liable: the staircase was only dangerous if unlit; and the brewery could not reasonably foresee that the publican would leave the stairs unlit. (And there was no evidence to suggest that the publican knew that the lightbulb was missing.)

EXPLAINING THE LAW

In *Wheat v Lacon*, there were two occupiers. The publican was concerned with day-to-day safety matters, like changing lightbulbs. The brewery, we might say, were concerned with more structural matters, like the safety of the stairs. The stairs were safe, if they were lit, and there was a light for just that reason. So structurally, the stairs were safe, and the brewery had done its job. There was no evidence that either the publican or the brewery knew that the lightbulb on the stairs was missing. Neither had behaved unreasonably. (Had they known that the lightbulb was missing, and ignored the problem, that might have been unreasonable.)

6 *Lewington v East Coast Main Line Co Ltd* [2021] All ER (D) 49 (Dec).

7 *Harrison v Bear Grylls Survival Race* [2021] EWHC 2396 (QB).

8 Occupiers' Liability Act 1984 s.1(2).

9 [1966] AC 552 (HL).

A landlord who has leased property to a tenant incurs no occupier's liability to the tenant or their guests (the landlord's liability arises under the Defective Premises Act 1972).[10] But otherwise someone can be an occupier without being in residence or otherwise attending the premises. In *Harris v Birkenhead Corp*,[11] the defendant local authority compulsorily purchased a house (as part of a clearance project), and then served on the tenant a notice of entry entitling the local authority to take possession. When the tenant moved out, the local authority did not send anyone to the house, even though it was their usual practice to brick up all ground-floor openings to prevent access by children and vandals. When a young child explored the house and fell out of an upstairs window, the local authority were liable as occupiers, since they had the immediate right of control over the premises.[12]

The corollary is that, just because someone is in attendance on site, it does not follow that they have sufficient control of the premises to incur liability as an occupier. For example, a single decorator painting the walls of a large exam hall is unlikely to be an occupier when a student entering the hall trips over an uneven floor tile in the middle of the room. (The university itself will remain the occupier.)

PREMISES

Premises typically consist of land or buildings. But they can include any fixed or moveable structure, including any vessel, vehicle, or aircraft.[13]

That said, not every moveable structure can sensibly be described as having an occupier beyond the person using it. For example, in *Wheeler v Copas*,[14] a builder was carrying out work for a farmer. The farmer supplied a ladder which the builder used. But the ladder was not strong enough, and when it gave way the builder fell, suffering injury. The court said that the farmer was not the occupier of the ladder; once the ladder was handed over, only the builder was the occupier. (Still, the builder could sue the farmer in negligence for supplying inadequate equipment. The builder was 50% contributorily negligent for not checking the ladder's suitability.)

VISITOR

A visitor is, technically, an invitee or licensee – in other words, someone who has permission to be on the premises.[15]

Someone who is exercising the 'right to roam' under the Countryside and Rights of Way Act 2000 is deemed *not* to be a visitor.[16] Nor is someone a visitor who is using a public right of

10 *Essex County Council v Davies* [2019] EWHC 3443 (QB).

11 [1976] 1 WLR 279 (CA).

12 This case was decided under the previous common law regime. The 1957 Act explicitly defers to the common law for a definition of occupier: s.1(2).

13 Occupiers' Liability Act 1957 s.1(3)(a).

14 [1981] 3 All ER 405 (QBD).

15 Occupiers' Liability Act 1957 s.1.

16 Occupiers' Liability Act 1957 s.1(4).

way.[17] However, someone who enters the premises pursuant to a right conferred by law, such as a policeman executing an arrest warrant, is deemed to be a visitor (whether or not they have permission from the occupier).[18] But these are technical examples. In most cases, a visitor is simply someone who has been given permission to be there.

A visitor might have express permission, like a guest invited to dinner. A visitor might instead have implied permission. For example, a postman has implied permission to walk up the path to the front door to deliver the mail, even though the householder has never said as much.

Implied permission can also arise where people make habitual use of the premises which the occupier tacitly allows. For example, if an occupier tolerates children playing on open ground, those children might be considered visitors with tacit permission to be there.[19] But where an occupier does try to restrain such access, for example by installing a fence and repairing it when damaged, there is no tacit permission just because the occupier knows that some people continue to go there despite the occupier's attempts to prevent them.[20]

Permission can be revoked, in which case a visitor must leave. They have a reasonable time in which to leave, and during that time they remain a visitor.[21] Afterwards, they become a trespasser.

Similarly, someone who was originally a visitor can lose that status, by going where they are not supposed to go, or staying longer than permitted, or doing something not permitted, like sliding down the bannisters instead of using the stairs.[22] But if a visitor has permission to be in one part of the premises, and the occupier wishes to exclude them from another part, then the occupier might need to make this obvious, otherwise the visitor retains permission throughout. For example, in *Gould v McAuliffe*,[23] when a pub customer, looking for a toilet, wandered mistakenly into the landlord's private area, without any notice saying, 'No entry', the customer was held to remain a visitor.

In contrast, a passenger on the London Underground ignored signs and a barrier to go where they were prohibited, and so was a trespasser, and remained so, even when they changed their mind, and tried to retrace their steps (but could not exit through a locked gate).[24]

---

17 *McGeown v Northern Ireland Housing Executive* [1995] 1 AC 233 (HL). Lord Keith said that, once a public right of way has been established, there is no question of permission being granted by the occupier (at 246). But as Lord Browne-Wilkinson said, surely a person might be a visitor after all if the only reason they are using the right of way is because the occupier asked them to come (at 248)? Note further that someone using a highway is not even owed a duty of care under the 1984 Act: s.1(7).

18 Occupiers' Liability Act 1957 s.2(6).

19 *Phipps v Rochester Corp* [1955] 1 QB 450 (QBD); *Jolley v Sutton LBC* [2000] 1 WLR 1082 (HL).

20 *Edwards v Railway Executive* [1952] AC 737 (HL).

21 In *Robson v Hallett* [1967] 2 QB 939 (DC), the court said that usually an occupier gives an implied licence to any member of the public on lawful business to come through the gate and knock on the front door. This included police officers. And when asked to leave, they had a reasonable time to do so, during which time, the police officers were still lawful visitors carrying out their duty.

22 *Geary v JD Wetherspoon plc* [2011] EWHC 1506 (QB); *The Carlgarth* [1927] P 93, 110 (Scrutton LJ).

23 [1941] 2 All ER 527 (CA).

24 *Ovu v London Underground Ltd* [2021] EWHC 2733 (QB).

MAKING CONNECTIONS

If someone is on another's land *without* permission, at least three things happen. First, that person commits the tort of trespass (see Chapter 12) and can be sued. However, this does not make them an outlaw, to whom anything might be done: the occupier must still take care for their safety. But second, a trespasser loses the protection of the 1957 Act. However, third, they are still protected by the 1984 Act (see below).

In criminal law, theft + trespass = burglary, which is important because burglary attracts a higher maximum punishment than theft. The trespass element is borrowed from tort law. So, for example, a customer has permission to visit a shop, but becomes a trespasser (and so a burglar) when, obviously without permission, they go where they are not supposed to – behind the counter in an attempt to take money from the cash register.[25]

11.2 LIABILITY TO VISITORS UNDER THE 1957 ACT

In this section, we consider the following topics: the common duty of care owed to visitors; how different visitors might have different needs; the extent to which an occupier is liable for dangers created on their premises by independent contractors (like a plumber or an electrician); what warnings might suffice to take care of visitors; and how the law regulates an occupier's attempt to exclude liability for harm suffered on their premises.

COMMON DUTY OF CARE

A customer at the supermarket slips in a puddle of spilt milk. Can the customer sue the supermarket? They might, for example, be able to sue in the tort of negligence. But they can also potentially sue the supermarket in its capacity as occupier of the building. Section 2 of the Occupiers' Liability Act 1957 sets out the duty imposed on occupiers as follows:

KEY LEARNING POINTS

- An occupier of premises owes the common duty of care to all their visitors.
- This is a duty to take such care as is reasonable in all the circumstances to see that the visitor will be reasonably safe in using the premises for the purposes of their visit.

25 *R v Walkington* [1979] 2 All ER 716.

The common duty of care is not just concerned with the personal safety of visitors: it also applies in respect of damage to another's property.[26] (We might say that the 1957 Act applies to visiting people and visiting property.) So, for example, the customer who trips on the hotel stairs might recover for their physical injury, and there might also be recovery for the broken bottle of wine the customer happened to be carrying (whether or not it belonged to them).

The occupier is only obliged to take reasonable care. The occupier does not guarantee a visitor's safety. For example, in *Laverton v Kiapasha*,[27] the claimant customer slipped on the wet floor of a takeaway restaurant, suffering injury. The court said that the restaurant had nevertheless taken reasonable care: there were slip-resistant tiles on the floor, a doormat for wiping feet, and a system for mopping up. The restaurant could otherwise not guarantee that the floor was dry when the shop was full of customers coming in from the rain.[28] In contrast, in *Ward v Tesco Stores Ltd*,[29] the supermarket left spilt yoghurt on the floor too long before mopping up, and so was liable when a customer slipped and hurt themselves.

EXPLAINING THE LAW

As McCombe LJ said in *Edwards v Sutton London Borough Council*,[30] not every accident is another's fault, and an occupier is not an insurer against injuries sustained on their premises.

In that case, the claimant fell over the side of a bridge in a park, suffering serious injuries. Perhaps that could have been prevented, for example by the defendant occupier installing additional guard rails on the bridge. But that would have been an unreasonable demand: there was nothing especially dangerous about the bridge itself, any risk of falling was obvious, and there had never been any prior accidents. The claimant simply lost his balance. It was a tragic accident, but the defendant occupier was not to blame.

In other words, just because it is technically possible to take further steps to prevent injury, that does not mean that it is reasonable to require an occupier to take those further steps. An occupier only has to do what is reasonable.[31]

26 Occupiers' Liability Act 1957 s.1(3)(b).

27 [2002] EWCA Civ 1656.

28 Similarly, in *Tedstone v Bourne Leisure Ltd* [2008] EWCA Civ 654, where a customer slipped in water at a spa, there was nothing to suggest that the defendant's regime for checking and cleaning was unreasonable. In *Richards v Bromley LBC* [2012] EWCA Civ 1476, where a pupil was injured when a door closed on her heel, there was nothing to suggest that the defendant's maintenance regime, or plans to overhaul the door in the vacation, were unreasonable. In *Cook v Swansea City Council* [2017] EWCA Civ 2142, where a customer slipped on ice in a car park, it was reasonable for the defendant only to grit the car park if a customer reported ice, rather than having to grit pre-emptively with every adverse weather forecast (either that, or shut the car park).

29 [1976] 1 All ER 219 (CA).

30 [2016] EWCA Civ 1005, [61].

31 Similarly, in *Bowen v National Trust* [2011] EWHC 1992 (QB), a school trip took shelter from the rain under a tree, when a branch fell off, crushing the children below. This was a tragic accident, but, said the court, the defendant occupier had taken reasonable care in its regime of tree inspection and maintenance. We might exaggerate, to make the point, that it would be unreasonable to demand every tree be chopped down just to preclude an unpredictable accident.

VARIETIES OF VISITOR

What an occupier has to do in order to ensure that a visitor is reasonably safe may well vary from visitor to visitor. Which is to say that some visitors require more care than others.[32]

For example, in *Pollock v Cahill*,[33] the claimant, who was blind, was an overnight guest at the defendant's home. Getting up in the morning, he lost his bearings, and seeking the door, instead fell from a window which the defendant had opened. That might have been an obvious danger for a sighted guest, but the defendant was liable for not providing a safe visit for this blind guest.[34]

Similarly, in *G4S Care and Justice Services (UK) Ltd v Manley*,[35] a prisoner reported a power failure in his cell, which meant that there was no light. When he slipped and hit his head while navigating his cell in the dark, the private prison was found liable, since it had taken unreasonably long to fix the power failure. The need for light was especially important for this prisoner because, having just had a hip operation, he was not very mobile (and so more exposed to slipping and injury).

An occupier must be prepared for children to be less careful than adults.[36] For example, children in a botanic garden might find berries tempting, so if the berries are poisonous, the occupier might need to warn or protect children against eating them.[37] Similarly, children might find a boat abandoned on land alluring to play upon, or even repair, so that the occupier of the land incurs liability when the boat collapses on top of the children.[38] But with very young children, an occupier can expect them to be accompanied by a responsible adult to protect them against obvious dangers.[39]

ANALYSING THE LAW

As Devlin J said, it would not be socially desirable if, simply by sending their children out of the house unaccompanied, parents were able to shift the burden of looking

32 Occupiers' Liability Act 1957 s.2(3).

33 [2015] EWHC 2260 (QB).

34 The claimant, a former Commonwealth Games medallist, limited his claim to the upper limit of his host's public liability insurance.

35 [2016] EWHC 2355 (QB).

36 Occupiers' Liability Act 1957 s.2(3)(a).

37 *Glasgow Corp v Taylor* [1922] 1 AC 44 (HL).

38 *Jolley v Sutton London Borough Council* [2000] 1 WLR 1082 (HL). The defendant local council conceded that children from a nearby block of flats were allowed to play upon the land where the boat was, so that the child injured was a visitor. It also conceded that it should have removed the boat because of the risk of children suffering injuries if the rotten planking gave way. The question was whether the council was liable for the more serious type of injury which the child suffered. The court held that it was so liable.

39 *Phipps v Rochester Corp* [1955] 1 QB 450 (QBD).

after their children to those who happened to have accessible bits of land.[40] Hence occupiers can expect young children to be accompanied. Having said that, would it not be a callous occupier who, knowing that children regularly entered its land unaccompanied, nevertheless did nothing until a child was seriously injured?

In contrast, an occupier may expect that a professional, in the exercise of their calling, will appreciate and guard against any risks ordinarily incident to that calling.[41] In other words, while children might require more care, a professional might require less care. For example, an electrician need not be told that electricity is dangerous, nor a window cleaner lectured on how to use a ladder.

A more extreme case is *Roles v Nathan*.[42] There the defendant occupier warned chimney sweeps about the dangers of carbon monoxide poisoning when working in the flue while the boiler was lit. They ignored the advice, saying that they knew better, and returned to work on the flue unannounced and unsupervised. They were later found dead from the fumes. The occupier was held not liable.

ANALYSING THE LAW

An occupier is entitled to expect professionals to guard against the risks of their profession. But it is something else when a so-called professional obviously flouts those risks. Can an occupier really just stand back and let the inevitable danger unfold? In another case, the court has hinted otherwise.[43] But perhaps the better analysis of *Roles v Nathan* is not to say that the occupier could rely upon the sweeps' professionalism (which was questionable at best), but rather that the sweeps voluntarily assumed the risks (in other words, there was a defence of *volenti*).

This does not mean that a professional can never sue. For example, a firefighter who suffers burn injuries might still sue the person who negligently started the fire, because a fire is always dangerous, even to people with special skills and training.[44]

INDEPENDENT CONTRACTORS

Where the danger on the premises was caused by the faulty construction, maintenance, or repair work of an independent contractor, the occupier will not be liable if (1) the occupier

40 Ibid, 472.

41 Occupiers' Liability Act 1957 s.2(3)(b).

42 [1963] 1 WLR 1117 (CA).

43 *Ferguson v Welsh* [1987] 3 All ER 777 (HL), but where it was also suggested that any liability would be incurred, not as occupier, but as joint tortfeasor with the employer who allowed the unsafe system of work.

44 *Ogwo v Taylor* [1988] AC 431 (HL), where the cause of action was negligence rather than occupiers' liability.

acted reasonably in entrusting the work to the contractor and (2) the occupier had taken reasonable steps (if any were needed) to satisfy themselves that the contractor was competent and the work properly done.[45]

For example, in *Haseldine v Daw & Son Ltd*,[46] the claimant suffered an injury when, visiting a block of flats, the lift they were travelling in broke and fell to the bottom of the lift well. The landlord incurred no occupiers' liability:[47] they had entrusted the maintenance of the lift to a reputable firm of engineers who made regular inspections. (But the claimant could sue the engineers because, on one of those inspections, the engineer negligently refitted the lift mechanism, which is what caused the accident.)

EXPLAINING THE LAW

On some large projects, like building a block of flats, there might be multiple independent contractors on site. While each independent contractor might be competent, nevertheless good practice often requires that the occupier take further steps to ensure that all the work is properly coordinated, for example by a site manager or architect. Some construction projects ordinarily, as a matter of industry practice, also involve final testing, like a new bridge, or a new ship,[48] before visitors are allowed on the premises. All of this is yet further example of how what constitutes *reasonable* care will vary according to the circumstances.

In *Gwilliam v West Hertfordshire NHS Trust*,[49] the defendant hospital organised a fund-raising fair. One of the attractions hired by the hospital was a 'splat wall', whereby participants bounced from a trampoline onto a Velcro wall. The claimant was injured because the equipment had been set up negligently by the contractor. The hospital remained potentially liable as occupier, since the fair was on its grounds. But it had discharged its duty of care by checking that the contractor had insurance: the availability and obtaining of insurance by the contractor in itself reflected well on the contractor's competence. (The claimant could sue the contractor in negligence.)[50]

Note that, while the 1957 Act refers to 'construction, maintenance or repair' work by a contractor,[51] the court in *Gwilliam*[52] was prepared to reason by analogy to apply the same

45 Occupiers' Liability Act 1957 s.2(4)(b).

46 [1941] 2 KB 343 (CA).

47 The case was decided on the common law before the passing of the 1957 Act.

48 *AMF International Ltd v Magnet Bowling Ltd* [1968] 2 All ER 789 (QBD), 803 (Mocatta J).

49 [2002] EWCA Civ 1041.

50 But it turned out that the contractor had insufficient funds, because the insurance had lapsed four days before the event. So, it seems that the contractor misled the hospital when it said that it had insurance. But, said the court, that was not the hospital's fault.

51 Occupiers' Liability Act 1957 s.2(4)(b).

52 [2002] EWCA Civ 1041, [11]–[12], [40].

principles to any type of work done by an independent contractor on the occupier's premises.

EXPLAINING THE LAW

Everyone makes mistakes occasionally, and that is partly what insurance is there to indemnify against. Indeed, taking out insurance for just such an eventuality might be considered prudent and responsible.

For example, even a good driver might be absent-minded for a moment. Hopefully no one gets injured as a result. But if they do, insurance is there to provide cover. The one-off negligent driver might face a higher insurance premium the following year, but there is no reason to doubt that the driver is generally competent. However, a driver who is regularly involved in accidents might soon be unable to obtain any insurance. That then is an indication of their general *in*competence. And if they continue to drive without insurance, that too speaks to their reckless disregard of others. The same goes for providers of fairground attractions and for building contractors: the fact that they are insured might be some evidence of their general responsibility.

WARNINGS

One way in which an occupier might seek to take care of any visitor is by issuing a warning, like 'Beware of the dog'.[53] However, a warning on its own does not absolve an occupier from liability unless the warning is enough to enable the visitor to be reasonably safe.[54] So it would not be much good warning 'Beware of the dog' if the visitor has no choice but to walk past the dog anyway.

To borrow a further example from Lord Denning,[55] a sign saying 'This bridge is dangerous' will not absolve the occupier from liability if, despite the sign, the visitor has to use the bridge because it is the only way off the premises. But a sign which says 'This bridge is dangerous, please use the other bridge to your left' could be enough to ensure that the visitor is reasonably safe in leaving the premises.

There is no need to give warnings about obvious risks. For example, in *Darby v National Trust*,[56] the court said that there was no need to warn an adult of the obvious risk of drowning when they go swimming in a murky pond.

53 The condition of premises includes the presence of dogs. Dangerous dogs can mean unsafe premises: *Gould v McAuliffe* [1941] 2 All ER 527 (CA); *Hill v Lovett* [1992] SLT 994.

54 Occupiers' Liability Act 1957 s.2(4)(a).

55 *Roles v Nathan* [1963] 1 WLR 1117, 1124.

56 [2001] EWCA Civ 189.

EXPLAINING THE LAW

As May LJ said in *Darby v National Trust*, it cannot be the duty of the owner of every stretch of coastline to litter the coast with notices warning of the dangers of swimming in the sea.[57] And, we might add, the same could be said about the dangers of crossing roads, walking into lampposts, or tripping over tree roots in a forest. Which is to say that the law expects us to take some responsibility for our own safety when out and about facing the usual hazards of ordinary life.

EXCLUDING LIABILITY

An occupier can exclude or restrict (or even enlarge upon) the common duty of care, by agreement with the visitor or by other means.[58] Such other means, for example, might include a sign, like 'Visitors enter at their own risk'.

However, any attempt to exclude or restrict liability under the Occupiers' Liability Act 1957 must satisfy other statutory safeguards.

First, there is the Unfair Contract Terms Act 1977. Despite the title of the 1977 Act, it applies explicitly to the common duty of care imposed by the Occupiers' Liability Act 1957,[59] and to any attempt to exclude liability either by a contract term or by a notice.[60] However, the 1977 Act only applies in the context of business liability, that is, when premises are occupied for the business purposes of the occupier.[61] So, for example, the 1977 Act will apply if a customer visits a hotel, but not if a guest attends a dinner party at someone's private home.

Where the 1977 Act applies, the occupier cannot exclude or restrict *at all* liability for death or personal injury.[62] As for any other type of damage, the occupier can only exclude or restrict liability if the contract term or notice was reasonable.[63]

Second, there is the Consumer Rights Act 2015. This applies to contracts and notices between traders and consumers.[64] Under the 2015 Act, an unfair contract or notice is not binding

57 Ibid, [27].

58 Occupiers' Liability Act 1957 s.2(1).

59 Unfair Contract Terms Act 1977 s.1(1)(c).

60 Unfair Contract Terms Act 1977 s.2.

61 Unfair Contract Terms Act 1977 s.1(3). Business liability does not apply when a visitor to business premises does so, not for business purposes, but for educational or recreational purposes. An example might be a school trip visiting a supermarket. Of course, it is business purposes after all if what the business does is provide educational or recreational experiences, like a tutorial college or a holiday park.

62 Unfair Contract Terms Act 1977 s.2(1).

63 Unfair Contract Terms Act 1977 s.2(2). In relation to a notice, it must be fair and reasonable to allow reliance on it: s.11(3). Where the occupier seeks to restrict liability to a specific sum, regard shall be had to the resources which the occupier could expect to be available for the purpose of meeting the liability, and how far it was open to the occupier to obtain insurance: s.2(4). It is the occupier who must prove that the contract term or notice was reasonable: s.2(5).

64 Consumer Rights Act 2015 s.61.

on a consumer. A term is unfair if, contrary to the requirements of good faith, it causes a significant imbalance in rights or obligations to the detriment of the consumer.[65] In particular, a trader cannot exclude liability for death or personal injury resulting from negligence.[66]

However, the 2015 Act does not apply to a claimant who suffers injury due to the dangerous state of premises which are accessed for recreational purposes not part of the occupier's trade.[67] For example, if a person suffers injury while skateboarding for fun in a supermarket car park, due to the state of the tarmac, that situation might fall outside the 2015 Act: the supermarket does not provide the car park for skateboarding.

11.3 LIABILITY TO NON-VISITORS UNDER THE 1984 ACT

In this section, we consider the following topics: the duty of care owed to non-visitors; how warnings might suffice in the case of non-visitors; and how all this relates to the 'right to roam' the open countryside.

DUTY OF CARE

A person, taking a short cut home, crosses a building site and falls down a trench, injuring themselves. Can that person sue the construction company as occupiers of the building site? The claimant did not have any permission to be on the building site, so they cannot invoke the Occupiers' Liability Act 1957. But occupiers still owe a duty of care even to non-visitors. This is governed by the Occupiers' Liability Act 1984. Note that it applies only to personal injury, and not also to damage to property (unlike under the Occupiers' Liability Act 1957).[68] It provides as follows:

KEY LEARNING POINTS

- An occupier owes a duty to non-visitors to take such care as is reasonable in all the circumstances to see that the non-visitor does not suffer injury on the premises,[69] if the following conditions are met:[70]
- (1) The occupier is aware of the danger, or has reasonable grounds to believe it exists;[71] and (2) the occupier knows, or has reasonable grounds to believe, that the non-visitor is in the vicinity, or may come into the vicinity, of the danger; and (3) it is

65 Consumer Rights Act 2015 s.62.

66 Consumer Rights Act 2015 s.65.

67 Consumer Rights Act 2015 s.66.

68 Occupiers' Liability Act 1984 s.1(8).

69 Occupiers' Liability Act 1984 s.1(4).

70 Occupiers' Liability Act 1984 s.1(3).

71 Having 'reasonable grounds to believe' means, in effect, that the occupier has actual knowledge of the danger, or actual knowledge of facts from which a reasonable person would infer a danger: *Ratcliff v McConnell* [1999] 1 WLR 670 (CA); *Swain v Puri* [1996] PIQR P 442 (CA).

> reasonable in all the circumstances to expect the occupier to offer some protection to the non-visitor against this danger.[72]

So, for example, it is not enough to know of a danger if the occupier does not know that anyone would be near the danger. In *Donoghue v Folkstone Properties Ltd*,[73] the occupier of a harbour knew of an underwater hazard which would have been dangerous to people diving into the sea. But it had no idea that the claimant would dive into the sea when he did – at midnight, in mid-winter. It was not liable for his injuries.

EXPLAINING THE LAW

In *Donoghue v Folkstone*, the court said that a warning sign was all that was needed to discharge the occupier's duty. But we can take the following point from that case: there is no need to put up a warning sign until you know that there is anyone to warn. So, in the summer, maybe, a sign should have gone up. But since the injury occurred, unpredictably, in mid-winter, the occupier was not liable at that time.

ANALYSING THE LAW

A non-visitor is usually a trespasser.[74] Why should we take any care of trespassers?

First, not all trespassers attract the same moral opprobrium. Yes, burglars are trespassers. But so too are children exploring an abandoned house. And you can even be a trespasser without meaning to be (see Chapter 12).

Second, even if someone is acting unlawfully, that does not mean that we can do anything we like to them. For example, just because someone is burgling our shed, it does not mean that we can shoot them (see Chapter 13). Should we not always act with at least a minimum of compassion? Before the 1984 Act, the common law termed it the 'common duty of humanity'.[75]

WARNINGS

It may suffice, under the 1984 Act, simply that the occupier took reasonable steps to give warning of the danger, or to discourage people from incurring the risk.[76]

72 It is difficult to see what this subsection adds to the general proposition that an occupier has to take reasonable care. What counts as reasonable care will naturally vary according to the type of danger involved.

73 [2003] EWCA Civ 231.

74 *Ovu v London Underground Ltd* [2021] EWHC 2733 (QB) at [55].

75 *Herrington v British Railways Board* [1972] AC 877 (HL).

76 Occupiers' Liability Act 1984 s.1(5).

Thus, to return to an earlier example, a warning sign which states 'This bridge is dangerous: do not use' will unlikely suffice to protect visitors who must use the bridge if they are to visit at all. But it may well suffice to discharge any duty owed to non-visitors (who usually ought not to be using the bridge in the first place). Unless, for example, the sign is obscured by vegetation, or has become illegible in the rain, in which case it is not a reasonable warning after all.

Once again, there is no need to warn about obvious dangers, like the risk of injury when diving into shallow water:

KEY CASES

In *Tomlinson v Congleton Borough Council*,[77] the defendant was the occupier of a park, which included a lake in a disused quarry. Many families played on the shores of the lake, but the defendant sought to dissuade swimmers. There were prominent signs saying, 'Dangerous water: no swimming', and rangers were employed to warn people against swimming. Nevertheless, the claimant went swimming (which made him a trespasser). Standing in the shallow water, he dived and hit his head, breaking his neck. The court said that the defendant occupier was not liable in respect of such an obvious risk.

During evidence at trial, it transpired that the defendant had plans to dump ballast on the sandy shores of the lake, and plant it with reeds, to make the area unattractive, and further dissuade trespassers from swimming. But Lord Hoffmann was strongly against the idea that the shore, safely enjoyed by families, should be ruined just to safeguard a few irresponsible people against dangers which were anyway perfectly obvious.[78]

THE RIGHT TO ROAM

Recall that those exercising their right to roam under the Countryside and Rights of Way Act 2000 are deemed *not* to be visitors under the Occupiers' Liability Act 1957. But their position is not much better under the Occupiers' Liability Act 1984:

> An occupier owes no duty in respect of a risk resulting from the existence of any natural feature of the landscape, or any plant, shrub or tree, or any physical feature of coastal margins, or any river, stream, ditch or pond whether or not a natural feature, or a risk of suffering injury when passing over, under or through any wall, fence or gate, except by proper use of the gate or stile.[79] Unless, that is, the danger concerned is due to anything

77 [2003] UKHL 47.

78 Ibid, [46].

79 Occupiers' Liability Act 1984 s.1(6A)–(6B).

done by the occupier with the intention of creating that risk, or being reckless as to whether that risk is created.[80]

Even then, whatever residual duty is left must still take account of the fact that the right to roam ought not to place an undue burden (whether financial or otherwise) on the occupier. And it must also take account of the importance of maintaining the character of the countryside, including features of historic, traditional, or archaeological interest.[81]

EXPLAINING THE LAW

In *Darby v National Trust*, discussed above in the context of the 1957 Act, the court thought it absurd that the countryside and coastline should be littered with signs warning of obvious dangers. In *Tomlinson v Congleton BC*, discussed above in the context of the 1984 Act, the court was against ruining a lake shore to protect the irresponsible. Now we see how the right to roam should not result in the character of the countryside being diminished, nor access to historic features prevented, just in case a rambler suffers an accident. What comes across is a general notion that our natural environment is to be embraced and respected for what it is, dangerous but beautiful, rather than roped off or blighted by notices just because the occasional person makes a poor judgment, however tragic the consequences.

11.4 DEFENCES

In this section, we give particular consideration to the defences of *volenti* (or voluntary assumption of risk) and contributory negligence.

ASSUMPTION OF RISK

Both the 1957 Act[82] and the 1984 Act[83] state that there is no duty owed in respect of risks willingly accepted by the visitor. In effect, this is statutory confirmation that the common law defence of *volenti*, or voluntary assumption of risk, remains available in the context of occupiers' liability. It is a complete defence.

For example, in *Ratcliff v McConnell*,[84] a student decided to go swimming, at night, when the college pool was closed for the winter, and when swimming was thus prohibited, as he

80 Occupiers' Liability Act 1984 s.1(6C). An intentional harm could also involve the tort of battery, or the tort in *Wilkinson v Downton* (see Chapter 13) – or straightforward negligence.

81 Occupiers' Liability Act 1984 s.1A.

82 Occupiers' Liability Act 1957 s.2(5).

83 Occupiers' Liability Act 1984 s.1(6).

84 [1999] 1 WLR 670 (CA).

knew. The gate was locked, so he climbed over the fence, and dived in, although he knew the dangers of diving in shallow water. He hit his head and suffered serious injuries. The court held that he was aware of the risk and willingly accepted it.

EXPLAINING THE LAW

As we saw previously, occupiers do not usually need to warn of obvious dangers. In many ways, *volenti* is just the flip-side: a visitor who risks an obvious danger is usually taken to have assumed responsibility for the risk. So, for example, an occupier might not need to warn an adult swimmer of the risk of drowning in a murky pond; an adult who goes swimming in a murky pond will probably be taken as assuming the risk of drowning.

Similarly, in *Titchener v British Railways Board*,[85] the claimant was injured when crossing a railway line. The court said that the danger of being hit by a train was obvious to these intelligent adolescents, and the fence was a further warning. When the claimant passed through a gap in the fence, to walk across the line, they had willingly accepted the risks involved.

In *Geary v JD Wetherspoon plc*,[86] a customer at a pub with a grand sweeping staircase decided to slide down the bannisters. She fell off and fractured her spine. The court said that the risk of injury was obvious, and that the claimant had made a genuine and informed choice to run that risk anyway. She was held to be the author of her own misfortune.

However, there is a difference between, on the one hand, knowing a risk and taking it anyway, and on the other hand, voluntarily assuming the risk as one's own, which is the proper province of the defence of *volenti*. That might seem a fine line conceptually, but it marks an important pragmatic distinction. For example, when I cycle down the road, I am aware of the risk of being hit by a car, and yet I continue to cycle. But I certainly do not assume the risk as my own, to the exclusion of any liability on the part of negligent drivers.[87]

Thus, in *Bunker v Charles Brand & Son Ltd*,[88] a construction worker, navigating a tunnel to access cutting equipment, slipped on rails and suffered an injury. The defendant contractors, who supervised the site, were held to be occupiers of the rails, and liable for not providing a safer access route to the equipment (like erecting a firm walkway). The mere fact that the worker knew the risk involved in walking on the rails was itself not sufficient to absolve the defendant of occupiers' liability.

85 [1983] 1 WLR 1427 (HL).

86 [2011] EWHC 1506 (QB).

87 Similarly, under the Unfair Contract Terms Act 1977, just because a visitor is aware of a notice excluding or restricting liability, or even agreed to a contract term which excludes or restricts liability, that alone does not mean that the visitor voluntarily accepted the risk: s.2(3). Nor, of course, do they lose their right to challenge the reasonableness of the exclusion under the 1977 Act. There is similar provision under the Consumer Rights Act 2015 s.65(2).

88 [1969] 2 QB 480 (QBD).

> MAKING CONNECTIONS
>
> Cases like *Bunker v Charles Brand* straddle employers' and occupiers' liability. (A defendant can always be liable for the same harm under multiple torts.) We saw in the context of employers' liability (Chapter 10) that, just because an employee 'chooses' to go to work, it does not follow that they are deemed to assume the risk of injury at work. Rather, the employer must still take reasonable care of the employee. Similarly, just because a person is on premises, it does not follow that they have assumed the risk of injury occurring on those premises. Indeed, the well-informed lawyer knows that they can be confident in visiting premises precisely because the occupier must make them reasonably safe.

CONTRIBUTORY NEGLIGENCE

A visitor might suffer injury because of their own contributory negligence. To return to *Bunker v Charles Brand*, the construction worker who slipped on the rails was nevertheless held 50% to blame for not making use of the handrail which was provided. In *English Heritage v Taylor*,[89] the occupier was liable for failing to provide a warning sign where a sheer drop (into a castle moat) was not an obvious danger, but the visitor was 50% to blame for choosing to descend the very steep grass bank which led to the sheer drop.

In *White Lion Hotel v James*,[90] a customer at a hotel sat on a window sill, but then fell out of the open window. The court said that the customer was 60% to blame. Just because the customer took a risk by sitting on the window sill, said the court, it did not follow that the customer voluntarily accepted all the consequences, and waived any liability on the part of the hotel. The hotel was also to blame because a customer was likely to be relaxed and off-guard, and the way in which the window opened was a risk which was easy to fix. We might say that cases like this tend to show a reluctance by the court to apply the all-or-nothing defence of *volenti* when contributory negligence allows the court to divide up responsibility, even if one person is clearly more to blame than another.

> MAKING CONNECTIONS
>
> As we have just seen, the defence of *volenti* requires the claimant to voluntarily assume a known risk. If the risk was not known, but should have been, that might instead incur contributory negligence. If the risk should not have been taken, that too might incur contributory negligence. So, if *volenti* is not made out, contributory negligence might be a fallback. *Volenti* is a complete defence; contributory negligence is a partial or proportional defence.

89 [2016] EWCA Civ 448.

90 [2021] EWCA Civ 31.

11.5 REMEDIES

Those injured on premises usually seek compensation. That will be quantified in the same way as with negligence claims in general. This is because occupiers' liability, whether under the 1957 Act or the 1984 Act, is, in effect, a specialist negligence regime. So too the availability of damages will be subject to the same tests of causation and remoteness that we encounter with the tort of negligence (see Chapter 4).

APPLYING THE LAW

Selina goes to Topsham College. She has A-level coursework to do over the weekend. On Saturday night she remembers that she left her coursework at school. She goes back to school that evening to collect it. She takes her friend Rahul. The gate is locked, so they climb over the wall. Selina rips her jeans on the wall. Rahul falls off the wall and hits his head. Advise the parties.

Topsham College might incur liability as occupier for the harm suffered by Selina and Rahul as they climb over the school wall. Does Selina have permission to be on the premises of Topsham College? On the one hand, she is a student there. On the other hand, it is after

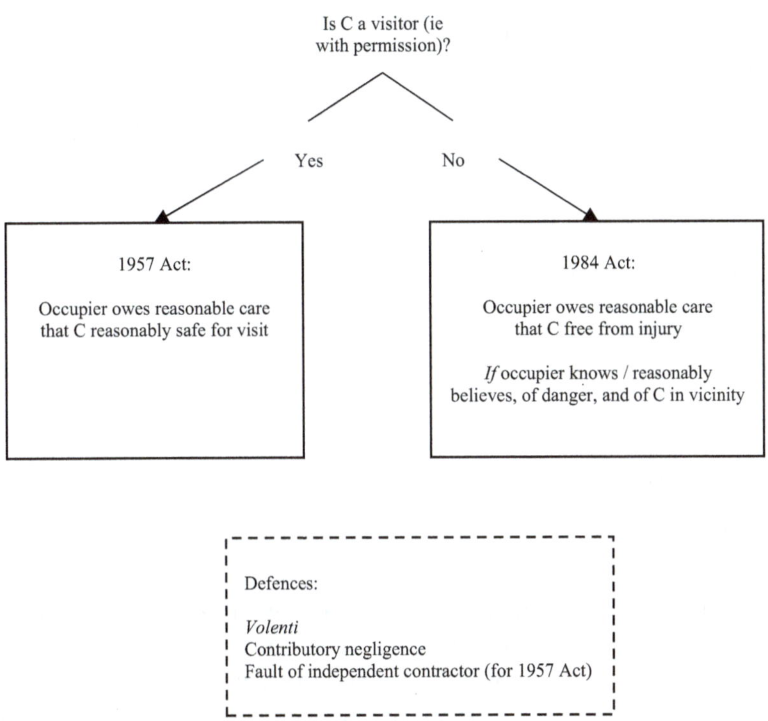

Figure 11.1 Overview of occupiers' liability

hours, and the school is locked up. At any rate, she is unlikely to have permission to climb over the wall. Probably she is a trespasser. The same would go for Rahul. (He would definitely be a trespasser if it turns out that he is not even a student at the school.)

Thus, it seems that liability is governed by the Occupiers' Liability Act 1984. The school will owe a duty of reasonable care to see that Selina and Rahul do not suffer injury. The 1984 Act does not cover injury to property (unlike the 1957 Act), so Selina cannot recover in respect of her ripped jeans. What about Rahul's injury? First, there is nothing to suggest that the school knew, or had reasonable grounds to believe, that Rahul would climb the wall. In which case, the school would owe him no duty of care under the 1984 Act. At any rate, second, what steps was the school supposed to take (but unreasonably failed to take)? Suffering an injury by falling off a wall is an obvious danger which surely called for no particular warning. Which is to say that there is nothing to suggest that the school has behaved unreasonably.

Further, there would likely be a defence of *volenti*, in that Rahul (and Selina) would surely be taken, as mature adolescents, to know the dangers involved in climbing a wall, and to have voluntarily assumed responsibility for those risks. That would provide a complete defence. Alternatively, there might be a partial defence of contributory negligence, since Rahul must take some blame for risking his own safety.

POINTS TO REVIEW

An occupier owes a duty of reasonable care, as regards the condition of their premises:

- Under the 1957 Act, to ensure that visitors (and property) are reasonably safe when using the premises for the purpose of the visit.
- Under the 1984 Act, to see that non-visitors do not suffer injury on the premises – but only if the occupier knew, or reasonably believed, that the danger existed, and that non-visitors were in the vicinity.
- Occupiers do not usually need to guard against or warn of obvious dangers. But different people with different needs may require different levels of care.
- Defences include *volenti*, where the claimant voluntarily assumed responsibility for taking a known risk, and contributory negligence, where the claimant failed to take reasonable care for their own safety.

TAKING IT FURTHER

Stapleton, J. 'Tort, Insurance and Ideology' (1995) 58 MLR 820
Free access: https://onlinelibrary.wiley.com/doi/abs/10.1111/j.1468-2230.1995.tb02054.x
What is the relationship between insurance and tort law? The author suggests that they are two different regimes, and that there is no necessary connection. We are free to decide the parameters of both. However, we might ask, are they so distinct? Obtaining insurance might be a sign of acting responsibly, indeed reasonably. And if a tortfeasor is ordered to pay compensation, usually they will claim on their own insurance (if they have

any) in order to meet the cost. Indeed, without insurance, a tortfeasor might not be able to afford compensation – which undermines the practical use of tort law (it is in vain to win compensation from a party who cannot pay it). Should insurance against occupiers' liability be compulsory?

Stevens-Hoare, M. and Higgins, R. 'Roam Free?' (2004) 154 NLJ 1846
Available on Lexis+

In explaining the remit of the Countryside and Rights of Way Act 2000, the authors note how limited the duty imposed on occupiers is – indeed, a landowner may owe a lesser duty to someone exercising their statutory right to roam than they owe to a trespasser. We might ask, does that seem appropriate? More generally, what is the best way of making open land available for public use: to allow its private ownership, but with a right to roam, or to have public ownership? Should open land be available for public use?

Murphy, J. 'Public Rights of Way and Private Law Wrongs' [1997] Conveyancer 362
Available on Westlaw

The author asks, how can a trespasser, who is not supposed to be there, be owed a duty of care by the occupier, but someone lawfully using a public right of way is owed no duty of care? He suggests that the occupier of land with a public right of way should owe a duty of care, at least where that occupier invites people onto it so as to derive a business benefit from them. We might give the example of a privately owned shopping mall, whose main 'street' is a public right of way. Surely the mall ought to keep the path safe?

12

CHAPTER 12
INTERFERENCE WITH LAND

This chapter discusses trespass to land, private nuisance, and the rule in Rylands v Fletcher.

If a defendant takes a shortcut by walking across their neighbour's garden, they may be liable in trespass. If a defendant hosts loud parties late into the night every Sunday, they may be liable to their neighbour in nuisance. If a defendant stores barrels of dangerous chemicals in their garage, and the chemicals leak onto their neighbour's property, they might be liable under the rule in *Rylands v Fletcher*. Thus, in this chapter, we consider three torts which respond to interference with another's land. The chapter proceeds as follows. First, we shall consider trespass to land. Second, we will discuss private nuisance. Third, we will explore the rule in *Rylands v Fletcher*.

AS YOU READ

- Identify the core or characteristic situation addressed by each tort in this chapter.
- Be aware that a given set of facts might lead to overlapping torts.
- Consider which of several overlapping torts might be the most suitable to govern the particular facts.
- Consider how the law might be improved or developed.

12.1 TRESPASS TO LAND

KEY LEARNING POINT

Trespass to land is an act which directly interferes, unlawfully, with land in another's possession.

In this section, we shall consider each of these topics in turn: what constitutes possession; what it means for interference to be direct; whether interference must be intentional; how interference must be unlawful; how trespass still applies, not just on the surface of land, but also in the air above land, and underground; finally, what defences and remedies might be available.

DOI: 10.4324/9781003480051-12

POSSESSION

It is the person in possession of the land who can sue in trespass. In *J A Pye (Oxford) Ltd v Graham*,[1] the court said that possession requires two things: a sufficient degree of occupation or control of the land; and an intention to possess, that is, to exclude anyone else from possessing it. For example, a home owner possesses the family home they live in. With a rented house, while the landlord owns the property, it is the tenant who has possession. Just because a home owner or tenant goes out for a day's shopping, they do not lose possession: for a start, they still intend to exclude others.

DIRECT INTERFERENCE

The defendant must interfere with another's land directly. Stepping onto another's land is a direct interference. Throwing litter onto another's land is also a direct interference. So too is leaning a ladder or a bike against another's wall.

In contrast, sensory interferences tend to be indirect, like smoke from a bonfire, or smells from a barbecue, or noise from trumpet practice. These indirect interferences do not ordinarily give rise to liability in trespass. But they could give rise to liability in nuisance (see below).

INTENTIONAL INTERFERENCE

Trespass usually involves intentional acts, that is, acts done on purpose or deliberately. So, if a defendant deliberately steps onto another's land, that might be trespass. It is irrelevant whether the defendant knew the land to be in another's possession. It is irrelevant whether the defendant thought it was their own land instead. It is no defence that the defendant thought they had permission to be there, if in fact they do not have permission.[2] The question is not whether the defendant intended to commit a trespass. The question is whether the defendant intended the movement. If for example the defendant intended to step onto a piece of land, and in doing so they happened to interfere directly with land in another's possession, then trespass is made out.

In contrast, in *Smith v Stone*,[3] the defendant was carried, against their will, onto another's land. That did not amount to trespass, since the defendant did not act intentionally.

What if the defendant found themselves on another's land negligently?

KEY CASES

In *League Against Cruel Sports Ltd v Scott*,[4] the claimant owned land which was kept as a wild animal sanctuary. The defendant repeatedly went deer hunting on

1 [2002] UKHL 30.

2 *Conway v George Wimpey & Co Ltd* [1951] 2 KB 266 (CA), 274.

3 (1647) Style 65, 82 ER 533.

4 [1986] QB 240 (QB).

neighbouring land. The defendant's hunting dogs repeatedly ran onto the claimant's land. The court said that the defendant would be liable in trespass if they intended the hounds to enter the claimant's land, for example by encouraging the hounds to enter the land, or if the defendant failed to take reasonable care to prevent the hounds from entering the land.

ANALYSING THE LAW

With trespass to the person, the case law suggests that, if a defendant fails to take reasonable care, the cause of action is in negligence; trespass to the person requires either intention or recklessness (see Chapter 13). It would be preferable if the law were consistent. Thus, trespass to land should require that the defendant act intentionally or recklessly.

That approach is probably compatible with the outcome in *League Against Cruel Sports v Scott*. In the past, the hunt had repeatedly happened near the claimant's land, and dogs had repeatedly entered the claimant's land. This makes the most recent incursion look, if not intentional, then at least reckless, that is, the defendant appreciated the risk, but took it anyway.

More generally, should someone who trips and falls onto another's land be liable in trespass? Perhaps that situation is better addressed through negligence – which only arises if there is damage. That said, someone who is negligently or unintentionally on another's land, perhaps like the defendant in *Smith v Stone*, still presumably commits trespass if they then refuse to leave.

UNLAWFUL INTERFERENCE AND PERMISSION

Trespass involves *unlawful* interference.

A defendant is on another's land *lawfully* when they have permission or 'licence' to be there. Permission can be express, like when a person invites a guest into their house. Permission can be implied. For example, most people are happy for a postal worker to walk up to their front door to deliver mail, even though they have never told the postal worker that this is acceptable.[5] All this is consistent with our discussion of 'visitors' in the context of occupiers' liability (see Chapter 11).

Permission can usually be revoked. At that point, the visitor has a reasonable time in which to leave the land, only after which they become a trespasser. But if the defendant's presence on

5 In *Robson v Hallett* [1967] 2 QB 939 (DC), the court said that usually a householder gives an implied licence to any member of the public on lawful business to come through the gate and knock on the front door. This includes police officers. And when asked to leave, they had a reasonable time to do so, during which time, the police officers were still lawful visitors carrying out their duty.

the land is governed by a contractual licence, it might not be possible to revoke permission inconsistently with that contract. For example, if a defendant pays for a ticket to the cinema or a night club, they have bought the entitlement to remain until the end, as long as they are behaving properly.[6]

Regardless of the landowner's permission, a person might have legal authority to be on another's land, like a police officer making an arrest.[7] However, when a person enters another's land with legal authority, but later abuses that authority (for example, by taking the opportunity, while there, to do something beyond what they had authority to do), then the law deems them to be a trespasser from the very beginning (known as 'trespass *ab initio*').[8]

> MAKING CONNECTIONS
>
> Whether a visitor or a trespasser, they are still owed a duty of reasonable care by the occupier of the premises (see Chapter 11). For example, a trespasser can be sued for committing a tort. But if, while trespassing, they suffer personal injury on the premises, they can sue the occupier for failing to take reasonable care for their safety. In other words, just because they are trespassers, it does not mean that they become outlaws who lose all their legal rights.

TRESPASS ABOVE AND BELOW

It is possible to trespass in the airspace above another's land.

For example, in *Kelson v Imperial Tobacco Co Ltd*,[9] the defendant had an advertising sign on the side of their building. This protruded eight inches into the airspace above the claimant's single-storey shop. That amounted to trespass. In *Anchor Brewhouse Developments Ltd v Berkley House (Docklands Developments) Ltd*,[10] the arm of a crane swung over the claimant's land as the defendant worked a neighbouring construction site. That too amounted to trespass.

However, there are limits. For example, satellites surely do not need permission to fly over another's land. So too in *Baron Bernstein of Leigh v Skyviews & General Ltd*,[11] the defendant flew in a plane over the claimant's country estate, taking photos which they then offered for sale to the claimant. The claimant sued for trespass. The court said that the defendant did not commit trespass. Instead, said the court, a claimant only has interest in the airspace above their land to a height necessary for the ordinary use and enjoyment of that land and the buildings upon it. Here, the defendant was flying at a height higher than that limit.

6 See *Hurst v Picture Theatres Ltd* [1915] 1 KB 1 (CA), discussed below.
7 See e.g. s.17 of the Police and Criminal Evidence Act 1984.
8 *The Six Carpenters' Case* (1610) 8 Co Rep 146a, 77 ER 695.
9 [1957] 2 QB 334 (QB).
10 [1987] 2 EGLR 173 (Ch).
11 [1978] QB 479 (QB).

Further, by section 76 of the Civil Aviation Act 1982, it is neither trespass nor nuisance to fly above property at a reasonable height in the prevailing weather conditions. But the plane is liable for any damage it causes.

ANALYSING THE LAW

Does this mean that land with tall buildings commands a greater height of airspace? The world's tallest building is the Burj Khalifa in Dubai at 828 metres, which opened in 2010. How much extra airspace would it need and own? Meanwhile, the world's smallest skyscraper is the Newby-McMahon Building in Texas at 12 metres tall, built in 1919. Supposedly the engineer tricked investors into thinking it might be 480 feet high, when the blueprints show it to be only 480 inches high. What remedy might the investors have had?

It is also possible to trespass beneath another's land.

For example, in *Bocardo SA v Star Energy UK Onshore Ltd*,[12] the defendant was drilling for oil. It drilled down from its land diagonally, and so underneath the claimant's land. There was no harm to the claimant's land, and the claimant had no right to the oil. Still, this amounted to trespass.

ANALYSING THE LAW

Presumably, given that the Earth is a sphere, a claimant's interest underneath their land ought to be wedge-shaped and tapering inwards, stopping at the centre of the Earth.

The court in *Star Energy v Bocardo* said that there must come a point at which it is absurd to talk about owning land that far down, because no one can reach it or do anything with it. Yet that did not stop the law, historically, from asserting that people owned the air above their land to an infinite height – until the technology of airplanes came along. So might the view change, of how far down land is owned, as technology develops which allows us to access deep underground?

DEFENCES

In this section, we focus on the defences of private and public necessity. In effect, the defendant says that they only committed trespass because it was necessary. But only some types of necessity provide a defence.

12 [2010] UKSC 35.

We start with **private necessity**. To invoke this defence, usually there must be a danger of death or serious injury to the defendant. The defendant's response to the danger must be reasonable, and without lawful alternatives. The defence is precluded if the danger was caused by the defendant's prior negligence.

For example, in *Esso Petroleum Co Ltd v Southport Corp*,[13] the defendant's oil tanker was stranded, and risked breaking her back on the embankment. This posed a threat of death or serious injury to the crew. The ship discharged the cargo of oil, which lightened the ship, allowing her to refloat safely. The oil washed up on the claimant town's foreshore. The claimant pleaded trespass and nuisance. The court said that the defendant had a defence of necessity. The defendant had acted to save the lives of the crew, and there was no evidence that it was the defendant's own negligence which had caused the ship to be stranded in the first place.

The defence of necessity is usually expressed in terms of permitting only temporary use of another's property. However, the more honest approach is probably to recognise that some persistent problems can only fairly be addressed collectively at a political level, rather than allowing defendants to trespass with impunity. Homelessness might an example. In *Southwark London Borough Council v Williams*,[14] the court said that necessity did not permit a homeless person to squat in empty houses owned by the claimant council.

There is a related defence of **public necessity**. Whereas in private necessity the defendant acts to save themselves, in public necessity the defendant acts to save another person or for the public benefit more generally. For example, this might cover a police officer who goes onto another's land to investigate cries for help. In *Dewey v White*,[15] the defence was available to fire officers who, attending a fire, pulled down a chimney to stop it falling onto passers-by, even though in doing so they damaged neighbouring property.

Another case of public necessity is *Rigby v Chief Constable of Northamptonshire*.[16] In that case, a psychopath had broken into a gun shop. To flush him out, the police fired gas canisters into the shop. This caused a fire and serious damage to the shop, whose owners sued in trespass and negligence. The court said that the use of the gas canisters was covered by the defence of necessity. However, the operation was not reasonably carried out, because the police had insufficient firefighting equipment to hand. So, the police were held liable for the *extra* damage which could have been avoided by having sufficient equipment to hand to deal with the fire.

13 [1953] 2 All ER 1204 (QB), upheld [1954] 2 QB 182 (CA) and [1956] AC 218 (HL).

14 [1971] Ch 734 (CA).

15 (1827) M & M 56, 173 ER 1079.

16 [1985] 2 All ER 985 (QB).

EXPLAINING THE LAW

Not every plea of public necessity is justiciable before the courts. In *Monsanto plc v Tilly*,[17] the defendants uprooted the claimant's genetically modified food crop. They said that they were acting out of necessity to protect the public from the dangers of genetically modified food. The court said that it was ill-equipped, in a private dispute, with limited resources, to decide whether genetically modified food was a danger. Constitutionally, said the court, the growing of genetically modified food involved policy questions which were properly suited only to Parliament.

ANALYSING THE LAW

Monsanto v Tilly tends to suggest that acts of protest, however genuine, are probably still tortious. In *City of London Corp v Samede*,[18] as part of the Occupy movement, a tented camp was set up in St Paul's Cathedral churchyard in London as a protest against social inequality. In issue were the protesters' rights under the European Convention on Human Rights, article 10 freedom of expression, and article 11 freedom of peaceful assembly. But the court said that the protesters' views, however sincere, were largely irrelevant. The longer the duration of any protest, the more likely it was outweighed by the breach of domestic law and the interference with the human rights of the landowner and other members of the public. In *Samede*, the landowners could get an injunction to remove the protesters. In *HS2 Ltd v Persons Unknown*,[19] the High Court issued an injunction against protesters on land to be used for the HS2 project. What use is the freedom of peaceful assembly without land to assemble on?

REMEDIES

In this section, we consider the remedies of ejection, recovery of land, and injunction. Damages are addressed in the following section.

A person in possession of land may use reasonable force in defence of the land against a trespasser. In other words, there is a self-help remedy of **ejection**: a trespasser can be ejected from the land by the person in possession. However, this self-help remedy can be perilous.

For example, in *Holmes v Bagge and Fletcher*,[20] a cricket captain sought to eject someone from the cricket field. However, this was not lawful, because the cricket captain himself did not

17 [1999] All ER (D) 1321 (CA).

18 [2012] EWCA Civ 160.

19 [2022] EWHC 2360 (KB).

20 (1853) 1 El & Bl 782, 118 ER 629.

have possession of the land (it was the club committee who had possession). In *Revill v Newbery*,[21] it was unreasonable force when the defendant, protecting his allotment shed, negligently shot a burglar.

MAKING CONNECTIONS

If person A seeks to eject person B, but B is not a trespasser, or if A uses too much force, then A commits battery against B (see Chapter 13).

For example, in *Hurst v Picture Theatres Ltd*,[22] a patron bought a cinema ticket. This gave them permission to enter the cinema. Having bought this permission, it could not be revoked, except in accordance with the terms of the contract. As long as the patron was behaving properly, they were entitled to stay until after the end of the film. When instead the cinema threw him out early, wrongly thinking that he was misbehaving, that itself was a tort against the patron.

The self-helper might incur further liability too, beyond trespass to the person. For example, the burglar in *Revill v Newbery* sued the shed owner in negligence, and pursuant to occupiers' liability (see Chapter 11).

ANALYSING THE LAW

In Canada, the law has further developed such that it might not be lawful to eject someone who cannot take care of themselves. For example, a pub might not be able to throw out a drunkard if the drunkard cannot get home without risking serious injury. And a host might not be able to turn out a sick dinner guest if their illness means that they cannot get home safely. Should English law follow suit?

Further, note that reasonable force is to be used defensively (to eject people), rather than assertively (to gain access). Thus, it is an offence, without lawful authority, to use or threaten violence to secure entry to any premises, when there is another person present on the premises opposed to that entry, as the would-be entrant knows – except where the entrant is a displaced residential occupier.[23] Instead, the person seeking entry, and to regain possession, should obtain a court order for **recovery of land**, rather than take matters into their own hands.

Another remedy is **injunction**: the court has a discretion to make an order which prohibits the defendant from committing any further trespass. For example, in *League Against Cruel*

21 [1996] QB 567 (CA).
22 [1915] 1 KB 1 (CA).
23 Criminal Law Act 1977 s.6.

Sports v Scott, the court granted an injunction restraining the defendant from continuing to hunt near the claimant's land. In *Kelsen v Imperial Tobacco Co*, the claimant obtained an injunction requiring the defendant to take down the projecting advertising sign. In *Anchor Brewhouse v Barclay House*, an injunction was granted prohibiting the crane arm from swinging above the claimant's land. In *INEOS Upstream Ltd v Persons Unknown*,[24] an injunction was granted to curtail the action of people trespassing to protest fracking. (Once again, we see how protest, however sincere, does not usually excuse a tort.) As noted by the Supreme Court in *Wolverhampton City Council and others v London Gypsies and Travellers and others*,[25] injunctions can also be granted against people who are not, at the time of injunction, committing (or threatening) a trespass, hence the court can act against future trespasses.

Trespass is 'actionable per se', which means that the tort is made out without needing the claimant to have suffered any loss. (In contrast, for example, the cause of action in negligence is only complete when the claimant suffers damage.) Put plainly, with trespass, the defendant simply has no right to be there. But if the claimant *has* suffered loss, then they can also seek damages.

DAMAGES

Damages can be quantified in a range of ways:

Compensatory damages reimburse the claimant's financial loss. For example, if a trespasser knocks down a door to gain access to a house, then the claimant can recover the cost of mending the door. In *Shepherd v Collect Investments Ltd*,[26] the owner of an industrial site terminated the defendant's licence and gave notice to quit. The defendant instead remained on site, even using it as a rubbish dump. Damages included the lost revenue (the land could have been leased to someone else) and the cost of clearing the rubbish.

Restitutionary damages disgorge the defendant's gain. For example, in *Inverugie Investments Ltd v Hackett*,[27] the defendant appropriated the claimant's hotel. The defendant was ordered to pay a rental price (also called 'mesne profits')[28] for the period of dispossession.

EXPLAINING THE LAW

A defendant who makes use of another's land has benefitted by getting this for free. It was not the defendant's land to take. They should have to pay for using it. It does not matter that the claimant suffered no loss because they themselves were not using it at the time.

24 [2017] EWHC 2945 (Ch).
25 [2023] UKSC 47.
26 [2018] EWCA Civ 162.
27 [1995] 3 All ER 841 (PC).
28 'Mesne' is pronounced 'mean'.

Similarly, it does not matter that the defendant did not make very good use of the land. In *Inverugie Investments v Hackett*, the defendant appropriated the claimant's hotel, and ran it as such. When the claimant sued for damages, the defendant argued that they should only have to pay their actual profit, because they were only able to rent some of the rooms, some of the time. In effect, the court said 'tough luck' – if you take a whole hotel, you must pay for a whole hotel.

ANALYSING THE LAW

If land is not being used at all, should others still be precluded from using it? There used to be a rule in Spain that if a farmer did not bring in their crops, anyone else might take them for themselves, rather than see the crops go to waste. In England, there is a limited 'right to roam' the countryside (see Chapter 11). Does that go far enough in sharing the land?

Another type of damages is the **hypothetical licence fee**. For example, in *Enfield London Borough Council v Outdoor Plus Ltd*,[29] the defendant erected an advertising hoarding which encroached on the claimant's land, without permission. The claimant was awarded a hypothetical licence fee – in other words, the court's best estimate of what a fair price might have been for the claimant to charge the defendant for use of the land.

EXPLAINING THE LAW

It is a 'hypothetical' licence fee, because the parties never agreed a price. Indeed, the fact that the parties are now in court tends to show that the claimant would never have agreed to the defendant using the land, perhaps for any price. This does not prevent the court from awarding a hypothetical licence fee.

ANALYSING THE LAW

On the one hand, awarding damages on a hypothetical basis seems questionable. After all, the law should not be founded on make-believe. On the other hand, presumably what the claimant wants is, first, an end to the trespass, and second, money. How is that money to be quantified? Surely the rental value of the land is a good proxy for what the claimant has lost, and the free use which the defendant should disgorge.

29 [2012] EWCA Civ 608.

Aggravated damages are available when the claimant has suffered humiliation or injury to feelings, or an affront to their dignity. Thus, only a person, not a company, can recover aggravated damages.[30] Usually, trespass to land would need to be accompanied by high-handed, insulting, or oppressive conduct in order to attract aggravated damages.[31]

For example, in *Drane Evangelou*,[32] a tenant was unlawfully evicted by the landlord. The court said that aggravated damages would have been available for the 'monstrous' way in which the eviction had been arranged. (The tenant did not claim aggravated damages, but was awarded exemplary damages.)

Exemplary damages go further, and punish the defendant for outrageous behaviour, to mark the court's disapproval of that behaviour, and to act as a deterrence. Exemplary damages are available at common law in the following circumstances: (1) for oppressive, arbitrary or unconstitutional actions by government servants (for example, the police); or (2) where conduct is calculated by the defendant to make a profit which would likely exceed any compensation they might otherwise have had to pay (in other words, to make sure that tort, like crime, does not pay).[33]

For example, in *Razman v Brookwide Ltd*,[34] the defendant simply expropriated part of their neighbour's property, in order to sell it. This also deprived the neighbour of a source of income (the property was being run as part of a restaurant). The court awarded exemplary damages for this trespass to land. Even if the parties were arguing over who owned the property, the defendant's behaviour was a 'totally unacceptable way of resolving the ownership of property in a democratic society subject to the rule of law'.

12.2 PRIVATE NUISANCE

There are two types of nuisance: private and public. *Public* nuisance is primarily a crime. It is where a defendant endangers the life, health, property, or comfort of the public, or obstructs the public in the exercise or enjoyment of rights common to all. A private citizen can only sue in the tortious version of public nuisance when they have suffered special damage beyond that suffered by the public in general.

However, this section is concerned instead with the tort of *private* nuisance, which a private citizen can invoke as a matter of course. Here are some possible examples of private nuisance. A defendant mows their lawn early every Sunday morning, waking up their neighbours.

30 *Eaton Mansions (Westminster) Ltd v Stinger Compania de Inversion SA* [2013] EWCA Civ 1308.

31 *Horsford v Bird* [2006] UKPC 3.

32 [1978] 1 WLR 455 (CA).

33 *Rookes v Barnard* [1964] AC 1129 (HL), 1226–1228. In that case, the cause of action was the tort of intimidation. Additionally, the court noted, exemplary damages are available when authorised by statute.

34 [2011] EWCA Civ 985.

A defendant puts fresh manure on their flower bed, and the smell brings tears to their neighbour's eyes. A defendant renovates their upstairs flat, and the vibrations from the drilling cause pictures to fall off the walls in the flat below.

In this section, we shall consider the following topics: who can sue (the claimant); who can be sued (the defendant); briefly, what particular rules apply to landlords; what types of interference are actionable; the 'common and ordinary' use of land; and finally, what defences and remedies might be available.

THE CLAIMANT

To sue in private nuisance, the claimant must have an interest in the land affected by the interference. In *Hunter v Canary Wharf Ltd*,[35] the court said that ordinarily the claimant would be the person with the right to exclusive possession of the land. This might include an owner-occupier, or a tenant.

THE DEFENDANT

First, the defendant is responsible if they create the nuisance, for example if they themselves play loud music late at night. Further, if two people each make noise, which on its own would not be a nuisance, but which combined is a nuisance, both are responsible (and can be restrained by injunction).[36]

If the defendant created the nuisance on another's land, for example, they turned on a tap and the water continued to run, it is no defence that the defendant is no longer able to stop the nuisance, because they have no permission to access the land.[37] They should not have created the nuisance in the first place. (Accessing the land without permission would make them trespassers.)

Second, the defendant is responsible if they authorise someone else to make the nuisance, for example if they allow their house to be used for late-night band practice.

Third, the defendant will be responsible if they have actual or presumed knowledge of the nuisance on their property, and fail to take reasonable steps to bring it to an end. This principle applies even where the nuisance is created by a trespasser or by nature.

For example, in *Sedleigh-Denfield v O'Callaghan*,[38] a drain pipe on the defendant's land became blocked by leaves. In heavy rain, water overflowed the drain onto the claimant's land. This was a nuisance. It did not matter that the defendant had not installed the drain pipe. In fact, it was installed by the local council inadvertently trespassing on the defendant's land. Nevertheless, the defendant, a monastery, was taken as knowing about the drain pipe and the potential blockage, since one of the monks was actually tasked with cleaning the ditch where the drain pipe was located. Also, the defendant could easily have fixed the problem.

35 [1997] AC 655 (HL).

36 *Lambton v Mellish* [1894] 3 Ch 163 (Ch).

37 *Thompson v Gibson* (1841) 7 M&W 456, 151 ER 845.

38 [1940] AC 880 (HL).

Similarly, in *Goldman v Hargrave*,[39] a lightning strike set a tree on fire on the defendant's farmland. The defendant cut down the tree and left it to burn out. When the wind changed, the fire revived and spread to the claimant's land. Nuisance was made out. It was no defence that the nuisance was created by an act of nature. The defendant should have put out the fire with water. In *Leakey v National Trust*,[40] a hill on the defendant's land had intermittently suffered landslips onto the claimant's land below. After a dry summer and wet winter, a large landslip damaged the claimant's property. This too was held to be a nuisance, even though it was a naturally occurring phenomenon.

ANALYSING THE LAW

What if the defendant does not have the financial resources to address the nuisance created by a trespasser or by nature? In *Goldman v Hargrave* and in *Leakey v National Trust*, the court said that the defendant only had to take reasonable steps. What might reasonably be expected of the defendant, said the court, also depends on their finances. The defendant might behave reasonably, said the court, by asking their neighbour for a financial contribution.

But if a claimant wants their land protected from the random dangers of nature, as in *Goldman v Hargrave*, should the claimant themselves not bear the cost and carry out the protective work? Why should the defendant protect the claimant's land from the consequences of lightning? Why should it make a difference that lightning strikes the defendant's land and then spreads, rather than strikes the claimant's land directly?

LANDLORDS

Slightly different rules appear to apply to landlords. Thus, a landlord will not be liable for a nuisance created by its tenant, unless the landlord itself had directly participated in committing the nuisance, or there was a very high degree of probability that letting the property to this tenant would result in a nuisance. It is not enough that the landlord was aware of the nuisance, but took no steps to prevent it.[41]

EXPLAINING THE LAW

A party who creates or authorises a nuisance is liable. Similarly, a landlord who creates a nuisance, or participates in a nuisance created by its tenant, will incur liability. However, a landlord does not authorise a nuisance simply because it has leased its

39 [1967] 1 AC 645 (PC).

40 [1980] QB 485 (CA).

41 *Lawrence v Fen Tigers Ltd (No 2)* [2014] UKSC 46.

property to a tenant who turns out to be a nuisance. The landlord will only incur liability where it was highly probable from the outset that this tenant would be a nuisance. Further, just because the landlord now knows this tenant to be a nuisance, it is not the landlord's responsibility to police against the tenant's own tortious behaviour.

ANALYSING THE LAW

Why is the landlord not liable on principles analogous to *Sedleigh-Denfield*? Perhaps the answer is this. With a lease, the right to exclusive possession usually transfers to the tenant. In a real sense, it is the tenant's property. It is the tenant who can exclude trespassers, and the tenant who can complain about other people's nuisance. The corollary is that the tenant must take responsibility for what happens on the property. In contrast, in cases like *Sedleigh-Denfield* and *Goldman*, it remained the defendant's property when the nuisance arose.

In contrast, in *Cocking v Eacott*,[42] a house owner allowed her daughter to live there rent free. The daughter was a mere licensee, not a tenant, so the owner retained the right to possession. The owner was held to be the occupier (not a landlord), and so liable for the nuisance created by the constant barking of her daughter's dog, which the owner failed to take reasonable steps to abate. The principles of *Sedleigh-Denfield* did apply in this case.

TYPES OF INTERFERENCE

There are three principal types of interference covered by private nuisance: physical injury to land or chattels, encroachment (for example, from overhanging branches, or spreading roots), and sensory interference (like loud sounds or bad smells) which affect the use of the land.

While trespass is actionable per se (see above), nuisance requires damage to complete the cause of action. Physical injury to land or chattels is an obvious example. And when it comes to sensory interference, to repeat, it must ultimately affect the land. For example, if a defendant plays their bagpipes loudly (is there any other way of playing the bagpipes?), the claimant might be unhappy to sit in their garden because of the noise. It is not, strictly, the claimant's unhappiness to which nuisance responds. Rather, the noise means that the garden becomes less useful or valuable. This harm to the land is damage which sounds in nuisance.

42 [2016] EWCA Civ 140.

MAKING CONNECTIONS

In *Kelsen v Imperial Tobacco Co*, the defendant's advertising sign protruded into the claimant's airspace. This amounted to trespass (see above). But it did not amount to nuisance, because there was no interference with the claimant's use or enjoyment of the airspace; there was no damage.

In *Hunter v Canary Wharf*, the court said that nuisance does not cover injury to people on the land. So, if the claimant has suffered personal injury, like a hit on the head, they have no claim in nuisance, although they might have other causes of action, such as trespass to the person, or negligence.

EXPLAINING THE LAW

If a defendant plays football in the garden, and the ball regularly comes over the fence, and hits the claimant on the head, the claimant cannot sue in nuisance for any head injury. But if the fear of being hit on the head means that the claimant no longer makes use of their garden, that diminishes the use of the land, and so might sound in nuisance.

With private nuisance, the most common type of interference tends to be indirect and sensory interferences, like loud sounds or bad smells, which either tend to be repeated, like a bonfire every weekend, or which tend to be ongoing, like a loud party which lasts several days. But can a one-off or isolated escape, like an explosion, support a plea of nuisance?

There is a requirement that nuisance only applies to continuing interferences and not 'one offs' although the difference between these have not always been clear. For example, in *Midwood & Co Ltd v Mayor of Manchester*,[43] a problem with one of the defendant's electricity lines, laid under a road, caused it to heat the surrounding bitumen, which volatilised into an inflammable gas, which then exploded. Although the explosion was a one-off, the court said that the prior build-up of gas was an ongoing state of affairs which sounded in nuisance (although it lasted only three hours). What about if a 'one-off' event happens but the defendant fails to clean up from the event and therefore causes a lasting interference?

KEY CASE

The case of *Jalla v Shell International Trading and Shipping Co*[44] involved a spillage from an oil pipeline which was quickly shut off, albeit with oil already spilled and eventually

43 [1905] 2 KB 597 (CA).

44 [2023] UKSC 16.

reaching the shoreline within a week and remaining, having not been cleaned. The Supreme Court noted that a continuing nuisance was 'where, outside the claimant's land and usually on the defendant's land, there is repeated activity by the defendant or an ongoing state of affairs for which the defendant is responsible which causes continuing undue interference with the use and enjoyment of the claimant's land'.[45] Applying the law, the Supreme Court held that the spillage of oil was a 'one-off event or an isolated escape',[46] and therefore a claim for nuisance would not be made out.

Most often, emanations from a defendant's land are sensory, like smells or sounds. However, even people can count as emanations. In *Halsey v Esso Petroleum Co Ltd*,[47] the defendant was liable in nuisance for the noise their trucks made when leaving the depot and driving down the public road past the claimant's house. In *Lippiatt v South Gloucestershire Council*,[48] the defendant council was potentially liable in nuisance when travellers, whom it had long failed to evict as trespassers from its land, went forth causing loss and damage to neighbouring properties.

Recently in *Fearn v Board of Trustees of the Tate Gallery*,[49] the Supreme Court found that visual intrusion could be a nuisance. This case involved the use of the Tate Gallery's Blavatnik viewing platform by visitors in London, who would look (sometimes with binoculars or cameras) into the flats opposite, which had floor-to-ceiling glassed windows. The Supreme Court stated that the use of the viewing platform to visually intrude on the flats opposite, rather than the platform itself, which made it a nuisance.[50]

MAKING CONNECTIONS

++++++++++++++++++

In *Fearn v Board of Trustees of the Tate Galleries*[51] the Supreme Court cited Lord McMillan in the well-known negligence case of *Donoghue v Stevenson*[52] (this is discussed in Chapter 2) who stated that 'the categories of negligence are never closed'.[53] and likewise noted that 'the categories of nuisance are not closed'.[54] The Supreme Court further stated that, 'Anything short of direct trespass on the claimant's land which materially interferes with the claimant's enjoyment of rights in land is capable of being a nuisance'.[55] Could there be new categories of nuisance which we are not aware of yet, that will arise in the next few years? Could we see an increase in nuisance claims?

45 [2023] UKSC 16, [26] (Lord Burrows).
46 [2023] UKSC 16, [37] (Lord Burrows).
47 [1961] 2 All ER 145 (QB).
48 [2000] QB 51 (CA).
49 [2023] UKSC 4.
50 Ibid, [92] (Lord Leggatt).
51 [2023] UKSC 4.
52 [1932] AC 562.
53 Ibid, 619 (Lord McMillan); see [2023] UKSC 4, [12].
54 [2023] UKSC 4, [12] (Lord Leggatt).
55 Ibid.

'COMMON AND ORDINARY' USE

At some point, all of us interfere with our neighbours to a greater or lesser extent. We all make noise. Some people light bonfires. Some practice musical instruments. All this is to be expected as part of everyday life. Private nuisance is not about the claimant getting everything their own way. There must be a balance between neighbours. Decisions have been made by courts through whether the defendants use of land was *reasonable.*

For example, in *Andreae v Selfridge & Co Ltd*,[56] the defendant was demolishing and rebuilding. This produced noise and dust. One must expect land and buildings to undergo occasional renovation. But here the noise continued during unreasonable hours, and the dust was excessive. Nuisance was made out.

KEY CASE

In *Fearn v Board of the Trustees of the Tate Gallery*, the Supreme Court were asked to determine whether a nuisance was committed by Tate Galleries through its viewing platform attached to the side of the Blavatnik building. While the Tate Galleries is preliminarily an art gallery, over a hundred thousand visitors per year would visit the viewing platform, which has views over parts of London. Opposite the viewing gallery are apartments with floor-to-ceiling windows visible to viewing platform visitors, some of whom used binoculars and took pictures showing the inside of the flats.

In its judgment, the Supreme Court noted the lack of 'explanatory power' of reasonableness in determining whether an interference was a nuisance,[57] and that this is another term for whether the interference was unlawful.[58] In determining this, the Supreme Court asked whether the defendant's use of land was a 'common and ordinary' use of land.[59] In this case, a viewing platform with a hundred thousand visitors a year was deemed not a common and ordinary use of an art gallery, with the Supreme Court noting the intensity of the interference.

Furthermore, the rule has usually been that a claimant cannot complain just because they themselves are unusually sensitive. For example, in *Heath v Brighton Corp*,[60] the claimant, who ran a church, complained that the humming noise from the defendant's electricity substation interfered with the use of their land for quiet prayer. This was not a nuisance. In *Fearn v Board of Trustees of the Tate Gallery*, the Supreme Court made it clear that compensation could not be provided unless there was a 'substantial interference with the claimant's ordinary use of land'.[61] This is very much about

56 (1938) ch 11.
57 [2023] UKSC 4, [18] (Lord Leggatt).
58 [2023] UKSC 4.
59 Ibid, [35] (Lord Leggatt).
60 (1908) 24 TLR 414 (Ch).
61 [2023] UKSC 4, [21] (Lord Leggatt).

reciprocity, and in this case, the claimants were using their land in an ordinary way, and a hundred thousand visitors to the viewing platform with some using binoculars and cameras caused a 'substantial' interference with that ordinary way.

Furthermore, the Supreme Court noted that while the claimants' need to put up with increased interference with their land due to the floor-to-ceiling windows, as the Tate Gallery viewing platform with such visitor numbers was far from being a common and ordinary use of land, this was still a nuisance.

Of course, in day-to-day life there will be some interference by neighbours with each other's enjoyment of land, and neighbours will need to live with some interference. As noted in *Fearn v Board of Trustees of the Tate Gallery*, any interference with the claimant's land needs to be 'substantial', and this is an objective test.[62]

It is worth noting that people must expect different levels of interference in different places. Locality is relevant in terms of whether the defendant's use of land is common and ordinary.[63] Someone who lives in an industrial area can expect more factory noise than someone who lives in a rural, non-industrial location. This, however, does not provide immunity to businesses which would usually make noise. For example, it would unlikely be common and ordinary for a factory to make large amounts of noise at 2am in a residential area. Timing and duration are also relevant in determining whether something is common and ordinary. In *De Keysers Royal Hotel v Spicer Bros Ltd*,[64] the use of a piledriver overnight was held to be a nuisance.

KEY CASES

In *Lawrence v Fen Tigers Ltd*,[65] the defendant received planning permission to build a stadium for motor sports. Decades later, the claimant bought a house nearby, and then complained about the nose. The defendant carried out work to reduce the noise level, but the claimants said that there was still too much noise. The court said that the claimant had to expect some noise from a motor-racing stadium which was an established part of the locality. However, it was no defence that the stadium was there first, and the claimant was the one who had moved nearby. The stadium was still making too much noise and could be restrained to races which produced lesser levels of noise.

62 [2023] UKSC 4.

63 Note that locality is considered in relation to the defendant's 'common and ordinary' use and not in relation to whether there is a 'substantial' interference. See e.g. *Dennis v Head Start Day Nursery* [2024] EWHC 1248 (Admin).

64 (1914) 30 TLR 257.

65 [2014] UKSC 13.

Thus, *Lawrence v Fen Tigers* also stands for the proposition that a defendant might commit a nuisance even though it has planning permission to do what it is doing. By way of further example, in *Wheeler v JJ Saunders Ltd*,[66] the defendant obtained planning permission for a pigsty to be located on the edge of his property. The neighbouring claimant suffered from the smell. Nuisance was made out.[67]

EXPLAINING THE LAW

Planning permission has a number of roles. These include promoting safety standards, advancing development, and protecting heritage. Further, the evidence available to planning officers, when they decide to grant planning permission, and on what terms, might also be relevant evidence when the court decides whether the defendant's activities are a nuisance. But otherwise, as Lord Neuberger said in *Lawrence v Fen Tigers*,[68] planning officers are not judges of tortious liability, and by granting planning permission they cannot deprive a landowner of their tortious rights.

Malice is also clearly relevant in determining whether a nuisance has been committed. In *Christie v Davey*,[69] the claimant made a living giving music lessons. The neighbouring defendant took offence at the noise, and so beat trays and banged on the walls for no purpose other than to disrupt the lessons and annoy in revenge. The court said that the claimant's music lessons were no nuisance, but the defendant's banging was.

Similarly, in *Hollywood Silver Fox Farm Ltd v Emmett*,[70] the defendant had plans to develop a field into bungalows, but thought that the claimant's sign, proclaiming a neighbouring fox fur farm, would be detrimental to the project. The claimant refused to take down the sign, which was on the claimant's own land. So, the defendant, from their land, fired guns in order to startle the foxes and prevent breeding. The fact that this was done maliciously was a significant factor in determining that this was a nuisance.

SUMMARY

Let us summarise this section so far. Whether the defendant's use of land is a 'common and ordinary' use of land needs to be considered and whether there is a 'substantial interference with the defendants ordinary use' also needs to be discussed. The tort of nuisance is about striking a balance between neighbours. What is 'common and ordinary' can depend on the

66 [1996] Ch 19 (CA).

67 Similarly, in *Barr v Biffa Waste Services Ltd* [2012] EWCA Civ 312, which concerned smells from a refuse site, the fact that the defendant had a waste permit from the Department of the Environment did not entitle it to commit a nuisance.

68 [2014] UKSC 13, [90], [95]–[97].

69 [1893] 1 Ch 316 (Ch).

70 [1936] 2 KB 468 (KB).

character of the location – but neither locality nor planning permission gives immunity to a defendant who goes too far. Interference made maliciously is more likely to be a nuisance.

Finally, we have mainly been discussing sensory interference. But it seems that the courts take a stricter line when it comes to physical damage to property.

For example, in *St Helen's Smelting Co v Tipping*,[71] it was a nuisance when noxious fumes from the defendant's factory harmed the claimant's trees. The court even suggested that locality was *not* a relevant consideration in the context of physical damage to property. In *Halsey v Esso Petroleum Co Ltd*,[72] it was a nuisance when smuts from the chimneys of the defendant's boilers at its oil depot caused damage to clothing hanging in the claimant's garden – and even damage to the paintwork of his car parked outside his house in the street. In *Crown River Cruises Ltd v Kimbolton Fireworks Ltd*,[73] it was a nuisance when a barge, moored on the River Thames, suffered fire damage, caused by falling debris from a firework display.

ANALYSING THE LAW

No doubt the law should restrain factory fumes so noxious it kills plants. But fireworks? All fireworks are, it seems, a potential nuisance. Who knows where they might fall, and upon what? It is only a matter of luck whether or not they cause damage. Are firework displays a part of British life for which there should be give and take? Or should they be banned? Perhaps more to the point, who should insure against damage caused by fireworks: the person who lets them off, or the property owner on whom they land?

DEFENCES

In this section, we focus in particular on the defences of prescription and statutory authority. Otherwise, note that **necessity** might be a defence to nuisance just as it is to trespass (see above).

There is a defence of **prescription** if the defendant has been making a nuisance for 20 years. In which case, the defendant is entitled to continue. This is not the same as saying that the defendant has been making a noise for 20 years.

For example, in *Sturges v Bridgman*,[74] the defendant was a confectioner. Making sweets involved pounding with pestle and mortar. The claimant neighbour was a doctor who built a consulting room at the end of the garden next to the defendant's workshop. The claimant then complained about the noise. The defendant said that it had been making that noise

71 (1865) 11 ER 1483 (HL).
72 [1961] 2 All ER 145 (QB).
73 [1996] 2 Lloyd's Rep 533 (QB).
74 (1879) 11 Ch D 852.

for 20 years. But the court said, with no previous adjacent neighbours, the noise had not previously been a nuisance. Only if the defendant had been making a nuisance, not merely a noise, for 20 years, would the defence arise.

EXPLAINING THE LAW

It is *no* defence merely that the claimant came to the nuisance. Yes, the defendant might have been there first, doing what they are still doing. But the claimant is there now, and they both have to get along. In *Bliss v Hall*,[75] it was no defence that the claimant chose to buy next door to a smelly candle factory. So too, in *Lawrence v Fen Tigers*, it was no defence that the claimant chose a house near to a motor-racing stadium. Only if the defendant has been making a nuisance for 20 years is it entitled to continue.

Time runs against the *land*. If a claimant moves into a house and complains about the noise from a neighbour, the defence of prescription would work if 20 years' worth of previous owners of that house had also been bothered by the neighbour's nuisance. The 20 years' nuisance need not be made against the same person, just the same land. (This is because nuisance is about interference with land, and not interference with any person.)

ANALYSING THE LAW

Does the decision in *Sturges v Bridgman*, in effect, render the defence of prescription redundant? How likely is it that neighbours would put up with an actionable nuisance for 20 years?

In *Lawrence v Fen Tigers*,[76] Lord Neuberger suggested that the outcome in *Sturges v Bridgman* might have been different had the claimant there run a different argument. Lord Neuberger suggested that if a defendant's activity is not a nuisance before, it cannot be turned into a nuisance just because the claimant changes the use of their own property.[77] That approach is perhaps analogous to the principle that a defendant commits no nuisance just because the claimant is sensitive. In *Sturges v Bridgman*, the claimant did change the use of their property, by building at the bottom of the garden, a place more sensitive to the noise.

More generally, we might ask this: if someone has been behaving tortiously for a long time, surely the law should now say that enough is enough, rather than giving them the right to continue misbehaving forever?

75 (1838) 4 Bing NC 183, 132 ER 758.

76 [2014] UKSC 13, [56].

77 In *Fearn v Board of Trustees of the Tate Galleries*, the Supreme Court noted that this may need to 'revisited' [46].

A nuisance might be **authorised by statute**. In *Allen v Gulf Oil Refining Ltd*,[78] statutory authority was given for the development of an oil terminal. The court said that this also authorised any nuisance which was an inevitable consequence of carefully developing and running that oil terminal.

There has been significant discussion in terms of nuisance and sewage pollution. In *Marcic v Thames Water Utilities Ltd*,[79] the claimant suffered when sewage water regularly backed up through his drains onto his property. But the court said that the whole question of sewerage was regulated by a statutory scheme, which the claimant did not invoke, and which was incompatible with any residual common law right to sue in nuisance.[80]

However, this case was distinguished by *Manchester Ship Canal Company Ltd v United Utilities Water Ltd*,[81] which involved the pollution of a watercourse by a sewerage undertaker. One of the key differences between these cases was that *Manchester Ship Canal*, concerned 'causing or adopting a nuisance',[82] because the defendants,'sewerage system is designed in a way that deliberately involves the discharge of effluent into the canal when the hydraulic capacity of the system is exceeded',[83] whereas in *Marcic* this was 'a continuing nuisance by failing to take reasonable steps to avert it by constructing a new sewer',[84] and that 'such a duty to construct a public sewer could only arise under statute'.[85] Finally, the Supreme Court held that where an injunction could cause problems for legislation, damages could instead be provided.[86]

In *Rapier v London Tramways Co Ltd*,[87] the defendant was empowered by legislation to operate a tramway. But, said the court, the statute said nothing about authorising any nuisance. In which case, the common law still applied and nuisances were actionable. Thus, even though horses were needed to pull the trams, the bad smell from the stables was a nuisance. (And it was no defence that the defendant had taken care to prevent that smell.)

REMEDIES

In this section, we consider the remedies of abatement, injunction, and damages.

78 [1981] AC 1001 (HL).

79 [2003] UKHL 66.

80 The claimant had argued, under the ECHR, that his right to private and family life (art 8), and peaceful enjoyment of possessions (Protocol 1, art 1), had also been infringed, but the court disagreed. Instead, said the court, the statutory scheme for sewerage sought to strike a balance between the needs of individuals and the needs of society, and this balancing meant that the scheme did not fall foul of the ECHR.

81 [2024] UKSC 22.

82 Ibid, [136].

83 [2024] UKSC 22, [136] (Lord Reed and Lord Hodge).

84 [2024] UKSC 22, [135] (Lord Reed and Lord Hodge).

85 Ibid.

86 [2024] UKSC 22.

87 [1893] 2 Ch 588 (CA).

Abatement is a self-help remedy: the claimant is entitled to stop the nuisance themselves. For example, in *Lemmon v Webb*,[88] the court said that a neighbour might cut down any tree branches overhanging their land.

MAKING CONNECTIONS

The court in *Lemmon v Webb* stressed that abatement in that case was only available where the branches could be cut from one's own land. Going onto the neighbour's land, said the court, would be trespass. Note, however, that a party might possibly have a defence to trespass, for example necessity, if there were an urgent need to abate a dangerous nuisance (like a gas leak).

Alternatively, the claimant might obtain an **injunction** to restrain future or ongoing interference. For example, a noisy builder might be ordered not to work before 8am or after 4pm, or not at all on Sundays. In *Lawrence v Fen Tigers*, the defendant stadium was prohibited from running activities which exceeded a certain noise level measured in decibels.

An injunction is a discretionary remedy which the court might refuse. The *Shelfer* criteria were once prominently used in tort to determine where compensation might be used instead of an injunction. These were

> (1) if the injury to the plaintiff's legal rights is small, (2) And is one which is capable of being estimated in money, (3) And is one which can be adequately compensated by a small money payment, (4) And the case is one in which it would be oppressive to the defendant to grant an injunction: – then damages in substitution for an injunction may be given.[89]

Lord Neuberger in the Supreme Court in *Coventry v Lawrence* stated that that the application of tests should not be 'mechanical' and that even where the criteria are not all met, it does not mean that an injunction should be granted.

Public interest nevertheless can be a reason why the court may determine that damages are more appropriate. An example of public interest is *Dennis v Ministry of Defence*.[90] In that case, the claimant's land bordered an RAF airbase which flew Harrier fighter jets, often at low altitude, producing considerable noise. This was a nuisance. But an injunction was refused. The court said that it was in the public interest to train air force pilots. However, said the court, it was unfair that the claimant alone should suffer for the public benefit. The

88 [1895] AC 1 (HL).
89 *Shelfer v City of London Electric Lighting Co* [1895] 1 Ch 287 (CA), 322–323.
90 [2003] EWHC 793 (QB).

government was required to pay significant damages of nearly £1 million to compensate for all past and future interference.[91]

EXPLAINING THE LAW

An injunction is a discretionary remedy, and the courts are empowered to award damages instead.[92] However, 'the Court has always protested against the notion that it ought to allow a wrong to continue simply because the wrongdoer is able and willing to pay for the injury he may inflict'.[93] Put crudely, rich parties should not be able to buy permission to behave tortiously.[94]

Damages are available to compensate for any harm done to the claimant's property. For example, if noxious fumes kill plants, or emissions damage clothing, or flooding ruins a crop, then the claimant might obtain damages measured as the replacement cost of the plants or the clothing, or the lost sale price of the crop.

ANALYSING THE LAW

In *Halsey v Esso*, the claimant recovered for damage to chattels (their clothing and car), but in *Hunter v Canary Wharf*, the court said that a claimant cannot recover for injury to people. Does this distinction make sense? For example, what if the pollution in *Halsey v Esso* not only damaged the claimant's washing, but also damaged the claimant's health?

The claimant can also recover a sum of money to compensate for any reduced use or enjoyment of their land. In *Bone v Seale*,[95] the claimant was awarded damages for the personal discomfort of the smell emanating from the defendant's pig farm – even though the claimant's land itself had not depreciated in value. In *Andreae v Selfridge & Co*, the claimant was awarded damages to compensate for lost custom to their hotel caused by the defendant's nearby demolition work.

91 But note *Peires v Bickerton Aerodromes Ltd* [2017] EWCA Civ 273, where noise from helicopter training flights at the neighbouring aerodrome was held to be covered by the Civil Aviation Act 1982 s.76, which provides, to repeat, that no action shall lie in respect of trespass or nuisance, by reason only of the flight of an aircraft over any property at a height above the ground which, having regard to wind, weather, and all circumstances of the case, is reasonable.

92 Senior Courts Act 1981 s.50.

93 *Shelfer v City of London Electric Lighting Co* [1895] 1 Ch 287 (CA).

94 In *Anslow v Norton Aluminium Ltd* [2012] EWHC 2610 (QB), an injunction, which in effect would have shut down a foundry, was refused, not least because the defendant was spending serious money trying to fix the problem (rather than, for example, just allowing the problem to persist while 'buying off' any complainant with compensation).

95 [1975] 1 All ER 787 (CA).

KEY LEARNING POINT

To recover damages in nuisance for past loss, the harm must have been reasonably foreseeable.

For example, in *Cambridge Water Co Ltd v Eastern Counties Leather plc*,[96] the defendant used chemicals at its tannery. Small amounts were occasionally spilled. Those chemicals found their way into the claimant's water supply. But the court said that it was not reasonably foreseeable that the chemicals would have escaped through the defendant's concrete floor, without evaporating, and enter the water table and there remain in detectable quantities. The defendant was not liable for past damage.

Similarly, in *Network Rail Infrastructure Ltd v Morris*,[97] the defendant's railway signalling system produced an electromagnetic field which caused interference when electric guitars were played at the claimant's recording studio 80 metres away. The claimant sued for lost business. But the court held that it was not reasonably foreseeable that the defendant's signalling system would have interfered with the claimant's business at that distance.[98]

EXPLAINING THE LAW

The defendant might not be liable for past damage, if the harm was not reasonably foreseeable, but that does not provide an immunity for all future interference. A claimant can obtain an injunction to prevent future interference. But in *Cambridge Water*, there were no ongoing spillages, and in *Network Rail*, the claimant explicitly sued only for past loss.

MAKING CONNECTIONS

Under the European Convention on Human Rights, enacted in English law by the Human Rights Act 1998, every person has a right to private and family life (article 8), and a right to peaceful enjoyment of their possessions (Protocol 1, article 1). If these rights are breached, the court may award 'just satisfaction'. However, the (English) court has said that it would be unlikely, in situations of nuisance, that just satisfaction would allow for recovery greater than damages available at common law.[99]

96 [1994] 2 AC 264 (HL).

97 [2004] EWCA Civ 172.

98 The need for past loss to be reasonably foreseeable was also recently reiterated in *Northumbrian Water Ltd v Sir Robert McAlpine Ltd* [2014] EWCA Civ 685.

99 *Dobson v Thames Water Utilities Ltd* [2009] EWCA Civ 28.

An interesting issue arises in terms of diminution of value of land. *Davies v Bridgend CC*[100] involved Japanese knotweed, which, while it can be treated, can be disturbed and regrow. This can therefore continue to reduce the value of the land even after treatment. The knotweed encroached onto the claimant's land from the defendant's land long before the defendant owned the land, when the defendant moved onto the land, they were not aware of the knotweed even though they ought to have been and failed to treat it. The Supreme Court held that as a matter of causation, the defendant's failure to treat the knotweed was not the 'but for' cause of the diminution of value of the land, and the claim failed.

Finally, a claimant is under the usual duty to mitigate their loss. For example, if land is flooded, a claimant must take reasonable steps to address the problem. If they fail to take reasonable steps, then the defendant is not liable for the extra damage which the claimant could have avoided. (On mitigation, see Chapter 9.)

APPLYING THE LAW

Dinesh lives next to Carl, and both Dinesh and Carl are freehold owners of their houses. Carl has used his garden shed for fixing furniture. This makes a lot of noise and can go on until 2am or 3am for most days of the week and is disturbing Dinesh while he is trying to sleep.

Is this nuisance? First, we can see that Dinesh is a freehold owner of the land and so can sue. This would be a sensory nuisance. Carl can clearly be sued here as the creator of the nuisance. While fixing furniture is probably a 'common and ordinary' use of land, the fact that Carl is doing this until 2am or 3am, and that this is happening for most days of the week, is not common and ordinary. Dinesh is clearly using his land in an ordinary way; sleeping is an ordinary use of land, and the interruption of Dinesh's sleep is also likely to be substantial. This is also clearly a continuing nuisance. Damages may well be recovered by Dinesh for previous inconvenience: a lack of sleep is likely to be a reasonably foreseeable consequence of late noise by fixing furniture. Dinesh might also obtain an injunction restricting Carl from fixing furniture during late hours.

12.3 THE RULE IN *RYLANDS V FLETCHER*

In *Rylands v Fletcher*,[101] the defendant engaged engineers to build a reservoir on their land. As the reservoir filled, water flooded into the claimant's neighbouring mines. The defendant had not been negligent (their engineers were a reasonable choice). Nevertheless, the court said

100 *Davies v Bridgend County Borough Council* [2024] UKSC 15.
101 (1868) LR 3 HL 330.

that the defendant was liable on the following basis: if a defendant brings onto their land, in a non-natural use of that land, something likely to be 'mischievous' or dangerous if it escapes, then if it does escape, the defendant is liable for resulting damage.

This liability has since been called the rule in *Rylands v Fletcher* which is deemed a 'sub-species of nuisance'.[102] The parameters of the rule have been developed in subsequent cases, as we shall see.

ANALYSING THE LAW

The court in *Rylands v Fletcher* did not appear to consider itself to be making new law. Subsequent cases like *Cambridge Water v Eastern Counties Leather* and *Transco v Stockport* have treated this liability as part of the law of private nuisance. But the tests are different: for a start, nuisance does not require the defendant to bring anything onto their land. Certainly, the two torts are strongly related and have ingredients in common, and both might apply on a given set of facts – but we should not ignore their differences. Whether we still need both torts, however, is a different question.

In *Rylands v Fletcher*, the court said that it was no defence that the defendant had taken reasonable care to keep the water on their land. The defendant remained liable, despite any reasonable care, simply if the dangerous thing escaped. For this reason, the rule has sometimes been described as strict liability. However, in *Cambridge Water v Eastern Counties Leather*, the court said that, as with nuisance, so too with the rule in *Rylands v Fletcher*, the defendant will only be liable for harm caused by the escape if the harm was reasonably foreseeable.

For the rest of this section, we consider the following topics: what is meant by non-natural use of land; what must escape; who can sue (the claimant); who can be sued (the defendant); and what defences might be available.

NON-NATURAL USE AND DANGER

In *Rylands v Fletcher*, the court indicated that non-natural use meant bringing onto the land something which was not naturally there. In that case, by building a reservoir, the defendant accumulated more water than would naturally have occurred. Other examples given by the court included: bringing cattle onto one's land, when the cattle then escape to trample neighbouring land; and sewage leaking from one's 'privy' (an old-fashioned word for a toilet located in an outside shed). And in *Cambridge Water v Eastern Counties Leather*, the court said that storing large quantities of chemicals on land would be an almost classic case of non-natural use – even though the land in that case was being used for a manufacturing industry in which those chemicals were common.

102 *Transco v Stockport Metropolitan Borough Council* [2003] UKHL 61.

ANALYSING THE LAW

If land use is measured against a state of nature, then almost anything brought onto the land will be a non-natural user. That makes all modern life non-natural: for example, houses have supplies of electricity and gas and water. All these things are potentially dangerous if they escape. It is no surprise, then, that the courts have since updated the concept of non-natural use to soften the potential liability of modern landowners.

In *Transco plc v Stockport Metropolitan Borough Council*,[103] a water pipe supplied a block of flats. The water pipe burst, washing away the soil, which in turn damaged the claimant's gas pipe by leaving it without adequate support. The claimant sued for the cost of repairing the gas pipe, but unsuccessfully. Non-natural use, said the court, was an extraordinary and unusual use which posed an exceptional risk of danger. There was nothing extraordinary or unusual or exceptionally risky about a water pipe which supplied domestic quantities of water to a block of flats.

In *Gore v Stannard*,[104] the defendant's business was supplying and fitting car tyres. To this end, the defendant stored large numbers of tyres at its premises on an industrial estate. An electrical fault caused a fire, eventually setting the tyres alight, which made the fire rage further, burning down the claimant's adjoining premises. The defendant was held not liable. One reason was because it was a natural use of land that a tyre-fitting business on industrial premises would store tyres.

EXPLAINING THE LAW

There is a tension between non-natural use and bringing something dangerous onto the land. Both are needed for liability under *Rylands v Fletcher*. Bringing something dangerous onto the land is not enough. So, if the court feels that what is brought onto the land is very dangerous, the temptation will be to say that it is also a non-natural use of the land, otherwise the defendant might escape liability. Chemicals, like those in *Cambridge Water v Eastern Counties Leather*, are potentially dangerous, which is probably why the court said that their presence was also a non-natural use, even though they were common in such factories. In *Gore v Stannard*, the court said that storing tyres on the premises was a natural use in the circumstances, but it probably helped that the tyres themselves were not dangerous (it was the fire which was dangerous).

In light of *Cambridge Water v Eastern Counties Leather* and *Transco v Stockport*, we can characterise the rule in *Rylands v Fletcher* as follows:

103 [2003] UKHL 61.
104 [2012] EWCA Civ 1248.

KEY LEARNING POINT

If a defendant brings something dangerous onto its land, in an unusual or extraordinary use of that land, then the defendant is liable, under the rule in *Rylands v Fletcher*, for reasonably foreseeable harm caused by its escape.

ESCAPE

The dangerous thing must escape from the defendant's land. In *Read v J Lyons & Co Ltd*,[105] the claimant was an inspector of munitions. They were injured by exploding ordnance when inspecting the defendant's munitions factory. The defendant was not liable under the rule in *Rylands v Fletcher*. The whole event occurred on the defendant's land; the dangerous munitions did not escape onto another's land.

So too in *Gore v Stannard*: the defendant had brought tyres onto its premises and the tyres had increased a fire, but the tyres did not escape; the fire escaped, but the defendant did not bring the fire onto its land. In other words, what the defendant brings onto their land must also be the same thing which escapes onto another's land.

In contrast, in *Rylands v Fletcher*, the water which the defendant had collected on their land was what escaped into the claimant's neighbouring mines. And in *Cambridge Water v Eastern Counties Leather*, the chemicals which the defendant had brought into its factory were what escaped by leaching into the claimant's water supply (although the defendant was not liable since the harm was not reasonably foreseeable).

MAKING CONNECTIONS

If somehow the dangerous thing escapes – however unlikely or unpredictable that might have been – then the defendant could be liable under the rule in *Rylands v Fletcher*. But additionally, if the defendant had not taken reasonable care to prevent the escape, they might also be liable in negligence. And if the defendant deliberately releases the dangerous thing onto another's land, they might be liable for an intentional tort like trespass.

THE CLAIMANT

The claimant can sue if they have an interest in land which is damaged, or if chattels on their land have been damaged.

What about personal injury? In *Rylands v Fletcher*, the court appeared to countenance recovery for personal injury, for example caused by escaping cattle, at least where the defendant knows that the cattle had a propensity to attack people. Subsequent cases have allowed recovery for

105 [1947] AC 156 (HL).

personal injury. For example, in *Hale v Jennings Bros*,[106] the claimant was a tenant running a stall at a fairground. They were hit when a chair, with its occupant, became detached from the defendant's neighbouring fairground ride. The court held that the claimant could sue for personal injury under the rule in *Rylands v Fletcher*.

However, in the subsequent case of *Read v Lyons & Co*,[107] the court doubted whether a claim in personal injury could sound under *Rylands v Fletcher* (as opposed to in negligence). Recent strong statements by the court in *Cambridge Water v Eastern Counties Leather*, *Transco v Stockport*, and *Gore v Stannard* indicate clearly the opinion that personal injury is not recoverable under *Rylands v Fletcher*. That further aligns the rule in *Rylands v Fletcher* with private nuisance.

ANALYSING THE LAW

Is the rule in *Rylands v Fletcher* about protecting land, or about protecting against dangerous escapes? If it is about protecting land, then fine, no action for personal injury (leave that to negligence, for example). But if it is about protecting against dangerous escapes, then surely it should provide a cause of action to anyone or anything injured by the escape of something dangerous. The latter idea, of a more expansive role for the tort, was discussed but rejected in *Transco v Stockport*. Would the tort be fairer or more useful if that wider role were reconsidered?

THE DEFENDANT

The defendant is the person who occupies or controls land onto which they bring the dangerous thing; or the person who authorises or enables this to happen. In *Rylands v Fletcher*, the water came of its own accord, but the defendant had procured that it should remain in large quantities by appointing engineers to build a reservoir.

DEFENCES

In this section, we consider in particular the following defences: statutory duty, *volenti*, contributory negligence, acts of third parties, and acts of God.

If a party has a **statutory duty** to store dangerous things, like a gas company, then this might provide a defence against non-negligent escapes. As we discussed with the defence to nuisance of statutory authority, much will turn on the proper interpretation of the relevant statute.

There may be a defence of **volenti** (that is, voluntary assumption of risk) if the *claimant* caused the dangerous thing to escape (from the defendant's land). Thus, if a claimant releases

106 [1938] 1 All ER 579 (CA).
107 [1947] AC 156.

the dangerous thing on purpose, they would probably have to accept the consequences. If a claimant releases a dangerous thing accidentally, they might have any award of damages reduced for **contributory negligence**.

There may be a defence if the dangerous thing was released by a **third party**. In *Rickards v Lothian*,[108] an unknown third party had deliberately blocked up a sink and then set the tap running, which caused water to leak into the premises downstairs and damage the claimant's goods. The court held that the owner of the premises upstairs was not liable. (Also, it was a domestic supply of water which escaped, and the court said that this was a natural use of land anyway.)

MAKING CONNECTIONS

If it was foreseeable that a third party might release the dangerous thing, and the defendant failed to take reasonable steps to prevent this, then the defendant might be liable in negligence.[109] Further, the third party, if they can be identified, might also incur liability: they could be liable to the defendant for trespassing on the land; and they might be liable to the claimant in negligence or trespass.

There is, in theory, a defence of **act of God**, which usually means extreme acts of nature. The defence is set at such a high level that it can apply only very rarely. In *Greenock Corp v Caledonian Rly Co*,[110] a municipal authority, in laying out a park, constructed a concrete paddling pool for children in a stream. This altered and obstructed the usual flow of water. This in turn caused the stream to overflow during a major storm, damaging the claimant's land. Although this was a 'flood of extraordinary violence', it was not an act of God. Serious flooding, said the court, must be anticipated even occasionally.

ANALYSING THE LAW

Perhaps as a modern example, the defence of act of God might have applied (had events happened in England) when an offshore earthquake caused a tidal wave which damaged the Fukushima nuclear power plant in Japan, leading to radiation leaks. Now that it has happened once, obviously it is conceivable that it might happen again, however unlikely. Does that mean that act of God can never apply to a second occasion?

108 [1913] AC 263 (PC).

109 *North Western Utilities Ltd v London Guarantee Co* [1936] AC 108 (PC). In *Smith v Littlewoods Organisation Ltd* [1987] AC 241 (HL), vandals broke into an empty cinema and set fire to it. The fire spread to neighbouring properties. The court said that the owners of the cinema were not liable for the damage to the adjoining properties: they did not know of the vandals' presence, nor did the cinema otherwise pose a fire risk, and they had no duty to anticipate the possibility of the cinema being set on fire by vandals.

110 [1917] AC 556 (HL).

APPLYING THE LAW

Simone collects sports cars. She keeps a large tank of petrol in a barn in order to refuel her cars. An electrical fault starts a fire. The tank of petrol explodes, sending pieces of barn raining down on a neighbouring house, causing roof damage. Advise Simone.

Keeping a large tank of petrol in a barn is probably a non-natural use of land. It is unusual, since most people refuel their cars at petrol stations. It also poses a much higher risk of danger. Indeed, petrol is dangerous, and Simone brought it onto her land. However, the petrol itself did not escape. What escaped were pieces of barn, and it is not unusual to have building structures, like a barn, on one's land. So, Simone is not liable under the rule in *Rylands v Fletcher*. However, she might be liable in negligence if she failed to take reasonable care to prevent the explosion. More safety steps might reasonably be expected of Simone, given the higher risk of danger she created by storing petrol in her barn.

POINTS TO REVIEW

- Trespass to land is an act which directly interferes, unlawfully, with land in another's possession.
- For nuisance, physical damage to land or chattels is likely to be a nuisance. Malicious interference is likely to be a nuisance. Otherwise, at least for sensory interference, a balance is to be struck between neighbours. Whether there is a common and ordinary use of land is important.
- Where a defendant brings something dangerous onto their land, in an unusual or extraordinary use of that land, then the defendant is liable, under the rule in *Rylands v Fletcher*, for reasonably foreseeable harm caused by its escape.

TAKING IT FURTHER

Lee, M. 'What Is Private Nuisance?' (2003) 119 LQR 298
The author argues that there are three different forms of liability dressed up in the language of nuisance: physical harm caused by negligence; physical harm foreseeably caused during the course of certain forms of activity (a modern version of the rule in *Rylands v Fletcher*); and amenity harm (like noises and smells), which is private nuisance proper – whose rules, says the author, continue to be inherently vague. We might ask, would it be tidier simply to abandon nuisance and *Ryland v Fletcher*, and instead deal with all those matters through the tort of negligence?

Nolan, D. 'The Distinctiveness of *Rylands v Fletcher*' (2005) 121 LQR 421
The author argues that the rule in *Rylands v Fletcher* is not an offshoot of private nuisance. Nor should it be merged with private nuisance, because its differences will strain private nuisance. Nor should it be developed into a general liability for dangerous activities. As technology develops, what counts as dangerous? And whether an activity

is dangerous depends on whether reasonable care is taken to offset the risks – which is more like negligence than strict liability. The best option, says the author, is to abolish the tort. Do you agree?

Steel, S. 'The Locality Principle in Private Nuisance' (2017) 76 Cambridge LJ 145
In the law of private nuisance, what noises one might be expected to reasonably endure can depend on locality: more noise in the factory district, less noise in the library district. The author suggests that this might be unfair. For example, factories benefit everyone, so why do only local residents have to put up with the noise? We might ask, how would we work out how much compensation to pay whom? Or is that already factored in, for example, by the fact that housing is cheaper to buy near a factory?

Goudkamp, J. 'Rethinking Fault Liability and Strict Liability in the Law of Torts' (2023) 139 LQR 269
The author discusses fault-based liability and strict liability and the problems with classifying torts as fault-based or strict liability. The author argues, for example, that some torts which look like strict liability have fault liability elements or defences, and some fault-based torts use strict liability elements. The author further argues that the classification of torts as strict may lead them to be limited in scope.

13

CHAPTER 13
INTERFERENCE WITH THE PERSON

What happens if someone is punched in a fight? Or if someone is restrained following mistaken identity? Or if someone is sent several threatening texts? There are potential remedies in tort through the torts involving interference with the person. This chapter discusses the torts of battery, assault, false imprisonment, harassment, and the tort in *Wilkinson v Downton*.

> MAKING CONNECTIONS
>
> The torts in this chapter are concerned with bodily interference, and interference with a person's mental well-being. Further, if a claimant suffers personal injury because a defendant breached their duty to take reasonable care, then the claimant can sue in negligence. Still further, there are other ways in which a defendant might interfere with another's personhood, for example by damaging a claimant's reputation (see Chapter 14).

This chapter proceeds as follows. It begins by introducing the umbrella term of 'trespass to the person'. Then it discusses those torts within trespass to the person, battery, assault, and false imprisonment. Then it examines the defences and remedies for those torts. It then discusses the tort of wilful infliction of harm, and finally, it considers the statutory wrong of harassment.

AS YOU READ

- Identify the core or characteristic situation addressed by each tort in this chapter.
- Be aware that a given set of facts might lead to overlapping torts.
- Consider which of several overlapping torts might be the most suitable to govern the particular facts.
- Consider how the law might be improved or developed.

13.1 TRESPASS TO THE PERSON

We have already considered trespass to land (see Chapter 12). But trespass is not just about intentionally or recklessly being on another's property without permission. It is also

DOI: 10.4324/9781003480051-13

concerned with interference with goods (for example, if I intentionally or recklessly scratch your car) and, in this chapter, intentional or reckless interference with the person.

Historically, if a person wanted to bring a legal claim, their choice was limited to a number of standard forms. Their complaint had to be compatible with one of those standard forms, otherwise the would-be litigant had to go without. Trespass was one of those standard forms. Today, most litigation begins with a Claim Form, a document almost without constraint: any complaint can be alleged and will be heard (whether the law ultimately recognises the complaint is another matter).

Thus, trespass to the person is not, strictly speaking, a cause of action. In other words, it is not a tort in its own right. Rather, it is a collection of torts which, historically, were actioned by using that same standard form.[1] Trespass to the person is an umbrella term which includes the torts of battery, assault, and false imprisonment.

As for the difference between battery and assault, by way of a loose example, getting punched would be battery, whereas noticing an imminent punch would be assault. In other words, battery is about contact, whereas assault is about perceiving contact. In popular speech, battery and assault tend to be used interchangeably. Thus, we might hear in the news how a victim was assaulted in the street when they were hit over the head. However, in law, battery and assault are distinct, with different technical requirements, and should be treated as such. Moreover, it is not always the case that a battery will also be an assault and vice versa, so a threat with no physical contact might be an assault but would not be a battery.

13.2 BATTERY

> KEY LEARNING POINT
>
> Battery is where the defendant intentionally or recklessly, and unlawfully, makes direct contact with the claimant.

In this section, we discuss the following topics: battery's requirement of intentional or reckless contact; how contact must be direct; how contact must be unlawful; how consent can make contact lawful; and the specific context of giving consent to medical treatment.

INTENTIONAL OR RECKLESS CONTACT

As for the meaning of intentional and reckless, we might take a lead from criminal law:

> According to *R v Woollin*,[2] an outcome is intentional when a defendant seeks that outcome on purpose. So, if I want to hit you with a snowball, and I throw the snowball,

1 *Wainwright v Home Office* [2003] UKHL 53, [8].

2 [1999] AC 82 (HL).

and it hits you, I achieve my goal, and my act was intentional, whether my motive was benign or malicious, and however unlikely I was to find my target.

Also, according to *Woollin*, it may be intentional when an outcome was virtually certain to be the consequence of acting, as the defendant appreciated. A frequent hypothetical example here is when a person puts a bomb on a plane, looking to blow up the plane in order to claim on insurance. They might hope that all the passengers survive, and they do not seek their deaths, but nevertheless they appreciate that passenger deaths are inevitable. In such a circumstance, the bomber can be deemed to intend their deaths.

According to *R v G*,[3] a person is reckless when they foresaw a risk, but took it anyway when to do so was unreasonable in the circumstances known to them. In that case, children set fire to some newspapers in a backyard, thinking the fire would burn out on the concrete floor. Instead it spread to the neighbouring shop. The children were not reckless, because they did not foresee the risk of the fire spreading. (If they *should* have foreseen that risk, they might be negligent, rather than reckless.)

To return to battery, the *contact* must be intentional or reckless. The claimant does not need to intend or be reckless in terms of the consequences. So, for example, if a defendant intends to push the claimant into a swimming pool, as a prank, that might be battery, because the pushing was deliberate, even though the defendant did not intentionally or recklessly cause the damage to the claimant.[4] Here is another scenario: if X takes hold of Y's hand to slap Z, then X commits battery (in effect, using Y as a weapon). Y does not commit battery, since they did not act intentionally.[5]

Tort law (like criminal law) recognises the notion of 'transferred malice'. For example, if the defendant intended to shoot X, but instead shot Y, because of bad aim, or just bad luck, the law deems it an intentional shooting of Y as well. In other words, the defendant's intent to make contact with X is transferred to the actual contact with Y.[6]

In criminal law, a battery can be committed intentionally or recklessly. It seems that, in tort law, a battery can also be committed recklessly,[7] as well as intentionally. But it probably cannot be committed negligently.

In *Letang v Cooper*,[8] the claimant was sunbathing on the grass car park of her hotel, when she was run over by the defendant in his car. The majority of the court said that if the contact was intentional, then the only cause of action was trespass, but if the contact was

3 [2004] 1 AC 1034 (HL).

4 *Williams v Humphrey* (1975) *The Times*, 20 February.

5 *Ward v Weaver* (1616) Hob 134, 80 ER 284.

6 *Bici v Ministry of Defence* [2004] EWHC 786 (QB).

7 Ibid, [67].

8 [1965] 1 QB 232 (CA).

unintentional, the only cause of action was in negligence. In other words, trespass and negligence are mutually exclusive causes of action.[9]

EXPLAINING THE LAW

It may be that trespass and negligence are mutually exclusive, but that does not prevent a claimant from suing upon them both in the alternative. For example, a claimant might say: 'First, the defendant made contact on purpose, which is trespass. But second, if you, the court, disagree with me on that, then alternatively the contact was unintentional, but negligent, so I should still get compensation'. A good lawyer must be aware of all available arguments.

ANALYSING THE LAW

Both negligence and trespass to the person protect against bodily interference. (Negligence protects against much more besides.) But there are differences in approach:

> For a start, trespass is 'actionable per se', which means that the cause of action is complete, and a claimant may complain, whether or not the claimant suffers any damage. The purpose of battery is primarily to respond to invasions of bodily autonomy. Negligence compensates for injury, and damage *is* an essential ingredient.

Also, trespass asks if the contact was intentional or reckless, and direct, whereas negligence asks if the contact was negligent, whether or not the contract was direct or indirect.

Now, let us distinguish two questions. First, can trespass include negligence? The case law in general tends to support *Letang v Cooper*: trespass cannot include negligence. Second, can negligence include intentional acts? Surely, the answer is yes. For example, a surgeon makes intentional contact, and without battery, given the patient's consent, but can still perform negligently, and be sued accordingly.

9 Under the Limitation Act 1980 (and its forerunners), a claim which includes personal injury, arising out of negligence, nuisance or breach of duty, must be brought within three years, otherwise the claim is barred (s.11). Most other tort claims must be brought within six years (s.2). In *Letang v Cooper*, the claimant sued after three years, and so thought that suing in trespass, rather than negligence, would avoid the shorter time bar. But the court held that trespass was a 'breach of duty' as well, and so also remained subject to the three-year time bar for personal injury. This approach has since been confirmed: *A v Hoare* [2008] UKHL 6.

In other words, intentional contact, as well as accidental contact, must still take reasonable care.

In summary, intentional and direct contact can be trespass, or negligence if harm is suffered. Unintentional or indirect contact cannot be trespass but can be negligence. Together, hopefully, both torts protect against the full range of possible interferences. And if there is a choice, which one should the claimant pick? The simple answer is, whichever cause of action is easier to prove on the facts or provides the most desirable remedy.

DIRECT CONTACT

Battery involves direct contact. Examples of direct contact include punching someone, or hitting them with a weapon or projectile. Digging a hole for someone to fall into would involve inflicting harm indirectly, because there is no proximate touching or contact. (It might still incur liability for wilful harm – see below – or in negligence.) The dividing line between direct contact and harm inflicted indirectly can be blurry.

For example, it is battery where the defendant strikes the claimant's horse, so that the horse bolts, throwing the claimant to the ground.[10] It is battery to overturn a chair upon which the claimant is sitting.[11] In *Scott v Shepherd*,[12] the defendant threw a lit squib into a crowded market.[13] It fell on X's stall, who threw it away. It then landed on Y's stall, who also threw it away. It then hit the claimant, and blew up in their face, causing injury. The court held the defendant liable for battery, as if the defendant had thrown it straight at the claimant, without the actions of X or Y breaking that chain of causation (not least because all they did was act foreseeably and instinctively).

UNLAWFUL CONTACT

Battery involves unlawful contact. Any contact is potentially unlawful: there is no minimum level of violence which the law condones. The least touching can be battery.[14] However, contact can be lawful when it is an acceptable or inevitable part of everyday life.[15] Examples might include the jostling common on busy commuter trains or in a crowded street, or tapping someone on the shoulder to get their attention. Horseplay among children at school might

10 *Dodwell v Burford* (1669) 1 Mod Rep 24, 86 ER 703.

11 *Hopper v Reeve* (1817) 7 Taunt 698, 129 ER 278.

12 (1773) 2 Black W 892, 96 ER 525.

13 A squib is like a firework. If a firework is wet, it might not light and explode. So, the phrase 'damp squib' refers to something which promises excitement, but fails to deliver. It has nothing to do with a damp squid, which is a cephalopod.

14 *Collins v Wilcock* [1984] 1 WLR 1172 (CA).

15 Ibid,; *Re F (Mental Patient: Sterilisation)* [1990] 2 AC 1 (HL).

similarly be lawful.[16] Of course, in all cases, the contact should not be taken too far, and the circumstances should not be misused cynically to provide an opportunity for unacceptable behaviour.

In *Wilson v Pringle*,[17] the court said that contact, to be tortious, must be 'hostile'. That is not a helpful designation. A kiss, meant affectionately, but unwanted, is still a battery. The better approach is simply to acknowledge, as the court did in *Collins v Wilcock*,[18] and then again in *Re F*,[19] that contact is lawful when it is an acceptable part of everyday life – but everything else remains potentially tortious (regardless of the defendant's motive or attitude).

> MAKING CONNECTIONS
>
> In criminal law, a defendant can still be guilty of battery even though any touching was not hostile, rude, or aggressive.[20] It would be strange if tort law were more demanding than criminal law in requiring a hostile motive.

CONSENT

Contact is lawful when the other person consents. Consent can be express, when a person says so, or implied. If a person extends their hand in greeting, they consent to it being shaken. If a person plays football, they consent to the contact, even injury, that comes with playing the game – but not to excessive contact, like a serious injury from a foul which is reckless and dangerous.[21]

In some situations, it might not be possible to obtain a person's consent. For example, if someone is about to be run over by a truck, there is probably not enough time to engage them in conversation. The right thing to do might be to push that person to safety. But pushing someone is ordinarily a battery. So in *Re F*,[22] the court recognised a further principle, sometimes characterised as a defence of 'necessity', which renders lawful any intervention which is in a person's best interests. The test is as follows:

> KEY LEARNING POINT
>
> There is a defence to battery, if it is not possible to obtain another's consent, when it is necessary to act, to preserve or advance the best interests of that other person.

16 *Wilson v Pringle* [1987] QB 237 (CA).
17 [1987] QB 237 (CA).
18 [1984] 1 WLR 1172 (CA).
19 [1990] 2 AC 1 (HL).
20 *R v Thomas* (1985) 81 Cr App R 331, 334.
21 *Condon v Basi* [1985] 1 WLR 866 (CA).
22 *Re F (Mental Patient: Sterilisation)* [1990] 2 AC 1 (HL).

EXPLAINING THE LAW

Reference to a defence of necessity crops up at various points in tort law. For example, we encountered it in the context of trespass to land (see Chapter 12). But our use of language could be clearer. We need to distinguish between two situations.

First, where the defendant acts upon the property of the victim, in the best interests of the *defendant*. For example, the defendant might run across another's property in order to escape attack. This is necessity proper: the law recognises a defence of necessity when using another's property to avoid serious harm to oneself (again, see Chapter 12). It is a defence whether or not the property owner consents to what the defendant did.

Second, where the defendant acts upon the victim's person or property, in the best interests of the *victim*. This is only available where it is not possible to obtain the victim's consent.

CONSENT TO MEDICAL TREATMENT

Of particular concern is consent to medical treatment. It is the consent of the patient which prevents the doctor who performs surgery from otherwise being liable in the tort of battery (or for the crime of inflicting grievous bodily harm). The courts will only recognise as true consent when the patient has been informed in broad terms about the nature of the procedure.[23]

MAKING CONNECTIONS

Where a patient has not been informed in broad terms about the nature of the treatment, then an action might lie in battery. Where the patient has been informed in broad terms, then the consent is properly given, and there is no trespass. But there is also a middle ground, where the information was enough to preclude trespass, but not as detailed as the patient was reasonably entitled to expect. In that case, the patient might be able to sue in negligence.[24]

23 *Chatterton v Gerson* [1981] QB 432 (QB).

24 Ibid. A doctor is under a duty to take reasonable care to ensure that a patient is aware of risks to which they are likely to attach significance. While a doctor can withhold information if they consider it detrimental to the patient's health, this exception does not entitle a doctor to withhold information just because the patient might make a choice which the doctor disapproves: *Montgomery v Lanarkshire Health Board* [2015] UKSC 11.

Statute provides that children aged 16 or over can consent to medical treatment.[25] At common law, children under 16 can also consent, provided that they have a sufficient maturity and intelligence to understand the nature and implications of the proposed treatment.[26] If a child refuses consent, the consent of the parents might suffice. But for serious medical interventions, it may be wiser for the doctor to seek a declaration of legality from the courts, who retain an inherent jurisdiction to order what is in the best interests of children, regardless of whether or not the child, or even the parents, refuse consent.

Some people cannot consent, for example because they lack sufficient mental capacity. That situation is now regulated by statute, which provides, for example, that care or treatment can go ahead after all, if it is in the best interests of the patient.[27] But when further medical treatment is no longer in the best interests of the patient, then no medical care is allowed, and must be withdrawn. This is when life support of those in persistent vegetative states can be (must be) switched off.[28]

ANALYSING THE LAW

When is it in someone's best interests to withdraw medical treatment? If the treatment is causing severe pain, it might be in the patient's best interests to go without. A shorter life without pain might be better than a longer life of intolerable pain. But a person in a coma might not feel any pain. The life-support equipment is keeping them alive. How can it be in their best interests to switch it off? Death is surely in no one's best interests. It is not possible to compare whether or not the patient is better off after death, because after death there is no patient at all. A patient only exists before death, not after, so there can be no before and after comparison. Put another way, after death, any patient is too dead to notice whether they are better off.

If a patient, who is mentally competent, refuses their consent, that is the end of the matter. The treatment cannot proceed. It would be battery. This is so, even if the patient's reasons for refusal are irrational, indeed even in the absence of any reasons.[29] Even if, for example, it puts at risk the life of the patient's unborn child.[30] Even if it risks the patient's own death.[31] This shows just how much importance the law attributes to bodily autonomy, that is, the right of each person to decide what happens to their own body.

25 Family Law Reform Act 1969 s.8(1).

26 *Gillick v West Norfolk and Wisbech Area Health Authority* [1986] AC 112 (HL).

27 Mental Capacity Act 2005 s.5. What is in the patient's best interests is not to be judged paternalistically, but from the viewpoint of the patient themselves: *Re J (A Minor) (Wardship: Medical Treatment)* [1991] Fam 33; *Portsmouth Hospitals NHS Trust v Wyatt* [2005] EWCA Civ 1181; *Aintree University Hospitals NHS Foundation Trust v James* [2013] UKSC 67.

28 *Airedale NHS Trust v Bland* [1993] AC 789 (HL); *Aintree University Hospitals NHS Foundation Trust v James* [2013] UKSC 67.

29 *Re C (Adult: Refusal of Medical Treatment)* [1994] 1 All ER 819 (Fam).

30 *St George's Healthcare NHS Trust v S* [1999] Fam 26.

31 *Re B (Adult: Refusal of Treatment)* [2002] EWHC 429 (Fam).

13.3 ASSAULT

KEY LEARNING POINT

Assault is where the defendant intentionally or recklessly, and unlawfully, causes the claimant to perceive an imminent and direct contact.

In criminal law, assault, like battery, can be committed recklessly as well as intentionally. That is probably true in tort law as well. Further, the tort of assault, like battery, is actionable per se, that is, without any requirement that the claimant has suffered damage. Indeed, it is still assault where the unlawful contact never happened, because, for example, the defendant was intercepted by another person before he could hit the claimant.[32] And it is still assault, even where the claimant has an escape route from the threatened harm. In *Read v Coker*,[33] the defendant threatened the claimant that, unless the claimant left the workshop, the defendant and his men would break his neck. That never happened because the claimant did indeed leave the workshop. Nevertheless, assault was made out.

It is possible to commit an assault by actions, like approaching someone with fists raised, or by words alone, such as saying: 'I'm going to hit you!' Indeed, it is even possible to commit an assault by silence, as where a defendant made silent telephone calls to a claimant who feared an imminent attack.[34] But words can also cancel out actions. In the old case of *Tuberville v Savage*,[35] in the course of an argument, the defendant laid his hand upon his sword, saying: 'If it were not assize-time, I would not take such language'. This meant that he would have used his sword, but not on this occasion, given that it was assize-time (that is, the court was in town). A modern example might be: 'I'd punch you if your friend was not over there!'

The direct contact must be perceived as imminent. If a defendant threatens to inflict harm in the future, that is not assault. But once again, the dividing line between imminent and future harm is blurry. Harm which might happen in the next minute or two can be sufficiently imminent to constitute an assault.[36]

MAKING CONNECTIONS

A repeated threat of harm (whether present *or future* harm) might constitute harassment – see below. And threatening someone in order to procure a change in their behaviour might ground the separate tort of intimidation.

32 *Stephens v Myers* (1830) 4 C&P 349, 172 ER 735.
33 (1853) 13 CB 850, 138 ER 1437.
34 *R v Ireland* [1998] AC 147 (HL).
35 (1669) 1 Mod Rep 3, 86 ER 684.
36 *R v Ireland* [1998] AC 147 (HL).

APPLYING THE LAW

Anton is playing football. He is tackled by Barry. The tackle causes Anton to fall over. The referee does not blow his whistle for a foul. Angry for what he perceives as a foul, Anton punches Barry. Now the referee does blow his whistle, and shows the red card. Furious, Anton storms towards the referee, but his teammates grab hold of him. Advise the parties.

Anton is tackled by Barry. Is this battery? Battery is an unlawful contact which is direct and intentional (or reckless). The tackle does constitute direct contact. Probably it was intended as well. However, it was probably not unlawful. In playing football, any player is thereby taken to consent, at least implicitly, to that ordinary contact which is incident to the game. This includes tackles, even fouls, as long as the foul is not excessive, that is, reckless or dangerous. Since the referee did not blow his whistle for a foul, it seems likely that this tackle was within the parameters of Anton's consent.

However, Anton punching Barry is battery. There is no excuse for this. When Anton marches towards the referee, this might be assault. The referee probably thought that he too might be hit – that is, he perceived an imminent battery. It is still assault, even though the referee might have run away, and even though Anton never made it to the referee because he was intercepted.

13.4 FALSE IMPRISONMENT

KEY LEARNING POINT

False imprisonment is where the defendant intentionally or recklessly, and unlawfully, restricts the claimant's freedom of movement totally.

In this section, we consider the following topics: how false imprisonment requires behaviour which is intentional or reckless; what is meant by imprisonment; how *false* imprisonment means *unlawful* imprisonment; which finally we contrast with lawful arrest.

INTENTIONAL OR RECKLESS

Since this tort falls within the family of trespass to the person,[37] false imprisonment can probably be committed recklessly,[38] as well as intentionally. An example of reckless

37 As noted, for example, in *Collins v Wilcock* [1984] 3 All ER 374, 378 (QBD) and *Wainwright v Home Office* [2004] 2 AC 406, [8] (HL).

38 *Iqbal v Prison Officers Association* [2009] EWCA Civ 1312, [73].

imprisonment might be a janitor locking up a school for the night, knowing that someone might still be inside, but without bothering to check.

What matters is an intention or recklessness to imprison, and not necessarily an intention or recklessness to falsely imprison. In other words, if a defendant imprisons someone, thinking that they were acting lawfully, when in fact they were acting unlawfully, false imprisonment is still made out, despite the good faith of the defendant.

For example, in *R v Governor of Brockhill Prison, ex p Evans (No 2)*,[39] the prison governor calculated the prisoner's release date by relying on guidance in the case law. The Court of Appeal subsequently, and retrospectively, corrected that guidance. This meant that the prison governor's calculation was wrong, and the prisoner should have been released earlier. Her claim for false imprisonment was successful. The court said that false imprisonment is 'strict liability', and it made no difference that the prison governor's mistake was made in good faith.[40]

IMPRISONMENT

False *imprisonment* does not require a literal prison, but a restriction on the claimant's freedom of movement. Tagging and a curfew can be false imprisonment.[41] The restriction must be total. This does not mean that the claimant cannot move at all. Rather, it means that the claimant is restricted to an area delimited by the defendant. Of course, the larger the area, the less likely that the claimant will be deemed to be imprisoned. Confining someone to a house would be false imprisonment. Confining someone to the land mass of the United Kingdom would not be false imprisonment.

KEY CASES

In *Bird v Jones*,[42] the defendant had cordoned off a public footpath by Hammersmith Bridge in order to erect an enclosure for paying guests to watch boat races. The claimant wished to pass along the footpath, but was turned away. This did not constitute false imprisonment: although the claimant was prevented from going where he wanted to go (and was otherwise entitled to go, it being a public footpath), he still had freedom of movement to go anywhere else. He was not, said the court, restrained to an area delimited by the defendant; the restraint was not 'total'. Put another way, we might say, the claimant could escape. But, said the court, escape must not involve unreasonable risks. The Supreme Court stated in *R (on the application of Jalloh) v Secretary of State for the Home Department* that 'it is also imprisonment if he is only able to leave the defined area by an unreasonable means or route, for example, by

39 [2001] 2 AC 19 (HL).

40 We might add that the prison governor's mistake was not only honest, but also reasonable, given that they were relying on guidance from the court itself. Yet still false imprisonment was made out.

41 *R (Gedi) v Secretary of State for the Home Department* [2015] EWHC 2786 (Admin), [2016] EWCA Civ 409; *R (on the application of Jalloh (formerly Jollah)) v Secretary of State for the Home Department* [2020] UKSC 4.

42 (1845) 7 QB 742.

jumping out of a first-floor window or risking prosecution by doing so'.[43] An example of an unreasonable escape can be found in *Hicks v Young*,[44] where the claimant jumped from a moving taxi after the driver thought that he was not going to pay (we will discuss this case later).

MAKING CONNECTIONS

There is no false imprisonment where the defendant locks the door to one room, but the victim can leave by another door, seemingly even if that route involves a trespass to land.[45] In other words, the victim has a reasonable means of escape. Presumably, the victim would have a defence of necessity to trespass (see Chapter 12).

False imprisonment is not just about locking someone in a room. A defendant might position themselves in a doorway to prevent someone from leaving the room.[46] Or a defendant might threaten violence if the claimant leaves, which could thus be both false imprisonment and assault.[47] Or a defendant might ensure that someone stays in a room simply by asserting their authority.[48] Where a claimant accedes to a show of authority, that does not necessarily mean that they consent to being detained.[49]

It is still false imprisonment, even where the claimant does not know at the time.[50] So secretly locking someone in a room is false imprisonment. (Of course, if they never find out, they will never sue.) Also, it might be false imprisonment where a person is rendered unconscious, for example by being punched (also a battery), or when their drink is spiked by drugs (also this could be wilful harm, or negligence), because their freedom of movement is thereby restricted.

UNLAWFUL IMPRISONMENT

False imprisonment simply means *unlawful* imprisonment. As with assault and battery, it is not unlawful where the claimant consents. For example, a claimant might pay to be locked up as part of an 'escape room' experience. Or they might consent to the doctor administering a general anaesthetic.

The court has said that it is not unlawful to refuse to open the doors to a train when the train is between stations, even though a passenger is thereby restrained inside the carriage.[51]

43 [2020] UKSC 4, [41].

44 [2015] EWHC 1144 (QB).

45 *Wright v Wilson* (1699) 1 Ld Raym 739, 91 ER 1394.

46 *Walker v Commissioner of Police of the Metropolis* [2014] EWCA Civ 897.

47 *Collins v Wilcock* [1984] 3 All ER 374, 380 (QBD).

48 *Harnett v Bond* [1925] AC 669 (HL); *Meering v Grahame-White Aviation Co Ltd* (1920) 122 LT 44.

49 *Warner v Riddiford* (1858) 4 CBNS 180, 140 ER 1052.

50 *Murray v Ministry of Defence* [1988] 2 All ER 521 (HL); *Meering v Grahame-White Aviation Co Ltd* (1920) 122 LT 44.

51 *Herd v Weardale Steel, Coal and Coke Co Ltd* [1915] AC 67 (HL), 71.

We might put it this way: anyone who travels by train (or plane or ferry) is deemed to consent to the ordinary incidents of such travel, including limited opportunities to exit, and perhaps also the possibility of extended 'detention' due to delays during the journey.

ANALYSING THE LAW

In *Herd v Weardale Steel, Coal and Coke Co Ltd*,[52] a coal miner wanted to be taken to the surface earlier than his contract provided for. The company's refusal to take him up earlier was held not to be false imprisonment. But caution is needed here:

> For example, a train passenger, or a ferry passenger,[53] is governed by a contract of carriage. If they wish to leave the train or ferry at an earlier stop than they have contracted for, that might be a breach of contract. But, surely, they are entitled to leave at the next reasonable opportunity. In other words, the carrier ought presumably to give them any reasonable opportunity to exit earlier. The carrier can always sue in damages for loss, if any. (None is likely where a passenger has already paid the fare, and the train or ferry was going to stop anyway.) It cannot be an appropriate response to insist that the passenger remains against their will all the way to the final destination.

In contract law, when one party is in repudiatory breach, the other party can only keep the contract alive if they have a legitimate interest in persisting in the performance.[54] Surely there is no legitimate interest in imprisoning a passenger until their final destination. Or imprisoning a coal miner if there is a reasonable opportunity to take him to the surface earlier than planned.

MAKING CONNECTIONS

If a passenger on a train did ask to be let out between stations, and the train conductor simply opened the door and pushed them out, the train company would probably find itself liable in negligence for any harm caused. When releasing someone, the defendant must still take reasonable care of them.

LAWFUL ARREST

An obvious and important example of when it is lawful to restrict someone's freedom of movement is lawful arrest.

52 [1915] AC 67 (HL).

53 *Robinson v Balmain Ferry Co Ltd* [1910] AC 295 (PC).

54 *White & Carter (Councils) Ltd v McGregor* [1962] AC 413 (HL).

Police may arrest under a warrant issued by a magistrate; or without a warrant, pursuant to the Police and Criminal Evidence Act 1984, anyone who is about to commit, is committing or has committed an offence, or is so suspected on reasonable grounds. Private citizens can also make an arrest for crimes being committed or having been committed, but only in relation to indictable offences. (Those offences designated as indictable tend to be serious crimes.)

Where a prisoner is lawfully held, it is not false imprisonment just because the conditions are unsanitary.[55] (That might instead sound in negligence, or the tort of misfeasance in a public office.)

Note also that a master of a ship,[56] or the pilot of a plane,[57] can detain people during a voyage or flight when they have reasonable cause or grounds to believe it necessary for the safety of the passengers or the ship or aircraft.

APPLYING THE LAW

Edward is accused of cheating in an exam. He is escorted from the exam room, by campus security, to the office of the Vice-Chancellor. He is told to wait in the office until the Vice-Chancellor arrives. Campus security stay outside, to prevent Edward from leaving. Inside the office, Edward waits for 5 minutes, then climbs out of the first-floor window. Advise the parties.

There is presumably nothing wrong with ejecting Edward from the exam room for cheating. However, marching him to the office of the Vice-Chancellor might be false imprisonment, since campus security are now determining where Edward is allowed to go. They might not be manhandling him (which could otherwise be battery), or threatening to do so (which could be assault), but it could be enough that they are asserting their authority to control his freedom of movement. The mere fact that he does as he is told does not mean that he consents to any detention. When he waits inside the office, he might not know that security remain outside – but it does not preclude false imprisonment that a person is not aware at the time that they are prevented from leaving. However, Edward does eventually leave, by climbing from a window, this is probably not a reasonable form of escape, remember the Supreme Court in *R (on the application of Jalloh (formerly Jollah)) v Secretary of State for the Home Department*[58] stated in *obiter* that a first-floor window escape is unreasonable. But it seems likely, in the end, that any false imprisonment was for a short period of time. Accordingly, damages would likely be very low. (This does not prevent the university from visiting upon him the consequences of his cheating.)

55 *R v Deputy Governor of Parkhurst Prison, ex p Hague* [1992] 1 AC 58 (HL).

56 *Hook v Cunard Steamship Co Ltd* [1953] 1 All ER 1021.

57 Civil Aviation Act 1982 s.94.

58 [2020] UKSC 4, [21].

13.5 DEFENCES TO TRESPASS

As discussed above, if it is not possible to obtain another's consent, but it is necessary to act to preserve or advance the best interests of that other person, then the defendant acts lawfully.[59]

Otherwise, in this section, we consider the following defences in particular: how contributory negligence is *no* defence; the use of force (for example, in self-defence); the fact that the claimant was themselves behaving illegally; whether duress might be a defence after all; and how lesser evil necessity should probably not be a defence.

CONTRIBUTORY NEGLIGENCE

Contributory negligence is *no* defence to trespass. In *Co-operative Group (CWS) Ltd v Pritchard*,[60] a manager punched an employee. That was battery. The manager sought to reduce the damages payable by arguing that the employee was partly to blame, for provoking the manager. This was rejected by the court, which said that contributory negligence was no defence to intentional torts like assault and battery.

Thus, returning to our earlier example of the football match, when Anton punches Barry, it is no defence for Anton to say that Barry's tackle was somehow provocative.

> MAKING CONNECTIONS
>
> Can trespass include negligent acts? Recall that *Letang v Cooper* said that it could not. (Trespass only covers intentional or reckless acts.) *Co-op v Pritchard* is further support. If trespass did include negligent acts, then contributory negligence would be a defence. Since contributory negligence is not a defence, then trespass cannot include negligent acts.

USE OF FORCE

Lawful use of force can be a defence. Thus, a person falsely imprisoned may use reasonable force to free themselves.[61] (In which case, they would have a defence if their imprisoner complained of battery.) Similarly, by statute, a defendant can use reasonable force to prevent a crime, or to make a lawful arrest.[62] (In which case, they would have a defence if the criminal arrested complained of battery.) And at common law, a person can use reasonable force if necessary for self-defence.[63] (In which case, they would have a defence if their attacker complained of battery.)

59 *Re F (Mental Patient: Sterilisation)* [1990] 2 AC 1 (HL).

60 [2012] QB 320 (CA).

61 *Rowe v Hawkins* (1858) 1 F & F 91, 175 ER 640.

62 Criminal Law Act 1967 s.3.

63 Reasonable force is that which is not disproportionate – except in a 'householder case', when reasonable force is that which is not grossly disproportionate: Criminal Justice and Immigration Act 2008 s.76.

To return once more to our earlier football example, when Anton marches towards the referee, the other players grab Anton. This might be battery – except that the other players probably have a defence of using reasonable force to prevent a crime (that is, to prevent Anton from battering the referee).

What if a defendant thinks that they are under attack, but in fact they are not? Can they still plead self-defence, even though they are mistaken? In criminal law they can, as long as the mistake was honest. What about tort law? In *Ashley v Chief Constable of Sussex Police*,[64] the court held that a mistake must *at least* be reasonable as well as honest. But Lords Scott, Rodger, and Neuberger went further, and said that even a reasonable and honest mistake was not enough. In other words, according to them, a mistaken defendant could never plead self-defence in tort law. However, the point remains open.

ANALYSING THE LAW

If a defendant is attacked, they should be able to defend themselves. If they make an honest mistake, defending themselves when not actually under attack, incurring criminal liability would be harsh. After all, the defendant acted honestly. But tort liability is a different matter. If the defendant has injured the claimant, the defendant should pay compensation. What does it matter that the defendant was honestly, even reasonably, mistaken? Why should the claimant bear the consequences of the defendant's mistake?

Recall from *R v Governor of Brockhill Prison, ex p Evans (No 2)*[65] that mistake is no defence to false imprisonment. False imprisonment is a form of trespass. So, for consistency, mistake should be no defence to other forms of trespass. Thus, *ex p Evans* is in keeping with Lord Scott et al in *Ashley*: it would still be battery to hit someone in mistaken self-defence, even if that mistake was honest and reasonable.

ILLEGALITY

Illegality is a recognised tortious defence (see Chapter 9). However, just because a person is behaving illegally, it does not mean that anyone else can harm them with impunity.

For example, in *Revill v Newbery*,[66] the claimant was a burglar, breaking into a shed on an allotment. The defendant was waiting in the shed and, when he heard the burglar approach, fired a shotgun through a hole in the door. He only intended to scare the claimant, but

64 [2008] UKHL 25. See too: *Davis v Commissioner of Police of the Metropolis* [2016] EWHC 38 (QB).
65 [2001] 2 AC 19 (HL).
66 [1996] QB 567 (CA).

instead, he injured the claimant.[67] The court said that, just because the claimant was a burglar, it did not mean that the defendant could shoot him. (And the use of force was unreasonable, because it was a disproportionate response.)

In *Hounga v Allen*,[68] a domestic helper was physically and emotionally abused. It was no defence to say that she had entered the country illegally. Indeed, her employers had arranged that illegal entry. And the law against people trafficking was designed to protect the claimant, not abandon her when harmed.

In contrast, in *Cross v Kirkby*,[69] the claimant was a hunt protester, who was trespassing on the defendant's land. When the defendant ejected the claimant's partner, the claimant became angry, and attacked the defendant with a baseball bat. The defendant wrestled the bat from the claimant, and struck the claimant once, causing injury. In this case, the court said that the claimant's illegality would provide the defendant with a full defence.

ANALYSING THE LAW

Illegality as a defence must surely be teetering on the verge of redundancy, at least in the context of personal injury. To repeat, just because a person is behaving illegally, it does not mean that anyone else can harm them with impunity. We were all told at primary school that two wrongs do not make a right. Thus, occupiers still owe a duty of care to trespassers on their premises (see Chapter 11). And a person using force against illegal activity must still act reasonably and proportionately, unlike in *Revill v Newbery*, and probably without mistake, unlike in *Ashley*.

The better approach in *Cross v Kirkby* was probably *not* to say that the protester could be hit because he was behaving illegally. Rather, the more convincing approach is to say that the defendant's use of force was lawful, because reasonable and proportionate, either in self-defence,[70] or in ejecting a trespasser (see Chapter 12).

DURESS

In the old case of *Gilbert v Stone*,[71] it was held that duress by threats is no defence in tort. But it is a defence in criminal law, and by comparison, there is no good reason to deny its existence in tort law.

67 The defendant only intended to frighten the burglar. Since contact was not intentional, presumably that would have precluded a cause of action in trespass. At any rate, the burglar sued in negligence, and under the Occupiers' Liability Act 1984 (see Chapter 11). The defendant was found negligent, but damages were reduced for the burglar's own contributory negligence (that is, for behaving criminally in the first place).

68 [2014] UKSC 47.

69 [2000] EWCA Civ 426.

70 This was the alternative ground for the defendant's successful appeal in *Cross v Kirkby*. See too *Flint v Tittensor* [2015] EWHC 466 (QB).

71 (1641) Aleyn 35, 82 ER 902.

ANALYSING THE LAW

Duress by threats is, in general terms, where A threatens harm to B unless B harms C. Duress by threats is a defence in criminal law. In other words, although B in turn harms C, B incurs no criminal liability. But what about tortious liability? On these facts, C would be able to sue A, for procuring B's tort, or under the tort of causing loss by unlawful means. This means, in theory, that B could have a defence, and C would still have someone to sue. But what if A has no money? Should C be able to sue B after all? Who should bear the risk of A's insolvency? Is it B's bad luck to be threatened, or C's bad luck to be the ultimate target?

LESSER EVIL NECESSITY

Is there a defence of lesser evil necessity? The broad idea is this: there might be a defence if trespass against another's person avoids something even worse.

KEY CASES

In *Re A (Children) (Conjoined twins: surgical separation)*,[72] conjoined twins were taken to hospital. Without surgical separation, both would die. With separation, the weaker twin would certainly die, but the stronger twin would probably live. The hospital sought a declaration that separation would be lawful. The twins were too young to consent. The parents resisted the separation on religious grounds. Thus, the surgery would otherwise be battery, perhaps murder. But the declaration was given[73] and the operation carried out. (The stronger twin survived.)

Alone of the three judges, Brooke LJ justified the result as fulfilling the following test of lesser evil necessity: (1) the act is needed to avoid inevitable and irreparable evil; (2) no more should be done than is reasonably necessary for the purpose to be achieved; (3) the evil inflicted must not be disproportionate to the evil avoided.

ANALYSING THE LAW

The better view is that there should be no defence of lesser evil necessity, because the defence is problematic and unpalatable.

72 [2001] Fam 147 (CA).

73 Recall that the court has an inherent jurisdiction to decide what is in the best interests of children, and so override refusals of parental consent.

A first difficulty with this defence is that, as long as the good outweighs the bad, then the action is acceptable, no matter what happens along the way. Thus, it would also legitimise stealing from the rich to give to the poor, or, with less appeal to folklore, harvesting the organs of one healthy but unwilling person to save the lives of several sick people.

A second difficulty is the notion that, in applying such a test, judges would be empowered to decide policy questions, about what in society counts as evil, according to nothing more than their own unaccountable moral compass, without the broader public debate one ordinarily gets through Parliament. For example, is genetically modified food an evil,[74] or the war in Iraq,[75] so as to legitimise tortious acts of protest? And if so, evil for whom, and over what period, and according to what reckoning?

13.6 REMEDIES FOR TRESPASS

To repeat, someone falsely imprisoned can use reasonable force to secure their release.[76] Otherwise, they might issue a writ of **habeas corpus**. This is a process whereby the courts can summon any person to appear before them, to inquire into the reasons for their detention. If no sufficient reason is found, the prisoner is released. The writ can be sought by the prisoner, or even by a friend.

The claimant might obtain an **injunction**, for example prohibiting future battery, but realistically this is more likely in the context of a restraining order for harassment (see below).

DAMAGES

Trespass to the person is actionable per se, that is, without any requirement that the claimant has suffered any harm. In which case, the claimant might be awarded only **nominal damages**, that is, a token sum of money which, along with the court's judgment, records the vindication of the claimant's rights.

As for false imprisonment, to repeat, it is still false imprisonment, even where the claimant does not know at the time.[77] But if the claimant did not know, or the imprisonment was only for a short period,[78] then damages are likely to be much reduced. Hence, to return to our earlier example, this is why Edward remaining for only a short period of time in the Vice-Chancellor's

74 *Monsanto plc v Tilly* [1999] All ER (D) 1321 (CA), where the court said that such a question was for the legislature, and was not justiciable before the courts.

75 *R v Jones* [2005] Crim LR 122, on appeal at [2006] UKHL 16.

76 *Rowe v Hawkins* (1858) 1 F & F 91, 175 ER 640.

77 *Murray v Ministry of Defence* [1988] 2 All ER 521 (HL); *Meering v Grahame-White Aviation Co Ltd* (1920) 122 LT 44.

78 *Walker v Commissioner of Police of the Metropolis* [2014] EWCA Civ 897.

office, without knowing that campus security were outside, might only attract nominal damages. Note further, if a claimant could have been lawfully imprisoned instead, then that too might mean only nominal damages.[79]

If the claimant has suffered injury of some sort, then they can recover **compensatory damages**. For example, the claimant might have suffered personal injury from having been battered. Or they might have suffered personal injury while trying to escape a false imprisonment – but if the choice to escape was unreasonable, then no damages are recoverable for any personal injury after all.

For example, in *Hicks v Young*,[80] a taxi drove off without allowing the claimant to exit. This was because the taxi driver thought that the claimant would run away without paying. But keeping the claimant in the taxi amounted to false imprisonment. So, the claimant jumped out. But that decision, to jump out of a moving car, was unreasonable, and thus he could recover no damages, through the tort of false imprisonment, for his injuries.

MAKING CONNECTIONS

The claimant in *Hicks v Young* could recover in negligence, because the taxi driver failed to take reasonable care for the claimant's safety: he drove off while the claimant was trying to exit the taxi. Nevertheless, the decision to jump out reduced the claimant's damages, through contributory negligence, by 50%.

Damages for false imprisonment can include injury to reputation. In *Hook v Cunard Steamship Co Ltd*,[81] a sailor was confined to his quarters during a voyage, following an allegation against him of child molestation for which there was 'no vestige of ground in support'. False imprisonment was made out, and the sailor recovered damages, including to his reputation.

Aggravated damages are available when the trespass constitutes an affront to the claimant's dignity, causing them humiliation or injury to feelings. For example, in *Appleton v Garrett*,[82] a dentist performed unnecessary dental treatment on patients in order to make more profit. Because the patients were deceived, their consent did not count. Accordingly, trespass was made out. The court said that aggravated damages would be awarded for their feelings of anger and indignation and because they had suffered mental distress.

Exemplary damages go further and punish the defendant for outrageous behaviour – to mark the court's disapproval of that behaviour and to act as a deterrence. Exemplary damages

79 *R (Lumba) v Secretary of State for the Home Department* [2011] UKSC 12; *R (Aboro) v Secretary of State for the Home Department* [2018] EWHC 1436 (Admin).

80 [2015] EWHC 1144 (QB).

81 [1953] 1 All ER 1021.

82 [1997] 34 BMLR 23 (QB).

are available at common law in the following circumstances: (1) for oppressive, arbitrary or unconstitutional actions by government servants (for example, the police); or (2) where conduct is calculated by the defendant to make a profit which would likely exceed any compensation they might otherwise have had to pay (in other words, to make sure that tort, like crime, does not pay).[83]

For example, in *AT v Gavril Dulghieru*,[84] the defendants, pretending to assist the claimants with immigration, instead held them captive and forced them to work as prostitutes. The claimants were awarded aggravated and exemplary damages. In *Thompson v Commissioner of Police of the Metropolis*,[85] the claimant was unlawfully arrested, ostensibly on the grounds of pushing a police officer, but that was a lie. Then he was beaten, racially abused, detained in a police cell, and finally refused transport home despite bare feet. The claimant was awarded aggravated and exemplary damages.

MAKING CONNECTIONS

Under article 5 of the European Convention on Human Rights, enacted in English law by the Human Rights Act 1998, everyone has the right to liberty and security of their person – although they can be deprived of their liberty in a range of specified circumstances. Breach of this right entitles a claimant to 'just satisfaction'. This is an alternative way in which a claimant might pursue their complaint; it is *not* co-extensive with false imprisonment.[86] Thus, a plea under article 5 might succeed where a claim for false imprisonment fails.

13.7 WILFUL HARM

This tort was first recognised in *Wilkinson v Downton*, hence it is often called 'the tort in *Wilkinson v Downton*'. But it has evolved, through *Wainwright v Home Office*, and recently in *OPO v Rhodes*. We shall take each case in turn.

In *Wilkinson v Downton*,[87] the defendant told the claimant, as a practical joke, that the claimant's husband had been seriously injured. The claimant suffered nervous shock and resulting illness. Now, the claimant could not sue in trespass, since there was no physical contact (or perception of physical contact) between the claimant and defendant.

83 *Rookes v Barnard* [1964] AC 1129 (HL), 1226–1228. In that case, the cause of action was the tort of intimidation. Additionally, the court noted, exemplary damages are available when authorised by statute.

84 [2009] EWHC 225 (QB).

85 [1998] QB 498 (CA).

86 *Zenati v Commissioner of Police of the Metropolis* [2015] EWCA Civ 80.

87 [1897] 2 QB 57 (QB).

Nevertheless, the defendant was held liable on a new basis: that he wilfully did an act calculated to cause physical harm to the claimant, that is, infringe her right to personal safety, and which did in fact cause her physical harm. The judge said that an intention to cause harm could be 'imputed' to the defendant, in effect because it was so likely that harm would be the result of what he did. And there was no justification for what he did, said the judge, even though there was no malicious purpose to cause the harm.

In *Wainwright v Home Office*,[88] a mother and son sought to visit a second son in prison. They were required to undergo a strip search, which was conducted in breach of the Prison Rules. The mother sued, unsuccessfully, under the tort in *Wilkinson v Downton*, for her emotional distress.

The court said that, despite *Wilkinson v Downton*, an imputed intention was not enough. Rather, the defendant must have acted in a way they knew to be unjustifiable, thereby causing harm intentionally or at least recklessly (on the facts, the prison officers had no such state of mind). Further, said the court, a claimant could not recover for emotional distress unless it amounted to a recognised psychiatric illness (which was also not the case on the facts).

MAKING CONNECTIONS

In *Wainwright*, the son who was strip-searched sued successfully for battery (since he was touched). Both mother and son then appealed to the European Court of Human Rights for breach of their article 8 right to private and family life. The court agreed that their rights had been infringed. Article 8, said the court, was also concerned with a person's physical and moral integrity.[89] Today, the claimants would likely have a successful claim for tortious invasion of privacy (see Chapter 14).

In *Wainwright*, Lord Hoffmann expressed a preference that this tort be left to wither, with any injury for emotional harm instead being addressed through the tort of negligence or harassment. And yet, this tort has recently received a full reconsideration:

KEY CASES

In *OPO v Rhodes*,[90] a mother sued, unsuccessfully, claiming that publication of the autobiography of her estranged husband, a concert pianist, which recounted a history of sexual abuse at school, would emotionally harm their son. The tort was described as intentionally causing physical or psychological harm, or wilfully infringing the right to personal safety.

88 [2004] 2 AC 406 (HL).
89 *Wainwright v UK* [2006] All ER (D) 125 (Sep) (ECtHR).
90 [2015] UKSC 32.

The court said that it required words or conduct, directed towards the claimant, without justification or reasonable excuse. As for justification, on the facts, this book, although dedicated to the son, was intended for a wide audience, and there was a legitimate interest in the father telling his story and a public interest in hearing it. Also, said the court, the tort should not interfere with the give and take of ordinary human discourse, including unpleasant or heated arguments, or trenchant journalism. And usually, reporting the truth is justification in itself.[91]

Further, said the court, contrary to *Wainwright*, recklessness is not enough: there must be an intention to cause physical harm or severe emotional distress which results in a recognised psychiatric illness (there was no such intention on the facts).

Finally, Lords Neuberger and Wilson went further, and held open the possibility that significant distress, even if not amounting to a recognised psychiatric illness, should be enough on its own to fulfil this tort.

ANALYSING THE LAW

The court sided with the defendant in *Rhodes* for two reasons: (1) he did not intend to harm his son; and (2) he was justified in publishing his autobiography. But what sort of defence is 'justification'? What other acts, besides reporting a true event, might be justified? And if, for example, someone does intend to cause a recognised psychiatric illness, and succeeds, what possible justification could there be for that sort of behaviour? In particular, it is one thing to report an event, so as to put the truth out there, and surely quite another to report an event deliberately to cause another emotional harm. Is that not an abuse of rights?

In light of the restatement in *Rhodes*, we can define this tort as follows:

KEY LEARNING POINT

It is tortious where a defendant, without justification, intentionally causes the claimant physical harm, or severe emotional distress which results in recognised psychiatric illness.

The most likely remedy is damages. Given that this tort involves harm inflicted intentionally, that increases the possibility of an award of aggravated damages, for injury to feelings, especially when the defendant causes psychological harm. However, the case law suggests that this tort is rare and not usually successful.

91 Unless, for example, speaking out breaches confidentiality or privacy (see Chapter 14).

MAKING CONNECTIONS

If a defendant says that they are about to torture the claimant, that could be assault. If the defendant thereby intends to cause the claimant severe emotional distress, that could be the tort in *Wilkinson v Downton*. And if repeated, it could be harassment (discussed next). And it could also be negligence, since all this would hardly be taking reasonable care of the claimant. The potential here for overlap raises the question of whether we still need all these separate approaches.

13.8 HARASSMENT

Historically, the common law of England and Wales did not recognise a tort of harassment. Instead, it tried to provide some measure of protection by distorting the tort of private nuisance,[92] until Parliament intervened with the Protection from Harassment Act 1997. That statute makes harassment a crime and a civil wrong.[93]

KEY LEARNING POINT

It is a civil wrong to engage in a course of conduct which the defendant knows or ought to know amounts to harassment.

The statute is structured as follows:

> A course of conduct which amounts to harassment, and which the defendant knows or ought to know amounts to harassment, is prohibited (section 1(1)). As for what the defendant 'ought to know', the test is whether a reasonable person in possession of the same information would think it amounts to harassment (section 1(2)).
>
> The prohibition does not apply where the course of conduct is pursued for the purpose of detecting or preventing crime, or where pursued under any enactment or rule of law, or was reasonable (section 1(3)).

KEY CASES

In *Hayes v Willoughby*,[94] the court said that the defendant must have an honest belief that they are acting to detect or prevent crime, and furthermore, that belief must be

92 *Khorasandjian v Bush* [1993] QB 727 (CA).

93 Elsewhere, for example in Hong Kong, the common law has now developed a tort of harassment.

94 [2013] UKSC 17.

grounded in rationality, that is, there must be some logical connection to the evidence, rather than the belief being arbitrary or perverse.

In that case, the defendant was making allegations against his former employer, of fraud, embezzlement, and tax evasion. The defendant engaged in a six-year campaign, writing to the police and the Department of Trade and Industry, among others. They all conducted their own inquiries, and concluded that there was nothing in the allegations. But when they shared their conclusions with the defendant, he continued to persist with the allegations. This amounted to harassment. There was no further rational basis to continue his 'investigations'.

Harassment is a crime (section 2). The statute also provides a civil remedy, for actual or apprehended harassment (section 3(1)). Damages may be awarded for anxiety and financial loss (section 3(2)). Harassment incurs liability for all direct losses, and not merely those which were reasonably foreseeable.[95] Further potential remedies include an injunction, and if that injunction is transgressed, the claimant may apply for an arrest warrant (section 3(3)).

A 'course of conduct' involves conduct on at least two occasions (section 7(3)). Harassment includes causing alarm or distress (section 7(2)). However, mere alarm or distress might not be enough; the defendant's behaviour must be oppressive.[96] In *Hayes v Willoughby*, harassment was described as a persistent and deliberate course of unreasonable and oppressive conduct, targeted at another person, calculated to cause, and in fact causing, alarm, fear, or distress.

ANALYSING THE LAW

The statute can be criticised for being unclear: harassment is behaviour which reasonable people know is harassment. This does not provide much guidance. It means that a defendant might not know in advance whether their behaviour has crossed the line. This is particularly objectionable when it comes to criminal liability: a defendant might only find out afterwards that their behaviour risks imprisonment.

In *Majrowski v Guy's and St Thomas' NHS Trust*,[97] the court said that there is a difference between behaviour which is unattractive, and behaviour which is oppressive and unacceptable. Irritations, annoyance, and upset, said the court, arise in everybody's day-to-day dealings with other people, whereas harassment must cross the boundary from regrettable to unacceptable.

95 *Jones v Ruth* [2011] EWCA Civ 804.
96 *R v O'Neill* [2016] EWCA Crim 92.
97 [2006] UKHL 34.

EXPLAINING THE LAW

When do bad manners become harassment? For civil liability, the court has stressed that, since the selfsame harassment is a crime as well as a civil wrong, the behaviour must be so bad as to warrant criminal censure. In other words, liability in tort requires a *criminal* level of harassment.

Another case to illustrate what amounts to harassment is *Ferguson v British Gas Trading Ltd*,[98] in which the defendant, British Gas, made repeated computer-generated demands for money. If the money was not paid, it said, it would litigate, and inform credit reference agencies about the debt. But the money was not owed. Indeed, the claimant no longer had an account with British Gas, and her repeated telephone calls and letters explaining this had no effect. The continuing letters from British Gas amounted to harassment. It was no defence that the demands were computer generated.

Finally, it is not necessary that the victim themselves be the target. To repeat, liability is incurred where the defendant engaged in a course of conduct which they knew, or ought to have known, amounted to harassment. So, in *Levi v Bates*,[99] although the husband was the target of the harassment, the wife could also sue, because it was foreseeable (the defendant ought to have known) that she too would have been harassed by the defendant's conduct.

APPLYING THE LAW

Claudia used to be in a relationship with Daria, but they have broken up. Claudia is upset, and wants Daria to feel her pain. Claudia writes hurtful letters to Daria, accusing her of being cruel. Claudia then writes letters to Daria's employer, falsely accusing Daria of stealing. Claudia begins telephoning Daria at home, threatening violence against her. Daria is now signed off work with depression. Advise the parties.

Claudia might incur liability for harassment. Writing hurtful letters is probably not harassment. It may be unattractive behaviour, but it is a regrettable yet common incident of ordinary relationships. However, making a false accusation of theft to Daria's employers is serious. Nor is there anything to suggest that Claudia believes she

98 [2009] EWCA Civ 46. See too *Worthington v Metropolitan Housing Trust Ltd* [2018] EWCA Civ 1125, where the landlord sent repeated letters threatening legal proceedings to evict tenants, when no legal proceedings ever materialised.

99 [2015] EWCA Civ 206.

is detecting crime, let alone that there are rational grounds for the allegation. It is also serious to threaten Daria with violence. This happens on at least two occasions, and so constitutes a course of conduct. Claudia probably knows this is harassment, since she wants Daria to 'feel her pain'. At any rate, a reasonable person would likely consider this harassment. Daria could get an injunction to restrain Claudia. She could also get damages reflecting her suffering, and any costs associated with treating her depression and being off work.

Further, Claudia might incur liability under the tort in *Wilkinson v Downton*. It seems that she was intentionally seeking to cause Daria distress. However, liability requires an intention to cause *severe* emotional distress, which results in recognised psychiatric illness. Daria is suffering from depression, which is a recognised psychological condition. But did Claudia intend severe emotional distress? If so, there is no justification for Claudia's behaviour: the breakdown of their relationship might explain her conduct, but does not excuse it. However, it would be hard to prove such an intention. Harassment seems easier to make out.

Threatening violence might also be trespass to the person, namely assault, if Claudia intended Daria to perceive an imminent battery. Although she was making threats over the phone, Claudia might have intended that (or been reckless whether) Daria might believe that Claudia could appear in person within a minute or two, depending on where Claudia was calling from.

When Claudia writes letters to Daria's employer, falsely accusing Daria of stealing, that might constitute defamation (see Chapter 14).

POINTS TO REVIEW

- Battery is where the defendant intentionally or recklessly, and unlawfully, makes direct contact with the claimant.
- Assault is where the defendant intentionally or recklessly, and unlawfully, causes the claimant to perceive an imminent and direct contact.
- False imprisonment is where the defendant intentionally or recklessly, and unlawfully, restricts the claimant's freedom of movement totally.
- It is tortious where a defendant, without justification, intentionally causes the claimant physical harm, or severe emotional distress which results in recognised psychiatric illness.
- It is a civil wrong to engage in a course of conduct which the defendant knows or ought to know amounts to harassment.

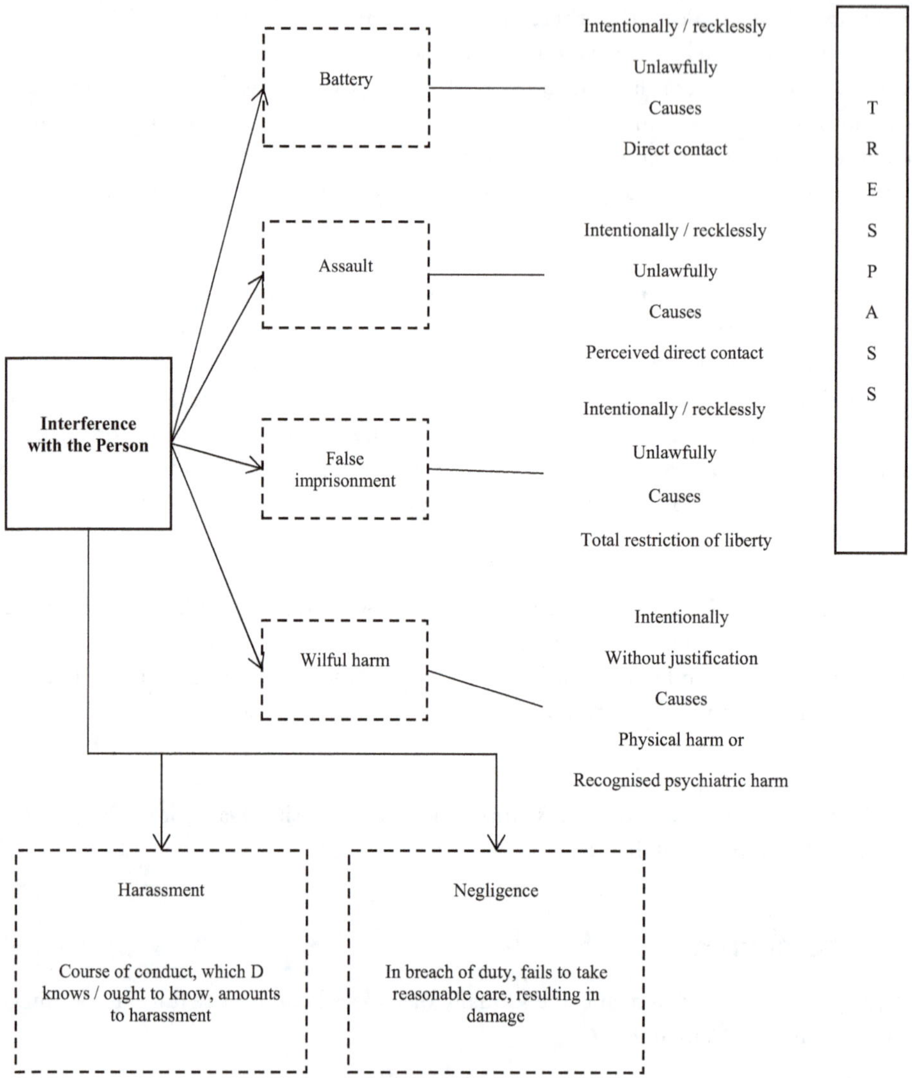

Figure 13.1 Overview of interference with the person

TAKING IT FURTHER

Beever, A. 'Transferred Malice in Tort Law?' (2009) 29 Legal Studies 400
The author argues that there should be no doctrine of transferred malice in tort law (despite its presence in criminal law). Where, for example, A shoots at B, but hits C, liability might still ensue: by recognising that a defendant still acts intentionally if they foresaw the outcome (hitting C) as virtually certain (even if they did not want it, or seek it deliberately); or because a defendant who mistakenly hits C has usually behaved recklessly (by shooting at B when C was nearby); or simply by C suing in negligence

(rather than trespass). We might ask, what are the reasons for keeping an intentional tort like battery if the situation might be captured anyway by the lower threshold of negligence?

Goudkamp, J. 'Insanity as a Tort Defence' [2011] Oxford J Legal Studies 727
Insanity is recognised as a defence in criminal law, but not in tort law. The author argues that it should be recognised as a defence in tort law too, because an insane person does not act with free will, and because tort liability is a sanction which it would be unfair to impose on an insane person. Additionally, we might ask, should we have a minimum age for tortious liability (just like we have a minimum age for criminal responsibility)?

Murphy, J. 'The Nature and Domain of Aggravated Damages' (2010) 69 Cambridge LJ 353
The author argues that aggravated damages are not about punishing the defendant, nor about compensating the claimant for mental distress, but are best regarded as reparation for harm to one's dignity. Such harm arises when a defendant acts with disregard for the innate value of the claimant's personhood, for example by deliberate humiliation or objectification. We might ask, instead of piggybacking humiliation as aggravated damages onto an existing tort, should we recognise a new tort of humiliation?

Keown, J. 'Restoring Moral and Intellectual Shape to the Law after *Bland*' (1997) 113 LQR 482
In the context of switching off life-support machines, the author says that a distinction must be drawn between, on the one hand, whether medical treatment continues to be worthwhile, which he says is a legitimate question, and on the other hand, whether the patient's life is worthwhile, which the author says is not a legitimate question. But, we might ask, does this distinction work? After all, whether medical treatment is worthwhile will in large measure be judged by its impact on a particular individual's life. For example, kidney dialysis is futile in curing the underlying condition, but it does keep the patient alive: A. McGee, 'Finding a Way through the Ethical and Legal Maze: Withdrawal of Medical Treatment and Euthanasia' (2005) 13 Medical L Rev 357.

14

CHAPTER 14
DEFAMATION

This chapter discusses, in the first half, what constitutes the tort of defamation, and in the second half, the defences to defamation.

What if someone writes a newspaper article accusing you of sexual misconduct? What if they suggest that you are a lawyer who embezzles client money?

Defamation is the tort which protects a person's reputation, that is, the regard which others have of that person. (This is not necessarily the reputation which the claimant deserves, or thinks they deserve.) For example, if a newspaper publishes an allegation that the claimant is a drug smuggler, the claimant might be able to sue in defamation. A statement is defamatory if it tends to lower the claimant in the estimation of right-thinking members of society.

There is a balance to be struck between, on the one hand, protecting one person's reputation, and on the other, promoting freedom of expression. Article 10 of the European Convention on Human Rights states that everyone has the right to freedom of expression, including freedom to hold opinions, and to receive and impart information and ideas. But it also states that the exercise of these freedoms carries with it duties and responsibilities, and so may be subject to such restrictions as are prescribed by law and necessary in a democratic society for the protection of the reputation or rights of others.[1]

Previously, defamation actions were tried before a judge, who would decide questions of law, and a jury, who would find the facts and decide the amount of compensation. Now, trial is before a judge alone, without a jury, unless the court orders otherwise.[2] More generally, there have been significant legislative developments to the law of defamation, specifically in the Defamation Acts of 1996 and 2013.

Finally, to repeat, a statement is defamatory if it tends to lower the claimant in the estimation of right-thinking members of society. That is all. The statement does not have to be false. It could be true. But 'truth' is a defence. This point reveals how much heavy lifting is done in defamation law by the defences. In effect, the law puts the burden on the person saying anything derogatory to justify what they have said, rather than putting the burden on the person insulted to prove that the insult was undue. The tort of defamation tells us: if you have nothing nice to say, do not say anything at all – but if you do say something, be ready to justify it.

1 The European Convention on Human Rights has been enacted into English law through the Human Rights Act 1998.

2 Defamation Act 2013 s.11.

DOI: 10.4324/9781003480051-14

The first half of this chapter is concerned with the long list of ingredients needed to make out a claim in defamation and the available remedies. The second half discusses the defences.

AS YOU READ

- Identify all the elements needed to make out a case of defamation.
- Keep in mind the two distinct steps of defamation and defence.
- Be aware that recent statutory developments often overwrite the previous common law positions.
- Consider how the law might be improved or developed further.

14.1 THE INGREDIENTS OF DEFAMATION

There are a large number of ingredients necessary to make out the cause of action in defamation. Is the statement a libel or a slander? (Each has slightly different requirements.) What does the statement mean? Is that meaning defamatory? (In other words, does it tend to lower the claimant in the estimation of right-thinking members of society?) Does the statement refer to the claimant? Is the claimant the type of person who can sue? (Not everyone defamed has standing to sue.) Has the statement been published to third parties? Finally, what remedies are available? We shall take each in turn.

14.2 LIBEL AND SLANDER

Slander is defamation in a temporary form, like words spoken in a conversation. Libel is defamation in a permanent form, like a newspaper article. In *Monson v Tussauds*,[3] it was libellous for the defendant to exhibit a waxwork of the claimant, holding a gun, in an anteroom to the Chamber of Horrors, the clear message being that the claimant was an evil criminal. (His previous prosecution in Scotland for murder had been returned 'not proven' by the jury.) Words, images, or gestures in the course of performance of a public play can constitute libel[4] – so too broadcasts on television and radio.[5] More generally, a defamatory statement can consist of words, pictures, visual images, gestures, or any other method of signifying meaning.[6]

3 [1894] 1 QB 671 (CA).

4 Theatres Act 1961 s.4.

5 Broadcasting Act 1990 s.166.

6 Defamation Act 2013 s.15.

Note: there is a difference between harm caused to reputation and the consequences which flow from that. For example, a ruined reputation might have as a consequence that the claimant has a lucrative job offer withdrawn.[7] Harm to reputation is one thing; consequential harm, or 'special damages', is another.

Previously, at common law, libel was actionable without proving that the claimant had suffered any special damages, whereas slander required proof of special damages. There were two exceptions when slander did not require proof of actual loss. First, imputation of a criminal offence punishable by imprisonment.[8] Second, any slander calculated to disparage, or cause pecuniary damage to, the claimant in their profession or business.[9]

Now, a statement is not defamatory unless its publication has caused, or is likely to cause,[10] serious harm to the reputation of the claimant.[11] And as regards a body that trades for profit, like a company, serious harm means serious financial loss.[12]

The cumulative effect of all this seems to be as follows. Libel, and the exceptions to slander, must at least be likely to cause serious harm to reputation. Slander must otherwise also result in special damage.

ANALYSING THE LAW

Previously, libel was considered more serious, because of its permanent form, and so likely to cause damage that the law presumed it. But is slander really less serious, given how quickly rumour can spread? Would it not be more sensible to have only one test of defamation, and ignore the form it takes? Is a photograph published on Snapchat permanent or temporary?

What about a post on X (formerly Twitter) which is deleted soon after? In *Monroe v Hopkins*,[13] discussed further below, the claimant complained about two tweets. The first tweet had been deleted within a couple of hours, but it was still categorised as libel. Further, the court said that it was not so much a matter of how long the tweet existed, as the impact it had when first read by others.[14] All of which suggests that the historic distinction between libel and slander is perhaps no longer justifiable.

7 *Lachaux v Independent Print Ltd* [2017] EWCA Civ 1334, [27].

8 *Webb v Beavan* (1883) 11 QBD 609.

9 Defamation Act 1952 ss.2–3.

10 'Likely to cause' means has a tendency to cause: *Lachaux v Independent Print Ltd* [2017] EWCA Civ 1334, [50].

11 Defamation Act 2013 s.1(1).

12 Defamation Act 2013 s.1(2).

13 [2017] EWHC 433 (QB).

14 [2017] EWHC 433 (QB), [71(2)].

Finally, what counts as 'serious harm'? The courts have given the following guidelines.[15]

First, injury to feelings alone, however grave, will not be sufficient in the absence of serious harm to reputation. Put another way, just because the statement is seriously defamatory (it says something awful), that does not mean that serious harm will follow (for example, if no one reads it or believes it).[16]

Second, mass media publications of seriously defamatory allegations are likely to render the need for evidence of serious harm less necessary. In other words, serious harm could be treated as a given. The internet can be particularly pernicious; statements posted online are easier to spread (the 'percolation effect'), and even when a web page is taken down, the statement can continue in screenshots or internet archives.[17] However, it is not a numbers game: very serious harm to reputation can be done with publication to just one person. (An example might be giving a defamatory reference to a single potential employer.)

Third, the courts acknowledge the difficulties in the claimant finding witnesses to say that they now think less of the claimant. The claimant is not likely to want to spread the defamation by asking friends if they have read it, and those who are not friends are unlikely to support the claimant's litigation.

Overall, the need for 'serious harm' is perhaps best viewed as a threshold requirement, to weed out those claims which, while technically viable, are undeserving because they do not involve actual serious harm to reputation.[18]

ANALYSING THE LAW

'Serious' sounds like a weighty word. But perhaps it is merely being used as an antonym for 'trivial'.[19] Thus, a defamation action might proceed only in cases of non-trivial harm to reputation. Just how much harm is suffered will be reflected in the amount of compensation awarded. Analogously, perhaps, summary judgment can be given on any case (in defamation or otherwise) where there is no real prospect of success, but a 'real' prospect of success means only that the claim is non-fanciful.[20]

15 *Sobrinho v Impresa Publishing SA* [2016] EWHC 66 (QB), [46]–[48]; *Monroe v Hopkins* [2017] EWHC 433 (QB), [67]–[69].

16 *Lachaux v Independent Print Ltd* [2019] UKSC 27.

17 *Schofield v Politicalite Ltd* [2024] EWHC 543 (KB) at [38].

18 *Theedom v Nourish Training* [2015] EWHC 3769 (QB), [15].

19 See *Lachaux v Independent Print Ltd* [2017] EWCA Civ 1334, [43].

20 Civil Procedure Rules 24.2.

14.3 WHAT DOES THE STATEMENT MEAN?

Before we can say whether a statement is defamatory, first we have to decide what the statement means. So, the first task is to establish the natural and ordinary meaning of the words. It does not matter what the author meant to say, but rather what meaning would be understood by reasonable people.[21]

It is, perhaps, sometimes the mark of great literature or poetry that different readers can understand it in different ways. But in defamation law, there can only be one natural and ordinary meaning of a statement.[22] The court must identify that meaning. This is known as the 'single meaning' rule.[23]

In *Jeynes v News Magazines Ltd*,[24] the court gave the following guidance on interpretation:

> The governing principle is reasonableness. The hypothetical reader is representative of those who would read the publication in question. They are not naïve, nor unduly suspicious. They can read between the lines. They can read in an implication more readily than a lawyer, and may indulge in a certain amount of loose thinking. But they are not avid for scandal, and do not select one bad meaning where other non-defamatory meanings are available. The article must be read as a whole, and any 'bane and antidote' taken together.[25] In delimiting the range of permissible defamatory meanings, the court should rule out any meaning which can only emerge as the produce of some strained or forced interpretation.

Different forms of publication might require different approaches to interpretation. For example, in *Monroe v Hopkins*,[26] Katie Hopkins, the outspoken journalist, posted twice on Twitter (now called X), the social network website, accusing Jack Monroe, the food writer and activist, of vandalising war memorials. Now, any post on Twitter was originally constrained to only 140 characters (it has now been increased to 280 characters). In that context, said the court, an 'elaborate analysis' of the words would be wrong, whereas an 'impressionistic approach' was more fitting, and might also take account of the wider Twitter conversation in which the post appeared.

---

21 *Capital and Counties Ban Ltd v Henty* (1882) 7 App Cas 741.

22 This is not necessarily the literal meaning, because some statements involve metaphor.

23 *Slim v Daily Telegraph Ltd* [1968] QB 157 (CA). For heavy criticism of the single meaning rule, and its rejection in the related tort of malicious falsehood, see *Ajinomoto Sweeteners Europe SAS v Asda Stores Ltd* [2010] EWCA Civ 609.

24 [2008] EWCA Civ 130, [14].

25 In other words, where a statement both defames (bane) and praises (antidote) the claimant, both must be taken together to consider the overall message. If the article sets out the truth, a claimant cannot sue only upon a misleading headline: *Spicer v Commissioner of Police of the Metropolis* [2019] EWHC 1439 (QB).

26 [2017] EWHC 433 (QB).

Similarly, a comment posted on Facebook saying that 'he tried to strangle me' is likely to be read casually, meaning that 'he grasped my throat', rather than given a technical meaning of attempted murder.[27]

To complicate matters, not only do words have a natural meaning, but also it is possible to 'read between the lines', by which a statement communicates an implied meaning. In defamation law, this implied meaning is called 'innuendo'. There are two types of implied meaning. First, what a reasonable person might imply, having only a general knowledge. (Sometimes this is called, unhelpfully, a 'false' or 'popular' innuendo.) Second, what might be implied by someone having special knowledge. (Sometimes this is called a 'true' or 'legal' innuendo.) A statement can have both a (single) natural and ordinary meaning, *and* an implied meaning.

To develop an example from Lord Devlin in *Lewis v Daily Telegraph Ltd*,[28] the statement 'X pays to have sex with prostitutes' has a clear, natural meaning. As for the statement 'X regularly visits brothels', that too has a literal meaning, albeit perhaps rather narrow, since it does not say expressly what X does at the brothels he visits. (Perhaps X is a doctor who performs medical check-ups for the prostitutes.) But without any further explanation, the statement 'X regularly visits brothels' might cause a reasonable person to infer that X pays to have sex with prostitutes by visiting brothels. That might be the first type of implied meaning or innuendo. As for the statement 'X regularly visits the Rising Sun, a house in New Orleans', the implication that X pays to have sex with prostitutes might only occur to those people who have a special knowledge that the Rising Sun is a brothel. That might be the second type of implied meaning or innuendo.

It is sufficient to prove that there are people with special knowledge who might understand the words in a defamatory sense, without having to prove that any person did in fact understand them in that sense.[29]

EXPLAINING THE LAW

On the one hand, it does seem strange that a statement might only be defamatory with special knowledge, and yet the claimant does not have to show that anyone with special knowledge actually gave it that defamatory meaning. But on the other hand, a claimant cannot be expected to know all the people who might have read or heard the defamatory statement, so really it is an exercise in showing what a possible reader might have thought. Nevertheless, the fewer such possible readers, the less likely the claimant will be able to show 'serious harm' to reputation.

27 *Stocker v Stocker* [2019] UKSC 17.

28 [1964] AC 234 (HL).

29 *Hough v London Express Newspaper Ltd* [1940] 2 KB 507 (CA).

ANALYSING THE LAW

All this seems unnecessarily complicated. For a start, why have a single meaning rule when we also acknowledge implied meanings, and when those implied meanings can be based on general knowledge *or* special knowledge, and when it is not even necessary to show that anyone with special knowledge actually understood that implied meaning?!

Perhaps a more straightforward approach might be: first, could anyone reasonably attribute the meaning which the claimant complains about; second, how many people would likely attribute that meaning; and third, is that enough to cause non-trivial harm to reputation?

14.4 IS THE STATEMENT DEFAMATORY?

Having determined what the statement means, the next question to ask is this: is the statement defamatory?

KEY LEARNING POINT

A statement is defamatory if it tends to lower the claimant in the estimation of right-thinking members of society.

The test of what is defamatory has sometimes been put in other ways: does the statement tend to expose the claimant to hatred, contempt, or ridicule;[30] might it cause the claimant to be shunned and avoided?[31] But undoubtedly the leading test is whether it tends to lower the claimant in the estimation of right-thinking members of society.[32]

For example, in *Berkoff v Burchill*,[33] it was defamatory for a critic to call an actor 'hideously ugly'. In *Tolley v JS Fry & Sons Ltd*,[34] it was defamatory to publish a caricature of a famous golfer with a chocolate bar, because it implied that the golfer, for money, had consented to the advertisement, and so flouted his amateur status.

30 *Berkoff v Burchill* [1996] 4 All ER 1008 (CA).

31 *Youssoupoff v MGM Pictures Ltd* (1934) 50 TLR 581 (CA).

32 *Sim v Stretch* [1936] 2 All ER 1237 (HL).

33 [1996] 4 All ER 1008 (CA).

34 [1931] AC 333 (HL).

EXPLAINING THE LAW

Attitudes change. Today, golfers often accept sponsorship deals. And would it lower a person in the public's estimation to know that they went to brothels (to revisit an earlier example)?[35] To do so might be hypocritical, for example, for a politician who preached 'traditional' values – but then the disparaging element of the statement (sometimes called the 'sting') would be not so much the visit to the brothel itself as the allegation of hypocrisy.[36] Without a jury, how might a judge keep up to date with current social attitudes?

What matters is the view of *right-thinking* members of society. At school, a child might be called a 'teacher's pet' for always handing in their homework on time. Other children might tease. But the law would find nothing disparaging in an accusation of always doing the right thing.

KEY CASES

In *Byrne v Dean*,[37] a member of a golf club informed the police that the club had unlicensed gambling machines. As a consequence, the machines were removed. The claimant was suspected of being the informant, and this allegation was posted on the club's noticeboard, along with the hope that he would 'byrnn in hell and rue the day'. The claimant took objection to the pun and sued the club in defamation (for failing to remove the notice). The court held that, although some in the club might think less of the claimant, it was not defamatory to assert that he had set in motion the proper machinery for suppressing crime.

It is no defence that the defendant did not intend the statement to be defamatory. In *Baturina v Times Newspapers Ltd*,[38] the defendant newspaper alleged that the claimant, a Russian billionaire, had bought a house in London (through an offshore company). The defendant argued that this was defamatory because it implied that she had broken Russian law: in Russia, one had to list all one's assets, and she had not listed this house. (She denied owning the house

35 In *Brown v Bower* [2017] EWHC 2637 (QB), the court said that it raised difficult questions as to contemporary social values, as to whether paying for sex, or enjoying rough sex, was defamatory.

36 Similarly, in *Modi v Clarke* [2011] EWCA Civ 937, the defendant accused the claimant of acting to destroy the structure of cricket (by introducing a Twenty20 League to England). That in itself was not defamatory, since changing the structure of cricket need not be a bad thing. But the sting of the accusation was that the claimant was behaving in an underhand or dishonourable way, for example by approaching clubs directly, rather than acting through the established cricket institutions, when the claimant himself held official positions in those institutions. That imputation of dishonour could be defamatory.

37 [1937] 1 KB 818 (CA).

38 [2011] EWCA Civ 308.

at all.) It was no defence that the defendant did not know the technicalities of Russian law on this detail. (Of course, the statement that the claimant owned a house in London could only be defamatory to those with special knowledge of Russian law – so this could be another example of a 'legal' innuendo.)

EXPLAINING THE LAW

The moral of *Baturina* is this: publish an alleged fact at your peril. Even if you think that the fact is harmless, it may turn out to be derogatory, especially in a modern world which is highly connected and multicultural. If the fact is true, or is false but your research was thorough, you may have a defence (see below).

It is no defence that the statement was published to people who already have a dim view of the claimant. There is a difference between, on the one hand, an audience generally disliking the claimant, and on the other, the audience now liking the claimant even less because of a specific allegation.[39] If a statement reduces a bad reputation even lower, that can be defamatory.

14.5 DOES THE STATEMENT REFER TO THE CLAIMANT?

There is no difficulty if the statement refers to the claimant by name. But otherwise, and once again, a reasonable person with special knowledge might understand that a statement about an unnamed person might actually refer to the claimant, and that can suffice for defamation.

For example, in *Morgan v Odhams Press Ltd*,[40] a newspaper alleged that a girl had been temporarily kidnapped. In fact, she had been staying with the claimant. The court held that the article could be defamatory of the claimant, at least to those who knew that the girl was staying with him at the time, since it implied that he was a kidnapper. (But the court also said that the smaller the group who appreciated the defamation, the lesser the award of damages.)

If the statement defames a group, and the claimant is a member of that group, the claimant cannot sue unless the statement was capable of referring to them personally – which might be the case if the group is very small or the allegation very specific.[41] But to say, to borrow

39 *Banks v Cadwalladr* [2023] EWCA Civ 219.

40 [1971] 1 WLR 1239 (HL).

41 *Knuppfer v London Express Newspaper Ltd* [1944] AC 116 (HL).

an example from Willes J, that 'all lawyers are thieves' is too general to be defamatory of any particular lawyer.[42]

Again, it is no defence that the defendant did not intend to refer to the claimant. In *Hulton & Co v Jones*,[43] a newspaper published a humorous story about a fictional character called Artemus Jones – which turned out to be the name of a real barrister. The court held that (some) reasonable people might believe that the article to referred to him. In *Newstead v London Express Newspapers Ltd*,[44] a newspaper reported a conviction for bigamy of Harold Newstead of Camberwell – which was true, except that there was a second Harold Newstead of Camberwell who could sue for defamation (the newspaper needed to distinguish more clearly between the two).

In contrast, in *O'Shea v MGN Ltd*,[45] a newspaper published an advertisement for a pornographic website. The fact that the model in the photograph happened to look like the claimant was insufficient to constitute defamation of the claimant.

ANALYSING THE LAW

The approach in *O'Shea* must be right, otherwise, taken to its full conclusion, one person, who happens to look like another person, would always be at risk of defaming that other person.

For example, Alex walks down the street wearing a T-shirt saying 'I like hamburgers', and Alex happens to look like Bill, and Bill has a reputation as a vegan. Surely Bill cannot sue Alex in defamation, just because some onlookers mistakenly think that Alex is Bill. Surely Alex can wear whatever t-shirt he wants to wear (as long as he is not trying to pass himself off as Bill).

In turn, this suggests that the approach in *Newstead* goes too far, because, by parity of reasoning, one person, who happens to share a name with another person, would similarly be at risk of defaming that other person.

In the modern world, with billions of people, with similar names and faces, all readily searchable on the internet, surely no one can claim that their own name or face is the one that deserves protection (from what the others do).

But what about the newspaper that deliberately uses a lookalike to fool its readership into believing that the photograph is of the actual celebrity?

42 *Eastwood v Holmes* (1858) 1 F & F 347, 349, 175 ER 758, 759.

43 [1910] AC 20 (HL).

44 [1940] 1 KB 377.

45 [2001] All ER (D) 65 (May) (QBD).

14.6 WHO CAN SUE?

A natural person, like you or me, can sue for defamation. But the action in defamation does not survive death (either for the benefit of the claimant's estate or against the defendant's estate).[46] A company, or charity, can sue for defamation, because its good name is a thing of value which the law deems proper to protect.[47] (Remember, a body which trades for profit must show that the defamation has caused, or is likely to cause, serious financial loss.)

Local and central government cannot sue for defamation, because of the highest public importance that a democratically elected body be open to uninhibited public criticism.[48] Similarly, a political party cannot sue.[49] And yet, an individual politician can sue.[50]

EXPLAINING THE LAW

How can we criticise the acts of government, without criticising the individual politicians who carry out those acts? In the United States, public figures can only sue for defamation on proof that the defendant knew that the statement was false, or acted with reckless disregard for its falsity. In English law, although it might be defamatory to disparage an individual politician, there are a range of possible defences, such as truth, honest opinion, or public interest. But is it better to put the burden on the politician to prove the defendant's bad faith (as in the United States) or to put the burden on the citizen to prove that their criticism of a politician was fair (as in England)?

14.7 PUBLICATION

It is not defamatory for a person to shout abuse at their television in the lonely privacy of their home. Nor is it defamatory for one person to be rude to another person. Rather, the defendant must publish the defamatory statement to a third party. (Although, for historical reasons, it does not suffice merely for one person to tell their spouse.[51])

46 Law Reform (Miscellaneous Provisions) Act 1934 s.1.

47 *Jameel v Wall Street Journal Europe Sprl* [2006] UKHL 44.

48 *Derbyshire County Council v Times Newspapers Ltd* [1993] AC 534 (HL).

49 *Goldsmith v Bhoyrul* [1998] QB 459 (QBD).

50 *Bookbinder v Tebbit* [1989] 1 WLR 640 (CA). Bookbinder was the leader of the Derbyshire council. In *Burgon v News Group Newspapers Ltd* [2019] EWHC 195 (QB), an individual MP sued successfully for it being wrongly suggested that he was in a rock band which delighted in using Nazi symbols.

51 *Wennhak v Morgan* (1888) 20 QBD 365 (DC).

MAKING CONNECTIONS

To lie to someone might be fraud. To lie about someone to a third party might be defamation. To be rude to someone, or threatening, might be assault or harassment (see Chapter 13). To be rude about someone to a third party might be defamation.

To complicate matters, it is possible to harass someone through a course of defamatory conduct! This might lead to aggravated damages for the defamation (rather than separate sums of compensation for the defamation and for the harassment).[52]

Sometimes, publication is unintentional. But once again, the defendant might still incur liability. The test is: was it reasonably foreseeable that a third party would see the statement? Yes, said the court in *Theaker v Richardson*,[53] when the defendant sent an abusive letter to the wife, which was opened at home by the husband, who mistook the brown envelope for an election circular. No, said the court in *Huth v Huth*,[54] when the mail was opened by the butler, out of curiosity, but in breach of his duty.

If writing an abusive letter, the better approach is to mark it 'private and confidential', and not to send it by postcard or telegram, which anyone might read.[55] (The best approach is not to send abusive letters.)

A person might be liable for publishing a defamatory statement even though they were not the original author. For example, if an unknown person pins a defamatory statement on a club notice board, the club might incur liability if they fail to act reasonably in taking it down.[56] An internet search engine is not liable for the hits it returns, even if they contain defamatory statements.[57] But an internet service provider can be liable for defamatory statements in a news service it provides to subscribers,[58] or a blog it supports,[59] at least if it does not act appropriately when responding to complaints about the post. It can even be ordered by the court to take down a web page.[60] There are, however, defences for innocent dissemination (see below).

REPEATING ANOTHER'S DEFAMATION

52 *Shakil-Ur-Rahman v ARY Network Ltd* [2016] EWHC 3110 (QB).
53 [1962] 1 WLR 151 (CA).
54 [1915] 3 KB 32 (CA).
55 *Sadgrove v Hole* [1901] 2 KB 1 (CA).
56 See *Byrne v Deane* [1937] 1 KB 818 (CA), but where the words were held not defamatory.
57 *Metropolitan International Schools Ltd v Designtechnica Corp* [2011] 1 WLR 1743.
58 *Godfrey v Demon Internet Ltd* [2001] QB 201 (QBD).
59 *Tamiz v Google Inc* [2013] EWCA Civ 68.
60 *Blackledge v Person(s) Unknown* [2021] EWHC 1994 (QB).

If *Origin* says to *Repeater*, 'Phil is a thief', and *Repeater* then tells their friend, both *Origin* and *Repeater* might be liable for that repetition.

1 Whether *Origin* is liable for the repetition is a matter of causation. Did *Repeater*'s repetition amount to an intervening act which broke the chain of causation, so exculpating *Origin*? Alternatively, was the repetition sufficiently foreseeable that *Origin* remains liable for the further damage which the repetition causes?

KEY CASES

In *McManus v Beckham*,[61] Victoria Beckham, the former singer, told others in a memorabilia shop that the signed photographs of her husband, David Beckham, the footballer, were fake. Predictably, this was repeated in the press. The court said that the original defamer would be liable for damage caused by a repetition if they were actually aware that what they said was likely to be reported, or they should reasonably have appreciated that there was a significant risk of repetition and increased damage.

2 As for *Repeater*, the law considers it just as bad to repeat someone else's defamatory statement as it is to make that statement in the first place.[62] Not least because it spreads the statement further and increases the damage.[63]

For example, in *Lord McAlpine v Bercow*,[64] following an accusation on television against an unnamed politician of sexual abuse, the defendant tweeted a comment which implicitly connected the claimant to that accusation. Although the defendant had only supplied the name, she was taken as having adopted the whole of the accusation.

(And while on the topic of Twitter, we might again note the likelihood of a post being re-tweeted, and so spreading the defamation, and extending the liability of the original author as well as the re-tweeter.)

All this, of course, is subject to defences, like truth or qualified privilege. But note: if *Origin* tells *Repeater* that Phil is a thief, and *Repeater* then says to their friend, 'According to *Origin*, Phil is a thief', to rely on a defence of truth, *Repeater* must prove not merely that *Origin* called Phil a thief, but that Phil is in fact a thief.[65] In this way, someone who repeats another's defamatory statement is treated as adopting that statement as their own.

61 [2002] EWCA Civ 939.

62 *Lewis v Daily Telegraph Ltd* [164] AC 234, 260 (Lord Reid).

63 *Mark v Associated Newspapers Ltd* [2002] EWCA Civ 772, [28]–[29].

64 [2013] EWHC 1342 (QB).

65 *M'Pherson v Daniels* (1829) 10 B & C 263, 109 ER 448 (where the defamatory statement was that X was insolvent).

REPUBLISHING THE SAME DEFAMATION

An action in defamation must be brought within one year from the date on which the cause of action accrued.[66] The court has a discretion, if equitable, not to apply that time limit.[67] Where a defendant publishes a statement, and then subsequently publishes another statement which is substantially the same, time runs only from the first publication.[68] (It does not start again from the subsequent publication.) This is sensible, given how much is now archived online, and can be accessed, and so republished, again and again, delving back far into the past.

In considering whether a subsequent statement is 'substantially' the same, or instead materially different, the court will consider the prominence and extent of the subsequent publication.[69] So, for example, something promoted from a footnote on page 94 of a magazine to a front-page spread is likely to be regarded as a new publication (which starts time running all over again).

14.8 REMEDIES

If a person is defamed, what remedies might they obtain?

The court can order a summary of its judgment against the defendant to be published.[70] It can order the operator of a website to remove a post, and it can order anyone who is not the author, editor or publisher of the statement to stop distributing, selling, or exhibiting it.[71]

The court might grant an **injunction** prohibiting the continuation or republication of the defamatory statement. A claimant might prefer to obtain an injunction to prevent the original publication in the first place, but under section 12 of the Human Rights Act 1998, no relief, which might affect the exercise of the Convention right to freedom of expression, is to be granted to restrain publication before trial, unless the court is satisfied that the applicant is likely to establish that the publication should not be allowed. In this context, the court is to have particular regard to freedom of expression in matters journalistic, literary, or artistic.[72] All of which is a rather technical way of saying that, in the context of defamation, injunctions pre-publication are rare.

There is a **summary procedure** for quick and cost-effective resolution of claims.[73] This is available when there is no realistic prospect of the claimant's success, alternatively of the

66 Limitation Act 1980 s.4A.

67 Limitation Act 1980 s.32A.

68 Defamation Act 2013 s.8.

69 Defamation Act 2013 s.8(5).

70 Defamation Act 2013 s.12.

71 Defamation Act 2013 s.13.

72 See the further discussion of this provision in Chapter 14.

73 The summary procedure was successfully utilised in *Brett Wilson LLP v Persons Unknown* [2015] EWHC 2628 (QB), where a law firm was listed on the website 'Solicitors from Hell'.

defendant's defence.[74] Available remedies include an order to publish a correction and apology, and damages not exceeding £10,000.[75]

This principal remedy for defamation is **compensatory damages**. In *John v MGN Ltd*,[76] a newspaper published a prominent story about Elton John, the singer, claiming that he had an eating disorder which involved him chewing food but not swallowing. The newspaper made no efforts to verify the accuracy of the story. The claimant was awarded damages, whose function the court explained as follows:[77]

> The sum is to compensate for damage to reputation, and to vindicate the claimant's good name. It will take account of the distress, hurt and humiliation which the publication caused. The more closely the libel touches the claimant's personal integrity or professional reputation, the more serious, and so the higher the damages. The extent of publication is also relevant, so that higher damages will be awarded if the libel is published very widely.

In setting awards, the court said that some comparison can be made to personal injury awards. (In other words, damages to reputation should not lose perspective by exceeding what might be recovered for a lost limb or permanent disability.) When there are multiple defamations from the defendant, a single overall award might be appropriate (rather than trying to quantify damages for each individual defamation).[78]

Damages to vindicate reputation will be reduced if the reputation is not deserved – for example, where the claimant has engaged in misconduct at trial by presenting a deliberately false case.[79]

Aggravated damages are available for additional injury to the claimant's feelings. This could be due to the way in which the defendant ran their defence, for example, insisting that the publication was true (when the court finds otherwise), or when the defendant would have known the defences not to be true,[80] refusing to apologise, or cross-examining the claimant in court in a wounding or insulting way.[81]

For example, in *Sutcliffe v Pressdram Ltd*,[82] the magazine *Private Eye* made allegations that the wife of the Yorkshire Ripper was prepared to cash in on her husband's notoriety by selling her story to the press. Although she objected, the magazine continued to make repeated

74 Defamation Act 1996 s.8.
75 Defamation Act 1996 s.9.
76 [1997] QB 586 (CA).
77 [1997] QB 586, 607.
78 *Shakil-Ur-Rahman v ARY Network Ltd* [2016] EWHC 3110 (QB).
79 *Wright v McCormack* [2023] EWCA Civ 892.
80 *Singh v Weayou* [2017] EWHC 2102 (QB), where defamation occurred in an internal work email.
81 *John v MGN Ltd* [1997] QB 586 (CA); *McCarey v Associated Newspapers Ltd* [1965] 2 QB 86 (CA).
82 [1991] 1 QB 153 (CA).

allegations over several years, a 'prolonged and vicious persecution' – and yet at trial adduced no evidence to support its case. Such conduct could attract aggravated damages.

A claimant might also obtain **exemplary damages**. In *Cassell & Co Ltd v Broome*,[83] the defendant published a book which made allegations against a naval officer that failings in his command had led to the fatal destruction of a convoy in World War II. The court said that exemplary damages might be available where a defendant, knowing the defamatory statement to be false, or with reckless disregard, publishes the statement anyway because the anticipated profit to be gained (from selling the book) will outweigh the possible damages.

But note that exemplary damages are not routinely awarded: they should only be awarded where compensatory damages are not sufficient to punish the defendant, to show that tort does not pay and to deter others from acting similarly.[84]

APPLYING THE LAW

Barry is seeking a new job. His former employers, Lawyers LLP, send a reference to his prospective new employers, Attorneys Inc, in which Barry is described as 'managing somehow to be both tight-fisted and light-fingered at the same time'. The recipient at Attorneys Inc thinks this reference so funny that they post it on Facebook. Advise the parties.

The reference is in writing. So too is the post on Facebook. This is libel. At the least, Barry will need to show that the statement is likely to cause serious harm to his reputation.

The statement has a literal meaning (about the physical condition of Barry's hands). But it is the implied meaning to which Barry objects: that he is not generous with money ('tight-fisted'), while also likely to steal from others ('light-fingered'). This implied meaning is likely to be understood by reasonable people reading the reference or Facebook post. It would likely lower Barry in the estimation of right-thinking members of society, and so be defamatory. Indeed, it is likely to hinder his job prospects, and for that reason serious harm to his reputation can probably be presumed.

The reference will obviously refer to Barry by name. So, Barry could sue Lawyers LLP for defamation. However, the Facebook post might only contain that part of the reference which the recipient found funny, rather than the whole post. In which case, no one reading it on

83 [1972] AC 1027 (HL).

84 *Cassell & Co Ltd v Broome* [1972] AC 1027 (HL); *McCarey v Associated Newspapers Ltd* [1965] 2 QB 86 (CA); *John v MGN Ltd* [1997] QB 586 (CA). But see the Crime and Courts Act 2013 s.34: no exemplary damages can be awarded against a publisher who is a member of a regulator approved under Royal Charter, unless the decision of the regulator on the complaint was manifestly irrational. Only one regulator has been thus approved, IMPRESS, and most national newspapers are not members.

Facebook would likely know that it referred to Barry. Even those with special knowledge, who happen to know that Barry had applied for a job with Attorneys Inc, are unlikely to be sure that the Facebook post refers to Barry (rather than any other candidate to Attorneys Inc, or, for that matter, any other candidate to any other company which Attorneys Inc simply happened to come across). So, it is unlikely that Barry could sue Attorneys Inc for defamation for the post (or Facebook, for enabling the post).

But even if Barry could sue Attorneys Inc for defamation, their act of posting the reference on Facebook would likely break the chain of causation so that Attorneys Inc (or Facebook) is liable for that wider damage caused by the Facebook post. Lawyers LLP would only be liable for the damage caused by sending the letter to Attorneys Inc. There is nothing to suggest that Lawyers LLP knew, or should have known, that Attorneys Inc would post it on Facebook, or that there was a significant risk of this happening.

Barry might seek from the court an order to remove the post from Facebook, an injunction to restrain Lawyers LLP from sending a similar reference in future, and an injunction to restrain Attorneys Inc from republishing the reference. He can also seek compensatory damages to vindicate his reputation. Damages against Lawyers LLP would be quantified by reference to the lost job with Attorneys Inc. Damages against Attorneys Inc (or Facebook) would likely be much higher, for spreading the defamation far and wide on social media. (As for possible defences, see below.)

14.9 DEFENCES

There is a large range of defences to defamation. The statement might be true. Or it might be an honest opinion. It might have been in the public interest to make the statement (even though it turns out not to be true). The defendant might be able to say that their dissemination of the statement was done innocently (such a plea avails a defendant who is not the author, editor, or publisher of the statement). The defendant might have already made an offer of amends. Or the statement might have been made on a privileged occasion (these are occasions when the law deems it important to be able to speak freely, without fear of subsequent litigation). We shall take each defence in turn.

14.10 TRUTH

By section 2 of the Defamation Act 2013, it is a defence to show that the imputation conveyed by the statement complained of is substantially true.

What does 'substantially' true mean? For example, in *Alexander v North Eastern Rly Co*,[85] the defendant reported that the claimant had been convicted of dishonesty with three weeks'

85 (1865) 6 B & S 340, 122 ER 1221.

imprisonment. This was substantially true, even though the sentence was only two weeks' imprisonment. In *Begg v BBC*,[86] the claimant imam was accused of preaching extremist Islam at East London Mosque in 2013. This was substantially true, given that he had preached extremist Islam on a number of occasions, albeit not at East London Mosque, and not in 2013.

In contrast, in *Wakely v Cooke*,[87] the defendant called the claimant a 'libellous journalist', in a context which suggested that the defendant habitually published libels, out of malice. It was insufficient for the defendant to show that the claimant had one libel judgment against him.

If a defamatory statement has multiple implications, and some are shown to be substantially true, the defence succeeds if the remaining implications do not seriously harm the claimant's reputation.[88]

So, for example, if the defendant says that the claimant stole four items from their employer, but can only prove that they stole three, the defence might succeed. But if the defendant says that the claimant is violent and a thief, yet they can only prove theft, the allegation of being violent might remain defamatory.

Another way of putting this is to say that a number of allegations might have a common theme or 'sting' – for example, that the claimant is dishonest or corrupt. If that common sting can be justified, by reference to certain instances, it may be that unproven instances nevertheless leave the claimant without any residual reputation to protect.[89]

If a statement is only partially true, that is no defence, but it might reduce the amount of damages payable, because the claimant's reputation would only have been partially tarnished. However, if a defendant runs the defence of truth, but fails at trial, that might increase damages, because it continues to give the statement additional publicity.[90] Further, if the defence run is disgraceful, that might lead to aggravated damages for the affront to the claimant's dignity.[91]

14.11 HONEST OPINION

By section 3 of the Defamation Act 2013, it is a defence that the statement was one of opinion (rather than fact) – but only if an honest person could have held that opinion, on the basis of any fact which (1) existed at the time or (2) was asserted in a privileged statement.

86 [2016] EWHC 2688 (QB).

87 (1849) 4 Ex 511, 154 ER 1316.

88 Defamation Act 2013 s.2(3).

89 *Rothschild v Associated Newspapers Ltd* [2013] EWCA Civ 197.

90 *Cassell & Co Ltd v Broome* [1972] AC 1027, 1125 (Lord Diplock).

91 In *FlyMeNow Ltd v Quick Air Jet Charter GmbH* [2016] EWHC 3197 (QB), it was the *claimant's* conduct which was disgraceful, its own conduct playing a significant part in causing the defendant to publish an untrue statement. The claimant was awarded damages of only £10.

KEY CASES

In *British Chiropractic Association v Singh*,[92] decided before the Defamation Act 2013, the defendant, a scientist, wrote an article in a newspaper stating that the claimant chiropractic association had 'not a jot of evidence' that its treatments cured a range of ailments. At trial, both sides presented the court with reports of various experiments. Whether those experiments were reliable, and what conclusions might be drawn from them, said the court, was a matter of opinion, on which people might differ.[93]

ANALYSING THE LAW

It is indeed the case that different people put different emphasis on the results of different scientific experiments. But surely the court can judge between them. Evaluating rival claims, on the balance of probabilities, is what the court does every day. If the court is brave enough, and capable, of branding someone an extremist, in the highly controversial arena of religious belief, as in *Begg v BBC* (discussed above), surely it can decide whether a purported medical procedure has a sound scientific basis.

The statement of opinion must also include the basis of the opinion.[94] This means that the opinion must indicate the facts upon which it comments, so that a reader can understand what the comment is about. But it is not necessary to give sufficient details for the reader to make their own judgment.[95] So, for example, it is not sufficient simply to say, 'Viktor is a disgrace'. To plead honest opinion, a defendant needs to explain why: 'Viktor is a disgrace *because* he never revises for exams'.

The defence is lost if the claimant shows that the defendant did not hold that opinion.[96] If the defendant has published another's opinion, the defence is lost if the claimant shows that the defendant knew or ought to have known that the other person did not hold that opinion.[97] If a defendant argues that their stated fact is true, or amounts to an honest opinion about that fact, then if the defence of truth fails (because the statement is false after all), then so too does the defence of honest opinion about that fact.[98] In other words, one cannot have an honest opinion based a false fact. (But there still might be a defence of public interest.)

92 [2010] EWCA Civ 350.

93 The defendant in *Singh* relied on the common law defence of fair comment, which was abolished and replaced by s.3 of the Defamation Act 2013.

94 Defamation Act 2013 s.3(3).

95 *Spiller v Joseph* [2010] UKSC 53.

96 Defamation Act 2013 s.3(5).

97 Defamation Act 2013 s.3(6).

98 *Riley v Sivier* [2021] EWCA Civ 713.

14.12 PUBLIC INTEREST

Previously, the common law derived from *Reynolds v Times Newspapers Ltd.*[99] In that case, the Irish Prime Minister sued over allegations that he had misled the Irish Parliament. The court held that a newspaper could claim qualified privilege when reporting on such matters, depending on the seriousness of the allegations, if it was a matter of public concern, and depending on what steps were taken to verify the information, the urgency of publishing and whether it also put the claimant's side of the story. This was refined in *Jameel v Wall Street Journal Europe Sprl*,[100] to ask whether the subject matter was in the public interest and whether the publication met the standards of responsible journalism.[101]

Now, the matter is regulated by section 4 of the Defamation Act 2013. It is a defence to show that the statement was on a matter of public interest, and that the defendant reasonably believed that publishing it was also in the public interest.

The statement does not have to be true – otherwise the defendant would rely on the defence of truth. Rather, this defence accepts that the statement now turns out to be false, but asserts that, in the meantime, it was worth having the public discussion. Of course, if the defendant knew at the time that the statement was false, the defence would not avail, because it is not in the public interest to publish knowingly false statements.

EXPLAINING THE LAW

If a matter is of public interest, when is it not in the public interest to publish it? That sounds like a paradox. (Section 4 is not the clearest of legislative drafting.) So here is perhaps an example. An allegation that the Prime Minister is a murderer would certainly be in the public interest (and would certainly be defamatory). But to publish that allegation, without any investigation, would not be in the public interest, for it simply spreads distracting and speculative rumour. So, whether publication is in the public interest might come down, once again, to notions of responsible journalism and what investigations were carried out. Indeed, in *Economou v de Freitas*,[102] the court said that a belief, that publishing was in the public interest, could only be reasonable after conducting such inquiries and checks as it was reasonable to expect of the particular defendant in all the circumstances of the case.[103]

99 [2001] 2 AC 127 (HL).

100 [2006] UKHL 44.

101 See also *Flood v Times Newspapers Ltd* [2012] UKSC 11.

102 [2016] EWHC 1853 (QB), affirmed [2018] EWCA Civ 2591.

103 In that case, the court said that more checks might be expected from a journalist writing up an article, and fewer checks from someone merely acting as a source of information for that journalist (the source might legitimately rely on the journalist to double-check some of the allegations).

Thus, we might paraphrase the law here as follows. First, is it in the public interest to hear this allegation? Second, has the allegation been sufficiently checked before publication? It is not in the public interest to debate gossip or unfounded rumour.

14.13 TYPES OF INNOCENT DISSEMINATION

There is a range of defences potentially available to those who were not the author, editor, or publisher of the original defamation. There are particular rules too for website operators. We shall take each in turn.

NOT THE AUTHOR, EDITOR, OR PUBLISHER

A court does not have jurisdiction to hear an action for defamation brought against a person who was not the author, editor, or publisher of the statement, unless satisfied that it is not reasonably practicable for an action to be brought against the author, editor, or publisher.[104]

Further, it is a defence to show that the defendant was not the author, editor, or commercial publisher[105] of the statement, and that the defendant took reasonable care in relation to the publication, and did not know, or have reason to believe, that they caused or contributed to the publication of a defamatory statement.[106] Such a defence might avail, for example, a printer, distributor, seller, copier, exhibiter of film or sound recording, or live broadcaster.[107]

As regards taking reasonable care in relation to the publication, for example, the more controversial the author is known to be, the more scrutiny the defendant might need to pay to the content before associating themselves with the project.

WEBSITE OPERATORS

The law relating to the operators of websites is now governed by section 5 of the Defamation Act 2013. It is a defence if the operator itself did not post the statement. But the defence is defeated if the claimant shows that it is not possible for the claimant to identify who did post the statement and, having given notice of complaint to the operator, the operator then fails to act in accordance with regulations.[108] Those regulations state that the operator must contact the poster for comment, and if they cannot, or receive no comment, then they must remove the statement within 48 hours. If the poster wishes the statement to remain, they must give their name and address to the operator, who can pass it to the complainant if the poster consents or the court orders.

104 Defamation Act 2013 s.10.

105 A commercial publisher is one whose business is publishing material to the public: Defamation Act 1996 s.1(2).

106 Defamation Act 1996 s.1.

107 Defamation Act 1996 s.1(3).

108 Defamation (Operators of Websites) Regulations 2013 (SI 2013/3028).

14.14 OFFER OF AMENDS

The defendant may make an offer of amends. To qualify as a defence, it must be in writing, contain an offer to publish a correction and apology, and pay such compensation as may be agreed by the parties or determined by the court. If the offer is accepted, then, in effect, the parties have reached a settlement agreement. If the offer is not accepted, then it is a complete defence, unless the claimant proves that the defendant knew all along, or had reason to believe, that the statement was false and defamatory.[109] 'Reason to believe' means that the defendant was reckless in publishing, in the sense of not caring whether or not the statement was false, rather than merely negligent.[110]

If the defendant raises offer of amends as a defence, then they may not rely upon any other defence.[111] But instead of relying upon it as a defence, the offer could be relied upon when it comes to assessing damages.[112] First, an offer which should have been accepted shows that the claimant has failed to mitigate their loss. Second, an apology is also likely to reduce the damage which the claimant might otherwise have suffered, by retracting the defamation.[113] Indeed, an apology might even reduce or prevent damage to the claimant's reputation to such an extent that the claimant is no longer likely to suffer 'serious' harm – thus falling below the threshold of establishing an actionable defamation in the first place.[114]

14.15 PRIVILEGE

There are two types of privilege. Absolute privilege attaches to those occasions when it is so important to speak freely that there should be no fear of being sued. Qualified privilege attaches to those occasions when it is still important to speak freely, but not so important that the claimant who goes too far should be free of all responsibility. Both statute and the common law each have something to say about which occasions attract what type of privilege.

This section considers the following issues: when an occasion attracts absolute privilege; when an occasion attracts qualified privilege under statute, and when under common law; and when qualified privilege is lost because it is exceeded or because the defendant has acted maliciously.

109 Defamation Act 1996 ss.2–4. In practice, this supersedes the older law which still provides a defence where the defendant shows that it acted without malice, or gross negligence, has published an apology and paid a sum of money into court by way of compensation: Libel Act 1843 s.2; Libel Act 1845 s.2.

110 *Milne v Express Newspapers plc* [2004] EWCA Civ 664.

111 Defamation Act 1996 s.4(4).

112 Defamation Act 1996 s.4(5); Libel Act 1843 s.1.

113 For example, in *Lisle-Mainwaring v Associated Newspapers Ltd* [2017] EWHC 543 (QB), there was a 40% reduction in damages for an early offer of amends. In *Barron MP v Collins MEP* [2017] EWHC 162 (QB), there was a 10% reduction for a belated offer.

114 *Cooke v MGN Ltd* [2016] EWHC 931 (QB).

ABSOLUTE PRIVILEGE

There are two broad categories of occasion which attract absolute privilege: Parliament and court.

Speech, debate or proceedings in **Parliament** are absolutely privileged.[115] So too are reports, papers, votes, and proceedings ordered to be published by Parliament.[116] So too are communications between officers of state, in the course of their official business, relating to state matters,[117] although this might not apply below the rank of Minister.[118]

KEY CASES

In *Makudi v Baron Triesman of Tottenham*,[119] the defendant made comments about the claimant, and corruption in FIFA (the international football federation), to a House of Commons committee. Then, at the committee's request, he repeated those comments to a barrister conducting a review of the allegations on behalf of the FA (the English football association). The proceedings before the House of Commons attracted absolute privilege. That extended, said the court, exceptionally, to the FA review, because there was a public interest, which the defendant ought reasonably to serve, in repeating the allegations; and the defendant's obligation to speak on the second occasion was reasonably foreseeable at the time of the first occasion, and the purpose in speaking was the same on both occasions.

Oral or written statements made in **court** in the course of judicial proceedings – for example, by judge, jury, counsel, parties, or witnesses – are absolutely privileged. This extends to the preparation of witness statements in advance of trial.[120] But it does not extend to the fabrication of evidence by police officers during the investigative process.[121] Fair and accurate reports, published contemporaneously, of public proceedings in any court or tribunal are also absolutely privileged.[122] But it can be tortious to use court documents out of court and out of context in order to defame someone.[123]

115 Bill of Rights 1688 art 9. The Act actually received Royal Assent in 1689, but was attributed to 1688 according to the custom whereby Acts without an express start date were attributed to the year in which that Parliamentary session began.

116 Parliamentary Papers Act 1840, s.1.

117 *Chatterton v Secretary of State for India* [1895] 2 QB 189 (CA).

118 *Szalatnay-Stacho v Fink* [1946] 1 All ER 303 (KBD), a point not considered on appeal at [1947] KB 1 (CA).

119 [2014] EWCA Civ 179.

120 *Watson v McEwan* [1905] AC 480 (HL).

121 *Darker v Chief Constable of West Midlands Police* [2001] 1 AC 435 (HL).

122 Defamation Act 1996 s.14.

123 *Hameed v Sheikh* [2023] EWHC 2845 (KB).

QUALIFIED PRIVILEGE: STATUTE

A statement in a peer-reviewed scientific or academic journal is privileged, unless made with malice.[124] This would not have helped the defendant in *British Chiropractic Association v Singh*, since he published in a newspaper (hence the alternative defence of honest opinion).

Any fair and accurate report, of the type of proceedings listed in Schedule 1 of the Defamation Act 1996, on a matter of public interest, is privileged, unless made with malice.[125] The list in the Schedule includes proceedings of any legislature, court, public inquiry, international conference, local authority, press conference, general meeting of a public company, or academic conference.

EXPLAINING THE LAW

There are overlapping rules here. Proceedings in Parliament are absolutely privileged, reports of proceedings of a local authority attract a qualified privilege, central and local governments cannot sue for libel, but individual politicians can. Contemporaneous reports of public proceedings in court attract absolute privilege, other reports of court proceedings enjoy only qualified privilege, whereas participants in court, like witnesses, enjoy an absolute privilege. What we have is a criss-cross of rules bestowing sometimes full, sometimes partial, immunity. Could this be structured in a more straightforward way?

QUALIFIED PRIVILEGE: COMMON LAW

At common law, the position can be summarised as follows:

KEY LEARNING POINT

Communications attract qualified privilege, where A has a duty (legal, moral, or social), or interest, in communicating with B, and B has a corresponding interest or duty in receiving that information, unless A has exceeded the privilege, or acted with malice.

Examples of occasions of qualified privilege include the following. A son-in-law can write to his mother-in-law about the character of the person she proposes to marry.[126] A person can complain about the misconduct of a public official, if made to the proper authority.[127] A former employer can send a reference about a past employee's character to the prospective new employer.[128]

124 Defamation Act 2013 s.6.

125 Defamation Act 1996 s.15.

126 *Todd v Hawkins* (1837) 2 M & Rob 20, 174 ER 200.

127 *Harrison v Bush* (1856) 5 E & B 344, 119 ER 509.

128 *Spring v Guardian Assurance plc* [1995] 2 AC 296 (HL).

MAKING CONNECTIONS

A defamatory statement in a reference might be subject to qualified privilege. But the author might still incur liability in negligence. In *Spring v Guardian Assurance plc*,[129] an employee was dismissed by his former employer, and sought work with a new employer, who asked for a reference. The old employer provided a reference which alleged that the employee was dishonest. As a consequence, the employee was not hired by the new employer. The court found that the authors of the reference honestly believed the allegation of dishonesty, and acted without malice.[130] But they failed to make reasonable investigations which would have revealed the employee was not dishonest after all. The court held that the former employer could be liable in negligence for failing to take reasonable care in the preparation of the reference. It would have to pay compensation for any loss caused.

In *Osborn v Thomas Boulter & Son*,[131] the claimant pub landlord was complaining to the defendant brewery about the quality of the beer supplied. The defendant replied that the cause of the problem was the claimant watering down the beer. That statement, though defamatory, was subject to qualified privilege, which can be explained in two ways:

> First, the parties had a common interest in establishing the quality of the beer they bought and sold with each other, facilitated by a frank sharing of views as to the cause of any problems.

Alternatively, it was in the defendant's interest to defend itself (against the accusation that its beer was of poor quality), and in the claimant's interest to receive and consider that defence.

Extending the latter point, it is sometimes suggested that when A makes accusations about the character of B, then in self-defence B can make accusations about the character of A, this too being the subject of qualified privilege (and so also defeated by malice).[132]

EXCEEDING QUALIFIED PRIVILEGE

An occasion which attracts qualified privilege at common law does so for a reason: because of the shared interest in communicating something particular. If a defendant uses that occasion

129 [1995] 2 AC 296 (HL).

130 So, the employee's claim for malicious falsehood failed. The tort of malicious falsehood is distinct from defamation, although it has similarities. It is discussed below.

131 [1930] 2 KB 226 (CA).

132 *Laughton v Bishop of Sodor and Man* (1872) LR 4 PC 495. The bishop's title refers to the Isle of Man, a Crown Dependency, and Sodor, a corruption of the Norse word for Southern Isles, that is, the Scottish Hebrides, which were once, but are no longer, part of the diocese of Man. There is no island itself called Sodor. Noticing this on a visit to the diocese, Rev Awdry created the fictional Island of Sodor, between England and Man, as the setting for *Thomas the Tank Engine*.

to communicate something else as well, that extra something else is not protected by the privilege.[133] For example, if A sends a reference to B about an employee X, but uses the opportunity to say something defamatory about the character of Y, that latter statement would fall outside the privilege.

Similarly, it exceeds the privilege to communicate the information to extraneous people. For example, in *Watt v Longsdon*,[134] the defendant could make allegations about an employee's misconduct to the company chairman, but not to the employee's wife. In *Toogood v Spyring*,[135] the defendant tenant complained that a workman sent to do repairs had broken into his cellar, drunk his cider, and spoilt the work he was sent to do. He could make this complaint to the landlord, but not to another tenant. In *Clift v Slough Borough Council*,[136] the defendant council put the claimant on a violent persons register after an argument with an official. It was appropriate to circulate that warning to people who might have to deal with the claimant, but not to everyone in the council, or anyone outside.

We can summarise the position as follows:

> KEY LEARNING POINT
>
> Qualified privilege at common law is exceeded if the defendant refers to extraneous matters or publishes to extraneous people.

MALICE

To repeat, qualified privilege can arise under statute or at common law. Both statute and the common law provide that malice defeats a defence of qualified privilege. The meaning of malice has been left solely to the common law. It can be summarised as follows:

> KEY LEARNING POINTS
>
> - Malice can mean spite or ill will.
> - Malice can also mean that the defendant did not believe in the truth of their statement, or was reckless as to whether or not it was true.

It is not enough that the defendant's statement stems from unreasoning prejudice or is irrational – unless that causes the defendant to be reckless.[137] Similarly, if there are no reasonable grounds for the defendant's belief in their statement, that alone does not amount to malice – but it could be evidence of malice, because it questions the defendant's credibility.[138]

133 *Adam v Ward* [1917] AC 309, 349.
134 [1930] 1 KB 130 (CA).
135 (1834) 1 Cr M & R 181, 149 ER 1044.
136 [2010] EWCA Civ 1484.
137 *Horrocks v Lowe* [1975] AC 135 (HL).
138 *Clark v Molyneux* (1877) 3 QBD 237 (CA).

EXPLAINING THE LAW

If a defendant says that they honestly believed the truth of what they said, but can offer no grounds to support that claim, their credibility is called into question, and the judge might conclude that the defendant did not believe what they said after all.

Also, if the defendant uses language which is stronger than necessary to make the communication, that too is evidence of malice.[139]

MAKING CONNECTIONS

There is a related tort, where malice plays a key role, called malicious falsehood. It is when the defendant makes a false statement about the claimant, maliciously, to a third party, calculated to produce, and which does produce, actual damage.[140]

The principal differences between malicious falsehood and defamation are (1) malicious falsehood requires the claimant to prove malice from the outset, whereas in defamation a claimant need only show malice to defeat a defence of qualified privilege; and (2) in malicious falsehood, damages are payable to compensate the claimant for injury to their earnings, whereas injury to personal reputation can only sound in defamation. (It is possible to say something non-defamatory which nevertheless maliciously harms another's earnings.[141])

An example of the distinction between defamation and malicious falsehood is *Joyce v Sengupta*.[142] In that case, the claimant was accused by a newspaper of stealing personal letters from her employer, the Princess Royal. Obviously, this is defamatory. But instead the claimant sued in malicious falsehood, because her action could then be funded by Legal Aid. (Now, Legal Aid is not available either for malicious falsehood or defamation.) She was successful not because her reputation was tarnished in itself (which is a matter for defamation alone), but because the allegation of stealing from her employer impacted her future job prospects.[143]

139 *Adam v Ward* [1917] AC 309, 349.

140 It is not necessary to prove actual loss if the statement was calculated to cause pecuniary damage and published in permanent form, or calculated to cause pecuniary damage in respect of the claimant's profession or business: Defamation Act 1952 s.3. 'Calculated' means more likely than not to cause pecuniary damage: *Tesla Motors Ltd v BBC* [2013] EWCA Civ 152, [27]. See too *Davidoff and others v Google LLC* [2023] EWHC 1958 (KB).

141 In *Joyce v Motor Surveys Ltd* [1948] Ch 252 (Ch D), in an attempt to evict a business tenant, the landlord returned the tenant's mail, saying that the tenant no longer traded from that address. Such a statement says little about the tenant's reputation, but certainly caused loss to his business.

142 [1993] 1 All ER 897 (CA).

143 See too *Khodaparast v Shad* [2000] 1 WLR 618 (CA), where the defendant posted flyers of the claimant, purporting to show her offering sexual services. She recovered damages, not for the injury to her reputation itself, but for the loss of her future job prospects (and aggravated damages because of the defendant's continued insistence that the flyers were true).

APPLYING THE LAW

To repeat, Barry is seeking a new job. His former employers, Lawyers LLP, send a reference to his prospective new employers, Attorneys Inc, in which Barry is described as 'managing somehow to be both tight-fisted and light-fingered at the same time'. The recipient at Attorneys Inc thinks this reference so funny that they post it on Facebook. Advise the parties.

Let us now consider defences. The more serious part of the defamation is the accusation that Barry is 'light-fingered'. If it can be shown that Barry has in fact stolen from others, then there might be a defence of truth. But given the casual wording of the reference (rather than a report, say, of Barry's conviction), this seems unlikely.

The most likely defence for Lawyers LLP is qualified privilege. Lawyers LLP was under a moral duty to send a character reference to Attorneys Inc, who had a corresponding interest in reading it. Qualified privilege is defeated by malice, but there is nothing here to suggest that Lawyers LLP acted with spite, or knew, or was reckless, that the reference was false. The colourful language, rather than a more straightforward assertion of theft, might raise the question of whether Lawyers LLP was as serious in providing the reference as they should have been. But that is not enough to constitute malice. (Nor is a lack of reasonable grounds for Lawyers LLP's belief, or even irrational prejudice on their part.)

There seems little prospect of Attorneys Inc raising any realistic defence. In which case, Barry could always invoke the summary procedure against them – except that damages are capped at £10,000, and Barry is likely to recover far more than that from Attorneys Inc. As for Facebook, it is likely to have a defence as an operator of a website which did not itself post the defamatory statement (assuming it reacted properly to any complaint which Barry might have made to Facebook). This need not preclude the court from ordering Facebook to delete the post.

POINTS TO REVIEW

- The court must first identify the natural and ordinary meaning of the statement complained of, as understood by reasonable people. There may also be implied meanings.
- Such a meaning is defamatory if it tends to lower the claimant in the estimation of right-thinking members of society.
- The statement must refer to the claimant, and be published to a third party, and cause, or be likely to cause, serious harm to the claimant's reputation.
- There is a wide range of defences: truth, honest opinion, public interest, forms of innocent dissemination, offer of amends, and absolute and qualified privilege.
- At common law, communications attract qualified privilege, where A has a duty (legal, moral, or social), or interest, in communicating with B, and B has a corresponding interest or duty in receiving that information, unless A has acted with malice, or has exceeded the privilege by referring to extraneous matters or publishing to extraneous people.

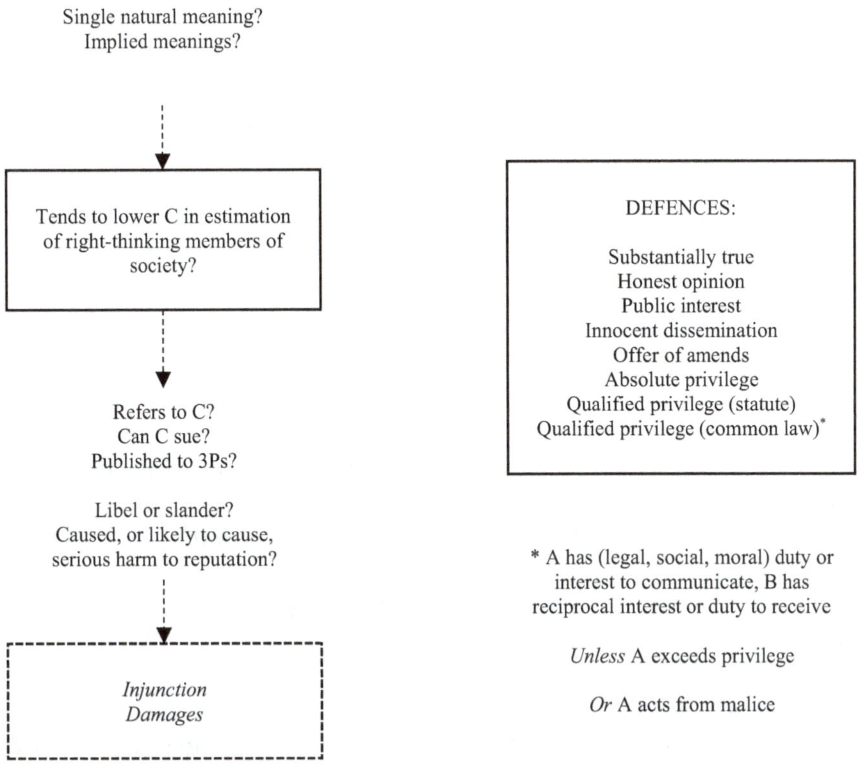

Figure 14.1 Overview of defamation

- Malice means spite or ill will, or that the defendant did not believe in the truth of their statement, or was reckless as to whether or not it was true.

TAKING IT FURTHER

Treiger-Bar-Am, K. 'Defamation Law in a Changing Society' (2000) 20 Legal Studies 291
Wiley online library: https://doi.org/10.1111/j.1748-121X.2000.tb00144.x
The author focuses on the case of *Youssoupoff v MGM Pictures Ltd* (1934) 50 TLR 581 (CA), where the court held that an imputation of rape could be defamatory. She suggests that this reflects the prejudices of society at the time, and that a finding of defamation might lend credence to those prejudices. Instead, she asks, should a court refuse a finding for defamation when based upon prejudices which ought not to be condoned? Should defamation law reflect society, or lead it forward?

Rowbottom, J. 'To Rant, Vent and Converse: Protecting Low Level Digital Speech' (2012) 71 Cambridge LJ 355
Cambridge Law Journal online: www.cambridge.org/core/journals/cambridge-law-journal/article/abs/to-rant-vent-and-converse-protecting-low-level-digital-speech/C86D33C0B35A25DEE100D01EC6539184

Given the ubiquity of social networks and other amateur digital content, the author suggests that there should be some recognition that communications which are casual and amateur should be held to a lesser standard (than, for example, a professional journalist) before attracting the intervention of the law. But, we might add, is there anything to suggest that the amateur context of a remark, say on Facebook, means it gets taken less seriously, or noticed by fewer people?

Descheemaeker, E. 'Protecting Reputation: Defamation and Negligence' (2009) 29 Oxford J Legal Studies 603
Oxford Journal of Legal Studies online: https://academic.oup.com/ojls/article-abstract/29/4/603/1404388?redirectedFrom=fulltext
The author suggests that reputation is not solely protected by defamation. For example, he says, damages to reputation can also arise in false imprisonment (see Chapter 13) and malicious prosecution. We can add, also for invasion of privacy (see Chapter 14). So why not, he says, in the tort of negligence? We might ask, would that not be a more sensible and straightforward approach than the overwrought complexity of defamation law?

Antoniou, A. and Akrivos, D. 'Homosexuality, Defamatory Meaning and Reputational Injury in English Law' in K. Horsey (ed), *Diverse Voices in Tort Law* (Bristol University Press, 2023)
Free access: https://repository.essex.ac.uk/35810/
The authors discuss whether misidentifying someone as gay should today be considered defamatory (when historically it was defamatory).

Dee, J. 'Fighting Back: Is Defamation Law a Double-Edged Sword for #MeToo Victims?' (2021) 55(2) First Amendment Studies 148–174
Free access: www.tandfonline.com/doi/full/10.1080/21689725.2021.1977160
When #MeToo victims name and shame their abusers, will they be sued in defamation by more powerful parties? Alternatively, when the victims are accused of lying, can the victims bring a defamation claim?

15

CHAPTER 15 ARTIFICIAL INTELLIGENCE

15.1 INTRODUCTION

Say an Artificial Intelligence (AI) provides the wrong advice to a doctor who then misdiagnoses a patient, or an automated vehicle crashes and injures the occupant of the vehicle. Who is liable in tort if an AI causes damage? This chapter focuses on the application of tort law to AI. Tort has always had to deal with advancements in technology. For example, the tort of defamation has had to learn how to interpret social media posts.[1] Modern technologies such as AI will cause significant additional challenges, particularly due to AI's evolving, autonomous, and potentially unpredictable nature.

There is no definition of AI that is agreed by everyone. We will adopt the definition provided by the House of Lords, which is 'the theory and development of computer systems able to perform tasks normally requiring human intelligence, such as visual perception, speech recognition, decision-making, and translation between languages'.[2] It is important to mention machine learning here, a subset of AI, where the system develops and learns without human intervention.

AI can be found in several different contexts. For example, AI can be used in medicine to help diagnoses and treatment of illness. It can be found on smartphones and in voice assistants. It can be found in financial services talking with customers. It can steer motor vehicles and ships.

There are several parties involved in development of AI: designers of the AI, those who programme the AI, those who produce specific pieces of hardware or software, and suppliers of the AI. Moreover, there is also the end user. Who should be deemed responsible in tort if an AI causes damage? And what if the AI was doing things of its own volition?

Whereas in other chapters we have discussed the law and its application, the difficulty with regards to AI is that there is no AI-specific tort law. So we begin by considering how some existing torts might apply to AI: strict product liability and negligence – although there are some difficulties even here. Then we will look more widely at reform, focusing for example on comparisons with the European Union as well as potential use of vicarious liability.

1 E.g. see *Stocker v Stocker* [2019] UKSC 17.

2 House of Lords 'Artificial Intelligence: Development Risks and Regulation', (2023) Artificial intelligence: Development, risks and regulation – House of Lords Library (parliament.uk) (https://lordslibrary.parliament.uk/artificial-intelligence-development-risks-and-regulation/).

DOI: 10.4324/9781003480051-15

AS YOU READ

- Be aware of how AI continues to evolve.
- Identify how existing torts might apply to AI.
- Identify where existing torts might struggle to apply to AI.
- Consider how tort law needs to adapt, and what reforms could be necessary, to regulate damage caused by AI.

15.2 STRICT PRODUCT LIABILITY

A potential claim against manufacturers could be through strict product liability. Strict product liability is regulated by the Consumer Protection Act 1987 (CPA 1987), which implemented the European Union's Product Liability Directive.[3] This renders manufacturers liable in relation to defective products and could be an avenue for redress in relation to damage caused by defective AI.

KEY LEARNING POINT

- Where damage is caused by a defect in a product, the producer and importer of the product are liable (section 2, CPA 1987).

Strict product liability is primarily about manufacturers' liability: claims against the user of the product should be under another tort, for example a claim in negligence. Fault does not need to be proven, which provides an advantage over a claim in negligence where fault is required.

However, will a 37-year-old (at the time of writing) piece of legislation be fit for the future of technology and AI? Reform is likely going to be needed in several areas.

PRODUCT

For example, a requirement in strict product liability is that there is a 'product', defined in section 1(1)(c) of the CPA 1987: 'a product means any goods or electricity and (subject to subsection (3) below) includes a product which is comprised in another product'.

Whether something is classed as a product is usually relatively straightforward. My non-AI lawnmower is a product: if it catches fire due to a defect and injures me, then I may be able to claim in strict product liability. A product is usually something tangible, and as my lawnmower is clearly tangible, it is a product.

3 Council Directive 85/374/EEC of 25 July 1985 on the approximation of the laws, regulations, and administrative provisions of the Member States concerning liability for defective products.

However, if software which has been downloaded to my lawnmower causes my lawnmower to malfunction, will this mean a claim fails in strict product liability?[4]

KEY CASE

In *Computer Associates UK Limited v Software Associates*,[5] Gloster LJ held that only software on a tangible medium, like a USB stick, could be classed as 'goods',[6] but software downloads 'over the air' and other intangible mediums could not. However, when this case went to the Court of Justice of the European Union (CJEU),[7] the CJEU stated that software on an intangible medium could be classed as a 'good'. While this may be applied by English courts in the future in a strict product liability setting, it may be beneficial for the definition of 'product' to be updated in legislation, to provide certainty to manufacturers and consumers.

As will be discussed later, the EU has adopted a new directive on strict product liability to include software.

DEFECT

The claimant must also prove that the product is defective. Under section 3(1) of the CPA 1987, a product is defective 'if the safety of the product is not such as persons generally are entitled to expect'. This is a reasonable expectations test. The test is objective, so it is not based on the subjective expectations of a consumer, but rather considers the safety 'that the public at large are entitled to expect'.[8]

The reasonable expectations test in some situations may seem rather straightforward: for example, say an AI robot catches fire soon after purchase and causes injury without any user involvement; it is likely that the robot is defective (although this would still need to be proven).

In determining whether the 'reasonable expectations test' is met, the court will look, for example, at any warnings or labels on the product,[9] and 'what might reasonably be expected to be done . . . with the product'.[10] Adequate warnings are likely to be important with AI,

4 This was discussed in some detail in relation to automated vehicle updates in Matthew Channon and James Marson, 'The Liability for Cyber Security Breaches of Connected and Automated Vehicles', (2021) Computer Law and Security Review.

5 [2018] EWCA Civ 518.

6 Note that this was not concerned with strict product liability but rather the EU Commercial Agents Directive.

7 (Case C-410/19) EU:C:2021:742. note that while this case was heard after the UK left the EU, the facts occurred while the UK within the jurisdiction of EU law).

8 *Wilkes v Depuy International Limited* [2016] EWHC 3096.

9 Consumer Protection Act 1987 s.3(2)(a).

10 Consumer Protection Act 1987 s.3(2)(b).

due to its nature, and the user may not always have experience of how to engage with it, or know the consequences of AI potentially learning through interaction. If the product is being used in a way which is clearly inappropriate and against manufacturer's clear instructions, then it probably should not entail liability on the manufacturer.

Difficulties in proving product defect have been found in several non-AI strict product liability cases. For example, in the Supreme Court case of *Hastings v Finsbury Orthopaedics Ltd*,[11] a claim was made in relation to hip protheses provided to patients in surgeries. The hip prosthesis would eventually need to be replaced. In some situations, metal debris would shed and cause damage. There were 'serious professional concerns'[12] shown by surgeons, in relation to a brand of the prosthesis and 'high revision rates'[13] and 'potential difficulties in carrying out revision operations' in relation to some prosthesis.[14] Moreover, a product was withdrawn, and notices issued in relation to the products. Despite this, the claimant failed to prove that the prosthesis was defective, particularly because there was a lack of statistical information to prove defectiveness on a balance of probabilities.

If it can be difficult to prove that a tangible product is defective, it can be even more difficult with AI, if what is being asserted is that a programme code or algorithm is defective. Such proof would require considerable expertise – and the investigation of what a defendant might seek to claim is confidential information. And can a manufacturer be said to have created defective AI if the AI correctly learns something which turns out to be ill-advised (perhaps with what it learned having come from another human source)?

CAUSATION

The defect must also be the cause of the damage. How easy is it to prove that a product defect has caused the damage? This concerns the usual 'but for' test (this was discussed earlier in the book at Chapter 4): but for the defect in the product, would the damage have occurred? There can be multiple reasons for failure. There might be internal reasons, like faulty manufacturing or software, or external factors including third-party interference, or misuse of the AI by the user. Proving causation in relation to AI can be challenging and again will require understanding of how the AI worked. It is worth remembering that it is the claimant who has the burden of proving both defectiveness and causation.

ANALYSING THE LAW

We can think of some of causation and strict product liability issues that will be present in relation to automated vehicles. For example, as these vehicles may involve both vehicle and

11 *Hastings v Finsbury Orthopaedics Ltd* [2022] UKSC 19.

12 *Hastings v Finsbury Orthopaedics Ltd* [2022] UKSC 19, [42] (Lord Lloyd-Jones).

13 Ibid.

14 Ibid.

user control,[15] proving what caused the damage if a crash occurs when control of the vehicle is being handed over between the human and machine would be a substantial challenge.

The UK introduced law in relation to automated vehicles to address issues around victim compensation. The Automated and Electric Vehicles Act 2018 (AEVA 2018)[16] provides that the claimant who is injured or has had their property damaged will receive damages from the insurer (which will cover product and user in one insurance policy).[17] The insurer will recover direct from the person (or persons) responsible, which can include, for example, the manufacturer.

Say for example Alex is sat in an automated vehicle and has the necessary insurance policy. The vehicle crashes into a lamppost when it is driving itself and injures Alex. Alex may make a claim against his insurer under section 2(1) of the AEVA 2018 so long as Alex's injury was 'as a result' of the accident. If Alex negligently allowed the vehicle to drive itself when it was 'not appropriate' to do so, and the accident that the vehicle caused was 'wholly' due to Alex's negligence in allowing the vehicle to drive itself, then the insurer will not be liable (section 3(2) of the AEVA 2018).

If not, then the insurer will then be able to claim against any person responsible for the injury to Alex. In this instance, this may be brought against the vehicle manufacturer under section 5(1)(a) of the AEVA 2018.

If Alex is the insured person and had ignored a 'safety critical' software update, then the insurer may refuse to compensate Alex (section 4(1) AEVA 2018) and could recover compensation if they have been forced to pay another party (section 4(4) AEVA 2018). If the vehicle was Alex's, then the Act states that Alex could not be compensated for damage to his vehicle (section 2 (3)(a) AEVA 2018). There is also a contributory negligence provision within the Act which may apply (section 3(1) AEVA 2018).

The Act is not without its difficulties.[18] An interesting difficulty concerns liability for cybersecurity breaches: should a manufacturer or insurance company be found liable for potentially huge costs if a vehicle or group of vehicles are hacked and cause

15 See SAE J3016, 'Taxonomy and Definitions for Terms Related to Driving Automation Systems for On-Road Motor Vehicles' for levels of vehicle automation.

16 The Act has been analysed in detail in literature; e.g. see M. Channon, L. McCormick, and K. Noussia, 'The Law and Autonomous Vehicles' (Informa 2019); M. Channon, 'Automated and Electric Vehicles Act 2018: An Evaluation in Light of Proactive Law and Regulatory Disconnect', (2019) 10(2) European Journal of Law and Technology; J. Marson, K. Ferris, and J. Dickinson, 'The Automated and Electric Vehicles Act 2018 Part 1 and Beyond: A Critical Review', (2020) 41(3) Statute Law Review 395–416; F. Boon, 'The Bites of a Peculiar Cherry? Res Judicata, Time Bar and Illiquid Debts: Insurer Recoveries Under the Automated and Electric Vehicles Act 2018' (2022) 133 British Insurance Law Association Journal.

17 Section 2(1) Automated and Electric Vehicles Act 2018.

18 See for example work from Felix Boon, who has highlighted substantial difficulties with the Act. F. Boon, 'Two Bites of a Peculiar Cherry? Res Judicata, Time Bar and Illiquid Debts: Insurer Recoveries Under the Automated and Electric Vehicles Act 2018', (2022) 133 British Insurance Law Association.

damage?[19] Compensation schemes have been suggested to manage potentially significant compensation for very significant damage in relation to AI, as these compensation schemes spread the loss.[20]

Overall, the stand-alone system of insurance for automated vehicles provides an interesting example of ways in which victims can receive compensation for damage caused.

DEFENCES

So, if we return to strict product liability and its application to AI, there are several defences available to the manufacturer.

Section 4(1)(d) of the CPA 1987 provides that it is a defence where the 'defect did not exist in the product at the relevant time'. This seems a rather sensible defence for non-AI products: if a defect in a product is introduced later which was not in the product at the time of manufacture, for example if the product was interfered with by a third party later, then surely a manufacturer should not be deemed to be liable for the product.

However, if the manufacturer is aware of the potential of the product becoming defective later, or of the potential for third-party interference, should the manufacturer address the problem by providing software updates? After all, the manufacturer may well have some control of the product to enable them to make updates to the product even though the product has been sold.

Moreover, the 'development risks' defence provides under section 4(1)(e) CPA 1987 that it is a defence where

> the state of scientific and technical knowledge at the relevant time was not such that a producer of products of the same description as the product in question might be expected to have discovered the defect if it had existed in his products while they were under his control.

ANALYSING THE LAW

It is perhaps fair in relation to non-AI products that a manufacturer should not be liable for a defect which they could not have discovered – but the difficulty with AI is in its potential unpredictability. AI develops and learns, perhaps beyond what was envisioned by the manufacturer. As scientific and technical knowledge develops, do you think there should be more protection for claimants against self-learning AI?

19 In M. Channon and J. Marson, 'The Liability for Cyber Security Breaches of Connected and Autonomous Vehicles', (2021) Computer Law and Security Review.

20 See N. E. Vellinga, 'Rethinking Compensation in Light of the Development of AI', (2024) International Review of Law, Computers and Society 1–22.

OTHER DEFENCES

Contributory negligence is also a defence to strict product liability. This defence has already been discussed in Chapter 9 in relation to negligence and is a partial defence.

Further, damage to the product itself is not covered within strict product liability.[21] Should a manufacturer be required to pay when their product has damaged itself?

15.3 NEGLIGENCE

Negligence was discussed in previous chapters, and requires a duty of care, breach of duty, and causation. We discuss each of these in turn, and then defences.

DUTY OF CARE

It has long been held since *Donoghue v Stevenson*[22] that manufacturers of products owe a duty of care to the end users of products not to cause injury to them or to property.[23] Claims can and have been brought against manufacturers in negligence. The manufacturer of an AI system will therefore likely owe a duty of care to end users of such system – for example, a duty of care to ensure that the AI model is appropriately tested and that the components of the AI are assembled correctly, with warnings and instructions also.

Moreover, the user of AI might owe a duty of care to others. For example, a doctor might use AI in diagnosing a patient, or a school might use AI to safeguard students. In such cases, there are layers of care: the doctor must take reasonable care in diagnosing the patient; it must therefore be reasonable to use AI at all; and then the AI must be used with reasonable care.

BREACH OF DUTY

A manufacturer must take reasonable care in manufacturing AI, and a user must take reasonable care when using AI. But whether there has been breach of duty – whether anyone has behaved without reasonable care – entails several different factors, such as the likelihood and seriousness of harm caused. A non-AI example is *Abouzaid v Mothercare.*[24] A strap, meant to fasten a sleeping bag to a pushchair, slipped from the grasp of the claimant. The strap's buckle then hit him in the eye. The court rejected an allegation of negligence: the risk of recoils from any strap generally was very small, and there were no reported accidents with this particular type of strap. This was simply an unfortunate accident rather than a negligently made product. Similarly, must we expect that sometimes damage caused by AI is just an accident, rather than a result of negligence?

21 Section 5(2) Consumer Protection Act 1987.

22 [1932] AC 562.

23 See e.g. *Howmet Ltd v Economy Devices Limited, Electrochemical Supplies Limited, MJD Supplies Limited* [2014] EWHC 3933 (TCC).

24 *Abouzaid v Mothercare (UK) Ltd* [2000] All ER 2436.

CAUSATION

Did the manufacturer's negligence cause the damage? Was this damage reasonably foreseeable? Or was the damage caused by another such as the AI's user? These could be particularly challenging questions; for example with machine learning, is the AI manufactured in such a way that it would likely learn errors?

DEFENCES

Contributory negligence might be relevant where a claimant has misused AI. But there might be a further question, whether it was even reasonable to rely on the AI in the first place (even if it had been properly used). For example, when is it reasonable to let an autonomous car do all the driving? Should a patient using an AI device at home (for example, to regulate their insulin levels) check any diagnosis made by AI, and if so, how, and how often?

15.4 APPLICATION OF OTHER TORTS?

We have focused primarily on strict product liability and negligence. However, one can think of a several other potential torts which could apply to AI, and we can detail a couple of examples here. For example, we can discuss the torts of trespass to land and private nuisance (which we addressed more generally in Chapter 12). Could an AI which moves onto another's land be classed as a trespass? If the user of the AI acts intentionally or recklessly, then possibly yes.[25] It is also important to repeat here that in relation to drones, there are limits in terms of trespass and nuisance through section 76 Civil Aviation Act 1982.

AI could also be used for example to commit a nuisance. For example, if an AI caused substantial amounts of noise, then the owner of the AI could be found liable in nuisance for the interference with another's enjoyment of land.

15.5 REFORM OF THE LAW

While there is existing law already that can apply to new technologies, is there a need for more substantial law reform such as legislation for tort liability in relation to AI? The UK Government published a policy paper titled 'A pro innovation approach to AI regulation' in 2023,[26] but civil liability was discussed very briefly with limited detail.

25 The position could be similar to *League Against Cruel Sports v Scott* [1986] QB 240.

26 Department for Science, Innovation and Technology, 'A Pro Innovation Approach to AI Regulation' (2023, 815).

On the other hand, the European Union has already introduced a Product Liability Directive[27] which has been adopted and have proposed a Non-Contractual Civil Liability Directive. We shall take each in turn.

STRICT PRODUCT LIABILITY

In terms of the newly adopted Product Liability Directive, this includes software within the definition of product (article 4(1)). Thus, products are no longer limited to tangibles (as discussed above).

The Directive provides a number of factors to consider when determining whether a product is defective, such as 'the effect on the product of any ability to continue to learn or acquire new features after it is placed on the market or put into service',[28] and 'relevant product safety requirements, including safety-relevant cybersecurity requirements'.[29]

There is a presumption of *defectiveness*, for example where 'the claimant demonstrates that the damage was caused by an obvious malfunction of the product during reasonably foreseeable use or under ordinary circumstances',[30] or where 'the claimant demonstrates that the product does not comply with mandatory product safety requirements laid down in Union or national law that are intended to protect against the risk of damage suffered by the injured person'.[31] The difficulty with the former is in determining what will be classed as 'reasonably foreseeable use' and 'ordinary circumstances'. And will a malfunction always be 'obvious'?

There is a presumption of *causation*, where a defect has been proven and 'the damage caused is of a kind typically consistent with the defect in question'.[32] But how will we know if the damage is consistent with the defect?

Finally, the 'development risks defence' has been maintained as an exception:[33] the manufacturer is not liable for any defect beyond the discovery of current scientific techniques. Is this defence too generous, not least because AI is (for now at least) necessarily at the forefront of technological development?

27 Directive 2024/2853 of the European Parliament and of the Council of 23 October 2024 on liability for defective products and repealing Council Directive 85/374/EEC.

28 Directive 2024/2853 of the European Parliament and of the Council of 23 October 2024 on liability for defective products and repealing Council Directive 85/374/EEC, Article 7.

29 Directive 2024/2853 of the European Parliament and of the Council of 23 October 2024 on liability for defective products and repealing Council Directive 85/374/EEC, Article 7(1)(f).

30 Directive 2024/2853 of the European Parliament and of the Council of 23 October 2024 on liability for defective products and repealing Council Directive 85/374/EEC, Article 10(2)(c).

31 Directive 2024/2853 of the European Parliament and of the Council of 23 October 2024 on liability for defective products and repealing Council Directive 85/374/EEC, Article 10(2)(b).

32 Directive 2024/2853 of the European Parliament and of the Council of 23 October 2024 on liability for defective products and repealing Council Directive 85/374/EEC, Article 10(3).

33 Directive 2024/2853 of the European Parliament and of the Council of 23 October 2024 on liability for defective products and repealing Council Directive 85/374/EEC, Article 11(1)(e).

NON-CONTRACTUAL LIABILITY

The EU has proposed a new Non-Contractual Liability Directive. This also includes a presumption of causation: for example, where a claimant has shown fault of the defendant (article 4(1)(a)),[34] and 'it can be considered reasonably likely, based on the circumstances of the case, that the fault has influenced the output produced by the AI system or the failure of the AI system to produce an output' (article 4(1)(b))[35] and that 'the claimant has demonstrated that the output produced by the AI system or the failure of the AI system to produce an output gave rise to the damage' (article 4(1)(c)).[36] The EU also designates some types of AI as 'high risk',[37] and subjects them to higher safety requirements.[38]

VICARIOUS LIABILITY

A final solution that could be implemented in terms of tort law which we will mention briefly is vicarious liability. As we have analysed in Chapter 10 of this book, an employer can be held liable for the acts of its employees (or those in a relationship akin to employment) and when there is a close connection with the employment. Could such a relationship be transposed to relationships involving an AI and its owner, or the manufacturer of the AI?

POINTS TO REVIEW

- There is currently no specific law of torts applying to AI.
- The application of strict product liability to AI can be a challenge – for example, whether software is a 'product', or whether machine learning can be 'defective'.
- Negligence could be relevant: for example, whether AI has been manufactured with reasonable care, or used by the defendant with reasonable care. But there is also a question of contributory negligence: to what extent should a claimant rely on AI?
- Reform has been proposed and a new Directive adopted by the EU so that product includes software, and introduces presumptions of defectiveness and causation to assist claimants. Should the UK follow suit?

34 Proposal for a Directive of the European Parliament and of the Council on adapting non-contractual civil liability rules to artificial intelligence (AI Liability Directive).

35 Ibid.

36 Ibid.

37 Regulation (EU) 2024/1689 of the European Parliament and of the Council of 13 June 2024 laying down harmonised rules on artificial intelligence and amending Regulations (EC) No 300/2008, (EU) No 167/2013, (EU) No 168/2013, (EU) 2018/858, (EU) 2018/1139, and (EU) 2019/2144 and Directives 2014/90/EU, (EU) 2016/797, and (EU) 2020/1828 (Artificial Intelligence Act). Article 6.

38 Regulation (EU) 2024/1689 of the European Parliament and of the Council of 13 June 2024 laying down harmonised rules on artificial intelligence and amending Regulations (EC) No 300/2008, (EU) No 167/2013, (EU) No 168/2013, (EU) 2018/858, (EU) 2018/1139, and (EU) 2019/2144 and Directives 2014/90/EU, (EU) 2016/797, and (EU) 2020/1828 (Artificial Intelligence Act). Section 2 (Articles 8–14). Also see section 3, 'Obligations of providers and deployers of high-risk AI systems and other parties'.

TAKING IT FURTHER

Glavanicova, D. and Pascucci M. 'Vicarious Liability: A Solution to a Problem of AI Responsibility?' (2022) 24 Ethics and Information Technology 27

The authors discuss issues with liability and AI and propose different vicarious liability models. If a programmer commits a tort, then the first model involves the manufacturer and programmer, and the second involves vicarious liability in relation to the manufacturer and the AI.

INDEX

Note: Page numbers in **bold** type refer to tables
Page numbers followed by 'n' refer to notes

For Product Safety Concerns and Information please contact our EU
representative GPSR@taylorandfrancis.com
Taylor & Francis Verlag GmbH, Kaufingerstraße 24, 80331 München, Germany

www.ingramcontent.com/pod-product-compliance
Lightning Source LLC
LaVergne TN
LVHW082342011026
849160LV00025B/1533

* 9 7 8 1 0 3 2 7 6 7 7 4 1 *